Gerhard Uhlhorn

The Conflict of Christianity with Heathenism

Gerhard Uhlhorn

The Conflict of Christianity with Heathenism

ISBN/EAN: 9783743317185

Manufactured in Europe, USA, Canada, Australia, Japa

Cover: Foto ©Lupo / pixelio.de

Manufactured and distributed by brebook publishing software (www.brebook.com)

Gerhard Uhlhorn

The Conflict of Christianity with Heathenism

THE

CONFLICT OF CHRISTIANITY
WITH HEATHENISM

BY

Dr. GERHARD UHLHORN

ABBOT OF LOCCUM, AND MEMBER OF THE SUPREME CONSISTORY
IN HANOVER

Edited and Translated

WITH THE AUTHOR'S SANCTION

FROM THE THIRD GERMAN EDITION

BY

EGBERT C. SMYTH AND C. J. H. ROPES

NEW YORK
CHARLES SCRIBNER'S SONS
743 AND 745 BROADWAY
1879

COPYRIGHT, 1879,
BY CHARLES SCRIBNER'S SONS.

FRANKLIN PRESS:
STEREOTYPED AND PRINTED BY RAND, AVERY, AND CO.,
BOSTON.

PREFACE.

THE work of which a translation is now offered to the public has been highly commended by leading reviews in Germany, and has been received with much popular favor. It has also been translated into the Danish and Swedish languages. Its author's name is familiar to scholars through his contributions to the first edition of Herzog's Encyclopædia of Protestant Theology, as well as to the one now issuing; through his work on the Clementine Homilies and Recognitions; and through other historical and apologetic publications, one of which has been translated into English by the Rev. Charles E. Grinnell, and published under the title: "The Modern Representations of the Life of Jesus." At home Dr. Uhlhorn is known also as an eminent preacher, and as one of the most prominent of the Lutheran clergy. Several volumes of sermons have lately appeared from his pen, and also a collection of addresses on important topics of religious and social life.

Gerhard Uhlhorn is the son of a shoemaker, and was born in Osnabrück, Feb. 17, 1826. From the gymnasium of his native city he went to the University of Göttingen, where he studied theology from 1845 to 1848. He then became a private instructor in the University, and served successively as a "*Repetent*," and as a "*Privatdocent*," until 1855. During this period, besides preparing and publishing a volume of sermons, he was engaged in a critical and thorough study of the early Christian history. In 1855 he became assistant preacher at the royal Schlosskirche in Hanover, and subsequently First Preacher to the Court, and a member of the Supreme Consistory of Hanover. In 1878 he was installed as Abbot of Loccum, a mediæval Cistercian Abbey which, toward the close of the sixteenth century, accepted the principles of the Lutheran Reformation, and is now a Seminary for the education of evangelical preachers. Its abbot is *ex officio* president of the principality of Kalenberg, and at the head (*der erste Geistliche*) of the Lutheran Church in Hanover.

The subject which Dr. Uhlhorn has treated in the following work is fitted to call into exercise his best powers, — his quick and broad sympathies with humanity, especially the poor and wretched, his ample and thorough learning, and his ability to clothe his thoughts in forms fitted to interest wide circles of readers. Dr. Channing, in his Essay on Fénelon, has recognized the grandeur and importance of this theme, and its need of juster treatment. It is of permanent and universal interest. We are transported to an ancient battle-field, but the cause is our own. Christianity, from the beginning, had to encounter active, skilful foes. Judaism and Heathenism were no abstractions, but armed warriors. The struggle was a vital one, — not a question of mere organization, or subsidiary doctrine, but of the origin,

PREFACE. 7

essence, authority, and power of the Gospel. The contest was also protracted. As it went on, all the forces which could be arrayed against the new religion had time to reach the field of conflict, and mingle in the strife. The victorious Roman, the acute and versatile Greek, the Oriental theosophist, the Jewish legalist, the power of the Empire, the learning of Alexandria, vested interests, wit, ridicule, sarcasm, reverence for the past, the pride of human reason, the cunning of covetousness, the accumulated resources of human wisdom and human depravity, were all marshalled and taxed. A conflict so real, so strenuous, so continuous and vital, deserves the careful attention of every student of history and lover of truth. And it has special claims in an age like our own, when the question of the supernatural origin and power of Christianity is so widely discussed.[1]

In its treatment of this subject Dr. Uhlhorn's book may be specially commended in the following particulars: (i.) its abundant use of the new materials which have been accumulated by the special investigations of Marquardt, Mommsen, Friedländer, Boissier, De Rossi, Keim, Overbeck, and others; (ii.) the vividness with which the principles and

---

[1] The German edition of this volume bears the secondary title: *Bilder aus der Vergangenheit als Spiegelbilder für die Gegenwart*, Pictures from the Past as Illustrations for the Present. This resemblance of the ancient conflict to the modern has also been noticed, on its Apologetic side, by Dr. Shedd, *History of Christian Doctrine*, vol. i., p. 103; and by Mr. Bolton in the Introduction to his useful collection and classification of the arguments of "the Apologists down to Augustine." Mr. Bolton also sketches the peculiar characteristics of the earlier contest, — to some of which, in broader relations, I have alluded.

progress of the conflict are conceived, and the skill with which they are illustrated by apt citations from the writings of those engaged in it, and by the introduction of striking personal experiences and incidents of the period; (iii.) the success with which the author preserves the unity of his theme, and the consequent distinctness of impression which is produced.

If these merits are justly attributable to the original work, and are not seriously impaired in its translation, it invites the attention of a much larger number of readers than those who may be supposed to have a professional interest in its subject. I cannot but hope that it will prove adapted to the wants of such persons; that intelligent laymen will deem it not without freshness and value, that pastors may find it helpful in their provision of reading for some who may consult them, and that it may fill a useful place in town and village and parish libraries. I shall be especially gratified if any young persons who have not as yet been attracted to the study of Church History may be allured by this volume to these rich fields of thought and knowledge. Desiring also that it may promote the study of this History in its sources, special pains has been taken to make the references to authorities exact and copious.

The latter half of the translation (from page 244), with the corresponding notes, has been prepared and edited by the Rev. C. J. H. Ropes of Ellsworth, Me. The translators have endeavored so far to assimilate their work that the unity of the original may not seem to have been greatly impaired in its English form.

E. C. S.

ANDOVER THEOLOGICAL SEMINARY,
    October, 1879.

CONTENTS.

BOOK FIRST.
The Powers in Conflict.

CHAPTER I.
THE RELIGIOUS CONDITION OF THE HEATHEN WORLD.

		PAGE
1.	The Commingling of Nations in the Roman Empire	13
2.	Decline of Religion	29
3.	Foreign Rites, and the Longing for Redemption	62
4.	Judaism	81

CHAPTER II.
THE MORAL CONDITION OF THE HEATHEN WORLD.

1.	Faith and Morals	92
2.	Marriage and Family Life	97
3.	Labor and Luxury	104
4.	Public Games	119
5.	Slavery	131
6.	The Need of Moral Renewal	141

CHAPTER III.
THE CHRISTIANS.

1.	The Preaching of the Gospel	150
2.	Worship and Church-Life	160
3.	Conduct of the Christians	165
4.	Benevolence of the Christians	191
5.	Martyrdom	205

BOOK SECOND.
The Conflict.

CHAPTER I.
THE FIRST ENCOUNTER.

1.	Preliminary Survey	217
2.	The Persecution under Nero	241

CHAPTER II.

THE CHRISTIANS BEFORE THE TRIBUNALS.

1. Trajan's Legislation against the Christians 251
2. The Increasing Influence of Christianity 264
3. The Persecution under Marcus Aurelius 282
4. The First Signs of Victory 297

CHAPTER III.

THE RE-ACTION.

1. The Internal Re-action in Heathenism 308
2. The Internal Re-action in Christianity 336

CHAPTER IV.

THE GENERAL PERSECUTIONS.

1. From Marcus Aurelius to Decius 355
2. From Decius to Gallienus 365

BOOK THIRD.

The Victory.

CHAPTER I.

THE DECISIVE STRUGGLE.

1. The Work of the Church among the Heathen 385
2. The Restoration of the Empire 393
3. The Persecution under Diocletian 407

CHAPTER II.

THE VICTORY. 420

CHAPTER III.

THE LAST EFFORT OF HEATHENISM. 445

Notes 481
Index 501

BOOK FIRST.

THE POWERS IN CONFLICT.

"Greater is He that is in you, than he that is in the world." — 1 JOHN iv. 4.

THE CONFLICT OF CHRISTIANITY WITH HEATHENISM.

CHAPTER I.

THE RELIGIOUS CONDITION OF THE HEATHEN WORLD.

"But, when the fulness of the time was come, God sent forth His Son, made of a woman." — GAL. iv. 4.

I. THE COMMINGLING OF NATIONS IN THE ROMAN EMPIRE.

MELITO of Sardis, one of the earliest Apologists, calls attention to the fact that Christianity was born at the same time with the Roman Empire.[1] Indeed the simple statement, in the story of our Lord's birth, of the decree of taxation issued by the first Roman Emperor, affords one of the plainest indications that the fulness of the time had come. The name of the Emperor Augustus marks the meridian of the ancient world; for the ancient world culminated in Rome, and Roman history in the rise of the Empire. And just at this culmination of the old world, which was also the beginning of its decline, He appears whose coming was the point of transition from the ancient era to the new, the turning-point of the ages. As in Nature new shoots do not first start when the plant they are appointed to succeed is wholly dead, but while it is still outwardly vigorous put forth and grow, feeding upon the life whose dissolution they hasten, so was it here. The Christian world, did not first appear when the old world was already decayed. To human eyes at least, although destroying forces were secretly at work, it still stood in full splendor and bloom when the germ of the new life was implanted, and henceforth the progressive decline of the old life, and the aspiring growth of the new, went on in constant and reciprocal interaction.

The task of Rome was to unite, — to unite, we may say as confidently, for Christ. Born at the same time, the Roman Empire and the Christian Church were also providentially appointed for each other. The kingdom of heaven is like a grain of seed. If the seed is to be sown the field must be prepared. The Roman Empire was the prepared field. The kingdom of heaven is like leaven. If the leaven is to be mixed with the meal, the meal must be shaken together. The Roman Empire was the shaken heap of meal appointed first of all to take up the leaven. All the peoples of the old world which hitherto had lived and labored apart, all their gains and achievements, their riches and treasures, their works of art and scientific results, their ancient traditions and legends, their gods and rites of worship, all existing elements of culture and forces of civilization, were now comprised in one Empire. Other empires have exceeded this in territory and in population, but there has never been a second empire in the whole course of history which so united in itself all the cultivated nations of its time.

The establishment of this kingdom was the historical task of the Romans. Rome's geographical position gave her the expectation of becoming the head of such an Empire. Around the Mediterranean, the central sea of the ancient world, dwelt the cultivated nations.

Far into the midst of this sea projects the long peninsula of Italy, and in the middle of this peninsula stood Rome, the centre of the centre. From this point the world was conquered and controlled. For this were the Romans endowed. They were not a people of peace but of war, not a nation of thinkers but of deeds, not rich in arts but great in bravery and political sagacity, equipped with a rare power of assimilation, a marvellous gift for organization, and a strong instinct for legislation and government. They produced no philosophical systems, but they carried law to its highest perfection; they built no Parthenon, but they constructed roads and bridges to bind countries together, and walls and castles to protect them. They were "the robbers of the globe," but in the divine counsel their robberies, unknown to them, had a higher purpose of union, and their Empire, brought together by reckless violence, was constrained by a superior will to serve the kingdom which Eternal Love has undertaken to establish in the world.

When the Republic ended, the conquest of the world was at least substantially accomplished. Then it received, in the Emperor, one ruler. From this point began the fusion of the heterogeneous mass of countries and peoples which at first were only externally united. The first Emperor, Augustus, erected in the Forum at Rome a golden milestone. It stood as a symbol that there was the centre of the world. A net-work of artificial highways, even then nearly completed, extended from this point through the entire Empire. From Cadiz in Spain, through France, through Italy, away up to the Cataracts of the Nile, from the lands of the Danube even to the pillars of Hercules, the traveller could journey over well-built roads, and find everywhere, at certain distances, *mutationes* for change of horses, and *mansiones* for lodging at night. These roads were so many cords binding the conquered world to the centre, Rome, so many channels for the impulses which streamed forth from it. On these roads marched the legions to keep under control a subjugated world, and to protect the boundaries; on these roads Proconsuls and Prætors went into the provinces to administer law and justice, and swift couriers bore the edicts of the Emperor to the extreme circumference of the broad Empire; over these highways commerce moved, and Romans of distinction journeyed to gain knowledge of the world; over these highways, too, went the messengers of the Gospel, bearing from city to city the joyful tidings of a manifested Redeemer.

A vast interchange now began through the entire Empire. Hitherto War alone had brought men together; now for the first time this was accomplished by Peace. For after the fearful assaults and revolutions of the Civil Wars the Empire was really peace: "Now land and sea are safe, and cities flourish in concord and peace," exults an inscription in honor of Augustus. "All which has hitherto been concealed comes now into general use," says Pliny. And Philo: "The noxious elements are driven to the remotest distances, the salutary are gathered together from the ends of the earth into the Empire of the world."[2] To be sure, as compared with the commercial intercourse of to-day, that of the Roman world was but small. The imports, for example, from Asia into England from 1861 to 1869 amounted annually, on an average, to nearly seventy millions of dollars, while the entire Roman Empire, according to an estimate found in Pliny, made use of only about five and a quarter million dollars' worth of merchandise from the East. Yet, in comparison with earlier times, traffic very largely increased during the age of the Emperors, and was of more importance in bringing the nations nearer together because mercantile intercourse was much more personal then than now. Like the great commercial cities of the East, — Alexandria, Antioch, Ephesus, Smyrna, Corinth, — Rome was a centre of traffic, as no city has been before or since. Every thing rushed to Rome. Whoever had any thing in art or science whose claims he wished to have recognized, whoever hoped to gain any thing by being near persons in power, whoever sought his rights in the highest tribunal of appeal, whoever expected through honest business, or even through adventure and fraud, to become rich, or whoever had obtained wealth and wished to see with his own eyes the wonders of the capital, and to share in the pleasures and luxuries which it afforded, went to Rome. On the streets of this matchless imperial city met the finely cultured Greek who sought here the sources for some history, and the half educated provincial who would gladly pass for a genuine Roman; the Alexandrian merchant, brought here by the corn trade, and the half savage African who perchance had come with an invoice of lions for the next hunting-show; the wily Syrian who hoped to propagate the worship of a new god, or sold amulets and charms, and the Gaul who, proud of the Roman citizenship recently presented to him, offered his homage to the eternal city; the Jew who for the sake of some pecuniary gain, or even to win proselytes, shunned not the long journey, and the Illyrian and Thracian who followed the Roman eagles.

The current toward Rome had a corresponding one outward into the provinces which, no less than the other, promoted the fusion of the nations. The administrative officers who went forth to govern the conquered lands in accordance with Roman laws, the knights who were drawn to the provinces by their financial operations, the armies and the colonies which Rome sent forth, all promoted that great process of assimilation which was now accomplishing with astonishing rapidity. In its numerous colonies Rome extended itself into the provinces. They were a part of Rome in the midst of Spain, Gaul, or Greece. The colonists carried with them their right of citizenship and their Roman law. Often foreigners were received into the colony, and even when they formed within it a separate community they still came under the constant influence of the Roman spirit. The stations of the legions on the Rhine and in Syria, in Britain and on the Danube, were so many points of support for this Romanizing process. And since the legions were obliged to recruit themselves increasingly from the provinces, they were consequently all the more a school of civilization, especially as it was a principle never to station auxiliary troops in their native cantons. Separated from the soil of their birth by long years of military service, the strangers became Romans, and regarded Roman citizenship as their highest reward. How rapidly this transformation was accomplished in the provinces can be seen in the case of Britain. This country was re-occupied in the year 43. Tacitus gives us a description of it in the year 61. How changed is every thing in these eighteen years! A net-work of camps and castles stretches over the conquered Southern part, individual chieftains have wholly adopted Roman manners, and govern as prefects; the bloody Druid worship is exterminated, Roman customs are diffused; the colony of Camulodunum (Colchester) has grown to an important city, in the midst of which rises a temple of *Divus* Claudius. We find circuses, theatres, marble goddesses of victory. Londinium is an influential commercial city, where the fabrications of Roman industry and the products of Gaul find a market, and the people are already accustomed to Italian pleasures.

This assimilation to Rome would naturally advance more rapidly and powerfully in countries hitherto possessed of little or no culture. Spain, Gaul, North Africa, soon became wholly Romanized. It was otherwise in the East. Rome met in Greece a higher culture than its own. Externally the conqueror, it became inwardly more and more subjugated by the Greek mind. What France once was to Europe, Greece was at that time to the world. As philosophers and rhetoricians, as school-masters and physicians, as artists and artisans, even as men-servants and maid-servants, numerous Greeks came to Italy and Rome and diffused there the Greek language and philosophy, Greek morality and immorality. Conversely, it soon became a mark of *bon ton* to visit the seats of ancient Greek culture. As in the last century people went to Paris to receive the finest polish, so throngs of youths went to Athens, or even to Rhodes and Marseilles, to become acquainted with Hellenic science and art, often enough too with Hellenic excesses. Already gaining ground toward the end of the Republic, Hellenism made more and more rapid progress in the time of the Emperors, especially under Nero.

Thus Roman civilization, while it conquered the world, became itself more and more imbued with that of Greece. From this confluence of two streams issued a third, a new one, neither old Roman nor ancient Greek, but Græco-Roman; and it was this Græco-Roman culture which, adjusting the old distinctions, filled the great Empire. Latin, indeed, was the popular language only in the Western provinces, almost supplanting there the old native tongues; yet it was understood, as the speech of the dominant race, even in Palestine and on the Nile. More nearly even than Latin was Greek raised to the rank of a universal language. Whoever spoke it could count upon being able to make himself understood everywhere in the East and in the West. In the Common Law Rome gave the world another bond of union, whose influence became more powerful in proportion as it was developed. On this firm basis the world became more and more accustomed to the same forms of social life.

The East, true to the stable character it still preserves, adhered most firmly to its peculiarities. And though the Hellenized cities, Antioch, Nicomedia, above all Alexandria, were influential supporters of the Græco-Roman culture, still the transformation in these regions was far less complete than in the West. The Oriental indeed should be recognized as a third element with the Roman and the Grecian, especially in the sphere of religion, it being faintly discernible from the beginning of the time of the Emperors, and more and more clearly so in the second and third centuries. While the Roman spirit ruled in the domain of government and law, and the Greek in that of art and science, the Oriental impressed itself upon religious life. Thus this part of the mighty Empire had a share in its internal growth, and one all the more important since the real and highest end for which this Empire existed must be sought for in religious development.

It is hardly necessary to suggest what aids to religious progress, particularly to the extension of Christianity, these facts imply. A religious impulse given at one point now, was no longer in danger as it might have been centuries earlier, of perishing in the little circle of an isolated people. If it only had sufficient power it easily propagated itself through the entire Empire. It no longer found anywhere a limit. The abundant means of communication, the wide-spread understanding of the two leading languages, Latin and Greek, the community of interests, the common law, the greatly increased similarity of social customs and forms, all came to its aid. We need only glance at the life and labors of Paul to find this everywhere confirmed. A missionary activity like his was possible only in an Empire like the Roman.

But none of these particulars, however important each may be, is of chief moment. Of infinitely more consequence is it that there was now developing in the Roman Empire a Universalism hitherto entirely unknown, the first step to the Universalism of Christianity. At no point does the providential significance of the Roman Empire stand forth more strikingly than here.

The human race develops as nations in the Christian era, as well as in the pre-Christian. "God hath determined the times before appointed and the bounds of their habitation." With this word St. Paul, in his discourse at Athens, gives us a glimpse into the divine government and guidance of the nations of which they themselves are unconscious. But in the times before Christ, the significance of nationality was entirely unlike what it has been since. In the ancient era the nations were strictly separated from each other. Each nation lived for itself and labored for itself. There was no common work of civilization in which the nations reciprocally supplemented each other, and together made progress in a common development; but rather, one nation transmitted its work to another to be continued by it, the Oriental nations to the Greeks, and they to the Romans. In the modern era, on the contrary, nations are interdependent. No one is the sole possessor of culture, so that all the rest must repair to it. Each shares in the work of civilization, and all mutually give and receive. Though distinct as States, and though each preserves its own individuality, their culture is a common one. Nations which have a Christian civilization are united as members of a great whole. And their inner bond of union, however little inclination there may be in many quarters to-day to recognize this, is in reality their common Christianity. Rome is the connecting link between these two forms of national life, the transition from one to the other. In the ancient era we have only distinct nationalities, no unity; in the modern era distinct nationalities, yet above them a unity. In Rome, there were no longer distinct nationalities, for all were outwardly comprised in one State; yet a real inward unity, a common bond was still wanting, — it had yet to be developed.

In the Roman Empire the old nationalities declined more and more; not merely those of conquered nations, but that of Rome as well. The old Roman families died out; provincials took their places; and soon the Emperors, too, were from the provinces. Romans and non-Romans came to be regarded as equals, and the Roman right of citizenship was shared by provincials in an ever-widening circle. As ancient Roman art and morality had degenerated, so also had the old Greek character. The Greek spirit in its purity withdrew; Hellenism took its place. The Roman colony Corinth surpassed Athens, the Hellenized cities of Asia Minor were more important centres than the ancient seats of culture in Greece itself. More fully still did the subject nations of the West give up their nationality.

Since all development took a purely national course, a certain narrowness adhered to ancient life. Moderation was the chief virtue of Antiquity. In it was rooted the artistic sense of the old Greek, as well as the strict virtue of the old Roman. This narrowness now disappeared. Through the magnificent intercourse and interchange of the universal Empire, national consciousness expanded into one which was world-wide. In all departments of life there was manifested a freedom from restraints which resulted in a disappearance of the old established forms, in a widening of view and of the entire circle of thought. The sharply discriminated philosophical systems lost their distinctive peculiarities. A practical philosophy was developed, which, far inferior in acuteness and logical consistency to the earlier, obtained for this very reason far wider acceptance. The styles of art commingled. Grecian finish and Oriental massiveness met in the colossal edifices of the Empire. But when purity of art was thus lost, and the Age could no longer rival the creations of classic time, art gained instead a diffusion never before attained. Never before nor since, has the world been so opulent in treasures of art. To say nothing of Rome, even provincial cities so abounded in lofty edifices, statues, and other works of sculpture, as greatly to exceed those of our capitals which are richest in such treasures. Never again has art so penetrated men's homes, adorning even all the utensils of daily life, and its entire environment. In the countries on the Danube, and on the Rhine, manufactories of earthenware copied Grecian patterns; and the streets and public places of Roman colonial cities, in the midst of barbarous nations, were adorned with imitations of works of Grecian art whose originals, perchance, graced some place or palace in Rome.

Culture, in a word, now tended to become universal. Numerous schools afforded to multitudes opportunities for knowledge hitherto available to only a few. The cheapness of books, and easily accessible public libraries, subserved the same end. Martial speaks of books which cost four or six sesterces, a trifle more than twenty or thirty cents.[3] The equivalent of a page of print cost from about two to two and a half cents. The diffusion of books was also great. Pliny expresses pleasure that his works are sold by booksellers in Lyons. Already in Rome Cæsar had projected the plan of establishing a library. Asinius Pollio carried it into effect, founding in the temple of Liberty the first public library of Rome. Augustus established two others, to which a great number were afterwards added. Learning became somewhat encyclopædic; an educated man was expected to be well-informed upon all subjects. Every branch of knowledge was cultivated. Grammar,

Antiquities, Agriculture, and the science of war. Characteristic of the times was the special attention paid to Universal History and Geography. The view became broader, and whereas the ancient Greek or Roman cared only for his own people and land, the Roman of the age of the Emperors was interested in every thing, in foreign nations and countries, in the plants and animals of distant zones. In Rome unknown animals and other curiosities from far off lands were exhibited as shows to great throngs. Even the Emperors provided such sights. Successful attempts were made to acclimatize foreign plants and animals. The natural products of different countries were also interchanged. Southern fruits were transplanted to Rome, and still farther towards the North. In this way Gaul received the cultivation of the olive and vine. Journeys became the fashion. Whoever had not seen Greece, and visited the East, whoever had not been in Athens and Alexandria, hardly counted among persons of education; and just as we have to-day our guide-books for Italy and Switzerland, so had the Roman tourist his guide-book which pointed out all the various sights and designated the temples, statues, pictures, antiquities, which were of special interest. We see this fondness for travels, also, in the literature of romance; whose appearance is itself a sign of the altered spirit of the age. It delighted in narrating fictitious journeys; and "the incredible things beyond Thule," or the like, were eagerly read.

It has been disputed whether this whole development should be considered a decline or an advance. Men even of that time had a clear presentiment that Rome then stood at the height of its prosperity, and so at the beginning of its decline. "Heaven grant that I may prove a false prophet, but I see Rome, proud Rome, fall a victim to its own prosperity," says Propertius,[4] and Tacitus saw with a ken truly prophetic that the Germans would destroy Rome. Their freedom seemed to him more dangerous than the power of the Parthians.[5] Yet the controversy over the question of decline or progress is needless. Certainly that age, as compared with the palmy days of Greece and Rome, was one of decline. It was no longer productive as before. Feeling and reflection were stronger than energy of will. Nothing strictly new was produced. But must not the blossom fall before the fruit can ripen? Even if the commingling of nations, as of philosophical systems and of styles of art, which was accomplishing in the time of the Emperors, was a decline, it was also, as opposed to the earlier exclusiveness, a salutary result of the mutual intercourse which was taking place. This widening of view, of thought, of interest, beyond the former narrowness, was no longer, it is true, the genuine ancient life, and neither a Sophocles nor a Phidias, neither a Pericles nor a Scipio, could then have arisen; yet who will deny that this expansion of knowledge, this general diffusion of art was also a progress? For do not Science and Art exist for this very purpose that as many as possible may enjoy their fruits? Least of all can it be denied that this entire Universalism then developing was the first step to the modern Christian era. Antiquity went beyond itself and reached out its hands to the new epoch. Itself passing out from the ancient narrowness into a world-wide breadth of thought and life, the old world became capable of accepting the Universalism of

Christianity. The thought of a religion not national but for all races would have recoiled from the rocky masses of the unbroken nationalities of an earlier age. Now, when the old nationalities were demolished, the thought of a kingdom of God embracing all nations could strike root, and the idea of a universal Church, which would have been entirely unintelligible to an ancient Greek or Roman, was to the Roman of the age of the Emperors, though still strange, no longer incomprehensible now that in the Empire he had before his eyes a universal kingdom.

All this, indeed, was nothing more than preparation. The old world was not able to produce from itself a Christian universalism. The result of that great process of comminution which was wrought out in the vast Roman Empire was only uniformity, not true unity. True unity presupposes diversity. It is a comprehension of the manifold under a higher principle of organization. Here we encounter a limitation which was insuperable to the old world. It lacked the thought of Humanity, and since it knew not the whole, it could not rightly appreciate the parts. The unity of mankind, and the organization of the entire race in nations, — the great truths which Paul preached in Athens, the centre of ancient wisdom, — were hidden from it. Therefore the meaning of nationality was not rightly understood. At first it was exaggerated. There was only national life, and nothing more. Afterwards it was undervalued. In the Roman Empire the various nationalities failed to obtain their just rights. They were completely lost in the great whole. The result was, not a living universalism but only a shadowy one, an abstract cosmopolitanism which did not know how to appreciate the meaning of nationality as a compact organism.

The ultimate reason lies deeper. There was no religious unity. That which to-day holds cultivated nations in unity, notwithstanding all their diversity, is their common Christianity. Were this taken away their development in culture would gradually diverge, and the nations would again, as in ancient times, confront each other as enemies, — unless, indeed, power were given to one of them to force them all into one empire. This, in many quarters to-day, will not be conceded. Appeal is made to the multiplied means of communication which now exist, and the consequent approximation of nations. Stress is laid on their common culture, conceived of wholly apart from religion, — as if outward union could of itself create community of life! as if the kernel of this entire common culture were not their Christianity! The thought of a humanity whose members are nations, is only possible where there is faith in one God and one Redeemer. As long as Polytheism rules, as long also as religion is purely national, humanity is split up into a multitude of nationalities rigidly secluded from each other. Even the Universalism of the Roman Empire was possible only because, in its religious development, a monotheistic tendency had already begun even within the limits of paganism, — a tendency to be sure which could not advance beyond a shadowy Monotheism. The abstract pantheistic Deity which was the result of this tendency corresponds exactly to the abstract, and pantheistically colored, cosmopolitanism which took the place of the earlier and vigorous consciousness of distinct nationality. When, instead of a dead deity, was preached the living God, Maker of heaven and earth, the Father of our Lord Jesus Christ, then for the first time humanity was able to advance from this abstract cosmopolitanism into the true Universalism which rules the Christian era.

This brings us to the religious condition of the Age of the Emperors.[6]

II. DECLINE OF RELIGION.

After Paul had gone through Athens observing with attentive eye the life, and especially what was to him of deepest interest, the religious life of the renowned city, he summed up in the opening of his discourse the impression he had received in the phrase which Luther translates, somewhat inaccurately, "allzu abergläubig" (too superstitious), but which, no doubt, would be more correctly rendered, "too god-fearing" or "deity-fearing." A survey of the religious life of the Roman Empire must produce the same impression. What a host of gods and goddesses whom the nations serve, how countless the temples and holy places adorned with vast wealth and the glory of art, how endlessly varied the rites and forms of worship! In fact no reproach would be more unjust than to call the old world irreligious. On the contrary Christians, to the heathen, must have seemed irreligious; and often enough were they thus reproached, because they had no religious ceremonies like those to which the heathen were accustomed daily, and hourly, and at every step of life. The whole world was full of gods. Their temples rose in all places, — large and splendid edifices and little chapels, in cities and villages, in field and forest, on the verge of the wilderness and on the summit of the Great St. Bernard pass, where a temple of Jupiter[7] invited the traveller who had come thus far to offer thanksgivings and vows for a safe return home. "Our country is so peopled with gods," Petronius makes a woman from Campania say, "that it is easier to find a god there than a man."[8] Or there were at least sacred trees, stones, rocks which were decked by heathen piety with garlands and ribbons, and which no one passed by without some sign of reverence. The entire life was permeated by religion.

The State was founded upon religion. It was very well understood that there must be something which binds the conscience and disposes men freely to obey the laws. This was faith in the gods, in Providence, in retributive justice. "Sooner," says Plutarch,[9] "may a city exist without houses and ground, than a State without faith in the gods. This is the bond of union, the support of all legislation." Polybius praises the Romans especially for their piety. "Among them," he says, "the administration of public funds is more secure by means of the oath than elsewhere through the most extensive system of checks."[10] At every important public transaction the gods were consulted, sacrifices offered, and religious rites observed; every assembly of the people was opened with prayer. Augustus made an express decree that every senator, before he took his place, should go to the altar of the deity in whose temple the assembly was held, and offer a libation, and strew incense.[11] Down even to the last days of the Republic it was the looking up to the ancestral deities which inspired the army. When, before a battle, Pompey spoke to his soldiers of the art of war they remained unmoved, but when Cato reminded them of the *dii patrii* (though himself without faith in them), he inflamed the whole army, and the battle was a victory. And as the entire State, so also every community, every city, every circle of cities, had its special cult, well-founded institutions, rich and distinguished colleges for priests, and special feast-days and sacrifices. Every province, every city, every village, honored with local rites its protecting divinity, and everywhere the various religious observances were most intimately connected with the civil constitution of the community and sustained by local patriotism.

In the same way all domestic and family life had a religious tone. Each period of life, every important event, was celebrated with religious services. Though the names of the numerous deities who are mentioned as presiding over domestic life designate rather functions of the deity than divine beings conceived of as having independent existence, yet these very names afford proof of what has just been stated. There was the goddess Lucina who watched over the birth of a child; Candelifera in whose honor at such a time candles were lighted; Rumina who attended to its nursing; Nundina who was invoked on the ninth day when the name was given; Potina and Educa who accustomed it to food and drink. The day when the child first stepped upon the ground was consecrated to Statina; Abeona taught it to walk: Farinus to lisp; Locutinus to talk; Cunina averted from it the evil enchantments lying in the cradle. There was a god of the door (Forculus), a god of the threshold (Limentinus), a goddess of the hinges (Cardea). There was a god for the blind (Cæculus), a goddess for the childless (Orbana).[13] "Even the brothels," exclaims Tertullian, "and cook-shops and prisons have their gods."[13] Every household festival was at the same time a divine service; each class had its gods whom it invoked, and from whom it expected help and protection in its work. From the niche of a rafter, Epona, the goddess of horses, looked down upon the stable; on the ship stood the image of Neptune; the merchants prayed to Mercury for successful bargains. All tillage of the soil began with prayer. Before harvest a pig was sacrificed to Ceres, and the labor of felling a forest was not commenced until pardon had been supplicated from the unknown gods who might inhabit it.[14]

This whole rich religious life of the ancient world makes at once an impression of the greatest variety. What diversity wherever we observe it, whether on the shores of the Nile or the Orontes, in the cities of Greece or at the Roman Capitol. How entirely different were the gods invoked by the Egyptian and Syrian, the Greek and the Roman.

The Orient degraded the deity to the level of Nature. A materialistic tendency pervaded the religions of Egypt and Anterior Asia. Therefore they found so many adherents in the materialistic age of the Emperors. Sexual life, procreation, and death, were attributed to deity, and consequently the service of these monstrous beings was on the one hand gloomy and stern, dark and cruel, as they themselves, and on the other full of intoxicating pleasure. Moloch delighted in the agonized cries of the children burned in his honor, while in Melytta's temple prostitutes enticed to lewdness, and virgins sacrificed their chastity to the goddess. The Osiris myth in Egypt, the Adonis myth in Syria reflect the thoughts of death and resurrection which governed these religions. Adonis was killed in the hunt by a boar. The quickly withering little gardens planted at his festival were symbolic of his fate. By the side of the bier on which lay the image of Adonis with the open, bleeding wound, a cultus of mourning-rites was celebrated with expressions of the most frantic grief. Women wailed: Alas, Lord! his glory is gone! They tore their hair, and lacerated their breasts. Seven days the mourning lasted: then arose the cry, Adonis lives! Adonis has ascended! and festivals of wildest joy succeeded the mourning.

The Greeks took the opposite course. They idealized Nature. An idealistic tendency ruled their cultus, as a materialistic tendency ruled the cultus of the Orient. The holy God was hidden from them also. Instead of holiness, beauty took the supreme place. Unlike the Orientals, the Greek revered his gods, not as monstrous beings, but as human types of perfect beauty. Their worship was bright and cheerful. It lacked the earnestness pervading Oriental worship, which, with all its distortions, was more profound, and contained unconscious presages of the Deity who has indeed in birth and death descended to redeem us, but it was free from the gross materialism, the cruelty and licentiousness, which offend us in the temples of Asia. Upon the Greek dawned the presentiment of a moral order of the world. Is Baal, after all, only the sun who creates life, and then again parches and destroys what he himself has created, Zeus is also the guardian of justice. Does Aschera represent only the sensuous impulse of nature, Here is the protectress of marriage and domestic life. All here is purer, for in respect to chastity the Japhetic nations were in advance of the early corrupted descendants of Ham. This, their fairest inheritance, the Greeks very early squandered; and, as the result, exhibited a wanton frivolity which was the exact opposite of Oriental earnestness. To his humanized gods the Greek in his rich mythology imputed human failings and vices, and Olympus, with its carousals and conflicts, its craft and violence, its amorous intrigues and ambitious striving, is but a picture of Greek national life itself. While the Oriental was subject to his gods, the Greek knew himself to be lord of his. He had himself made them; their images were the workmanship of his artists, their legends the creations of his poets. Greece was also the land from which proceeded unbelief. As the Greeks, and the Romans whom they infected, lost their faith in the Olympian gods, the monstrous Oriental deities became again more powerful. They were still believed in; and therefore they gained a marvellous power of attraction for those who no longer had faith in Zeus and Here, in Jupiter and Juno.

Still differently was the religious life of Rome formed and developed. In Rome the State was every thing, therefore religion was interwoven with public life to a degree never elsewhere realized. "Our ancestors," says Cicero,[15] very significantly, "were never wiser, never more inspired by the gods, than when they determined that the same persons should preside over the rites and ceremonies of religion and the government of the State." The priest, who had so important an influence in the East, was completely overshadowed in Rome by the statesman. The Consul offered sacrifices, and though he was surrounded by priests, they were mere masters of ceremonies who showed what was to be done and what words were to be used.[16] In Rome the State, Rome itself, was honored as the supreme deity. In the times of the Republic the State was represented by the Capitoline Jupiter. The conquerors marched to his temple, and brought to him their thank-offerings. When, however, Monarchy, Cæsarism, had supplanted the Republic, the Emperors became representatives of the State, and thus, to a certain extent, took the place of the Capitoline god. With perfect logical consistency the Emperors themselves became gods, and the official worship of these Emperor-gods became the proper State religion.

The Roman religion, like the Roman character, was somewhat prosaic and abstract. It lacked imagination. The Roman gods, unlike the Greek, had no rich legendary endowment. Every thing was practical, and controlled by a strong juridical bias. A Roman's religious duties were prescribed for him with the greatest exactness, and to the last detail. What god he was to invoke, in what way, with what words, all this was definitely settled by ancient tradition. In these particulars he was excessively punctilious, whereas he was entirely unconcerned as to the state of his soul while performing these ceremonies. He was deemed religious who best knew the ritual, and most exactly observed it. Such a man expected the divine blessing as his right. "Whom the gods like, they favor." And because his religion was thus purely external (*Ceremoniæ Romanæ* was the expressive name of the Roman religion), devoid of imagination and appeals to feeling, the genuine Roman had so profound a dread of all excess in religious matters. *Superstitio*, immoderate piety, was hated by him as much as *impietas*, impiety. He kept his accounts with the gods in order, would not remain in debt to them; but would only pay what he owed. It is important to realize this character of the Roman religion, for the Romans were the ruling nation, and from this point of view can be judged how unintelligible, how rejectable must have appeared to a genuine Roman that Christianity which in his eyes was only a reprehensible *superstitio*.

But however manifold, however variegated and rich a development Heathenism attained in the ancient world, it was still everywhere fundamentally the same. "They worshipped and served the creature more than the Creator,"—this was always its essential character in all its forms. And because of this homogeneity these dissimilar forms could interchange, intermingle, and enter into new combinations. While the Monotheist of necessity regarded all gods, save the one only God, as idols to be utterly rejected, the Polytheist readily acknowledged gods everywhere, even though they were not his own. Indeed he was disposed to find his own in foreign gods, and to recognize them in all places even in the strangest disguises. The Roman easily persuaded himself that the Olympian gods were identical with his own. Zeus was the same as Jupiter, Here as Juno; even the grotesque deities of the Orient were not alien to him. Everywhere he sought and found his native gods, easily blended their forms with those of other deities, and transferred the symbols and names of the one to the other. Cæsar [17] found among the Gauls Mercury, Mars, Apollo; indeed Pliny relates that the inhabitants of the distant island Tapobrane (Ceylon) worshipped Hercules.[18] A combination of deities arose which led at last to a pantheistic divinity.

An abstract Monotheism hovered more or less distinctly over Polytheism. As the commingling of nations gave rise to an abstract Universalism, the first step to a Christian universalism, so the blending of religions produced an abstract Monotheism, the first step to Christian monotheism.

Here also appears the significance of Rome as the collecting or uniting power. Arnobius justly calls Rome "the worshipper of all divinities."[19] It was a maxim of the Roman State to tolerate all religions. Upon the conquest of a province, or city, its gods were invited with a solemn formula to come and take their seat in Rome. "If there be a god or goddess who has taken this people and city, N. n., under its protection, Deity, whosoever thou mayest be, I pray thee, I adjure thee, to forsake this people and city, to withdraw from this city and its temples, and come to Rome to me and mine, that our city, our temples and sacrifices, may be acceptable to thee. If thou wilt do this, I vow to thy divinity temples and games."[20] The gods were not taken away captive, and while the whole conquered nation and territory were regarded as at the free disposal of the conqueror, Rome acknowledged their deities. The Athenians retained their Athene, the Syrians their Syrian goddess, the Jews their Jehovah. However rigidly Rome centralized, in the religious domain the cities preserved what was peculiar to them, their *pontifices* and *flamines*, their local rites and institutions, which could not easily be alienated from their original design. This was not mere political sagacity; it was founded on the idea that the gods of other nations were also gods who if badly treated might harm the Romans. It was therefore held to be a duty even to honor them. Augustus declared to the Alexandrians that he spared their city in honor of the great god Serapis.[21] He also sent presents to the temple in Jerusalem, and had sacrifices offered there for himself.[22]

However foreign it would have been to the Romans to deprive subjugated nations of their religions, they nevertheless took their own gods into the provinces. The armies, the public officers, the colonies carried with them the Capitoline Jupiter, the *ceremoniæ Romanæ*, and required for them as friendly a recognition as they themselves extended to the local deities. This was all the more exacted because the official religion of Rome now culminated in the divine homage paid to the Emperor. In the adoration of the *Divus* Augustus, and the other *Divi*, a universal State religion was constituted which had more profound significance than is commonly supposed. In this way there was effected in the provinces a strange medley of Roman and local deities. The soldiers, especially, were largely instrumental in bringing this about. Ordinarily they were very superstitious. If they remained a long time in a country, they worshipped its gods and took them with them on their return. Very often the Roman and the local deities were associated. A cavalry officer in an inscription between Syene and Phylæ, gives thanks for his fortunate discovery of some new marble quarries to Jupiter Ammon Anubis and Juno *Regina*, the protectress of mountains.[23] Another, "zealous for all holy things," makes in Egypt a vow "for the welfare of his wife and children" to the great god Hermes Paytnuphis.[24] On the other hand the provincials were inclined to recognize and honor the Roman gods while they also retained their own. Thus under Tiberius a corporation of seamen in Paris erected to Jupiter *Capitolinus* an altar on whose socle may be also seen the names of the old Celtic deities Esus and Tarvus.[25] Temples have been found which were consecrated jointly to Apollo and the Gallic goddess Sirona, to Mercury and Rosmerta.[26]

Moreover the gods worshipped in the provinces migrated to Rome. Every thing worthless and disgraceful, says Tacitus,[27] flows from all quarters into Rome, and is there honored. The gods of the whole earth gathered together in the chief city of the world; and however strenuously the genuine Roman spirit, as expressed by Tacitus, at first rejected foreign rites, and numerous as were the edicts issued for their suppression, or at least restriction, that commingling of deities which began as early as the decline of the Republic, and which characterized more than all else the period of the fall of Heathenism, went on uninterruptedly to its completion. As all nationalities dissolved and became fused in one mass, so there was also a dissolution of religions. A religious chaos unparalleled in history took the place of the national religions in order that out of this chaos a new world might be created.

This entire process presupposes that the pagan faith was in its decline. Had it still retained its fresh, youthful vigor, such agitation, such restless fluctuation, would not have been possible. On the other hand it should not be overlooked that this process sprang from a strong religious need, and in a certain sense contributed to the strengthening of the popular religion. The multitudinous forms of Heathenism arrayed themselves as a unit against Christianity their common foe. And since the Roman gods had borrowed somewhat from the Oriental, they were better fitted to appease the religious need, and consequently better able to resist the new faith.

In general we must beware of the representation that Christianity, at its advent, found the religious life of the pagan world already dead, or even in complete decay. Victory was not made so easy for it. The usual statements as to the decay of religion in the earlier years of the period of the Emperors, are, I am convinced, greatly exaggerated, and need in more respects than one essential qualification. This much is true: the decline had already begun, but its completion went on very slowly, constantly retarded by mighty forces, and interrupted by seasons of new progress, such as for instance was the time of the Empire when compared with the last days of the Republic. If we would endeavor to trace a picture of the religious condition of that time we should do well first of all to realize how difficult it is to estimate the general state of faith in an age. This is one of the hardest of tasks even when copious contemporary materials are at command. How much more difficult is it when we possess only fragments of its literature, isolated and as it were accidental remains, inscriptions, and the like. The literature of the time bears indeed a strongly marked sceptical and rationalistic (aufklärerischen) character, but this is no certain test since a people can have more faith than their literature indicates, for this always proceeds from a particular class; while, if we take into account inscriptions and similar memorials, we should always bear in mind that in public documents, in accordance with traditional custom, a faith is often confessed which in reality no longer exists. The two sources must be combined if we would obtain a correct insight into the religious life of Heathenism at that time.

It would certainly be a mistake to suppose that Paganism was already in manifest outward decline. On the contrary there was as yet no visible sign of decay. The temples still stood in all their splendor,— those destroyed in the civil wars having been restored with great magnificence,— and were visited by thousands. Feasts and sacrifices were celebrated with great pomp. The altars were not without suppliants and seekers for aid. The oracles were still consulted; and though they had lost their political importance, Pythia in Delphi, and many others, still responded to the inquiries of persons in private life. How large was the number of sacrifices can be inferred from the fact that in Rome alone, on the accession of the Emperor Caligula, 100,000 animals were slain in sacrifice in three months. Countless inscriptions prove sufficiently that there were yet believers who bestowed rich gifts upon the temples and priests. Here an officer gives 100,000 sesterces (about $5,000) to build for a goddess a new chariot to be used in processions; there some one gives to Father Liber a golden necklace weighing three ounces, or another presents a silver statue to Felicitas. When we consider how few comparatively of such votive inscriptions have come down to us, we can infer how great was the number of gifts, buildings, institutions, bequests, daily bestowed for religious purposes.

Heathenism had as yet by no means outlived itself. There was much which still assured to it for centuries a tenacious life. First, its union with the political and public life of Rome. Everywhere religion was intimately interwoven with the organization of the State; upon it rested outward morality, and even those advanced thinkers who personally no longer believed in the gods, but only in Nature, were of necessity pious after the Roman way as respected the whole mass of traditional usages, the national sanctuaries, the fire of Vesta, the haruspices and auguries, memorial services for the dead, or whenever they were officially present at sacrifices, and perhaps themselves obliged to conduct them. The Emperors in person performed solemn lustrations for the city. On special occasions, as under Nero after the Pisonian conspiracy, the gods were remembered with costly gifts. The Roman aristocracy, also, though at heart long estranged from the established cultus and disposed in private to smile at it, did not oppose it. On the contrary they deemed it of consequence officially to prove their Romanism by strict adherence to the State religion. They had moreover a personal interest in its maintenance beside that which arose from their membership in the many higher colleges of priests. As in Rome, so in all the cities religious life was most closely connected with the municipal constitution. In the East there were a great many municipal associations (the Koinon) which rested wholly on a religious basis, and were designed to secure the observance of common religious festivals. Naturally those in authority had an interest, of which they were well aware, to preserve what was established.

The general adherence of the people to the existing forms of religion cannot be doubted in view of the habitually conservative feeling in such matters of the masses. In the cities numerous associations formed so many centres for the worship of this or that god. The burial-clubs, the guilds of artisans, merchants, workmen of various sorts, all of which gained increasing importance to society during the Empire, bore at the same time a religious character. Each had some god or other as a patron, and was instituted, in part, for his worship. His image and altar stood in their place of assembly, and every meeting began with a sacrifice. That the country-people adhered even more firmly to the ancient religion, need scarcely be mentioned. They still recited with simple faith the old legends, and dreaded to meet Pan at noon in the field, or to find on their return home a faun on the hearth. In accordance with ancient custom they still observed the feasts of the gods, the festival of Anna Perenna, or of Juno in Faleria, which Ovid describes for us from personal experience. In the darkness of an ancient wood stood the rude altar of the goddess, her image was carried thither in procession, sacrifices were offered, booths constructed of branches, and then the day was spent in eating, drinking, merry-making, and dancing, with unrestrained joy.[28]

The old religion was also still firmly supported by family customs and usages. These are chiefly determined by the wife and mother, and the women at the time of which we speak were generally attached to the old faith. Cicero, who himself often enough ridicules the fables about the gods, deemed it perfectly natural that his wife should be pious, and did nothing to change her views. Plautus, in portraying the ideal wife, does not fail to mention, — together with *gravitas*, womanly dignity, respect for parents, obedience to her husband, — reverence for the gods.[29] "She was pious without superstition," is the highest praise which a husband pays to his deceased wife in a memorial inscription.[30] An estimable matron was still one who faithfully fulfilled her religious duties, did not stay away from prayers and sacrifices, and diligently frequented the temples.

Generally a man sooner cuts loose from his faith, than from established customs. Even where the father of a family belonged to the advanced thinkers the customary religious observances were never omitted at betrothals and marriages, at births and deaths. Lucretius is perhaps correct when he speaks of those who, so long as it went well with them, mocked at the gods, but at the first reverse of fortune hastened to the temples for the sake of sacrificing;[31] and to many would have applied the picture Plutarch draws of a man who inwardly estranged from religious ceremonies still outwardly joined in them. "Through fear of the multitude he feigns prayers without feeling any need, and utters words which contradict his philosophy. When he sacrifices he stands by the side of the slaying priest as by a butcher, and after the offering departs with the words of Menander: 'I have sacrificed to gods who do not care for me.'"[32]

Finally there were the countless local rites in which the old faith lived on notwithstanding all enlightenment. The recently discovered registers of a Roman local worship, that of the *Arvales*, afford an interesting view of the tenacious life of these cults. It continued unaltered through all changes of the city and the State down to the later centuries. The same litany to which the kings of Rome had listened was still chanted by the Arval Brothers when Elagabalus, the priest of the sun from Syria, sat upon the throne of the Cæsars. Still stood in their temples the antique jars, made without potters' wheels, which were used before bread was baked, and when corn was only pounded into meal. Rome from a village of peasants had become the metropolis of the world, its morning and its noon were past, its evening was already setting in, and still they sang, at every fresh return of Spring, in Latin which if spoken on the street no one could have understood, the primeval song:

> Help us, Lases! help!
> Mars! Mars!
> Suffer not Death and Destruction
> To rush in upon us:
> Be satisfied, dread Mars![33]

The chants and prayers of the Salian priesthood had become so unintelligible in the classical age that commentaries were written upon them. Even the learned could no longer explain them. Yet they were retained unaltered, and Marcus Aurelius knew them by heart in his eighth year.[34] The tough, conservative, spirit of the Romans showed itself, also, in religious things.

So was it everywhere. Not to speak of the Orient, whose thoroughly stable character is evinced also in its worship, how many primeval images of the gods, how many cults observed without change from time immemorial, had Greece. In Sparta was still shown the image of Artemis which Orestes, according to the legend, had carried away from the Taurian temple, and every year youths were found who were willing to be scourged before this image until their blood flowed. In Patræ, as had been the custom for centuries, the priest still rode, in the procession at the annual festival, upon a car drawn by stags, in order to burn animals alive on the altar of the goddess, and in Arcadia the priestesses still chanted before the altar the old magic songs which Medea was said to have sung.

While, however, there were few, if any, apparent traces of even an external decline of the old religion, something like the dusk of evening rested everywhere upon it. The times in which Pericles led processions up to the Parthenon, or the generals of the Republic brought as triumphers their thank-offerings to the Capitoline Jupiter, were irrecoverably gone. Doubtless there were even then devout souls, according to pagan standards, who with mystic fervor frequented the temples, brought thither their offerings, and repeated their prayers; doubtless there were many more upon whom the intoxicating splendor of the worship made at least a momentary impression: but, in general, religion was unquestionably sustained more from custom than from faith; and calm deliberation, cool calculation, regard for the masses, and the consideration that it had always been so, had more to do in securing its observance than mystic fervor. At least there was among the higher classes much open unbelief, which more and more found its way down to the lower strata of society; and even amongst such persons doubt and superstition flourished and grew rank, testifying just as strongly as unbelief that the time of simple faith had gone by. More or less clearly the feeling was awakened that the old religion no longer sufficed. New ideas were stirring, and while some persons gradually cut loose from all the gods, others sought after new ones only to find quickly enough that the new could satisfy the deepest needs of the heart as little as the old.

This unbelief was not of recent date. In Greece philosophy had long since undermined faith in the old deities, and Aristophanes had already made sport of the Olympian gods on the stage. The fickle Greek at evening in the Comedy laughed at the same gods to whom the next morning in their temples he offered sacrifice. With Greek culture and philosophy unbelief had come to the Romans, as in the last century Illuminism came to Germany from France. The first Roman writers who copied the Greek appropriated also their unbelief. Ennius thus expresses his sentiments: "I believe that there are gods in heaven, but I affirm that they do not concern themselves about the human race. If they did the good would prosper, the bad suffer. But now the reverse is true."[35] This was a practical argument which was then employed as often against the heathen faith as it is to-day against the Christian. Cato and Cæsar openly acknowledged their scepticism in the Senate, and numerous testimonies in the literature of the classic age prove unmistakably that amongst educated persons the majority were at heart more or less at variance with the old creed.[36] With glowing hate had Lucretius already pursued every religious faith. Each was to him nought but a gigantic spectre rearing itself from earth to heaven, with heavy foot trampling the human race ignominiously to the dust, while with menacing look it gazed down from on high until the bold spirit of Epicurus bade it defiance. He opened the gates of nature, pressed far beyond the flaming walls of the universe into the infinite, and as a conqueror brought to man the knowledge of the ultimate grounds of all being. Thus did he vanquish faith and exalt us by his victory to heaven. Acceptance of this doctrine did not necessarily imply frivolity and irreligion. On the contrary faith itself had often led to impious and criminal deeds. Agamemnon sacrificed his own daughter to Diana, "To so much harm could faith impel." To Lucretius the gods are but the offspring of fear, Providence a chimera, the world a result of the conjunction, mixture, and combination of atoms, life a product of primeval generation.[37] Deeply as this fanaticism of unbelief moves us we are equally if not more affected by the calmness with which Pliny sets forth as an assured result of science that there are no gods; for, he says, Nature alone is God, the mother of all things, the holy immeasurable universe; and with freezing unconcern he draws the comfortless conclusion inseparable from this view of the world: "There is nothing certain save that nothing is certain, and there is no more wretched and yet arrogant being than man. The best thing which has been given to man amid the many torments of this life is, that he can take his own life."[38] Put now with the fanatic, and the man of science, the courtier, the consummate worldling, Petronius, who was regarded at Nero's court as an arbiter in questions of taste, and who for a long time possessed the highest favor of the Emperor on account of his skill and inventive talent in the arrangement of sports, and we have three types of unbelief which doubtless were often enough repeated although with less cleverness and brilliancy. A life without God, a life of prosperity and of most highly refined enjoyment; not coarsely material but finely cultured and art loving, yet without any deeper meaning, this it is which is mirrored in the life and in the works of Petronius. His death was in keeping with such a life. Implicated in the

Pisonian conspiracy he determined to destroy himself. His veins were opened, and while the blood was flowing he conversed with his friends, not upon serious themes, upon immortality, like Pætus Thrasea, but on frivolous subjects. He caused ludicrous poems to be read to him, and when something especially laughable occurred he had his veins tied up again that he might thoroughly enjoy it.

Not all were so fanatical as Lucretius, so confident in their unbelief as Pliny, so frivolous as Petronius. We meet also men who strove to hold fast the old faith. Such was Tacitus, the great historian, who lived in the full conviction that the gods carry into effect the laws of nature, are active in the course of affairs, and by omens, — so many of which he himself relates, — foretell the future. Dionysius of Halicarnassus,[39] who shortly before the birth of Christ wrote a Roman history, admires in Romulus most of all that he held something to be the basis of the State of which many statesmen talk, but which few seek to secure, the good will of the gods, which when it exists disposes all for the best good of men. Notwithstanding many ridicule the idea he holds fast to this, that the gods concern themselves about men; and he relates with entire confidence an instance of such care, in which, through the intervention of the gods, the innocence of a falsely accused Vestal was brought to light. Especially does Plutarch everywhere appear, in a pagan way, believing and pious. Yet in this very case we cannot avoid the impression that this believing disposition, with its forced character, its constant complaint of the unbelief of the present, and its looking back to better times, has in it something artificial; while in the case of Tacitus, as his contempt of Christianity and of all forms of religion shows, political motives doubtless co-operated.

The majority were likely then, as at all times, to seek a middle way. Without wholly discarding the popular faith and openly breaking with it, they kept to themselves the higher knowledge peculiar to men of culture. Personally they no longer believed in the gods, but found it useful and conducive to conservatism to have the people believe in them. So they were cautious about openly acknowledging their unbelief, and hypocritically participated in the ceremonies, while at heart they imagined themselves to be wholly superior to all the old traditional rubbish. The irrational populace, Strabo[40] thinks, is allured, like children, by the fables of the gods. "For it is not possible to impart intelligence to the crowds of women and common people, and lead them by philosophical teaching to piety, reverence, and conscientiousness. This must be done by superstition which cannot exist without fables and marvellous tales. For, the thunderbolt, the trident, the dragons of the gods are myths, as is also all the old theology. Founders of states have approved such things as bugbears for the simple." "All that ignoble crowd of gods which the superstition of ages has collected, we will adore," says Seneca,[41] "in such a way as to remember that its worship belongs rather to usage than to reality. The wise man will unite in all these observances as commanded by the laws, not as pleasing to the gods." Varro[42] formally systematized this view by distinguishing three kinds of religion, the mythical for poets, the physical (Natural Religion) for philosophers, and the popular for the masses. In a similar way most persons discriminated between an esoteric knowledge belonging to the cultivated, and the exoteric religion possessed by the ignorant multitude. Sextus Empiricus was a complete sceptic. His entire doctrine amounts to this, that one can know nothing, that all is uncertain, even the existence of the gods; and yet he adds: " Following the custom, we affirm that there are gods, and that they exercise a providence and we honor them."[43] The Epicureans did not all share the hate of Lucretius; on the contrary most of them were indifferent. They did not deny the existence of the gods *per se*, but only that they cared for this world. The people might be left in peace with their gods, but the educated man had a right not to trouble himself about them. A real mediating theology, however, appears first in the Stoic school, at that time the most widely diffused of all. It sought to reconcile faith and philosophy by accepting in addition to the one supreme Deity, whom it conceived of pantheistically, numerous subordinate gods, the gods of the popular religions. Accordingly the Stoic could accept these religions with their countless deities, sacrifices, oracles, miracles, omens, and incantations, if necessary take part in them, and all the while hold fast to his esoteric knowledge of God.

As regards the educated classes we may perhaps come to this conclusion: faith in the gods of the old religions had disappeared. In its place had come sheer Atheism and Nihilism, though only, it may be among individuals (at least only such ventured openly to express it). The majority substituted a kind of Monotheism. They imagined something godlike above the gods, a divine first principle, or at least they had a presentiment of this without clearly discerning it, and especially without being able definitely to distinguish it from the world. This dissolving Polytheism led naturally to Pantheism. As the many deities of the heathen were all Nature-gods, so must the One Deity in whom these all met be a Nature-god. Nature itself is God; and the conviction which Strabo utters as his own was doubtless that of many: "The one highest being is that which embraces us all, which we call heaven, world, and the nature of the universe."[44] Doubtless there was in this Monotheism a presage of the true God, a longing and reaching forth by Heathenism after something higher, a testimony of the soul by nature Christian, as Tertullian says.[45] But the One was still only "the unknown God whom ye ignorantly worship." The heathen did not go beyond this. The Monotheism to which they came at last remained abstract, lifeless. The God vaguely conceived of as above the gods was no divine being who has talked with men, and who can be named and supplicated. Therefore this conviction, however widely it was diffused in cultivated circles, proved on the whole powerless. It gained no influence over public opinion and morals. The educated who shared it did not thereby attain to any higher worship, but remained continually in suspense between this their own better conviction and a hypocritical (we cannot otherwise term it) participation in the official rites. With this scepticism was often offensively combined a childish superstition. Caesar, who made no concealment in the Senate of his unbelief, never stepped into a carriage without first uttering a magical formula as a preservative against accident.[46] Augustus, of whom it was related that he had at a banquet openly scoffed at the gods, dreaded misfortune through the entire day when on rising in the morning he had put the left shoe on the right foot. He would never begin a journey on the *nundinæ*, nor undertake any thing important on the *nones*.[47] Pliny had lost faith in every thing, yet he believed in talismans. No one thought of bringing the great mass of the people to a better knowledge; in the pride of an esoteric wisdom this was regarded as plainly impossible. So far therefore as this wisdom, notwithstanding such an opinion, did affect the people, its influence was only destructive.

The exact limit of this process cannot be defined. It is true that a series of passages might be adduced from writers of the time which would lead us to conclude that literally no one any longer had faith in the gods. Indeed Juvenal contemptuously says that even the youngest children had ceased to believe every thing that was related of the lower world.[48] But we are too familiar from our own experience with such forms of speech as, Nobody believes that to-day! not to understand how little force they have as proof. Unbelief has had the skill in all ages to set forth its own views as alone valid, and universally diffused. All the facts are too strongly contradictory to allow the supposition that as early as the first century the mass of the people had been inwardly estranged from the heathen faith. On the other hand, however, we have unimpeachable witnesses whose testimony leaves no doubt that unbelief had already penetrated beyond the cultivated circles, and begun to make its way among the masses. The historian Livy speaking of an earlier time, says, "That neglect of the gods which prevails in the present age had then not yet spread,"[49] and Quinctilian, the renowned teacher of rhetoric, whose own convictions seem to have been very fluctuating, declares: "Even among our country-people there are only a few who do not either know something of Nature or seek to acquire this knowledge." [50] It was a bad sign, and indicative of a wide-spread indifference toward the old religion that so early as the time of Augustus there could no longer be found among free Roman families virgins who were willing to become Vestals. It became necessary to take freed persons, and Tiberius was constrained to increase the privileges and prerogatives of the Vestals in order to make attractive a service once so highly venerated. Even among the people confidence in the ancient deities had already much diminished and was daily decreasing. It could not be otherwise. The example of the higher classes is always determinative for the lower, and the endeavor to maintain amongst the ignorant a religion one has himself abandoned has never yet succeeded.

On the other hand we may not underestimate what was done by the upper classes to foster the old religion. Augustus consciously aimed at a restoration of the State-church. Much that had been destroyed in the turbulent times of the civil wars, was replaced. Temples were repaired and built anew, the priesthoods filled up, the festivals and sacrifices re-established, ancient traditions sought out. Virgil's poems by their piety promoted this object, and Ovid suffered severely for not entering into the movement. Even the bad Emperors of the Julian line held firmly to the maxim that the State-religion should be supported by laws and their own example. However indifferent Tiberius may have been personally, he still cared zealously for the official worship, was well instructed in the ancient usages, and would not tolerate any changes in them.[51] Claudius, at his triumph, ascended on his knees the steps to the Capitol.[52] When one day a bird of evil omen sat on the temple of Jupiter, all the people were summoned to make a solemn expiation, and the Emperor himself as *Pontifex Maximus* pronounced from a tribune the liturgical formulas which the people repeated after him.[53] Even Nero, whose own devotions were limited to a little idol given him by one of the common people, rigidly adhered to this fundamental principle of the Julian house. When a temple on the Capitol had been damaged by lightning he instituted elaborate ceremonies to appease the anger of the god.[54]

Accustomed as we are to regard religion as an inward life which cannot be evoked by any imperial edicts, it is natural for us to condemn in advance such efforts at restoration as futile. They were not so much so as we might readily suppose. The Roman religion did not consist of articles of faith, but of ceremonies. Belief cannot be decreed by authority, but ceremonies may be restored; and it is not to be questioned that in this respect the policy of the Julian house — which later Emperors, especially Vespasian,[55] continued — was not without effect. It is well to notice that just at the time when Christianity was born the pagan religion received a new impulse. As compared with the last days of the Republic Religion began with the Monarchy to acquire new strength.

A sure sign that the pagan religion was by no means as yet so devoid of life as is commonly supposed, is to be found in the new forms of worship which now appeared; as for example, the worship of the goddess Annona, the provider of corn. When the supplying of Rome with corn assumed greater importance than in earlier times, the impulse among the Romans to give to every branch of life a special deity, led them to create this new goddess. The worship of the Emperors is especially significant in this connection.

The deification of the Emperors seems to us, at first, like an effect of frenzy, and like boundless adulation. We are therefore inclined to regard it as of little importance, particularly as we find it hard to conceive that any one could have seriously believed in the divinity of the Emperor. But this is contradicted by the fact that the first apotheosis, that of Cæsar, proceeded from the people themselves, and though Augustus was, so to speak, regularly deified by a decree of the Senate, yet it was the conduct of the people which first gave the decree real validity. It would be a great misapprehension to regard the worship of the Emperors solely as an indication of the extent to which human folly can go, and as deserving only ridicule and scorn. In reality it exerted the greatest influence not only upon the religious, but also upon the social, life of that time; and became of the greatest importance in the conflict of Christianity with Heathenism.

The deification of the Emperors, which seems to us so strange, was deeply rooted in pagan modes of thought. The Orientals had long been accustomed to pay divine honors to princes. In Egypt, as an inscription attests,[56] Ptolemy Epiphanes was revered as a god, the son of a god and goddess. His image stood in every temple, and was carried about in procession with those of other gods. The idea that a man by illustrious deeds can become divine was by no means foreign to the Greeks (recall their hero worship), and if among the Romans no example of apotheosis occurs after

Romulus, still the veneration paid to ancestors, the cultus of the *dii manes*, was universal. When one so highly honored by the people as Cæsar sank beneath the daggers of his enemies, it was not so strange that they began immediately a cultus of the *divus* Julius, erected to him an altar, and paid him divine honor; that after the fearful storms of the civil wars the world, which now at last had attained repose, dedicated to Augustus even in his life-time temples and altars.

It is true the worship of the Emperors had its chief seat in the provinces. One was too near the Emperor at Rome. There, no doubt, it was difficult to believe in the divinity of Claudius whom, as Juvenal sneeringly says, his wife had sent to the skies, or in that of the *diva virgo*, a daughter of Nero, who lived but a few months and was deified by him after her death. It was otherwise in the provinces. Their inhabitants were thoroughly in earnest when they adored the *numen* of the Imperial house, and erected temples to the goddess *Roma*, and to Augustus. In so doing they honored the power which had given peace to the world, and to which they owed their security and their civilization. For them the worship of these *Divi* was a public attestation that they deemed themselves happy in being under the dominion of the Romans. And not without reason. The freedmen who had become rich, and who as merchants, or in other forms of business, peculiarly appreciated the value of the peace of the Empire, were also specially zealous worshippers of the divinity of the Emperors. The soldiers, who were accustomed to look up to their flags with the reverence for their imperial leaders produced by strict discipline, saw in them at the same time the gods whose hands held their entire fate. And if the masses worshipped the new gods with the same simple ignorance as they did the old, so the educated also found ways of adjusting themselves to this homage. It was the duty of a good Roman citizen, it was an act of patriotism, and, in the case of a good Emperor, an expression of gratitude. It was under the able Emperors who from Trajan on ruled the State for nearly a century that the worship of the Emperors became deeply rooted. It is the one, ancient and traditional way of testifying thankfulness, says Pliny.[57] Many, indeed, honored Plato in the same way, and Virgil.

Moreover — and this should be carefully noticed — this cult gained great political and social importance. It gave the provincial assemblies ($\varkappa o \iota v o v$, *concilium*), — which otherwise might have been objects of suspicion to the Emperors as dangerous to the unity of the realm, — a new and wholly unobjectionable character. They now became chiefly assemblies for worshipping the deity of the Emperors. Provincials deemed it the highest honor to be sent as delegates to such an assembly. Splendid festivals with costly games drew multitudes of people, and the worship of the Emperors as divine was the first step by which the provincial assemblies regained political importance, since it was natural that the delegates once convened, if opportunity occurred, should busy themselves with the interests of the province. Thus within the close centralization of the Roman State a provincial consciousness began again to develop, and the Emperor-cult gave it support.

Not less great was its social importance. To that large portion of the population which had been steadily kept down by the strongly aristocratic tendency of the earlier time, to all those who were excluded from municipal offices, and from the confraternities of priests of the old gods, the service of the Emperor-gods stood open, and they prosecuted it with zeal. In all the cities we find colleges of *Augustales*, or *Claudiales*, to which they could belong, and membership in such a fraternity was for them a way of regaining social importance. To the restoration of a middle class, as we can observe it in these centuries, the worship of the Emperors greatly contributed.

What we wish most to emphasize is, that this imperial cult supplied a worship which was common to the whole Roman Empire. All other religions contained something purely local. Every country, every city, with a certain jealousy maintained that its divinity was supreme. To the citizens of Ephesus there was no higher deity than the great goddess Diana, to those of Pergamus where Æsculapius was worshipped he was chief. Not one of the ancient deities could have secured a united worship, but all men did homage to the Cæsar-gods. In their service there arose a unity of worship entirely unknown to former times. Thus it came to pass that the worship of the Emperors eclipsed all other worships. "The statues of the Emperors are more reverenced than those of the ancient gods," testifies Melito.[58] In Spain the number of priests of the gods mentioned in inscriptions is insignificantly small in comparison with the priests of the Emperors, and in Africa the latter evidently far exceed the former in importance. Even in the ancient seats of worship in Greece arose images of the Emperors. In Delphi they had largely supplanted the ancient deities; in Elis, in Corinth, in Sparta could be found their temples; and even in the temple of Olympian Zeus, by the side of his renowned statue, stood an image of the Emperor. In many ways, also, the ancient cults combined and blended with the new. In Gaul the Emperor-god was honored with rites which were borrowed from the worship of the ancient gods, and the *Arvales*, assiduously as in other respects they cared for what was old, did not oppose this innovation; they even assigned the divine Emperor a place among the ancient gods.

In a certain sense it can be said that the religious development of the ancient world culminated in this imperial worship. It gave to Heathenism a centre of religious unity, and to this extent invigorated it. Thus now existed what hitherto had been unknown, a formal universal State religion in which it was the duty of the citizen to participate, and which he could not violate without committing at the same time a crime against the State. However tolerant one might be elsewhere, there could be no concession here. With what forbearance were the religious peculiarities of the Jews generally treated. Even the legions, when they entered Jerusalem, were obliged to leave their standards behind that they might not seem to bring idols into the holy city. Yet even the Jews were required to worship the Emperors. In Alexandria, the erection of an image of the Emperor in one of the synagogues occasioned a bloody insurrection; and the order of Caligula to set up his statue in the temple at Jerusalem would doubtless have caused great mischief had not the murder of the Emperor intervened. Here, therefore, was the point where the growing Christianity necessarily came into sharpest conflict with Heathenism. It could be tolerated that Christians worshipped neither this god nor that; the heathen themselves adored different gods: but that they scrupled to pay the Emperor the divine honor which was his due, was not to be endured. Not their abandonment of other religious rites of Paganism, but their refusal to strew incense to the Emperor, was what decided the fate of most of the martyrs.

The worship of the Emperor strengthened heathenism by giving it a common centre and by connecting together its diversified forms; yet it also sensibly weakened it. Men saw too plainly what the gods were to whom temples were erected and reverence paid. When the Emperor Claudius died, poisoned by mushrooms, as the report ran, he too was transferred to the gods. As was the custom, witnesses appointed for this purpose testified upon oath that they had seen his soul ascend into heaven. Seneca delivered an address which extolled him as a god. His apotheosis was celebrated with great pomp. And immediately afterwards the same Seneca, teacher and minister of the new Emperor, published a satire upon this deification under the title: " The translation of Claudius into the society of the pumpkins," [59] in which not only the memory of the Emperor was smirched with poor witticisms, but even the facts about his death were intimated quite plainly. Nero himself said with forced wit that mushrooms must be a divine food since Claudius by eating them had become a god. In Rome this was laughed at; yet none the less temples to the new god arose in the Capital and in the provinces, and it was a part of official piety to offer to him the usual homage. Nero had a daughter by Poppæa Sabina who died when three months old. She too was exalted to the *Divæ*, and was honored with temples and offerings. So with Poppæa

Sabina herself. Hadrian afterwards crowned the whole by deifying his beautiful page Antinous, for whom he entertained an unnatural affection. Monuments, temples, and statues, were dedicated to him, and even a city was specially set apart for his worship. And when in the provinces, as was not the case in Rome, at least in the beginning, temples and altars were erected to the Emperors during their life-time, what sort of an impression must have been made on their inhabitants when they came to Rome and saw the Emperor Nero, the god whose temple stood in their native city, appear before the people as a player on the cithera, or as a singer, exhibit his tricks, and then on bended knees submissively await the verdict of the assembly. What gods were these! Could the inquiry be repressed whether the other deities who were worshipped were any better and more worthy of confidence?

III. FOREIGN RITES AND THE LONGING FOR REDEMPTION.

Nothing shows more conclusively that the people also had begun to lose confidence in their gods, than the foreign cults which were more and more crowding in. For philosophical convictions do not take the place of a lost faith with the multitude as they do with the educated. On the contrary there arises either perfect indifference toward all religious rites, or, since such a vacuum soon becomes intolerable, the old gods are exchanged for new ones in the hope that the new may prove more powerful than the old. How changed was the religious life of Rome as early even as the beginning of the Empire. No longer were seen there merely the ancient and venerable brotherhoods of priests, austere Vestals who guarded the sacred fire, augurs and haruspices who searched into the future. Gauls went about the streets, — priests of the great goddess Cybele, now transferred to Rome. Howling and with dishevelled hair they lashed themselves to blood with thongs, struck their sounding cymbals, and offered for a hundred eggs to ward off the diseases of Autumn. Priests of the Egyptian Isis were also there, in long linen robes, with the dog-mask before their faces, and their peculiar rattle (*sistrum*) in their hands. Roman ladies thronged the synagogues of the despised Jews, and many a Roman observed the Jewish Sabbath in the hope of propitiating the great Jehovah. All sorts of soothsayers were there, — Chaldæans, astrologers, people pretending to possess Oriental wisdom.[60] There too Roman soldiers, while officially paying due honor to their own deities, revered, though at first only in secret, an entirely new god which they had brought back with them from some piratical war, Mithras, the Persian god of light. It was a perfect Babel of religions. Scarcely a type of worship could be found which had not its adherents. Even the lowest form of Heathenism, Feticism, reappeared. The Emperor Nero, having become tired of the goddess Astarte, no longer worshipped any deity, but only an amulet which had been given him.[54] The ruler of a world-wide Empire which embraced all culture had become the devotee of a fetish!

The Roman laws against foreign rites were very strict. Cicero[61] cites a regulation which forbade any one to have gods separately, or to privately worship new gods or foreign ones unless they had been legally sanctioned. This forbade not only the public introduction of a new cultus, but also its private observance at home and in retirement. Livy gives the law in a somewhat milder form. According to his statement foreign rites were prohibited only so far as they were practised in public, or in some sacred place.[62] The two accounts may be reconciled, perhaps, by supposing that Cicero states what was strictly legal, Livy the usual practice. The Romans were religiously scrupulous about interdicting outright the cult of any god. Significant, in this respect, is an opinion reported by Livy: "When the worship of the gods is used as a pretext for the commission of crime the soul is seized with fear lest in punishing the human wickedness, some divine right blended with it may be violated."[63] Even in the terrible suppression of the *Bacchanalia* the government did not venture to wholly prohibit this cult. Whoever deemed it a matter of conscience could obtain from the Prætor permission for its observance, on condition that not more than five persons should be present at the sacrifice.[64] This explains why the laws against foreign religions had so little force. No one ventured to execute them with rigor. It would have been lawful to enter private houses and forbid such worship even there; but this was not done, and therefore the foreign cults came out from the houses on to the streets, and the public places. There was, also, an inconsistency in acknowledging a foreign god in his own land, but not in Rome,—as when, for example, Augustus declared expressly that he spared the city Alexandria in honor of the great god Serapis, and then destroyed his temple in Rome.[65] Every nation, every province was expected to keep its own gods to itself. This religious decentralization, however, was not consistent with the intense centralization in political affairs. A blending of religions was as essential to the Roman Empire as a fusion of politics and of nationalities. Thus it came to pass that repeated efforts on the part of the State to suppress foreign rites, proved wholly ineffectual. However quickly the Chaldæans and astrologers, or the Jews, were expelled from Rome, however promptly the temple of Isis, or any other foreign god, was closed, or the laws against forbidden worships enforced anew, the current waxed stronger and stronger, until, a century later, Roman Emperors themselves built sanctuaries for Isis and Serapis side by side with the temples of Jupiter and Vesta; noble Roman ladies walked in the processions of Isis, shaking costly golden *sistra*, or, clad in linen robes and with bare feet, watched out the night in her temple to obtain expiation for their frivolous lives. And, later still, the sacred treasures of proud Rome herself, the Palladium and the eternal fire, were borne into the newly-built temple of some obscure god brought from some far off place in the East.

We stand here before one of the most significant of phenomena. The old world had become perplexed about its century honored gods, and grew daily more unsettled. The time of secure certitude was past; a day of seeking and questioning had begun. Men sought and asked for new gods, gods who could fulfil what had been promised in vain for the old. The greater the distance from which a god had been brought, the more ancient, the more mysterious and singular his cultus, so much the better, so much greater the hope that he would be the right one. Above all,—let us mark it well,—it was Oriental deities who found most adherents. The religious current flowed manifestly from East to West. It was a refluent tide. From the days of Alexander the Great Græco-Roman culture had penetrated deeply into the East. Olympian gods had their temples hard by the fantastic deities of Syria and the animal gods of Egypt, either crowding them out or at least throwing them into the shade. Now the stream flowed back, and the gods from the Orontes and from the Nile won a place in Greece and Rome, in Gaul and on the Danube. This, also, was a preparation for Christianity. To the world seeking for mightier gods was preached the true God. Men looked for a new god to the East; from the East, according to God's counsel, He was actually to be proclaimed to the world, as the Father of our Lord Jesus Christ.

Let us examine this momentous movement more closely. How came it to pass that the old world was perplexed about its gods? The fact is far too weighty and significant to allow of our even attempting to explain it either from any isolated causes, or from mere personal influence. The scorn and mockery of a sceptical literature surely could not have destroyed faith if it had still possessed a vigorous life. On the contrary, this scorn and mockery set in precisely because the old faith was undermined. The wonderful phenomenon can only be explained by the fact that a transformation had been effected in men's entire view of the world, in the fundamental ideas by which they were impelled and controlled. The gods were still the same that they had always been, but they could no longer be the same to men as heretofore because men themselves had changed, because they sought and asked for something else, and desired something different from their gods. Let us try to make this change clear. Here, especially, shall we discover that the heathen world was prepared for the acceptance of Christianity, that the fulness of the time was come.

Ancient life was directed to this world, not to the future. Pleasure in existence, joy in the ever new glory of the world, in the beauty and greatness of human life, was its fundamental characteristic. The belief in immortality, firmly held at least so long as pagan faith retained its vitality, did not at all change this. For the dead were thought of as still turning ever toward this life. This was the reason why men so gladly buried their dead upon the streets where many persons were accustomed to pass (recall, for instance, the rows of tombs on the Appian Way in Rome); they were to remain connected, as it were, with the living. So, likewise, many epitaphs represent the dead as continually holding intercourse with the living, as, for example, this one: " Titus Lollius Musculus is laid here by the way-side that those who go by may say: Hail! Titus Lollius!" [66] Another epitaph contains a formal colloquy between the buried man and the passers by: " Farewell, Victor Fabian! — May the gods heap blessings upon you, my friends. And you, also, travellers, may the gods protect you as a reward for having tarried a moment at the tomb of Fabian. May your journey and your return be free from accident. And you who have brought me crowns and flowers, may you be able to do this many years." [67] It was the custom for those who went by a grave to say: " The earth be light upon thee!" " Whatsoever wayfarer goes by, let him say at this burial mound: Rufinus! Greeting! The earth be light upon thee! that after his death one may also wish for him: The earth be light upon thee!" runs another inscription.[68] Sacrifices, also, and libations were offered, and meals eaten at the graves. Wreaths of roses and violets were laid upon them, and the dead were supposed to rejoice in the light of the grave-lamp and in the fragrance rising from the sweet-scented oil. The horrors of death were veiled from men. They lived joyously in the present with little concern about death and eternity. They knew not the word: "The wages of sin is death."

Sin, also, was still veiled from men. It was the times of ignorance, as Paul says (Acts xvii. 30); for as the tendency of ancient life was toward this world not the other, so it was occupied with what is without, rather than with that which is within man. Hence the inclination for art, especially for architecture and sculpture. Hence the taste for decoration, the fondness for the theatre, the predilection for spectacles of every kind, for pomps and triumphal processions. Hence, too, the absorption of the man in the citizen. Man as man had no value, the infinite worth of a human soul was not yet recognized. The word of the Lord: "What is a man profited if he shall gain the whole world and lose his own soul," is a wisdom that was hidden from antiquity. Men looked without not within, not into their own hearts, therefore they did not find sin. They did not attempt to look any more deeply into Nature. The natural science of the ancients did not go beyond mere external description. With a vivid sense of the beauty of Nature they lacked susceptibility to its grandeur and sublimity. The glory of the Alpine world never dawned upon the Romans.[69] They liked only gentle and pleasing landscapes. Christianity first unlocked the sense for Nature, by teaching us to understand a creation groaning with us, and by showing the connection of Nature with ourselves and our own life.

The great transformation which now took place was

the turning from what is without to what is within, from this life to the life to come. If we trace this change up to its origin we may say, it begins with the word of Socrates: "Know thyself." From this aphorism may be dated the dissolution of ancient life, from this point it turned to a new life which came into the world with the call of which that word of the greatest sage of Greece was only an anticipation: "Repent, for the kingdom of heaven is at hand." Man as man was now respected, the real *Ego* came to the front, the development of personality proper became of chief importance. Though at first apprehended only in a pagan way and with reference to the present life, the question of salvation arose: How may I become happy? how shall I attain peace? This was the great question which now occupied the wise, over which the centuries wearied themselves, to come at last to the conclusion that all is in vain. But when the ancient world had reached this point, it was able to listen to the message of salvation by grace.

Whoever will be happy must strive after knowledge. The wise, the well-educated man is the happy man. To him is the hidden nature of things revealed, and to him, the man of understanding, evil has become unreal. But can we know any thing? know with certainty? One philosophical school followed another. What one proclaimed for truth was denied by its successor; the end was complete scepticism, doubt, and despair of all truth. "What is truth?" asked Pilate, and with him multitudes of his contemporaries. In long array Cicero adduces the doctrines of different philosophers concerning the human soul, and then adds: "Which of these opinions may be true, a god may know; which may be only probable is a difficult question." [70] Ah! if one only might have a guide to truth, sighs Seneca.[71] Thus men now looked for guides; Plato, Pythagoras, the ancient philosophers, must be such. The quest went beyond the Greeks; Egyptian, Indian wisdom seemed to offer still greater assurance. Thus something brought from far, replete with mystery, inspired confidence at first. Here too men discovered that they were deceived. "We will wait," Plato had already said, "for One, be it a god or a god-inspired man, to teach us our religious duties, and, as Athene in Homer says to Diomed, to take away the darkness from our eyes,"[72] and in another place: "We must lay hold of the best human opinion in order that borne by it as on a raft we may sail over the dangerous sea of life, unless we can find a stronger boat, or some word of God, which will more surely and safely carry us."[73] The old world, convinced of the fragility of its self-constructed float, now desired this stancher vessel; confused by its own wisdom, it longed for a Revelation.

There were two leading ways by which happiness was sought. Enjoy! said Epicurus. Enjoy to the full the good things of this life, this is the way to happiness. Forego! exhorted the Stoic, or, to speak with the chief representative of this school in the age of the Emperors, Epictetus: Abstain and endure! True happiness is only to be found in tranquillity of spirit wherein man, renouncing all things and calmly accepting what fate appoints for him, allows nothing to disquiet him. The Stoic school was the leading one in the time of the Empire; all thought which dealt with the more serious questions belonged to it in greater or less degree. Happiness was not to be found in enjoyment, therefore it was sought in renunciation! The Scepticism, also, of which we have before spoken, was itself a renunciation — a despair of attaining to assured knowledge. The times, too, were no longer favorable to enjoyment, they preached abstinence loudly enough. For the world once so gay had become more and more gloomy. The days were past when in sunny Greece men built the Parthenon, and rejoiced in the creations of a Phidias and Praxiteles; departed, also, from Rome were the days of republican greatness when men lived and strove for father-land. The One, the Emperor, was now all, and there was no longer room for men like the Gracchi and the Scipios. To be sure it seemed as if society under the first Emperors, when men revelled in the treasures of a conquered world, was everywhere joyous. But it was not really so bright as it appeared. Men were not satisfied. That refined luxury, those voluptuous banquets, those orgies became themselves sources of pain. One symptom of such dissatisfaction was the widely-spread inclination to dream one's self back into simpler times, when the cows still pastured on the Palatine, and Senators, clad in the skins of animals, counselled on the meadow. It was precisely as in the last century, when men were enraptured by Rousseau.[74] The age in which the treasures of the world were squandered in luxurious pleasure, ran swiftly enough to its end. Under Emperors like Caligula and Nero, all property, all pleasure, life itself, became insecure. And while some, indeed, solicitous to spend all the more quickly an existence which was uncertain, sought in the most refined revelry compensation for the higher good life no longer afforded, from others were heard for this very reason all the more frequent complaints of the corruption of the world, and the vanity of all that is earthly. The view of life as a whole became more and more pessimistic.

Such tones were not unfamiliar to Greece, even in its palmy days. From Homer on, a low, yet distinct lamentation sounds through all its splendor, testifying to a presentiment that something was wanting, that the solution of the riddle of the world believed to have been found, could not be the right one. How Homer sighs over the frailty of men. They fade like leaves, no being is more miserable. Like shadows, says Pindar, like a dream, says Æschylus, they pass away. Ever recurs the thought: it were best never to have been born; the next best, to die early; and with profound sadness Sophocles gives expression to this sentiment in the *Œdipus at Colonus:*

> "Happiest beyond compare
> Never to taste of life;
> Happiest in order next,
> Being born, with quickest speed
> Thither again to turn
> From whence we came." [75]

These tones became unmistakably stronger and stronger, the lamentation louder, the resignation greater. According to Homer [76] two jars stand in the palace of Zeus, one with evil, one with good, gifts for men. Later, there were two with evil gifts, and only one with good, and, later still, Simonides says: "Sorrow follows sorrow so quickly that not even the air can penetrate between them." [77] Happiness was no longer the goal of Philosophy. Men despaired of attaining it. "The aim of all Philosophy," says Seneca, "is to despise life." Here, too, Heathenism ended in barrenness and sheer despair, and at last the only comfort was that men are free to leave this miserable world by suicide. *Patet exitus!* The way out of this life stands open! That is the last consolation of expiring Heathenism. "Seest thou," exclaims Seneca, "yon steep height? Thence is the descent to freedom. Seest thou yon sea, yon river, yon well? Freedom sits there in the depths. Seest thou yon low, withered tree? There freedom hangs. Seest thou thy neck, thy throat, thy heart? They are ways of escape from bondage."[78] Can the bankruptcy of heathenism be more plainly declared than in these words? Despairing of every kind of happiness it had no further consolation for the evils of this life than suicide, and it knew no other victory over the world than this flight out of it. But who does not also hear how the cry breaks forth ever louder and louder from the heathen world: "O wretched man that I am! who shall deliver me from the body of this death?"

If happiness cannot be found in this life, men look all the more longingly to the next. The thought of another world was not unknown to the ancient Greeks and Romans, but it was for them only one of shadows. This world alone was real, alone offered true happiness; the other was the gloomy, joyless, lower world. Ulysses, in Homer, sees the dead as shadows greedily drink the blood which for a moment at least restores to them real life, and he would rather linger here upon earth in the lowest station than be a king among the shades.[79] Men shuddered at the thought of that other world. The heathen through life were slaves to the fear of death. "My temples are gray," sings the pleasure-loving Anacreon,[80] "and white my head; beautiful youth is gone. Not much remains of sweet life. Therefore I often sigh, fearing Tartarus, dreadful abyss of Hades. Full of horror is the descent thither, and whoever has once gone down there never returns." But the less this world fulfilled what it promised, and the more its evil and its emptiness were felt, and the spirit of resignation was developed, the more was this view reversed. Life in this world began to be looked upon as shadowy, and the true life was sought first in the life to come. Joy in existence, in the beauty and glory of the earth and of human life, disappeared; the consciousness of weakness, of the limitations of human nature, the sense of the vanity of all earthly things, increased. The body was now spoken of as the prison of the soul,[81] and death, which Anacreon dreaded as a fearful descent into Tartarus, was extolled as an emancipation. "After death," says Cicero, "we shall for the first time truly live."[82] How often in the schools of the rhetoricians is this theme discussed: Death no evil! How often the thought recurs in Seneca, that the body is only an inn for the spirit, that the other world is its real home. Indeed, just as did the primitive Christians, he calls the day of death "the birth-day of eternity."[83] While, however, the glory of this world faded before the eyes of men, the other grew in distinctness and reality; and more than once we meet in literature and in works of art with pictures of the future life as one of joy, a symposium, a banquet, where the souls of the departed rejoice together with gods, heroes and sages. Already had Cicero in the *Dream of Scipio* thus described the other life, and Seneca paints it yet more vividly. Plutarch delights to contemplate it, and rejoices that there "God will be our Leader and King, and that in closest union with Him we shall unweariedly and with ardent longing behold that beauty which is ineffable and cannot be expressed to men."[84]

Is there then another world? Heathenism now stood face to face with this great question, and was wholly unable to make any reply. Many answered it with a resigned No! Cæsar, indeed, had once said in the Senate with cool composure: "Beyond this life there is no place for either trouble or joy," and Cato had approvingly responded: "Beautifully and excellently has Caius Cæsar spoken in this assembly concerning life and death, esteeming as false those things which are related of the lower world."[86] Indeed we find not a few sepulchral inscriptions which confirm the apostle's declaration that the heathen are "without hope." We read: "To eternal sleep!" "To eternal rest!" Or the oft recurring distich: "I was not, and became: I was, and am no more. This much is true, whoever says otherwise does not speak the truth, for I shall not be!" or, "We all, whom Death has laid low, are decaying bones and ashes, nothing else!" or, "I was nought, and am nought. Thou who readest this: Eat, drink, make merry, come!"[85] Many inscriptions blend with resignation a tone of frivolity. Thus we read on the grave-stone of a veteran of the Fifth Legion: "So long as I lived, I gladly drank; drink, ye who live!"[86] Complete resignation is expressed by Pliny:[87] "What folly is it to renew life after death! Where shall created beings find rest if you suppose that shades in hell, and souls in heaven, continue to have any feeling. You rob us of man's greatest good, death. Let us rather find in the tranquillity which preceded our ex-

istence, the pledge of the repose which is to follow it."
Still more decidedly Lucretius: "The fear of the lower
world must be driven headlong forth. It poisons life
to its lowest depths, it spreads over all things the blackness of death, it leaves no pleasure pure and unalloyed." Utter annihilation was its consolation. "When
we have ceased to be, nothing can excite our feelings,
nothing disturb our rest, even though heaven, earth,
and sea should be commingled." [88] Yet Plutarch had
already replied: "What is gained by substituting for
fear of the lower world dread of annihilation. It is
as if one should say to passengers in a vessel who are
frightened by a storm : Keep calm, the ship will soon
go to the bottom." [89] Others left it uncertain whether
all is over at death, or not. The celebrated physician
Galen, no doubt, only expressed the conviction of
thousands when, not venturing himself to decide the
question, he said that he intended as little to affirm as
to deny immortality; [90] and there is almost a touch of
pathos in what Tacitus writes in his life of Agricola:
"If there is a place for the spirits of the pious, if as
the wise suppose, great souls do not become extinct with
their bodies:" . . . [91] "If"—in that If lies the utter
disconsolateness, the whole torturing uncertainty, and
no less the ardent longing of Heathenism. If? Who
gave the answer? Men sought and asked here and
there; no other question so occupied all the profounder
minds as did the question of immortality; now they
believed that the Eastern religions would shed light,
for these religions revolved wholly about birth and
death; now they knocked at the gates of the under
world with magic formulas, adjurations and rites of
consecration. But no answer. The more joyless this

world became, the more every thing faded which in the freshness of youth had shone so brightly, the State, Art, Science offering no more satisfaction, public life affording no longer a field for activity, private life, property, pleasure, life itself becoming insecure, so much the more did men long for another world whose portals still stood closed before them. With what power then must have come the preaching of this word: "Christ is risen! The wages of sin is death: but the gift of God is eternal life through Jesus Christ our Lord." Nothing led more believers to Christianity, even from cultivated circles, than the sure answer it gave to the question respecting another world, and the hope it offered of eternal life to those whose earthly expectations had been destroyed.

But the question of a future life necessarily raises a further question. If there is another life how can men secure it? How may they attain to the communion of the blest? The consciousness of sin also now began to awake, and with it the same question. Strictly speaking the ancient world knew nothing of sin. It deplored the need, the misery, the transitoriness of human life; but it had no conception of the corruption of human nature. Sin as a defection from God, sin as guilt, was hidden from it. In this respect, too, there was now a change. Seneca discourses of the depravity of man in words which have often been thought to sound like Paul's. " We have all sinned, some grievously, others more lightly, some purposely, others accidentally impelled or led astray, and not only have we transgressed, we shall continue to do so till the end of life." " It was the complaint of our ancestors, it is our own, it will be that of posterity, that morals are subverted, that corruption reigns." Seneca sought for the cause of this in man himself. "The human mind is by nature perverse, and strives for what is forbidden. Our fault is not external to us, it is within us and cleaves to our souls." [92] Indeed Plutarch openly expresses the idea of an evil principle. "For, since nothing can arise without a cause, and good cannot be the ground of evil, therefore evil as well as good must have a special origin." [93] The conviction now became wide-spread that man as he is cannot enter into the society of the blessed, but only when he is purified and cleansed from sins, when he is transformed and renewed. For this the old gods and their cults were insufficient. The Olympian deities were gods for the prosperous; they satisfied men so long as life shone in the serene light of a beautiful present. A man conscious of sin, anxious for salvation found them inadequate to his needs. The Capitoline Jupiter, Vesta, Victoria, were State gods. They sufficed, so long as the man was absorbed in the citizen. They were gods for publicity. A man who turned his gaze in upon himself, who looked into the depravity of his own heart, who sought for peace, could no longer rest in them. This was the deepest reason why the heathen were perplexed about their gods, why men turned pre-eminently to the Oriental cults with their gloomy sadness, their penances and purifications, why the mysteries now became universal instead of local, and new ones were added to the old with ever increasing extravagance. It is the awakened need of Redemption which is mirrored in all this. Let us reflect a moment on the character of the Roman religion as above described. It was predominantly a ceremonial service. Men kept their accounts with the gods in order by the punctual performance of the prescribed rites. Priests, in the exact sense of the word, mediators between God and men, were unknown. The magistrates offered sacrifices; the priest was only a master of ceremonies. There were no expiations, properly speaking, — there was no sense of need of them, for there was no consciousness that man by sin is separated from God. There was no desire to approach the gods; nothing was more remote from the dry prosaic Roman cultus than such mystical excitements. Therefore, the more the consciousness of sin awoke, the less did the Roman cultus satisfy. What was lacking in it the oriental religions offered in richest measure. They had a priesthood which undertook to reconcile man with Deity; they had purifications and propitiations; they offered to man a religion which corresponded to what he now required, that he be brought into immediate contact with God. Hence the current that now set from the East to the West, hence the power which the religions of the Orient gained over men's minds.

In this way the anticipation became more general that Redemption would soon dawn. For this also men's eyes turned to the East. From thence was help to come. These presentiments clothed themselves partly in heathen garb. The cycle of the ages, it was said, is completed. The golden age has been followed by the silver, this by the iron. Now this, also, is passing away; then will the cycles begin anew, Saturn will again assume the government, and the golden age return. In part however these presages bore a Jewish coloring, and their origin in Hebrew prophecy can be more or less clearly perceived. Suetonius and Tacitus both report a wide-spread rumor that the Orient would become powerful, and the dominion of the world be assigned by Fate to the Jews. Even among the Roman legions which Titus led against Jerusalem there were indications of such thoughts. They looked on the holy city which they were come to destroy with a certain superstitious awe, and even during the siege there were not wanting deserters who could bring nothing else to the city encircled with iron arms than the expectation of some extraordinary divine aid, and the hope of participating in the dominion promised to it. Remarkably do these presentiments re-echo in the Fourth Eclogue of Virgil. The poet there celebrates a child who shall restore the Golden Age, in pictures which, directly or indirectly, are derived from the ninth and eleventh chapters of Isaiah. The boy descends from heaven, then peace prevails on the earth which without culture liberally yields its gifts, the herds are no longer afraid of the lions, the yoke is taken off from the ox, and the vine-dresser toils no more in the sweat of his brow. It is supposed that these words are to be applied to a son of Asinius Pollio. If this is correct the illusion was indeed great. This very child of whom Virgil sings as Messiah, when grown to manhood, became one of Nero's numerous victims, and starved himself to death in prison.[94]

So the prophecy of the coming salvation went forth from Israel into the heathen world. We come thus to an element which we have not yet considered, but which was of great importance among the religious factors of that age, Judaism.

IV. JUDAISM.

Israel's mission was twofold. It was to be the birthplace of the Christian Church, and to prepare a way for it among the heathen. At first glance the two seem essentially opposed, yet in Israel the apparent contradiction was wonderfully reconciled. In order to become the birthplace of Christianity, Israel was necessarily a chosen people, separated from all the heathen, indeed strongly antagonistic to them, as the sole possessor of a divine revelation, and alone knowing the living God whose will had been made known to them in the law. That they might pave the way for Christianity among the heathen, it was necessary that the Jews should be dispersed among them, dwell in their midst, and be in constant intercourse with them. In every respect the Jews were qualified to meet these, at first view, irreconcilable demands. The country assigned them as a dwelling-place was specially adapted to this end. Palestine was a secluded land, shut in like a garden by mountains, deserts, and sea, yet opening on all sides to other lands, and affording easy access to the chief centres of the world. The character of the people was suited to the same purpose. No nation possessed so marked an individuality, none at the same time was so endowed for universality; none preserved so tenaciously its own peculiarities, and remained, even in the midst of other nations, so distinct and exclusive, and yet none understood so well the art of everywhere pushing itself into favor, and adapting itself to circumstances. The Jew settled as a citizen in all regions, knew how everywhere to make a place for himself, and yet everywhere remained a Jew. The way in which the people had been led was another qualification. "Get thee out of thy country and from thy kindred." This call of Abraham was the beginning of Jewish history. It began with separation, and for centuries all God's dealings with the chosen people had this design, to set them apart, to seclude them, to establish their national character. Then there came a change, and every thing tended to their dispersion. The Captivity was the turning point. From this time on, with Palestinian Judaism appeared the Judaism of the Dispersion — the *Diaspora;* with the Temple, the ritual centre of the entire nation, the Synagogue, promoting doctrine more than ritual, yet creating in all countries and cities new centres of Jewish life; with the Hebrew Old Testament, the Septuagint, appointed to carry to the Heathen also the Law, the Prophets, and the Psalms of David. Palestinian Judaism, with the Temple and the Hebrew Old Testament, was in the highest degree a centralizing power. To it gravitated all the countless scattered Jewish congregations. The *Diaspora*, with the Synagogue and the Septuagint, was a widely operative centrifugal power; through it Israel became a messenger of God, a missionary to the heathen world.

Only a part of the Jewish people had returned from the Captivity. The larger portion had either remained in Babylon, or wandered to other lands. This number was continually increased, partly by those who had been carried away prisoners of war, and through their own industry, and because the Romans knew not what to do with such strange superstitious people, had acquired freedom and remained in foreign countries, and partly by those who had voluntarily left over-populous Palestine for purposes of gain elsewhere. Thus the Jews were scattered over the whole Roman Empire, and even beyond it. "Already," says the Geographer Strabo,[95] "a Jewish population has entered every city, and it is not easy to find a place in the habitable world which has not received this race, and is not possessed by it." Naturally they were most strongly represented in the Eastern countries, Babylonia and Eastern Syria. In Egypt, they constituted more than one-eighth of the entire population; and in Leontopolis they had a temple of their own, whose erection, it is true, was disapproved by those dwelling in Palestine, yet was carried through without actual schism. In Alexandria, that great commercial centre, they occupied two of its five wards; and were scattered throughout the others.[96] Not less numerous were they in Antioch, that metropolis on the other side of Palestine. Antiochus the Great had transplanted thousands of Jewish families to Phrygia and Lydia. From there they spread over all of Asia Minor, and thence found their way into Greece. Taurus in Cilicia, Ephesus in Asia, were centres of Jewish life. Throughout Greece, in Northern Africa, in Sicily and in Italy were Jewish settlements. In Rome under Augustus the Jews numbered perhaps 40,000, in the time of Tiberius perhaps 80,000. They occupied the fourteenth district, across the Tiber, and a part of the city near the Porta Capena, the beginning of the Appian way. Their residences stood, also, in the most aristocratic portion of the city. The existence of seven synagogues in Rome has been definitely established, and probably there were others. In Spain, in Gaul, even as far as Britain, representatives of the Jews were not wanting, and the recent discovery of one of their cemeteries of the first century proves their presence in the lands of the Danube.[97]

Their principal business was trade. Retailing, peddling, and especially the smaller money-transactions (the larger were carried on by the Roman knights, the bankers of that time) were almost wholly in their hands, and they prosecuted this traffic with such characteristic industry and shrewdness that the cities of Asia Minor complained to the Emperor that they were completely drained by the Jews. The wholesale trade, also, was in many places entirely under their control. In Alexandria they almost monopolized the corn-trade, and carried on an extensive traffic with the more distant East. Wherever money was to be made, there the Jew, especially if liberalized, was to be found. We meet him in Rome as scholar, poet, actor, and even singer. "The Jews sell every thing," says Juvenal.

Though in the writings of the Roman poet just named, and of others, the Jews appear as a beggarly race,[98] — the father buying old glass and other rubbish, the children peddling matches, — many of them obtained great wealth; and this wealth, together with their adroitness in improving every favorable opportunity to put themselves unconditionally at the service of whatever government was in power, though at heart unfriendly to the entire constitution of the State and indifferent to its weal and woe, had procured for them important privileges. They were exempt from military duty,[99] and from the payment of certain taxes, and could not be summoned on the Sabbath before a court. So far was this consideration for them carried, that the municipalities were obliged to pay them money instead of corn and oil which were regarded by them as impure. Indeed, when the delivery of these supplies fell on a Sabbath, payment to the Jews was required to be made on another day.[100] Above all, they had perfect freedom in their religious observances. Wherever they dwelt together in sufficient numbers they had a Synagogue, or at least a place of prayer (a *Proseucha*, Acts xvi. 13), formed a distinct communion under chosen presidents, and exercised a large autonomy which, in consequence of their religious and national isolation from the heathen among whom they lived, embraced not merely matters of religion, but much besides.

All these Jewish congregations were most intimately connected with each other, and with the centre of Judaism, Jerusalem. Every Jew, however far away he dwelt, regarded himself as a member of the chosen people, and strove to keep the bonds of union fresh and strong. He paid yearly his temple tax,[101] sent offerings and gifts to Jerusalem, and once, at least, in his life went up to visit the holy city and to keep the feast.[102] The Supreme Council in Jerusalem sent annually the calendar of festivals to the congregations of the Dispersion, communicated to them important decisions, and took care that they received information of all events which concerned the Jewish people. Since the Jews as merchants were great travellers, brethren often came bringing news of other congregations, and such guests were gladly permitted to speak in the Synagogues. In brief, whether one of their congregations was located on the banks of the Danube, or on the margin of the Libyan desert, it was a part of a universal society. The Jews well understood how to use this connection for the promotion of their own interests. If a Jewish congregation received any injury, all alike broke out into sedition, and this skill in exciting alarm had not a little to do in securing for them, notwithstanding the universal hate and contempt which they had to endure, the greatest respect from every Roman official up even to the Proconsul.

Apart from this, hatred and contempt were their usual lot. To the heathen their whole appearance was strange and utterly unintelligible, so entirely different were they in all respects from the other nations. If we would be convinced how unique this people was in history, if we would obtain an immediate impression of this, we need only recall the judgments of the heathen upon them. What marvellous tales concerning them were in circulation![103] Now they were said to have sprung from Mount Ida in Crete; now from lepers who had been expelled from Egypt. In the desert, when there was a great scarcity of water, an ass showed them a fountain; therefore they worshipped the head of an ass as God. Tacitus thinks that Moses, in order to make sure of the people, gave them new customs contradictory to all the usages of mankind. "They deem profane what we hold sacred, and permit what we abominate."[104] To the Romans the commandments about food and fasting appeared ridiculous in the extreme. The prohibition of swine's flesh was an inexhaustible theme for their wit. The Sabbath rest they could explain only by laziness. Juvenal[105] thus ridicules an idler:

> "His sire's the fault, who every seventh day
> Neglected work, and idled time away;"

and Tacitus relates with entire seriousness: "Afterwards when inactivity became agreeable the seventh year (the Sabbatical) was also given up to idleness."[106] Particularly offensive was their worship without images, and their entire faith was to the heathen the acme of superstition and credulity. "*Credat Judæus Apella,*" "A Jew may believe that,"[107] says Horace in order to characterize something wholly incredible.

This wide-spread hatred of the Jews,—to which countless bloody sacrifices were offered, especially during the Jewish war,—was doubtless, to some extent, a consequence of their hatred of the heathen. They were treated with contempt because they themselves despised the unclean Gentiles. The Jew had a large self-consciousness. He looked upon himself as a member of the elect people, who possessed, in contrast with the blind heathen, a divine revelation. This self-consciousness was intensified by his Messianic hopes. He was destined, he believed, soon to receive the dominion of the world, and he made no reserve of this expectation even when face to face with the heathen. The less its depressed and enslaved present harmonized with this hope for the future, the more absurd must it have seemed to the proud Roman that this filthy race of beggars should dream of such things. We need only glance at the writers of the Empire to meet everywhere witticisms about the circumcised Jews.[108] Wherever the Jew went or stood he was encompassed by pagan ridicule. In the theatre he was the object of coarse sallies, which were sure to call forth laughter; on the street he had frequently to endure brutal abuse.

Hatred and contempt might well be increased by the fact that the heathen could not be insensible to the wide and profound influence which the Jews were exerting. Seneca says of them, "the vanquished have given laws to the victors."[109] At a time when the old gods no longer satisfied the heathen, when so many longing spirits, anxious for happiness, were seeking peace by foreign gods, and secret doctrines and expiations, how attractive must Judaism have been! Here Monotheism, which wise men taught as an esoteric religion for the cultivated, appeared as a religion for the people; here was a spiritual cult infinitely superior to the wild, and often immoral, heathen cults; here was a revealed word of God; here were offerings and expiations.

It is true that only a small number of heathen passed, by circumcision, wholly over to Judaism, great as was the trouble the Pharisees gave themselves, compassing sea and land to make one proselyte (Matt. xxiii. 15). Those who were gained, were for the most part complete slaves of Pharisaism, allowing themselves to be led blindly by blind leaders, fanatics, proud saints, who afterward became the most zealous persecutors of the Christians. Often worldly advantages would come into play, particularly exemption from military service, for there was certainly a special reason why Tiberius, in the year 19 of our era, inflicted on the Jewish community in Rome precisely this punishment of recruiting from it. Our Lord, also, passed, in the passage just referred to, a severe judgment on these proselytes. The largest number by far of those who attached themselves to Judaism were only the so-called Proselytes of the Gate. Without receiving circumcision, and thus obliging themselves to keep the whole ceremonial law, they were bound merely to avoid idolatry, to serve the one God, and to keep the so-called precepts of Noah. On these conditions they had a part in the blessings of Judaism. They are the devout men and women so often spoken of in the book of Acts. They were, for the most part, souls anxious for salvation, who sought in the synagogues for that peace of heart which they had failed to find in the proud temples of Greece, and the intoxicating cults of the Orient. There was, in all the cities, a great number of such persons, for the most part women.[110] In Damascus, almost all the women are said to have belonged to this class, and, in Rome, there were many even from the higher circles. On the gravestones of Jewish cemeteries we read names from many an illustrious old Roman family, the *gens* Fulvia, Flavia, Valina, and others. The report spread that even the Empress Poppæa Sabina was a proselyte. Even without becoming exactly proselytes many attached themselves to the synagogue, fasted, prayed, kept the Sabbath, and lighted candles on Jewish festival days. In this there may have been much superstition. The experiment which had been tried with so many other gods was repeated with Jehovah. But on the other hand many a soul thirsting after the living God found there its refuge. A circle formed itself about the synagogue which, no longer pagan, nor yet Jewish, was in suspense and in a position of expectancy, and thus was prepared for the preaching of the Gospel. Those who belonged to it had renounced idolatry, had learned to hearken to a revelation. The Old Testament was known to them, the law had awakened in them a consciousness of sin, and prophecy a longing for salvation, and yet they did not share in that pride of Jewish descent and Pharisaic righteousness of the law which with the Jews themselves was so great a hindrance to the reception of the preaching of the cross. These devout heathen were everywhere, as at Philippi (Acts xvi. 14) and Thessalonica (Acts xvii. 4), the first to receive the message of Christ.

How wonderfully every thing here, also, was prepared for the Gospel. What Palestine was for the whole world, the synagogue was for every city. How could the youthful Christianity possibly have made its way through the unyielding, rock-like mass of Heathenism without the *Diaspora?* Now it found channels everywhere cut, a net-work of canals extending over the whole Roman Empire, and was able to diffuse itself rapidly in every direction. Knowing the chief seats of Judaism, we know already in advance the chief seats of early Christianity. Everywhere the ways were made ready for it, the centres determined. Moreover we should remember that the privileges of Judaism were at first of service to the Christian Church. So long as Christianity was regarded by the heathen as a Jewish sect, it appears to have been tolerated by them. Judaism served as a protecting sheath to the young plant, until it had gained sufficient strength to endure the storms.

Truly the times were fulfilled; the old world was ready, not to produce Christianity from itself, but to receive it. In Greece, in Rome, had been shown what the human spirit can accomplish in its own strength. It is capable of great things, and gloriously has it wrought, but all the greatness sank into ruin, all the glory paled, and one thing it could not do, it could not appease the longing of every human soul for the eternal, for God. The end of Heathenism, as respects religion, is complete inefficiency, perfect despair of itself. Man can know nothing with certainty, this is the end of all questioning. *Patet exitus!* This is the end of all search for happiness, suicide is the last consolation. But, in the act of expiring, Heathenism reaches forth to the new creation which God will provide. Everywhere coming events cast their shadow before them, the universality of Christianity is adumbrated in the universality of the Roman Empire, faith in the one living God in the Monotheism which through the labor of Philosophy and the mingling of national gods opens a way for itself into ever widening circles. Everywhere is disclosed a seeking and questioning which wait for their fulfilment and will find it, the seeking for Redemption in the Saviour of all nations, the questioning respecting the other life in the preaching of the risen One. And in the midst of the seeking heathen world Israel stands as a Prophet, fulfilling here also its mission to prepare a place for Him who is to come. Here, if anywhere, can it be perceived, not to say grasped with the hand, that every thing in the history of our race, according to the plan and counsel of God who is rich in mercy, finds its goal in Him in whom all the promises of God are Yea and Amen, in Christ the Lord.

CHAPTER II.

THE MORAL CONDITION OF THE HEATHEN WORLD.

"We ourselves also were sometimes foolish, disobedient, deceived, serving divers lusts and pleasures, living in malice and envy, hateful, and hating one another." — TIT. iii. 3.

I. FAITH AND MORALS.

AN age which has become unsettled in its faith is wont to lay all the greater stress upon morality. Our own age of Illuminism, for instance, — how prone it was to moralizing. What voluminous compends of Ethics, what a flood of moral sermons, moral tales, moral songs, what space was given in the catechisms to lessons on the virtues, of which too many could not be enumerated. There was a consciousness that something had been lost, and at the same time an unwillingness to acknowledge it; a misgiving that, with faith, morality also must decline, and a desire to prove, at least by words and looks, that this was not so. Men would gladly have kept the fruit although they had cut off the roots. They had so much to say about the fruit because they wished to persuade themselves that this was still uninjured. But soon enough it appeared that with the root the fruit as well was irrecoverably lost.

The first century was a similar period. If we survey its literature we shall feel ourselves tempted to regard it as moral to an extraordinary degree. Men moralized abundantly. Philosophy was wholly absorbed by Ethics. Casuistry was perfected, even to the minutest details, so that the wise man was provided with a rule of conduct for every relation and event of life. Seneca's purpose is not so much to teach philosophy as to prepare for a successful life.[1] Characteristic is his relation to Annæus Serenus, captain of the watch under Nero. Seneca regulates his life even to the smallest detail, points out what he shall read, how he may best spend the day. Serenus lays before him the state of his soul, and Seneca discusses it like a father confessor. So should Serenus attain tranquillity of mind, that blessed state in which the soul has inward peace, and exemption from all disquietude. Similar relations often appear. Indeed it became the custom to receive philosophers into the family as teachers, one might almost say as confessors and chaplains, in order to obtain from them counsel and guidance for the whole ordering of life; and how beautifully and admirably they could talk about all possible virtues. The ethical essays of Seneca, to mention only one of these philosophers, have appeared so excellent to many persons in later times that they have thought them explainable only on the theory of a Christian influence, and the story arose of a personal intercourse between the philosopher and the Apostle Paul.[2] But what are these moral sermons? Words, nothing but words. The same Seneca who could discourse so finely upon the abstemiousness and contentment of the philosopher, who on all occasions paraded his contempt for earthly things as nothingness and vanity, amassed, during the four years of his greatest prosperity and power, a fortune of three hundred millions of sesterces (over $15,000,000), and, while writing a treatise on Poverty, had in his house five hundred citrus tables, tables of veined wood brought from Mount Atlas, which sometimes cost as much as $25,000, and even $70,000. The same Seneca who preached so much about purity of morals was openly accused of adultery with Julia and Agrippina, and led his pupil Nero into still more shameful practices. He wrote a work upon Clemency, yet had, beyond question, a large part of Nero's atrocities upon his conscience. It was he, too, who composed the letter in which Nero justified before the Senate the murder of his own mother. What was accomplished, then, by such ethical homilies as Seneca's? Leaving entirely out of account that it was not in the least his intention to influence the mass of the people, what good did he do to individuals? He put their minds into a state of feverish excitement, induced habits of morbid introspection, but such results contained no power of moral renovation. That very Serenus whom he guided so like a father confessor was unable to withstand the infection of Nero's court; he it was who brought about Nero's amour with Acte. This period, as well as others, affords a proof of the indissoluble connection between faith and morals. Restricting the question to the imperfect morality of Heathenism, we see even here, that, when faith goes, morals perish with it. Not until we perceive the moral condition of the heathen world, do we discover the depth and completeness of its decay.

Such a view, however, it is difficult to secure. I might, indeed, simply refer to contemporary representations which portray the state of morals. What a picture it is! Seneca says, "All things are full of iniquity and vice. More crimes are committed than can be remedied by force. A monstrous contest of wickedness is carried on. Daily the lust of sin increases; daily the sense of shame diminishes. Casting away all regard for what is good and honorable, pleasure runs riot without restraint. Vice no longer hides itself, it stalks forth before all eyes. So public has iniquity become, so mightily does it flame up in all hearts, that innocence is no longer rare: it has ceased to exist."[3] Somewhat later Lucian exclaims: "If any one loves wealth, and is dazed by gold, if any one measures happiness by purple and power, if any one brought up among flatterers and slaves has never had a conception of liberty, frankness and truth, if any one has wholly surrendered himself to pleasures, full tables, carousals, lewdness, sorcery, falsehood, and deceit, let him go to Rome!"[4] Or, if we would have in addition to these somewhat rhetorical representations a sober and calm opinion, we may take that of the historian Livy: "Rome has become great by her virtues till now, when we can neither bear our vices nor their remedies."[5] But it may be replied: These are general representations, which proceed from pessimistic views, and from their very generality, are of little value; for it cannot be denied that they are not universally applicable, and that with the darkness which is all that is here recognized there was still some light.

Instead, then, of these general descriptions I might give details, an anthology of the horrors committed in that age. I might draw the portrait of a Messalina, or relate how Nero murdered his brother, his wife, and his own mother, how secretly plotting her death he first spun about her a web of intrigues, and, when this failed, used brutal violence, and himself sent the murderer to plunge the sword into the body of her who had borne him; how he then with lies justified to the Senate what had been done, and that assembly, transparent as were these lies, in slavish subjection decreed new honors for the Emperor, and offered prayers of thanksgiving in the temples of the gods; how, greeted by the Senate, and welcomed by the people arranged in tribes, with their wives and children in festal attire, the matricide entered Rome as a *triumphator*. I might describe the imperial frenzy of a Caligula, or the government of freedmen under Claudius, and then say: This is the Age! But with reason I should be answered, that in all ages we meet with individual instances of deeds of horror, and yet the error should not be committed of judging a whole period by such cases without further evidence. I might, it is true, reply in turn, that such atrocious crimes are but the summit of a pyramid whose broad base is in the life of the nation, that shapes like Messalina's are not to be encountered in every age, and that an Emperor who murders his mother, a Senate which decrees thanksgivings therefor, a people who go out to meet the murderer as a *triumphator*, do indeed presuppose, in order to the mere possibility of such occurrences, a universal and horrible decay of morals. And yet I concede that there is no poorer way of characterizing an age than that of sweeping all the dirt which can be found into one heap. Though every detail may be correct, the picture as a whole is false.

This much is clear. If we would obtain a tolerably correct impression of those times we must neither be content with mere generalizations which from their very nature imply that there are exceptions, nor look too exclusively at individual facts, since their significance for the entire period can always be called in question. The best course will be to go through the different departments of life, and thus at last, from a mass of details, compose for ourselves a comprehensive picture.[6]

II. MARRIAGE AND FAMILY LIFE.

We begin with that relation which is fundamental to all others, whose soundness, therefore, is a prerequisite to the healthfulness of a nation's life, whose stability is for this reason, the surest criterion of the moral character of an age — with Marriage and Family Life.

The Japhetic nations received as their choicest inheritance, shame, chastity, and modesty. It was these traits which distinguished them so definitely from the descendants of Ham, and elevated them so high in comparison. But they acted like the prodigal son. They wasted their portion. First of all, the Greeks. They too in their youth were not wanting in chastity and modesty (recall Penelope), but as early as the palmy days of Greece this treasure was already lost. Almost all their great men — not merely so notorious a libertine as Alcibiades,[7] but even a Themistocles and a Pericles — were impure. The female sex had a low position in Greece, was shut out from education, and took no part in any of the employments of men, in public life, in the affairs of their country. Plato[8] represents a State as wholly disorganized, where slaves are disobedient to their masters, and wives are on an equality with their husbands. Aristotle[9] expressly characterizes women as beings of an inferior kind. Family life, in the true meaning of the words, the Greek did not know. He was at home as little as possible, and sought happiness elsewhere than at his own hearth. "Is there a human being," asks Socrates of one of his friends, "with whom you talk less than with your wife?"[10] And Demosthenes[11] says, without the least embarrassment: "We have *hetæræ* for our pleasure, wives to bear us children and to care for our households." So the courtesan became the complement to the wife, and it is easy to understand why there is such an almost entire absence of noble women throughout the history of Greece, and so great prominence given to the position occupied by courtesans and the *rôle* which they played in the national life. They frequented the lecture-rooms of the philosophers, wrote books, and were on terms of intercourse with prominent statesmen. Even Socrates went to hear Aspasia.[12] Famous men collected their witty sayings, and wrote their histories. Aristophanes of Byzantium mentions one hundred and thirty-five of these *hetæræ*, Apollodorus a yet larger number.[13] They gave themselves also as models for images of the gods. Phryne — the courtesan who promised the Thebans to rebuild their walls if they would write on them in golden letters: "Alexander destroyed them, Phryne rebuilt them" — served Praxiteles as a model for his renowned statue of the Cnidian Aphrodite. Thus the Greeks lifted their hands to public prostitutes when they prayed in their temples, and the extent of this shamelessness is sufficiently shown by the fact that this very Phryne, at the festival of Poseidon in Eleusis, appeared as Aphrodite Anadyomene, and having laid aside her garments and unloosed her hair, descended into the sea before the eyes of applauding Greece.[14]

The Romans kept their inheritance much longer. Their power was rooted in chastity, modesty, and the strict morals of the earlier time. Nothing immodest was tolerated. No nude images of the gods violated the sense of shame. Marriage was considered sacred, and children grew up under the watchful care of chaste mothers in the simple relations of home. According to Plutarch it was 230, according to others it was 520, years before a divorce occurred in Rome.[15] The Romans were acquainted with true family life. When work was done they went home, and gladly remained in the bosom of the family. A genial profligate like Alcibiades could have gained no foothold in Rome, an Aspasia or Phryne could have played no part.

It was otherwise when, with Greek culture, Greek frivolity as well entered Rome, when the riches of the conquered world flowed thither, and the luxury of the Empire took the place of republican simplicity. The ancient simple domesticity disappeared. Chastity and modesty perished. Luxury in dress came into vogue, and with it a finicalness and unnaturalness such as perhaps have never since been equalled. A fashionable Roman lady protected her complexion with a fine artificial paste, which she laid at night on her face, and then bathed in ass's milk. Of artificial washes, sweet-smelling oils, salves, perfumeries, pigments, there was no end. Female slaves thoroughly skilled in all the arts of the toilet stood at her beck, and often, while dressing her, were roughly and cruelly treated, being pricked with long needles, or beaten. For each separate pigment a particular slave was appointed who had been perfectly trained to color the eyebrows black, or the cheeks red. The hair was dressed in the most artificial way, dyed, or entirely cut off and rep aced by false hair. Auburn hair was specially prized in the first period of the Emperors. The dealers could not procure enough of it from Germany. What magnificence, what changes of apparel, what wealth of gold, pearls, and precious stones, ear-rings, and bracelets! Lollia Paulina, the spouse of Caligula, wore at a marriage festival a set of emeralds which she was prepared to prove by documents was worth forty millions of sesterces ($2,000,000).[16] The famous necklace of Queen Marie Antoinette, which in the French Revolution became so fatal, cost but 1,600,000 francs, not one-sixth as much. They wear two or three estates suspended from their ears, says Seneca.[17]

Naturally there was a desire to display such ornaments. In earlier days a Roman wife remained at home, seldom allowed herself to be seen on the streets, and then only when veiled, or in a closed chair. Now, the motto was, as Tertullian says: "See, and be seen."[18] In their walks, at the theatre, the circus, and at entertainments, they exhibited themselves and their finery. Those who did not own what was necessary to such a show could hire clothes, jewels, a sedan-chair, cushions, even an old waiting-woman or a fair-haired lady's maid, for a day at the theatre or circus.[19] How demoralizing this must have been is obvious; all the more so because the performances in the theatre were thoroughly immoral, and everywhere at social entertainments mythological paintings on the walls, tables and utensils for food, representations of naked forms, pictures often positively immodest, surrounded the guests — to say nothing of the dances, shows, music and songs.[20]

The result was that domestic chastity and morality

almost wholly disappeared. Conceding that the representations of the satirists, of Juvenal and Persius, may be exaggerations, that much of what we read in Horace, and especially in Ovid, may be poetical embellishment, enough remains to warrant this conclusion. Marriages now were effected as easily as they were dissolved. Inclination was not taken into account. For a man, marriage was a financial transaction, for a maiden the longed-for means of escape from the narrow limits of the nursery (for usually the transition was almost immediate from the nursery to married life), and of becoming free. "There are women who count their years not by the number of Consuls, but by the number of their husbands,"[21] says Seneca. "They allow themselves to be divorced," mocks Juvenal, "before the nuptial garlands have faded;"[22] and Tertullian: "They marry only to be divorced."[23] Friends exchanged wives, and it was not considered in the least dishonorable to employ the name of friendship for the purpose of seducing a friend's wife. Seneca goes so far as to affirm that marriage is only contracted because adultery affords a new and piquant charm.[24] Matrimonial fidelity was made a subject of ridicule. "Whoever has no love affairs is despised," affirms the same Seneca.[25] Not only did the theatre and the circus offer opportunities for beginning and continuing amorous intrigues, the temples were not too holy nor the brothels too foul for them.[26] It came to pass (a more horrible symptom of demoralization can scarcely be imagined), that ladies of high birth had themselves enrolled in the police register of common prostitutes in order that they might abandon themselves entirely to the most wanton excesses. So frequently did this scandal occur that it became necessary to pass laws against it. The blessing of children was only a burden. Infanticide, and a yet more shameful practice, were not regarded as crimes, for according to heathen ideas the father had absolute power over his children.[27] Household employments were despised, and the children, as they grew larger, were left to the care of the slaves. Mothers were more concerned about their toilets, or what flute or cithara player would receive the crown in the next contest, what horse would win at the next race, what athlete or gladiator would come off victorious in the amphitheatre, than they were about the education of their children.[28]

As a matter of course marriage itself fell of necessity into deeper and deeper contempt. Who would marry merely for the sake of supplying a disobedient wife with means for extravagance? The men, too, preferred the freedom of single life. To such a degree did celibacy and childlessness prevail, that the State deemed it necessary to interfere. As early as Augustus laws were enacted imposing fines and increased taxes on those persons who remained unmarried beyond a certain age. These were at first opposed in the Senate, and the insubordination of women was pleaded as a reason for this aversion to marriage. Later still the laws were again and again renewed and made more severe, yet without removing the deep-seated evil. Many preferred to accept the penalties decreed against the unmarried, and the childless. A single life was wholly unrestricted; childlessness had its advantages. An unmarried man had something to devise, and was flattered and honored with all sorts of attention by those who counted on being remembered in his will.

Legacy hunting had become an established evil in the first period of the Empire, and was so much a matter of course, so little perceived to be contemptible, that Seneca, for example, in a letter of condolence to a mother upon the loss of her only son, does not hesitate to remind her, by way of special consolation, that she will now, as a childless widow, be so much the more honored and beloved by such as hope for an inheritance.[29]

It would be unseemly to lift the veil from the sins of impurity of which the heathen world was full. "God gave them up to uncleanness, through the lusts of their own hearts, to dishonor their own bodies between themselves," writes St. Paul (Rom. i. 24); and for every line of the frightfully dark picture which he there sketches, proofs can easily be adduced. In shapes like Nero's, we can clearly perceive how thirst for blood went hand in hand with sensuality; and in the orgies of the age, as for instance in the great festivals which the prefect Tigellinus gave on an artificial island in the lake of Agrippa, the shamelessness was so conspicuous that the wildest carousals of later times do not offer even a resemblance. We know not which is the more shocking, the effrontery with which sensuality came forth, or the cunning with which it sought what was more and more unnatural. Even the temples promoted lewdness, the priestesses were prostitutes, and, shameful to relate, this was esteemed and practised by the heathen as a part of religious worship.[30]

There were doubtless many exceptions. Even if the epitaphs did not prove it, we should assume that there were still good housewives and faithful marriages, especially among the middle classes, even while the higher orders were much more deeply corrupted. Not infrequently is to be read on some grave-stone erected by a husband to his wife: "She never caused me a pang but by her death,"[31] and the praise of domesticity, of piety, of chastity, is often expressed. Yet this much is certain, that married and domestic life were widely corrupted and destroyed, and a lawlessness and dissoluteness prevailed which far exceeded even the worst which is presented by our large cities of to-day. Nobler souls felt this. With what earnestness did Tacitus hold up as an example to his contemporaries the purity and modesty of German women. Effort after effort was made to repress the evil, but the stream of corruption spread wider and wider. Indeed it was favored by all the conditions of the age. The world was conquered, what had been won was now to be enjoyed. For a century and longer, pleasure was the motto with high and low, and greater seriousness did not return until the time of enjoyment was past, and the increasing need, the deepening misery, toward the end of the second, and during the third century had inclined the world to become more earnest again.

III. LABOR AND LUXURY.

Enormous wealth flowed from the conquered provinces to Rome, and immense sums were continually collected from the provinces even after the imperial government had introduced a stricter management of the finances. Especially when the treasures which for centuries had been accumulating in the East fell to the victors the influx of gold was such as before had never been thought of as possible. From the temple in Jerusalem alone Crassus plundered 10,000 talents

($11,316,600).[32] As Proconsul of Syria Gabinius exacted one hundred millions of denarii ($16,839,360).[33] From Ptolemy Auletes the same Gabinius took away 10,000 talents after Cæsar had already taken 6,000, in all, therefore, about eighteen millions of dollars.[34] The other provinces, Spain, Gaul, also contributed largely. Quintus Servilius Cæpio alone carried off from the Tectosagan city Tolosa 15,000 talents ($16,974,900).[35]

Wealth is not merely hazardous to the individual, it is also dangerous to a nation, doubly dangerous when it pours in suddenly, as in Rome, and has not been gradually acquired as the fruit of labor. In Rome it resulted in the ruin of the middle class, the accumulation of colossal wealth in the hands of a few, the impoverishment of the masses, and finally in unrestrained luxury and voluptuousness.

Antiquity had no knowledge of a middle class such as modern times are acquainted with, for labor, the basis of a sound middle class, was not regarded as honorable but as a disgrace. Plato[36] deemed it right to despise men whose employment did not permit them to devote themselves to their friends and to the State. According to Aristotle,[37] all forms of labor which require physical strength are degrading to a freeman. Nature has created for such purposes a special class; they are those whom we reduce to bondage that they may work for us as slaves or day-laborers. In Athens we can plainly trace the process by which the middle class was obliterated by slavery. In the earlier period of its history Athens had such a class composed of free laborers, but this was unable, when wealth increased, to maintain itself against the combination of capital and labor. The capitalists owned great factories in which the foremen as well as the operatives were slaves. Nothing was left to the free laborer but to work side by side with slaves in the factory, or to remain idle and depend on the State for support. Thus instead of a people living, as Solon intended, by labor, and treating labor with respect, there was a people prone to idleness, corrupted by contact with slaves, and involved in all the vices of Athenian life.

The course of things in Rome was similar. There, too, labor fell more and more into disgrace. There all work by which money is earned was despised as an ignoble bondage. Medicine, architecture and commerce were alone excepted as honorable employments for a freeman. "The mechanic's occupation is degrading. A work-shop is incompatible with any thing noble."[38] Again we see the curse of slavery. Where it exists free labor cannot be respected, nor a middle class arise consisting of free laborers.

In the country Italy had formerly possessed such a class in the free peasants who industriously tilled the arable land on small farms such as the soil of Italy requires for its cultivation. This free peasant class which formed the kernel of the legions had been annihilated by the civil wars. More than once the disbanded legions of the conqueror were rewarded with landed property in Italy. Sulla had distributed among twenty-three legions such *municipia* as had shown themselves hostile to him. The soldiers entered triumphantly into Florence, Præneste, and other places appointed for them, drove away the inhabitants, and took possession of houses and lands. Octavian had treated thirty-four legions in the same way. The old soldiers seldom became industrious farmers. What had

RUIN OF THE MIDDLE CLASS.

been easily won was easily squandered. Speculators bought up the farms. The Roman magnates, who had acquired wealth in the East, or in Gaul, invested in them their capital. Thus arose great *latifundia*, immense estates, often miles square. These could be worked more profitably with slaves than with free laborers. The slave therefore everywhere drove out the free laborer. Only in regions the most remote, where slaves could not be controlled, and under hard conditions, did the freeman, as *villicus*, maintain his position. At most he received one-fifth of the produce.[39] Or he was allowed a chance where the country was unhealthy and capitalists hesitated to take the costly risks involved in slaves. In consequence of the size of the landed property and the poor quality of the labor (a slave is always a bad and dear workman) the cultivation of the soil ceased to be profitable, and gave place to the raising of cattle, which required less labor, and offered a more sure reward. Where once luxuriant corn-fields waved and gardens stood full of delicious fruit, nothing ould now be seen for miles but a barren heath grazed by cattle. Where in earlier times numerous villages, in the midst of well-cultivated fields and gardens, had delighted the eye, stood now, at great distances apart, the *ergastula*, prison-like dwellings, which concealed hundreds of miserable slaves. The two maxims then often heard: " A purchased laborer is better than a hired one," and: " Grazing is more lucrative than farming,"[40] mark the steps in the progress of deterioration.

As the flat country became depopulated the large cities became crowded. Those who could no longer maintain themselves in the country flocked into the cities, especially into Rome. And what a population was there crowded together! We do not know with entire accuracy the number of inhabitants of Rome at the beginning of the Empire.[41] Some estimate it at one and a half, others, for instance Hoeck, at two millions and upwards. Of these perhaps only about 10,000 belonged to the higher orders, senators and knights; then, according to Hoeck, there were one million of slaves, and about 50,000 foreigners; the remainder constituted the *Plebs urbana*, who were absolutely destitute. Of service for hire there was little in Rome. For even here the free laborer had to come into competition with the slave, and here, too, the latter took away his work. What the rich needed in their homes was produced for them by their many slaves. Even large buildings were erected by slaves in the employ of contractors. Craftsmen thus had but few customers. The only other opportunities for earning money were those afforded by positions as inferior attendants upon the magistrates, as servants in the colleges of priests and assistants at funerals. There was no real middle class. Many sought their living as clients at the houses of the great, a living scanty enough, and little better than slavery. From early in the morning till late in the evening, whether it was hot or whether it snowed, the clients were obliged to be ready in their togas for service to their patron, waiting upon him in the house, and accompanying him by the way. For such attendance they received from him a gift, and were invited on festival occasions to his house that they might help swell the pomp. In other respects they were often subjected to most shameful and degrading treatment even from the freedmen and slaves of their lord. The great mass of the people lived in almost complete idleness and were supported by the State.

Even in earlier times corn was delivered to Roman citizens at a moderate price. In the year of the city 695 Claudius carried through a law which provided for its gratuitous distribution. During the Civil Wars the number of receivers of corn increased considerably, since every ruler naturally courted the favor of the people. In Cæsar's time this number rose to 320,000. Afterwards, through the sending away of colonies of the poor, it was reduced to 130,000, under Augustus to 100,000, but it always increased again. Inquiry was made into the need, but no attention was paid to morals and conduct. "The thief," says Seneca,[42] "as well as the perjurer and the adulterer receives the public corn; every one, irrespective of morals, is a citizen." On an appointed day of the month each person enrolled in the lists received the *tessera frumentalis*, a check for five bushels of wheat. This amount was then measured out in the magazines to every one who brought and showed the *tessera*. For this reason the checks were often sold, especially as the measure was so large that it was more than enough for one person. In addition to this gift of corn, largesses in money (*congiaria*) were distributed. These were either alms which were dispensed solely for the benefit of the recipients of grain, or they were presents which were bestowed upon all, down even to the boys; as, for instance, in the years of the city 725, 730, 742, when every one received 400 sesterces (about twenty dollars). Each *congiarium* of this sort cost the State 250,000,000 sesterces, about $12,500,000.

Such munificence the world has never again witnessed, but we do well to reflect that it was not benevolence. Not man, but the Roman citizen was taken into consideration; not the needy, but strong men, able to work, received the gift; not the individual, but the State was the giver; not love, but justice was the criterion. The *congiarium* was, after all, but each Roman citizen's share in the spoil of a conquered world, a premium which the rich out of fear paid to idleness. Hence what was received only increased the demand. In the days of Augustus the people clamored for wine in addition to corn. The Emperor replied: "The provision made by aqueducts is so ample that no one need thirst."[43] Later Emperors were obliged to do more. Septimius Severus caused oil to be distributed. Aurelian, at his triumph, gave bread. This remained the rule when the people demanded it. The Emperor would even have given wine. When the prætorian prefect remonstrated: "If we grant the people wine, we must also serve out to them chickens and geese," he desisted, but took care that wine should be furnished to the people at cheaper prices.[44] Such a system of largesses could only work demoralizingly. Love elevates the poor man, such gifts degrade him. Christianity first introduced true benevolence, and as it has ennobled labor so it has also honored innocent poverty.

Whilst the mass of the people lived by alms, the few who possessed wealth revelled in unheard of luxury. Down to the time of Augustus, Rome, compared with what it afterwards became, had been rather a poor city. Augustus could boast that instead of the city of brick which he found he had left one of marble. Not only public buildings, but also private dwellings show from this date an incomparable magnificence. A residence which with its appurtenances (gardens, etc.) embraced four acres, was considered small. What a splendid spectacle was offered by the *atria* with their lofty pillars, for which the most costly stones were collected from the whole world. Beams of Hymettian marble rested on pillars from Africa; the walls were formed of costly slabs of variegated marble, or alabaster bordered with green serpentine, brought from distant Egypt, or from the Black Sea. The arches glistened with mosaics of glass, the floors were artistically tessellated. In the intervening spaces were green shrubberies and plashing fountains, while high above, for protection from the sun, a crimson awning stretched from one pillared roof to another, suffusing the mosaic floor and the mossy carpet with a rosy shimmer.

All this was surpassed by Nero's Golden House, which was like a city in size. Its colonnades were each a mile long. In its vestibule stood a colossal statue of the Emperor 120 feet high. The other dimensions of the palace were on the same scale. It embraced fields and gardens, meadows and forests, and even a lake. The halls and saloons were overlaid with gold, and adorned with precious stones and mother-of-pearl, or with glass mirrors which reflected to the beholder his entire figure. Smaller apartments had walls which were completely covered with pearls. The banqueting-rooms were decorated with special magnificence, and the baths afforded the rarest luxury. The banqueting-rooms had gilded, carved, and painted ceilings which were changed to suit the various courses of the meal, and so constructed that flowers and perfumes could be scattered upon the guests. Water from the sea, as well as sulphurated water from the springs of the Tiber, was conducted to the baths through magnificent conduits, and flowed from gold and silver faucets into basins of variegated marble, so that it looked now red, now green, now white. "Now I am lodged as a man should be," said Nero when he took possession of it.[45] Otho granted three millions for an enlargement of this palace, and yet Vitellius found it still unworthy of an Emperor. Naturally these extensive houses rendered building sites extraordinarily dear, and there was as little room in Rome for the poor as there is now in our large cities. Under Nero a law was passed which forbade the purchase of houses for the sake of pulling them down and speculating with the sites.

Beside his city residence a wealthy Roman had a number of country houses in the mountains or by the sea, in Southern Italy or in the North. For miles away stretched the most magnificent parks, such as only a strongly developed taste for natural beauty, with enormous means at command, could create. If one had seen in his travels a landscape which seemed to him specially beautiful, he sought to imitate it, or found satisfaction in producing one under circumstances and in places where every preliminary condition was wanting. Where the sea had been, he made land, and laid out a villa on it, merely for the sake of being able to say that he had wrested it from the waters; or he had earth brought at an enormous expense and spread upon naked rocks in order to plant there a garden or a grove. Nature and art, wealth and taste, were combined to insure, in a land whose climate is enchantingly beautiful, an enviable existence for the rich. That these great villas drove the poorer class away from land and soil, withdrew the fields from the culture of corn, wine and fruit, products to which they were naturally adapted, and so helped increase the *proletariat*, what did the rich care for this?

Consider first the public buildings! A real frenzy for architecture ruled the age, and when pure art was declining men strove to supply the lack of genuine artistic perfection by colossal size and excessive decoration. We can scarcely imagine now the magnificence and splendor of a city like Rome. The most beautiful and wealthy capitals of modern times are far inferior to it. In comparison with such a profusion of works of art, of palaces and temples, of theatres and baths, of triumphal arches and statues numbered by thousands, they appear actually poor. And when we remember the many other large cities, some of which like Antioch and Alexandria, for instance, rivalled Rome, when we recall even smaller cities like Pompeii which a favorable fortune has preserved for us, we see everywhere such wealth of artistic decoration, and, apart from occasional defects of taste, such unvarying pleasantness, such cleanliness and neatness, that we find here continually our models. If we then represent to ourselves only approximately the grandeur of the public works, the bridges, streets, aqueducts, throughout the entire Empire, whose ruins in Africa and in the Eifel, in France and in Syria, still excite our admiration, the picture as a whole is indeed astonishing, and we obtain some idea of the power still resident in that imperial Rome to whom most of these works owed their origin.

The interior of the dwellings presented nothing of what we now call comfort, but, all the more, wealth and sumptuousness. Even here it is apparent, that the life of the ancient world was directed to what is external, not to what is within. We seek above all else in a dwelling an agreeable and comfortable home; the ancient world inclined everywhere, even in the house, to show. The occupant of a mansion desired most of all to make a brilliant display of his wealth and his importance. The rooms compared with ours were empty, containing, instead of a large amount of furniture for daily use, only a few articles which were so much the more superb and costly,—expensive tables with covers of citrus wood and resting on ivory feet, couches inlaid with gold and silver and covered with Babylonian tapestry, splendid vases of Corinthian bronze, or the somewhat enigmatical Murrha, vessels of which were worth $7,500 and even $37,500, Æginetan candelabra, sideboards with antique silver plate, and statues and paintings by renowned artists. Every thing, even down to the common household utensils, was, in an incomparably higher degree than with us, artistically formed and finished.

Then the life in these magnificent houses! Inordinate longing for enjoyment, effeminacy and voluptuousness, reigned supreme. Numerous slaves stood waiting the nod of their master, ready to render all kinds of service in order to relieve him of the slightest trouble. There were even some slaves who knew by heart Homer or Virgil, and standing behind the chair of their master whispered in his ear a citation from the classic poets whenever he deemed it appropriate to introduce such a passage into the conversation. Earnest labor was not thought of, at most only a *dilettante* occupation with the fine arts. Apart from this, life was one prolonged revel. Entertainments and feasts chased one another, each in turn more *recherché* than the preceding. The means of enjoyment were gathered from every quarter of the globe, and the more rare and costly they were the more highly were they prized. Men out-vied each other in the art of squandering at a single meal hundreds of thousands, until the Emperor Vitellius exceeded all by running through, in the few months of his reign, one hundred and fifty millions. That the pleasure of eating might be prolonged emetics were made use of. "They vomit to eat, and eat to vomit," says Seneca, "and do not deign to digest the feasts collected from all parts of the world." [46] What extravagance in yet other respects was committed at these banquets! Thousands were expended in a single day for flowers — roses and violets in the middle of winter — which were showered upon the guests, for ointments and fragrant waters. In every thing there was exaggeration even to unnaturalness, and often our belief is taxed as though we were in an enchanted castle, where, as fairy-tales relate, every thing is of silver and gold. As, for instance, when we hear that Poppæa Sabina, the wife of Nero, took with her on a journey five hundred asses in order that cosmetic baths might be prepared for her from their milk, and that these animals had gold and silver shoes, and that her husband, when he amused himself with fishing, used nets interwoven with threads of gold.

Only an age utterly wanting in earnestness, destitute of any high purpose or endeavor, and wholly abandoned· to sensual enjoyment, could have fallen into such practices. And, conversely, this life of pleasure must have proved increasingly destructive to morals. "Through dissipation," complains a contemporary, "the minds of indolent youth have become sluggish, and no one rouses himself to the trouble and toil of an honorable employment. Sleep and lassitude, and what is worse than both, zeal in wrong-doing, have taken possession of them. The disgraceful pursuit of song and dance makes them effeminate; their darling passion is to curl their hair, to weaken their voices to feminine accents of flattery, to vie with women in pampering the body, to excel in the foulest vices. Who of your contemporaries is full of spirit? Who is full of desire for knowledge? Who is even a man?" This was the race as Pliny and the physician Galen, in this matter a competent witness, depict it for us, "with pale faces, flabby cheeks, swollen eyes, trembling hands, enfeebled understanding, and ruined memory."[47] These were the people who, morally rotten, completely enervated, cringed before the Emperor in the Senate and answered every kick with new and studied flatteries, these aristocrats who boasted of their proud old names and their wealth, and yet in Nero's presence were mere slaves, or at most, in company with shameless women, plotted conspiracies which they could not find courage to carry out, even in death dastards or profligates.

How dull, how stale, life seemed to all this *blasé* race. Intoxicated with pleasure and sensual enjoyment, able to gratify every whim however absurd, they were nevertheless thoroughly discontented, and sought in vain by ever new devices to impart fresh zest to existence. Life, in the time of the Emperors, was utterly tedious and uninteresting. There were no elevating influences. Interest in public affairs had died out from the time that the Emperor alone ruled the world according to his own caprices, or, as might happen, allowed it to be ruled by women or *valets de chambre*. Religious life had disappeared. Philosophy had degenerated into a vain display of mere words. Between an inordinately wealthy aristocracy and a populace accustomed to be fed by its lords, there was no opportunity for creative, progressive labor.

In the absence of serious occupation life became filled with mere frivolities. Men ceased to work. The obligations of society and politeness assumed a ridiculous importance. "It is astonishing," Pliny writes in one of his letters,[48] "how time is passed in Rome. Take any day by itself and it either is, or seems to be, well spent; yet review many days together and you will be surprised to discover how unprofitable they have been. Ask any one: What have you done to-day? He will tell you: I was at a friend's who gave his son the *toga virilis*; another requested me to be a witness to his will; a third asked me to a consultation. All of these things appear at the time extremely necessary. But when we reflect that day after day has been thus spent, such employments seem trifling." Where life was not passed in frivolity and dissipation the most important occupations were writing, reading to others what had been written, hearing lectures, composing poems, and admiring those produced by others. "During the whole month of April," Pliny [49] relates, "there was scarcely a day in which some one did not recite a poem." "We suffer from a superfluity of sciences," Seneca had already remarked.[50] Instead of going to the Forum, or elsewhere, to important business, one went to hear some rhetorician declaim about morality, or to the baths — the clubs of that day — to talk about every thing and nothing. Or one was invited by a friend to hear some history or poem. They declaimed through life. The sense for true beauty became more and more impaired. If a poet or rhetorician succeeded in successfully imitating the works of the ancients, he received the highest applause.

A striking proof of the spiritual condition of many persons at that time is afforded by the beginning of Seneca's treatise "On Tranquillity of Mind." Serenus, the captain of the watch, already referred to, had disclosed to Seneca the state of his soul, and begged him to name the evil from which he was suffering. Seneca's reply describes what the outlook then was for many persons. It is an indescribable medley of energy and weakness, of ambition and impotence, a rapid succession of undefined hopes and groundless discouragements, a consuming *ennui*, an utter disgust with self, which allows no place of rest and finally renders every thing odious. The world seems monotonous, life uniform, pleasures fatigue, the least efforts exhaust, and this vague sadness becomes at last so heavy a burden that one contemplates escaping from it by death.[51]

I gladly acknowledge that the description I have given of the moral life of that age needs qualification on this side, or on that; that there were, beyond question, sounder and nobler elements; that, by comparison with other times which offer similar phenomena, much can be set in a milder light; and yet, after all such allowances are made, one thing must at any rate be admitted, of which all these details are only a symptom, and which itself is the most unerring symptom of the degradation of the old world: the exhaustion from life of every lofty purpose.

IV. PUBLIC GAMES.

This appears pre-eminently in the wide-spread passion among the higher classes for personally taking part in the theatre, the circus, the chariot-races, and the gladiatorial sports. Nero led the way in this by his example. Prouder than any *triumphator* he entered Rome with eighteen hundred and eight victors' wreaths which he had won in the Grecian games, and hung them on the obelisk in the Circus Maximus even while the Nemesis of his bloody deeds was already knocking at the gates. So general did this inclination become that more earnest Emperors endeavored to restrain it by legislation. It can be explained only by the craving for new and more powerful stimulants. Satiated with all possible enjoyments, people sought in the circus, and in the arena, for an excitement they no longer found elsewhere, and, grown indifferent to every thing, staked in the gladiatorial games a life which had ceased to have for them any value. In general the absorbing interest of this age in all sorts of spectacles was in the highest degree characteristic, and it is worth while to contemplate it somewhat more closely from this point of view, since, in this way, a profound insight can be obtained into the morality of that time, as well as of all antiquity.

Spectacles (taking the word at first in the broadest sense) had for ancient life generally a higher importance than for modern. Here, again, that tendency of the former to externals which has been already repeatedly noticed may be seen in its delight in artistic representation, and, consequently, in public parades and displays of all sorts. This is apparent even in public worship. The whole cultus had a theatrical tendency; processions constituted a large part of it. What an important place did the theatre occupy in the popular life of the Greeks. In this domain lie in part the highest achievements of Greek genius, in the dramas of an Æschylus, Sophocles and Euripides. To be sure, the day when such creations of genius were rejoiced in was long gone by. The tall figures in the cothurn and with the mask, with solemn step and solemn speech, had disappeared from the boards. The Greeks of that time, to say nothing of the Romans, would have found no pleasure in the Œdipus, nor in the Antigone. The later comedy continued longest in favor, at least the fineness of the acting proved attractive. Buffoonery and pantomimes became popular. The *Attellana*, a sort of Punchinello comedy with grotesque drollery and coarse jokes, the *Mimus*, a loosely connected representation of characters in common life, with jesters and much stage art, with rich decorations and astonishing scene shiftings, were now the favorite amusements. The lofty deeds of heroes were no longer held up for imitation, nor were the follies of the time derided; the adventures of deceived husbands, adulteries and amorous intrigues formed the staple of the plots. Virtue was made a mock of, and the gods scoffed at; every thing sacred and worthy of veneration was dragged in the mire. In obscenity, unveiled and unambiguous, in impure speeches and exhibitions which outraged the sense of shame, these spectacles exceeded all besides. Ballet dancers threw away their dresses and danced half naked, and even wholly naked, on the stage. Art was left out of account, every thing was designed for mere sensual gratification.

Apart from such exhibitions the theatre proper was decidedly out of favor. The popular taste inclined chiefly to the amusements of the circus and amphitheatre. These festivals, of religious origin and still connected with religious ceremonies, had acquired in the time of the Emperors a political significance. Those in power found it to be strongly for their interest to keep the people busy and diverted. Bread and Games! was the demand, and so long as Rome had enough to eat and was amused, the Emperor had little to fear. Hence the great watchfulness respecting the supply of corn, hence the pains taken to provide at so enormous an expense for games. The more political life decayed, the greater the place occupied by sports. The Emperors, therefore, good and bad without distinction, expended on them immense sums. The most economical felt obliged to have money for them, and the most inflexible and simple had to yield in this matter to the pleasure of the people.

In the times of the Republic games were observed within moderate limits. As early as Augustus they were celebrated for sixty-six days; under Marcus Aurelius the number had increased to one hundred and thirty-five. Besides these there were extraordinary festivals. Titus gave the people, at the dedication of the Flavian Amphitheatre, a festival which lasted a hundred days; Trajan, on the occasion of his Dacian triumph, one of one hundred and twenty-three days. So it was in Rome, where, to be sure, every thing was carried to extremes. Yet there were not wanting games in the provinces, although in a more moderate degree, as is proved by the ruins of numerous, and often colossal, amphitheatres in all parts of the Roman

Empire. Even in Palestine King Agrippa, to the horror of the Jews, caused a circus to be built, and his race horses are said to have contended for the stakes with the Roman. On the walls of Pompeii we see to-day the posters in which the holding of games was announced. It belonged to the most burdensome and pressing duties of municipal officers even in the medium-sized cities to provide games at their own expense, and we know accidentally of a gladiatorial show in an Italian city of middle rank at the beginning of the Empire, which lasted three days, and cost 20,880 dollars.

Often the people were feasted at the games, and entire days were appointed for magnificent banquetings. Slaves of the Emperor carried around viands and wine on broad platters and in large baskets. All the people, men, women and children, senators and knights, the court and the Emperor himself, ate at great tables in the broad public places of Rome. Or figs, dates, nuts and cakes were thrown among the people, — it rained roasted fowls and pheasants. Lottery tickets were distributed entitling to smaller or larger prizes, perchance articles of clothing or household furniture, gold and silver, houses too, and landed estates. Whoever had luck could become rich in a day. The people thronged to these games. Not unfrequently lives were lost in the crowd.

The greatest enthusiasm was felt for the chariot races in the Circus; there the passions were most fearfully excited. Which of the four parties designated by the colors worn by horses and drivers would win at the next race, whether the red or the green, the blue or the white, was a question which occupied Rome for days in advance. Wagers were often concluded for hundreds of thousands, for entire estates. Sacrifices were offered, soothsayers questioned, even magical arts employed, in order to obtain the victory for the favorite party. "Does the green lose," says Juvenal, "then is Rome struck aghast as after the defeat at Cannæ."[52] "Whether a Nero governed the Empire or a Marcus Aurelius," writes Friedländer, from whose representations of Roman life I borrow much, "whether the Empire was at peace or aflame with civil war, or the barbarians stormed at the frontiers, in Rome the question of chief moment for freemen and slaves, for senators, knights and people, for men and women, was whether the blue would win or the green."

Already on the night before the people streamed into the Circus in order to secure seats, for, immense as was the number of places provided, it was yet difficult to obtain one. In Cæsar's time the Circus had 150,000 seats; Titus added 100,000 more; finally there were 385,000.[53]

A religious service introduced the sports. From the Capitol, to the sound of trumpets and flutes, advanced a great procession, led by the magistrate who gave the games standing on a chariot as a *triumphator*, followed by images of the gods and emperors borne on litters and accompanied by the colleges of priests in full dress. Then the whole *pompa diaboli*, as Tertullian says, entered the Circus through the chief gate and moved with stately slowness over the course, the spectators rising to their feet and receiving it with jubilant cheering and clapping of hands. All eyes now turn in breathless suspense to the balcony from which the Prætor lets fall the signal for beginning the race. The white cloth flutters toward the course. *Misit! misit!* he has thrown it, calls one to the other, and as the rope which had hitherto closed the track is cast off, as the chariots burst forth and veiled in dust speed over the course, as now this now that faction has an advantage, and is applauded accordingly by its partisans among the spectators, spurred on with cheers, or loaded with curses, as the chariots often dash in pieces on the turning-post and horses and drivers roll on the ground in a confused heap, the excitement increases every moment even to frenzy and vents itself in infuriated roaring. At length the victor reaches the goal and is greeted with thunders of applause. Ribbons, favors, garlands fly to him. Before the seat of the Emperor he receives the prize-purse, filled with gold, and the palm branch, and amid the shouts of the people passes slowly along the course to the *porta triumphalis*. The race is ended, but only to be soon followed by another. Often there were twenty-four in succession with merely a short pause at noon. Even then many persons did not go home; they ate in the Circus and kept their places until evening brought the show to an end.

Another sort of spectacles was furnished by the Amphitheatres. Here occurred the gladiatorial contests, the hunting of animals, the representations of battles on land and sea. In the horse-races of the present day we have something like the chariot races of the Circus, but the spectacles of the Amphitheatre are wholly unlike any thing modern. In Christendom the only relic of them which can be found — and that but slight — is in the bull-fights of Spain.

On the walls of Pompeii we may still read the inscription: "If the weather allows, the gladiatorial bands of the Ædile Suetius Certus will fight, on the 30th of July, in the Arena at Pompeii. There will also be a hunt of animals. The place for spectators is covered, and will be sprinkled."[54] Such an amphitheatre must have been a splendid sight, the seats, rising one above another, all filled, below, people of rank, senators, knights, ladies magnificently arrayed, sparkling with gold and precious stones, Vestals in their sacred garb; higher up the other orders; at the top the common people, country-folk, soldiers, house-slaves. Far over the arena stretched an awning supported by masts gay with pennons, many colored tapestries covered balustrades and parapets, festoons of roses linked pillar to pillar, and in the spaces between stood glittering statues of the gods before whom rose from tripods fragrant odors. Every thing exhaled pleasure and joy. People laughed, talked, interchanged courtesies, spun love-affairs, or bet on this or that combatant. And yet what a horrible show it was at which the multitude lingered.

It began with a pompous procession of gladiators in full armor. Before the Emperor they lowered their arms and cried: "Hail, *Imperator!* they who are about to die salute thee." At first only a sham fight took place, then the dismal tones of the *tubæ* gave the signal for the combat with sharp weapons. The most varied scenes followed in rapid succession. Singly or in companies the *retiarii* came forward, almost naked, without armor, their only weapons a dagger and trident, and endeavored each to throw a net over the head of his antagonist in order to inflict a death-blow. The Samnites, with large shields and short straight swords, engaged the Thracians with small round shields and curved swords. Combatants clad in complete armor aimed at the joints in the armor of their opponents, knights tilted at each other with long lances, and others, in imitation of the Britons, fought standing on chariots of war.

All this was not for show nor in sport, but in downright, terrible earnest. If one fell alive into the hands of his opponent, the giver of the entertainment left the decision of life or death to the spectators. The vanquished begged for his life by holding up a finger. If they waved their handkerchiefs his life was granted him, if they turned up their thumbs this was a command for the fatal stroke. Women even, and timid girls, gave lightly and without hesitation the sign which doomed a man to death. The brave who despised death received abundant applause, the timorous excited the anger of the people who considered it an affront if a gladiator would not cheerfully die. They were trained for this in gladiatorial schools and learned there also how to breathe out their lives with theatrical grace. For this, too, the giver of the show had hired them from the *lanista*, the owner of the school. This fact appears in the Institutes as a question of law. A *lanista* furnished a private person a number of gladiators on the condition that he should pay for every one who returned from the fight uninjured, or without serious wounds, twenty *denarii*, for every one killed or badly hurt, one thousand *denarii*. The question arose: Was this purchase or hire? Caius decided: In the case of the first class it was hire, for they went back to their master; in the case of the second it was purchase, since they belong to him whom they have served, for what is the *lanista* to do with the dead or mutilated?

A right had thus been purchased in their death, and accordingly those who hesitated to die were driven into the fight with scourges and red-hot irons. Inflamed to madness the spectators screamed: Kill! lash! burn! Why does he take the death-blow with so little bravery? Why does he die so reluctantly?

At the first spilling of blood, the roar and acclamations of the crowd increased, it fairly thirsted for blood. Before the vanquished had time to implore mercy the cry for blood resounded, and the stroke followed which put an end to life. Officials in the mask of the god of the lower world dragged the still palpitating body with a hook into the death chamber, whilst the victors proudly flourished their palm branches, and the spectators, at the highest pitch of excitement, standing on the benches, shouted approval. In the pauses between the fighting the soil of the arena, saturated with blood, was turned-up with shovels, Moorish slaves threw on fresh sand, and smoothed again the place of combat. Then the shedding of blood began anew.

Together with the gladiatorial shows proper, fights with wild beasts were extremely popular, and were carried out on a splendid scale. Wild animals were hunted in all parts of the world in order to supply the Amphitheatre at Rome, and those of other great cities. The hippopotamus was transported from Egypt, the wild boar from the Rhine, the lion from Africa, the elephant from India. Even rhinoceroses, ostriches, and giraffes were not wanting. The beasts of the desert were brought not singly but by hundreds into the arena. Six hundred bears, five hundred lions, are mentioned at one festival. At the games given by Trajan in honor of the Dacian triumph in the year

A.D. 106, there fought in all eleven thousand animals of the most diverse species. There was also great variety in the contests. Now the wild beasts fought with one another, now with dogs trained for this purpose, now with men on foot or mounted.

Still more magnificent were the battles, especially the naval battles, which took place in the Amphitheatre arranged for their display, or on lakes excavated for this special purpose. Whole fleets engaged in these contests. Claudius exhibited on the lake Fucinus a sea-fight between vessels of three and four benches of oars, in which there were nineteen thousand combatants. Domitian had a new and larger lake dug, on which battles were fought by fleets almost as large as those commonly employed at that time in war. These were not mock-fights, but all real combats in which thousands fell or were drowned.

While these spectacles still impress us by their magnificence, the public executions, also exhibited as shows in the Amphitheatre, excite only emotions of horror and disgust. Wholly unarmed, or furnished with weapons solely that their torments might be protracted, the condemned were bound to stakes and exposed to famished beasts. There they lay bleeding and with torn garments, while the people shouted for joy. And yet worse than this occurred. Those under condemnation were used for theatrical spectacles at which all the arts of decoration in which that age was so proficient were brought into requisition — only in these plays death, sufferings, and agonies were not feigned, but actually endured. The unfortunate victims appeared in garments interwoven with threads of gold, and with crowns on their heads. when suddenly flames burst from their clothing and consumed them. There Mucius Scævola was seen holding his hand in a brazier of live coals; there Hercules ascended on Mount Œta his funeral pile, and was burned alive; there robbers, hanging on crosses, were torn limb from limb by bears. All this with complete theatrical machinery for the delight of a sight-loving people.[55]

We turn away from such scenes with abhorrence. Antiquity had no such feeling. We should search literature in vain for expressions which censure and repudiate this shedding of blood. Even a man like Pliny,[56] who usually manifests a nobler and more humane spirit, praises, in his *Panegyric* upon Trajan, games " which do not enervate the minds of men, but on the contrary inflame them to honorable wounds and contempt of death as they perceive even in slaves and criminals the love of praise and desire for victory." Seneca calls them a light amusement. Once only, when he had accidentally seen, in the recess at noon, that unpractised gladiators were allowed to engage in combats which were mere butchery, does he express indignation that men were permitted to slaughter each other merely for the amusement of those who remained during the interval in the Amphitheatre.[57] Ovid[58] even instructs those present at these sights to improve the offered opportunity for love making. One speaks to his neighbor and in the eagerness of conversation touches her hand, or asks of her the programme and bets with her on the issue of the combat. For women, too, beheld these sights, and while blood flowed in streams, and men wrestled with death in the arena below, those above engaged in thoughtless gallantries. Such eagerness was there for these spectacles, that even at social entertainments gladiatorial combats were held, and not infrequently at these carousals the blood that was shed mingled with the spilt wine.

This is Heathenism, and let us mark it well, not Heathenism uneducated and rude, but at the height of its culture. I know very well what in ancient culture is fundamental and exemplary for all ages, so that we read, and rightly, in our schools the Greek and Roman classics, and open to youth a view of the beauty and glory of the ancient world, but it would be one-sided and untrue, should we for this reason overlook its great defect. It lacked a genuine culture of the heart. With all the perfection of form the heart still remained the old, natural, undisciplined, human heart. A complete change of heart, a work of purification wrought by a man within himself, these were wholly strange conceptions to Heathenism. Herbart has said, that one object of classical instruction is to show the young that durable life was not attained in Greece and Rome. The heart was not satisfied.

The view which we thus obtain of the complete exhaustion from life of moral aims, is appalling. Life really had no longer an object. The one great end for which men had lived, the development of the State, no longer existed. From the time when the Emperor could say: "I am the State!" political life had ceased. All that was left — the assemblies of the people, the Senate, the offices derived from the Republic — was mere pretence. No wonder that men were wholly absorbed in enjoyment, and that "Bread and Games" became the motto for all classes. But there was a deeper reason yet for this exhaustion of life. Heathenism knew no goal in the life beyond, and consequently had no true aim in the present life. When a man has found the goal of existence in the other world, his one great task, however in other respects his life may shape itself, is always within his own heart. For him life continually retains the sublime significance of a school for the life to come, and in darkest seasons never becomes empty and unmeaning. The heathen knew nothing of all this. Therefore in times of decline, like those of the Empire, their only resource was amusement. This drove them to the circus and the theatre, and made it an event in their eyes whether the horses with red colors or those with green first reached the goal, whether this or that gladiator was victorious.

And if then, wholly inconceivable as this now seems to us, men and women, high and low, feasted their eyes on murder and bloodshed, and saw nothing therein but a light amusement, it was because they did not regard those who died in the arena amid horrible tortures as men, but only as barbarians, foreigners, prisoners of war, slaves, criminals, outcasts of the human race, worthless and dangerous. Antiquity lacked any genuine conception of humanity. The worth of man as man, a worth shared by all, even by foreigners and barbarians, which remains inamissible for all, even the most degraded criminal, which is to be honored in all, even in enemies, this was a truth hidden from the heathen. Here, too, was the root of slavery, which prevailed everywhere in Antiquity, and was considered by Greeks and Romans as a perfectly justifiable and ·indispensable institution.

V. SLAVERY.

A slave was not regarded by the ancients as a man, he had neither a free will nor any claim whatever to justice, nor any capacity for virtue. Plato, the noblest thinker of antiquity, wavers somewhat on this subject. He concedes that there are slaves who have practised virtue, and who have saved their masters by sacrificing themselves; he affirms that the question how slavery shall be estimated is a difficult one, but comes at last to the conclusion that it is a natural institution since Nature herself has destined some to bear rule, others to serve. Aristotle admits no objections at all. In a well-arranged household, he thinks, there are two sorts of instruments — inanimate and animate. The former are slaves without souls, the latter (slaves) are instruments with souls. But though a soul is thus attributed to slaves, it is explained to be imperfect, it is a soul without will. The Romans speak in precisely the same way. Florus [59] characterizes the slaves as another race of men. According to Varro,[60] in his work on Agriculture, there are three kinds of implements for tillage, those that are dumb, e.g. wagons, those that utter inarticulate sounds, e.g. oxen, and those that talk. The last are slaves. Even a man like Cicero does not rise above this. When his slave Sositheus, to whom he was much attached, died, he wrote to Atticus: "Sositheus is dead, and his death has moved me more than the death of a slave should,"[61] just as we sometimes apologize for ourselves when troubled by the death of a dog or a canary-bird. The Prætor Domitius caused a slave who made the mistake on a hunt of killing a boar at the wrong time, to be crucified as a punishment for his offence. Cicero passes merely this judgment thereupon: "This might, *perhaps*, seem harsh."[62]

These views were impressed with the greatest distinctness on the Roman law. The slave was not a person, but only a thing whose owner had in it all the rights of property, the right to use it or misuse it. The slave himself had no rights.[63] He could not hold property. Whatever he had belonged to his master. Hence he could not be prosecuted by the latter for theft. If a slave stole any thing from his owner, it was still his master's. He could contract no marriage, nor could any action be brought against him for adultery. Neither paternity nor kinship could be affirmed of him. The words might be used; it might be said, the slave has a father, or relatives, but such language had no legal meaning.[64] His testimony was inadmissible in a court of justice. If his deposition was needed, he was subjected to torture. Only in this way could his evidence have weight.

Though in many cases the actual treatment of slaves was milder than the laws, it corresponded in the main to the principles which have been stated. Slaves were bought and sold, given away as presents and exchanged, inherited and bequeathed, according to caprice or need. They were also lent and hired out. If the hirer treated a slave badly, if a slave suffered an injury, was maimed, or any thing of the sort, this was regarded simply as deterioration of property. The loss was made up to the owner, and the matter was considered as adjusted; no inquiry was made respecting the slave himself. The slave-market was managed as with us the cattle-market. The slaves, male and female, stood there, the more valuable ones apart, often upon a raised platform, those of less price in gangs. The vendor cried up his wares, and used all sorts of means to make them better looking; the buyers looked at them, handled and felt them, to be sure they were sound. The slaves were required to walk, run, leap, open their mouths, show their teeth, etc. When purchased they were assigned, according to ability or opportunity, to some handicraft or art, to agriculture or to begging, or even to the gladiatorial sports and the brothel. As porters they were chained in front of the gate as with us a house dog,[65] and at night were shut up in the *ergastula* like animals in stalls. Like them they were branded and marked;[66] they were also flogged and crucified, often on the least occasion.[67] So long as there was any hope of profit from them they were spared, and when dead they were cast into a pit with dead animals, unless indeed they had been previously exchanged, according to Cato's advice, for old oxen and cows.[68] As to-day a course of instruction in veterinary science forms a part of the education of a farmer, so then a large proprietor was obliged to have some knowledge of medicine for the treatment of sick slaves. Generally the old and diseased were turned off without concern, or they were killed outright as one kills a brute beast. In the city of Rome they were usually exposed on an island in the Tiber. Claudius enacted a law that those thus exposed should be free, and if they got well should not be obliged to return to their masters. Whoever killed his slaves, instead of exposing them, might be indicted for it.[69]

Not that the slaves were systematically abused. They were so much property, a costly capital, to be managed with the greatest economy. But the owners of this capital, regardless of the fact that it consisted of human beings, sought to make it as profitable as possible. Therefore they exacted the *maximum* of labor while they gave only the *minimum* of what was absolutely necessary for maintenance. The meanest laborer to-day is infinitely better off than the slave of that time.

The hardest lot was that of the slaves who cultivated the fields. There were many thousands of them, for the extensive plantations of the Roman magnates were carried on solely by slaves. It appears that a rich Roman, C. Cæcilius Claudius Isidorus, left over four thousand slaves, and others certainly had no less. But few had liberty of motion, and these found a dwelling, perchance, as Cato directed, near the feeding-place in the ox-stall. The majority worked in chains, and then spent the night on the damp ground of the *ergastulum*. These *ergastula* were slave-prisons, partially underground, filthy and unhealthy. Augustus once had them investigated, not however, as we should suppose, in the interest of humanity, but simply for the purpose of ascertaining whether strangers might not be unlawfully imprisoned in them. Nothing was said about improving the lot of the slaves, although the horrors of their condition were fully disclosed. Worse, if possible, was the state of the slaves who worked in the city in great factories, or who were otherwise employed. The field-slave enjoyed at least the free air; but they, scantily clothed, their heads half shorn, their breasts branded, were compelled to toil all day in the low work-house without respite. On the other hand the position of house-slaves, of whom there were often many hundreds in the palaces of Rome, was more tolerable. They were sometimes, especially at the Imperial court, persons of position and wealth, and had, even as slaves, and still more as freedmen, great influence with their masters. Still their lot too was hard, and in many cases horrible. Dumb and fasting such a slave must stand whole nights long behind the chair of his carousing master, wipe off his spittle, or quickly remove his drunken vomit. Woe to him if by whispering, or even by sneezing or coughing, he disturbed the peace of the feaster. He was exposed to every caprice of his owner. A word, and he was sent to the field-slaves in the prisons on one of his master's numerous estates, or scourged till blood came, or horribly killed, or thrown as food to the fishes. Caligula caused a slave who had made some trifling mistake at a public spectacle, to be thrown into prison, tortured for several days in succession, and then executed when at last the putrefying brain of the poor wretch diffused too strong an odor for the cruel monster. A Roman magnate condemned a slave, who carelessly broke a valuable vase at a banquet in the presence of Augustus, to be thrown to the fishes, and not even the Emperor's intercession could save him. Not merely the arbitrariness of a capricious master, but the law also dealt thus rigorously with the slaves. According to the old Roman law, when a master was killed in his house, the slaves who had passed the night under his roof were all executed if the murderer was not discovered. This law was still in force as late as the time of the Empire. When, under Nero, the city prefect Pedanius Secundus was murdered, four hundred slaves of every sex and age, down even to the smallest children, were put to death. To be sure opposition arose in the Senate, but a senator of distinction, C. Cassius, made a speech in favor of the old usage with such effect that the Senate decided to carry the law rigorously through, and it was even proposed to render it still more severe by requiring that all freedmen who had been in the house should be banished from Italy. The speech of Caius Cassius, preserved by Tacitus, gives us a deep insight into the customs of that age, as well as into the pernicious consequences of slavery. He reminded his hearers of the danger to which all masters of slaves would be exposed if the ancestral usage should in this case be forsaken. Whom will his own dignity secure when that of the prefecture of the city has been of no avail? Whom will the number of his slaves defend when four hundred have not protected Pedanius Secundus? It is impossible that the murderer could have planned and executed the deed without exciting suspicion. The slaves in the house must have observed some indications of the crime, but they have not divulged. The slaves must be brought to do this by fear. "If the slaves disclose we can live single among many, safe among the anxious, and, if we must perish, be not unavenged among the guilty. The dispositions of slaves were regarded with suspicion by our ancestors even when they were born on the same estates, or in the same houses with them, and from infancy had experienced the love of their masters. Now, however, when we have nations among our slaves with various rites, with foreign religions, or none at all, it is not possible to control such a rabble except by fear." Thus mistrust on the part of the masters and fear on the part of the slaves, were the principles in accordance with which the slave-holders, and in their interest the State also, were obliged to act. Should the objection be raised that thus innocent persons would perish, Cassius replies: " When every tenth person in a defeated army is put to death, some who have been brave draw the fatal lot. Every great example has something unjust in it, but this is counterbalanced by the public good." [70]

Never has an opponent of slavery set forth its demoralizing effects so clearly as did the representative of the slave-holders on this occasion in the Senate. The influence of slavery was necessarily disastrous on the morals of the higher classes. A man can exercise dominion over a brute without degradation, for it is subordinated to him, but to govern his fellow-man like a beast must lower him morally, for, since no restraint is laid upon him, he is always in danger of giving the reins to his passions. Slavery made masters cruel and hard, and not seldom even women, renouncing the gentleness of their sex, took pleasure in torturing their female slaves. Among their slaves the masters found pliant tools for every deed of shame, otherwise sins against purity especially could never have become so excessive and appalling. The low position of woman in Antiquity was also a consequence of slavery. Its effects upon children were even more injurious. They were wholly abandoned to the care of the slaves. The slave had no authority and was ready to please the child in every thing, otherwise he had reason to fear the anger of his master, or mistress. There must have been many a father who exclaimed to his slave like the father in the comedy: "Wretch, thou hast ruined my son!" The worst result of slavery was, that every form of honorable labor was despised, and became, as a service of slaves, a disgrace. Slavery did not allow the formation of a middle class, and so the check was wanting which might have restrained the wider diffusion of the moral ruin prevalent among the higher orders. That in

Rome the corruption proceeding from the Imperial court and a debased aristocracy penetrated so quickly and so deeply the entire people, is due, in no slight degree, to slavery.

The slaves, in return, became what their treatment made them. As they were deemed incapable of any virtue, and arbitrarily and capriciously treated, so they became low-minded, lazy, lying, and treacherous. The sly, perfidious slave is a constantly recurring character in Greek as well as Roman comedy. No one thought of improving the slaves morally. There was but one virtue for them, — absolute obedience to their masters, for good or for ill. A slave had no moral responsibility whatsoever. Conversely, the slaves looked upon their masters as only their enemies, and were inclined, whenever opportunity occurred, to revenge and insurrection. So many slaves as a man has, so many foes has he, was a saying often heard.

The freedmen were another very bad and pernicious element in the life of the Roman people. They were exceedingly numerous. During the civil wars many slaves had served in the army and had been rewarded by the victor with their liberty. Manumissions frequently occurred, also, in other ways; occasionally from attachment and gratitude, oftener from self-interest, — as those who were enfranchised had to furnish a ransom, or pay a heavy tax, from their earnings to their masters, — and from vanity, in order that great throngs of freedmen might parade in the funeral procession of their master. It became necessary to restrict manumissions by special laws. All classes of the population were filled with freedmen. From them were recruited the lower officials, mechanics, and tradesmen. Some acquired large wealth and shone as *parvenus* by a prodigality as senseless as extravagant. Many remained in the families of their former masters as valets, secretaries, or stewards, and played an important part, not merely in the houses of Roman magnates, but also at the Imperial court. The free Roman shunned every relation which implied service. He deemed it a disgrace even to serve the Emperor, and would rather be fed by the State as a proletary. Consequently the Emperors were obliged to seek their servants among the freedmen. The posts of secretaries, and treasurers, were regularly held by them under the Julian Emperors, and more than once freedmen actually ruled the State. Still the stain of their birth always clung to them; they never attained to the dignity of a freeman, and consequently did not possess the character and spirit of a freeman, but even as freed remained servile. Among them tyrants found their most manageable tools, and from their ranks helpers for every deed of violence could easily be obtained. At home in all classes of the population, they were specially influential in the diffusion of moral contagion.

We should, indeed, err, if we supposed that in Antiquity no one thought of the rights of the slaves as human beings. Such a sentiment is clearly and beautifully expressed by the older Greek poets. "Many a slave bears the infamous name whose mind, nevertheless, is freer than theirs who are not slaves," says Euripides,[71] and another Greek poet[72] says yet more positively: "Though he be a slave, he is, O master, none the less a man." The Stoic school with much greater energy began to advocate the human rights of the slave. This was a consequence of its doctrine of the unity of mankind. "Man is a sacred thing to man," says Seneca: "we are all formed from the same elements, and have the same destiny."[73] "He errs who thinks that slavery takes possession of the whole man. His better part is excepted. Bodies are subject to masters, the soul remains free."[74] He regards it as a misfortune if a man is born a slave, but this is not a determination of nature, and in one place he calls the slaves his "humble friends."[75] We shall see, further on, that such thoughts became increasingly prevalent in the heathen world, and more and more transformed Roman laws and customs. But at first they had little influence. Slavery was held to be absolutely necessary, and therefore justifiable. Notwithstanding all that was said, it had on its side established usage, law, and public opinion.[76]

Not until men were taught that whom the Son makes free, they are free indeed, not till He was proclaimed who Himself took the form of a servant and died the death of a slave on the cross, did the full day of liberty begin to break for slaves, a day which neither the theories of the Stoics, nor Seneca's fine words respecting the dignity of man, could ever have brought. Much is said, at the present time, about humanity, and it is opposed to Christianity as something higher, or at least it is brought forward as a substitute for Christianity which is assumed to be in a state of decrepitude. This is wholly to forget that true humanity is the product of Christianity.[77]

VI. THE NEED OF MORAL RENEWAL.

A gloomy picture has unrolled itself before us. I am conscious that I have not designedly painted it too dark, but that it may not seem blacker than the reality, let us not forget that in the midst of this fearful corruption some sounder elements must still have existed. Otherwise the Roman Empire could not have stood so long as it did. What we know of its moral life is derived chiefly from Rome itself, and unquestionably there, at the centre, the corruption was greatest, whilst in the provinces, and in the camps of the legions, it had not made so great progress. From thence accordingly came a reaction, which brought to the Empire, when the Julian house had passed away, a brilliant after-summer under the noble Emperors of the second century. We must remember, also, that in accounts concerning that time, as all others, the unfavorable aspects are very naturally the most emphasized. For goodness has always but little to say about itself, and in times of declension is peculiarly apt to be quiet. We may safely assume, therefore, that even then there were peaceful, decorous homes into which corruption had not penetrated, where the labor of the hands procured the simple fare, and the discreet house-wife reared her children as a good mother. Yet when all this is taken into account, the general conclusion must still be that the heathen world was ethically as well as religiously at the point of dissolution, that it had become as bankrupt in morals as in faith, and that there was no power at hand from which a restoration could proceed.

It has indeed recently been affirmed that the corruption of morals was not worse then than at many other periods; and parallels from later centuries have been adduced in justification of this assertion. Without doubt there are such. The court of Louis XIV., and those of the princes of his day, afford many a counterpart to the Imperial court in Rome. Yet two things should not be overlooked. First, that at no other period has moral corruption been so universal as in that of the Emperors. At the time when the greatest dissoluteness prevailed in the court at Versailles, what simplicity and strictness characterized the life of the people! Such an entire stratum of population not yet open to corruption, no longer existed in Rome. Secondly, — and this is of chief importance, — for Christian nations there is provided in Christianity a power which can restore the moral life again and again from the deepest degradation. The ancient world was destitute of any such power. After its palmy age — a time of comparative soundness — was gone, after corruption had once entered, it degenerated beyond recovery. Heathenism bore within itself no power of moral renewal.

Or, where can such a power be supposed to have resided? In Religion? We shall see that later, towards the end of the second century, there occurred a strong reaction of pagan faith. In place of the unbelief which prevailed in the first century, superstition gained the ascendancy, and this change reacted upon morals; but reaction is not regeneration. Though the pagan faith once more arose in might, and appeared, especially against Christianity, as an important power, it could not effect a moral transformation, because the relation which subsisted between heathen faith and morality was wholly unlike that which exists between Christian faith and Christian life. There was indeed a connection. The gods were regarded by the heathen as the protectors of the moral law; they punished evil and rewarded goodness. But there was this great difference between the two systems: the heathen deities were neither the authors of the moral law nor its exemplars. Just as little could they impart strength for its fulfilment. On the contrary, judged by its requirements, the gods themselves were the most heinous transgressors. What immoralities do the pagan myths relate of the gods, and instances are by no means wanting in which the heathen appeal, in justification of their iniquities, to the examples of the gods. Looking up to them had a demoralizing, rather than a purifying, effect. "If I could only catch Aphrodite!" once exclaimed Antisthenes, a friend of Socrates, "I would pierce her through with a javelin, she has corrupted so many of our modest and excellent women." [78] In the writings of Terence [79] an adulterer expressly pleads the example of Jupiter, an incident assuredly not merely invented, but taken from life. "If a god does it," so he concludes, "why should not I, a man?" From such deities no purifying influence could proceed. For his moral life the pagan was referred wholly to himself. This is the reason why there was no virtue in which the ancient world was so deficient as humility. It was utterly incomprehensible to a Greek or a Roman, for such virtues as he possessed were self-acquired without divine aid. Therefore he was proud of them, and boasted of them even in comparison with the gods. The Stoics deemed themselves as good as the gods. Even Seneca, who complains so often about human frailty, says: "Give your whole mind to Philosophy, be absorbed in it, cultivate it, and you will far surpass all other men, and be little inferior to the gods." [80] Still more characteristic is the maxim also to be found in the writings of Seneca: "Admire only thyself."[81] Repentance, renewal through contrition, were to the heathen utterly strange ideas. This is the profoundest reason why a reactionary movement might proceed from the heathen religion, but not a moral recovery, not a regeneration.

Or could such a restoration emanate from the State? This preserved, unquestionably, the best which that age had. There still remained, in a good degree, the old Roman bravery, patriotism, and readiness to make sacrifices for the public good. Among the legions which along the Rhine protected the frontier from the barbarians already storming against it, and which more than once bore their victorious eagles to Germany and beyond the sea to Britain, and on the North and East extended the boundaries of the Empire, making their camps at the same time centres of civilization, something of the old spirit still survived. For this reason the sovereignty naturally fell into their hands, and it was the soldier Emperors who had grown up in the camps, who, for a while, kept the structure of the old civilization from falling to pieces. But from this source a moral renewal could not come. The State was sick to the very marrow, and this dominion of soldiers was itself only a symptom of the disease. What the State lacked was the bond of conscience, which secures the obedience of citizens to the laws not merely from compulsion, but for conscience' sake. No State can exist without submission to the laws, but woe to the State which endeavors to secure this result simply by force, and whose citizens no longer render a willing obedience from conscientious regard to its authority. The heathen faith, the dread of the avenging deities, had been such a moral bond. This bond was loosened and from day to day became increasingly relaxed, the more religion declined. The State itself needed regeneration, if it was not to fall asunder; and the nobler Emperors of the later time, even down to Diocletian, sought for a religious basis, on which alone such regeneration was possible, sought for a new bond of conscience with which to unite again what was falling apart. They found none. Religion can quicken the life of the State so that it may flourish anew after temporary decay, but the process cannot be reversed. Never can the moral and religious life of a people be restored by any powers at the command of the State.

There remains Philosophy. Often looked upon distrustfully by the first Emperors, often persecuted outright because it was suspected that behind the philosopher was a republican, it grew in favor, until, in the person of Marcus Aurelius, the philosopher, it ascended the Imperial throne. It became indispensable to the culture of a Roman noble to frequent the schools of the philosophers. Such schools were promoted in every way, and even the salaries for their teachers were provided by government. The more philosophy was absorbed in ethics, and the philosopher's task was not merely to teach but to train in virtue, so much the more prevalent became the custom of taking such persons into families, and the house-philosopher became as regular an appendant of a household of rank as in the Middle Ages the castle-chaplain. The family philosopher, like a father confessor or pastor, was expected to be ready with counsel for those intrusted to his charge, and to impart consolation in the hour of death. This was a need which doubtless opened a way for Christianity, by which alone it could be truly satisfied. The philosophers discoursed even in the streets. In the midst of the tumult of sensual pleasures, to which the world was devoted, the voices of the Cynics rang out, proclaiming renunciation, and freedom from wants, as the way to peace. Not unlike the mendicant monks of the Middle Ages, they roved about without fixed habitation or family, often clad in a ragged mantle or simply a bear-skin, with unkempt hair and shaggy beard, a wallet slung over the shoulders, and alms their only means of support. In the Forum they stopped the rich to declare to them that nothing is more unhappy than a man who has never met with any thing untoward; on the street they stood in the midst of the rabble and discoursed of the corruption of the world. Often they were rewarded only with taunts, or even a cudgelling, but they took it calmly, for, they said, it is the will of the Deity, to which all things must be subordinated and sacrificed.

Certainly these phenomena make us feel that the old world was not contented with its condition. Here too its longing and yearning for renewal are apparent, and just as really, its inability of itself to bring this to pass. What sort of persons usually were these preachers of repentance? They inculcated renunciation and virtue, but if one offer them a piece of cake, mocks a contemporary, they lower their speech and evince their greatness of soul by accepting nothing small. And though there were nobler figures among the philosophers than these philosophasters, what was it, after all, that was cultivated in their schools? Rhetoric, nothing more. They discoursed about virtue, oh with how many fine words, with what art of facial expression and of gesture; they declaimed without end upon the old themes: "Death is no evil." "The wise man who keeps himself free from all needs is the happy man;" the old examples were praised; men plumed themselves upon the splendor of their own virtue; but in reality all this (as we have already seen in the case of Seneca) was mere words. How a man attains to the virtue which is praised so much, how he becomes another man, how he conquers death, no one of those who talked so finely could really tell. Upon the people Philosophy had at first no influence at all. They were even despised by these proud professors of an esoteric wisdom, and deemed incapable of any higher culture and virtue. "With its empty heaven, its single doctrine of duty, its sole reward in a satisfied conscience, its proud bearing toward the gods, from whom it asked nothing, and the annihilation which it contemplated without trembling, Stoicism was made for select souls, not for the masses."[82] For the heathen Philosophy can be claimed neither the glory which St. Paul ascribes to the preaching of the cross, that it was not in lofty words, but in demonstration of the Spirit and of power, nor that of the Gospel, that it was preached to the poor.

Thus there was nowhere to be found a power competent to the gigantic task of a moral renewal of the ancient world. This power must come from another source, from above. When to those who "were sometimes foolish, disobedient, deceived, serving divers lusts and pleasures, living in malice and envy, hateful and hating one another," the kindness and love toward man of God our Saviour appeared, then was first opened the fountain from which a new and healthful life flowed forth for diseased humanity; then the Gospel gathered communions the opposite of that which the heathen world had become, modest, chaste, diligent, their affections set upon things above, the salt of the earth, the light of the world. But obviously the more corrupt the world was in the midst of which they stood, the more terrible must have been the conflict, until, in place of the old pagan world, appeared a new Christian world, in which indeed sin is always present, and morality is only fragmentary, but in which grace is mightier than sin, in which the powers of the world to come rule as powers of regeneration, and in which, therefore, we can say: We WERE sometimes foolish, disobedient, deceived; we were, but are so no more. To God be praise and thanksgiving!

CHAPTER III.

THE CHRISTIANS.

" That ye may be without rebuke, in the midst of a crooked and perverse nation, among whom ye shine as lights in the world." — PHIL. ii. 15.

I. THE PREACHING OF THE GOSPEL.

NEVER in the whole course of human history have two so unequal powers stood opposed to each other as ancient Heathenism and early Christianity, the Roman State and the Christian Church. Apparently, the weakest of forces confronted the strongest. Remember the enormous power concentrated in the Roman Empire; consider not merely the material resources of the State, but, also, that Heathenism had possession of every sphere of life, public and private, that it filled the State and the family, and ruled all culture, and bear in mind, besides, the tenacious power dwelling in a cultus which has prevailed for centuries. Contrast with this the Christian Church as it was in its beginnings, totally destitute of all this might, possessing neither political power nor wealth, neither art nor science, a little company, in the world's judgment, of unlearned men, fishermen, publicans, tent-makers, with only the word of the cross, the message that the promised Messiah has appeared, that in the crucified and risen One there is salvation for all peoples. Verily, the kingdom of heaven is like a grain of mustard seed, small and insignificant; is like leaven, little as compared with the mass of the meal; but it is a living seed, it is a transforming leaven, it bears within itself an energy which is not of this world, and therefore is mightier than the whole world.

Think once more of Paul on the Areopagus in Athens. The glory of the ancient world surrounds him, before his eyes are the noblest works of art which Greece has produced, the Propylæa, the Parthenon, the masterpieces of a Phidias. In his wanderings through this city of ancient renown he has seen the numerous temples, the altars and images of the gods, and the zeal with which they are worshipped. Around him are philosophers reared in the schools of Grecian wisdom, Epicureans and Stoics, proud of their wisdom, masters of form and style. And yet this Jewish tent-maker stands forth and preaches to them that all this belongs to a past time, that now a new era has begun, and offers to make known to them something before which all that glory fades, all their worship proves futile, and all their wisdom is as foolishness. Such language expressed more than human courage; there was in it a joyfulness such as could have sprung only from the certainty of possessing in the Gospel a divine power able to cope with all those earthly forces, an assurance to which this same Apostle gives expression when he writes to the Corinthians (1 Cor. i. 25): "The foolishness of God is wiser than men, and the weakness of God is stronger than men."

From the beginning Christianity bore within itself the consciousness of universal dominion, and the full assurance of victory over all the powers of the world. "Ye are the salt of the earth, ye are the light of the world!" the Lord had said to the disciples, and, "Go ye and make disciples of all the nations," was his parting command. So they went forth to conquer the world for Him to whom they belonged, admitting no doubt that the victory would be theirs. "Greater is he that is in you, than he that is in the world!" and "our faith is the victory which hath overcome the world!" exclaims John; and in proof that the Christians, even after the times of the Apostles, in the midst of a conflict to human view so unequal, held fast this joyful assurance, it will be enough to recall the beautiful words of the Epistle to Diognetus: "What the soul is in the body, that are Christians in the world. The soul is diffused through all the members of the body, Christians are scattered through all the cities of the world. The soul dwells in the body, yet is not of the body, so Christians dwell in the world, yet are not of the world. The soul is imprisoned in the body, yet it holds the body together; so Christians are confined in this world as in a prison, yet they hold the world together." [1]

In truth all that Christianity had to oppose to the whole might of Heathenism was simply the word, the testimony, of Christ. But this testimony was preached from a living faith, with demonstration of the Spirit and of power, and was accompanied by the testimony of life and conduct as a palpable proof for all of the transforming and renewing power inherent in this word. The preaching of the love of God in Christ approved itself in the practice of love to the brethren, and what Christians confessed they sealed in suffering with their blood. Ye shall testify of me! was the Master's commission to His disciples, and thus He pointed out to them the way to overcome the world. The early Christians were also witnesses, and testifying of Christ by word and life, in their love and suffering they won the victory; or rather, He Himself conquered through His witnesses.

In the Roman Catacombs among the oldest pictures, which certainly are as early as the second century, there is a representation of the gift of water in the desert as Moses smites the rock with his rod, and the people, with vessels for drinking, press round the gushing water.[2] The picture unquestionably reflects the impression made at that time by the preaching of the word. In the barren wilderness of Heathenism where men had sought and dug for water so long that at last they were in despair of finding any, now welled freshly forth the fountain of living water springing up into everlasting life, and thus many a soul among the heathen thirsting for truth, many a seeker after wisdom in the schools of the philosophers, in the temples of gods the most diverse, or in Jewish houses of prayer, found here his deepest longing satisfied.

We possess two narratives of the conversion of heathen, which although not belonging to the very earliest period, are yet admirably adapted to show us the impression made by Christian truth upon susceptible spirits, and the ways in which they came to it. One of these narratives is contained in a kind of romance from the middle of the second century, the so-called Clementine Homilies, in which ostensibly Clement of Rome relates to us his history. "From my earliest youth," he says, "I thought much concerning death, and of what may be after death. When I die shall I cease to exist and be remembered no more? Has the world been made, and what was there before it was made? In order to learn something definite about these and similar questions, I used to resort to the schools of the philosophers. But nought else did I see than the setting up and knocking down of doctrines, and strifes and contentions, and artificial reasonings and invention of premises. Now the opinion prevailed that the soul is immortal, now that it is mortal. If the former I was glad, if the latter I was sorrowful. Perceiving that opinions were deemed true or false according to the ability of those who maintained them, and not according to their real nature, I was more than ever perplexed. Wherefore I groaned from the depths of my soul. For neither was I able to establish any thing, nor could I refrain from solicitude concerning such themes. And again I said to myself: Why do I labor in vain? If I am not to live after death, I need not distress myself now while I am alive. I will reserve my grief till that day when, ceasing to exist, I shall cease to be sad. But if I am to exist, of what advantage is it to me now to distress myself? And immediately another thought came to me. Shall I not suffer worse there than now? If I do not live piously, shall I not be tormented like Sisyphus and Ixion and Tantalus? And again I replied: But there is no truth in such stories. But if there be? Therefore, said I, since the matter is uncertain, it is safer for me to live piously. But I am not fully persuaded what is that righteous thing that is pleasing to God, neither do I know whether the soul is immortal or mortal, nor do I find any sure doctrine, nor can I abstain from such reasonings. What am I to do? I will go into Egypt, and seek and find a magician, and will persuade him with large bribes to conjure up a soul. And so I shall learn by ocular proof whether the soul is immortal." From this purpose he was dissuaded by a friendly philosopher, on the ground that the gods are angry with those who disturb the dead. Clement therefore remained without relief, until, hearing of Christ and his Apostles, he determined to seek them. He first found Barnabas, and was greatly impressed by the fact that in his preaching, Barnabas did not concern himself with the objections of the philosophers, their subtle questions and their ridicule of his simple and illogical discourses, but calmly declared such things as he had heard and seen Jesus do and say, and substantiated his statements by witnesses instead of by artificial demonstrations. Afterwards he found Peter, obtained from him a sure answer to his questions, and became a Christian. All this is only fiction, but the colors of the picture were certainly taken from life, and the imaginary narrative of Clement was doubtless the actual history of many.

In a similar manner Justin Martyr tells us of his fruitless wanderings through the schools of the philosophers in search of certainty and peace of mind. A Stoic, under whose instruction he first placed himself, asserted that the sure knowledge of God, which Justin chiefly longed for, was a subordinate question of philosophical speculation. A Peripatetic, of whom he next inquired, demanded, after a few days, as of primary importance, that he should settle the fee. This repelled Justin, and he went to a Pythagorean, who dismissed him immediately, because he had no knowledge of music, geometry and astronomy, an acquaintance with which the Pythagorean declared was pre-requisite to the study of philosophy, since they are the means by which the soul absorbed in earthly things may be purified. Justin then turned to a Platonist, and supposed that he had reached the goal, for his teacher introduced him to the Platonic doctrine of ideas, and the pupil already dreamed that he had become a sage and was near to the vision of Deity. Then, walking alone one day on the shore of the sea, he met an old man, a mature Christian, and fell into conversation with him on divine things. The venerable man showed him that God can be perceived only by a mind sanctified by the Spirit of God, and so affected him that all at once his proud dream of knowledge vanished. The old man, seeing his consternation, pointed him to the divine Word as the source of all true knowledge of God, and began to tell him of Christ. Following these hints, Justin found in Christianity that sure knowledge of God which he had sought for in vain in the different schools of philosophers.[3]

Doubtless, what principally attracted the heathen and held them fast, was the fact that with the Christians was to be found full assurance of faith on the basis of a divine revelation. They did not ask: What is truth? but they preached: "Grace and truth came through Jesus Christ." They did not dispute *pro* and *contra* as in the schools, nor was their final conclusion that we can know nothing with certainty, but: "That which we have heard, which we have seen with our eyes and our hands have handled of the word of life, that declare we unto you." They did not prate about trifles like the Rhetoricians, who with the most incredible affectation of far-fetched words now pronounced a eulogy upon obscurity or laziness, now discussed the dangerous illness of a member of the Imperial household as a welcome theme for rhetorical artifice, but they spoke simply and plainly upon the highest themes and such as are necessary to the salvation of the soul. They said nothing about artificial ways of attaining the favor of God, such as the wandering magicians and hierophants scraped together in order that they might with much mystification proclaim them as the only saving wisdom, — for example, when one of them tried to prove that the surest way to please God was always in libation to pour the wine exactly over the handle of the pitcher, as that is the only part which is not defiled by man's mouth. On the contrary Christians bore witness to facts, the facts of Redemption: "God was in Christ reconciling the world unto Himself;" Christ "was delivered for our offences, and was raised again for our justification." To all was made known the one true God, the Father of our Lord Jesus Christ, preached not as the result of philosophical speculation, but upon the basis of His word, not as a secret doctrine for a few wise men, but publicly to all, even the poor and the insignificant. "Not only the rich among us," says Tatian, "seek for wisdom, but the poor also enjoy instruction gratuitously." [4] "Every Christian laborer," says Tertullian, "both finds out God and manifests Him, though Plato affirms that it is not easy to discover the Maker of the universe, and when He is found it is difficult to make Him known to all." [5]

The sign which our Lord adduced in proof of His Messiahship: "To the poor the Gospel is preached," was now abundantly fulfilled. It is a characteristic of those times that the circle of the poor, the oppressed, the unprotected, the enslaved was so large. What an impression must have been made upon such persons, on all who were without possessions, who had no share in the wealth and pleasures of Rome, upon the obscure and down-trodden, on the artisans who, because they lived by the work of their hands, were regarded as of no account by the ancient world proud of its learning and culture, of whom even a Plato said their life serves no other end than the practice of their trade, and if they fall sick they must be left to their fate since they can no longer fulfill their calling, on the crowds of slaves in their lot so unworthy of human beings; what impression must have been made on these, when the poor Jesus, who Himself died the death of a slave, was proclaimed to them, and in Him access to a divine kingdom which embraces all men, in which there are no more masters nor servants, nor any who are trodden under foot. Even in the second century Celsus scoffingly says that workers in wool and in leather, and fullers, and persons the most uninstructed and rustic, were the most zealous ambassadors of Christianity, and brought it first to women and children.[6] But the mockery of the heathen bore witness, against their will, to the power of the preached word, and what was only a matter of scorn to cultivated pagans was to our Lord a subject of praise when He said: "I thank Thee, O Father, Lord of heaven and earth, because Thou hast hid these things from the wise and prudent, and hast revealed them unto babes. Even so, Father, for so it seemed good in Thy sight (Matt. xi. 25, 26)."

Another satire of the same enemy of the Christians,

Celsus, gives us a still deeper view of the power of the evangelical preaching. "Let us hear," he says, "what kind of persons these Christians invite. Every one, they say, who is a sinner, who is devoid of understanding, who is a child, him will the kingdom of God receive. They assert that God will receive the sinner if he humble himself on account of his wickedness, but that He will not receive the righteous man although he look up to Him with virtue from the beginning."[7] This seems to Celsus thoroughly absurd. "It is manifest to everybody," he thinks, "that no one by punishment, much less by showing mercy, could wholly change those who are sinners both by nature and custom."[8] It was precisely this preaching of grace which had such power over men's spirits. Now the consciousness of sin awoke in the heathen world, and a longing for redemption. Now many souls groaned under the burden of their sins and asked for a purification, for an atonement. Here they found what they had sought for in vain in the heathen temples, in manifold consecrations and lustrations, in numerous ascetic practices and acts of wearisome self-denial, which continually gained a larger place in the pagan cultus. In the blood of the Lamb of God they were offered the free forgiveness of all sins, and in Baptism a laver of purification which cleansed them from all defilement. The invitation of our Lord: "Come unto Me, all ye that labor and are heavy laden, and I will give you rest," preserved all the more its power since in the decaying world whose splendor and joy were daily fading, the number of the weary and heavy laden was daily increasing.

And at a time when the attention of men was turned

with greater longing to the other world, when, as we have seen, the question was more and more earnestly discussed: Is there another life? and how can we attain to a blessed existence there? what an impression must have been made when the Resurrection of Christ was proclaimed. Here was the answer to all such questions, not upon the basis of doubtful proofs and reasonings which, as Clement says, could be turned now for, now against immortality, but on the ground of a fact. Here was offered what the heathen world lacked, a living hope. It was attested at the graves of Christians. There were heard, not cries of lamentation, but the singing of psalms: "Precious in the sight of the Lord is the death of his saints," "Return unto thy rest, O my soul; for the Lord hath dealt bountifully with thee," "Yea, though I walk through the valley of the shadow of death, I will fear no evil; for Thou art with me;" there resounded a victorious "Hallelujah! death is swallowed up in victory!" and the inscriptions on the unpretending graves: "He lives!" "In peace!" show that Christians had become sure of eternal life. Even the attacks of the heathen, which were more vehement against this article of the Christian faith than any other, even the terrible scorn with which they exclaimed, as the bodies of the martyrs in Lyons were burned, and the ashes cast into the Rhone: "We shall now see if they will rise," sufficiently prove the power exerted upon men's minds by the preaching of the Resurrection and of eternal life.

II. WORSHIP AND CHURCH LIFE.

The religious services of the Christians also made a deep impression upon the heathen. Pagan worship was everywhere destitute of devotion. The Roman religion was a lifeless ritualism, a punctilious repetition of liturgical formulas, although the language used had ceased to be intelligible. Among the Greeks raillery and jests were practised in connection with their most solemn processions. When, at the celebration of the greater Eleusinian mysteries, the mystæ marched in procession to Eleusis, they were greeted at the bridge over the Cephissus with all sorts of jokes and gibes, many of them exceedingly coarse. Even at the chorus dance on the meadow near Eleusis, similar sport was made. The Oriental cults were, on the contrary, a sort of orgy, in which ecstasy, exaggerated often to frenzy, took the place of devotion.

The worship of the Christians was the exact opposite to this heathen cultus. Pomp and splendor were not to be found among persons so poor, but their service was a worship of God in spirit and in truth. No temples, no altars, no images, was their rule.[9] They needed no temple, they who were themselves, according to the testimony of the Apostle, the living temple of God, built upon the foundation of the Apostles and Prophets, Jesus Christ Himself being the chief corner-stone.[10] In houses here and there, in little narrow rooms, or in a hall when a wealthy member of the church possessed such an apartment, they were wont to assemble for singing, reading of the Scriptures, prayer, and celebration of the Lord's Supper. In the early days it often happened that one or another member of the congregation, who had received the gift, spoke a word of edification; but generally, and in later times exclusively, this service devolved upon the president. We possess several descriptions of this primitive Christian worship, which are as simple as was the service itself, yet in their simplicity testify to its vitality, its freedom from dead forms, its perfect truth. Pliny the Younger, while governor in Bithynia, instituted inquiries respecting the faith and the life of Christians, and also by tortures extorted confessions from some deaconesses. The information which he thus obtained he embodied in a letter to the Emperor Trajan. "The Christians," he says, "affirmed that it was their custom to meet on a stated day before sunrise, and sing a hymn to Christ as to a god; that they further bound themselves by an oath" (obviously the baptismal vow) "never to commit any crime, but to abstain from robbery, theft, adultery, never to break their word, nor to deny a trust when summoned to deliver it, after which they would separate and then re-assemble for the purpose of eating in common a harmless meal."[11] Still more exactly does Justin describe this worship:[12] "On Sunday, all who live in cities or in the country gather together to one place, and the memoirs of the Apostles or the books of the prophets are read, as long as time permits. Then, when the reader has ended, the president in a discourse instructs, and exhorts to the imitation of these glorious examples. Then we all rise together and send upwards our prayers. And when we have ceased from prayer, bread and wine and water are brought, and the president offers prayers and thanksgivings according to his ability. The congregation assent, saying Amen; and there is a distribution to each one present of the consecrated things, and to those who are absent a portion is sent by the deacons. And they who are well-to-do and willing give what each thinks fit, and the collected gifts are deposited with the president, who succors with them the widows and orphans, and those who through sickness or any other cause are in want, and those who are in bonds, and the strangers sojourning among us, in short, all who are in need." Connected at first with the Lord's Supper, afterwards separated from it, were the *Agapæ*, whose observance is hinted at in the letter of Pliny. The whole congregation met, like one family, at a common meal. Tertullian describes these feasts as they were observed in his day. "Our meal," he writes,[13] "explains itself by its name. It is designated by the Greek word for love (*Agape*). Whatever it costs, our outlay is gain if we thus benefit the poor. This is the honorable occasion of our repast. By this judge its further regulations. As it is an act of religious service, it permits no vileness, nor excess. We do not go to the table until we have first tasted of prayer to God; we eat as much as satisfies the hungry; we drink as much as is profitable for the chaste. We satisfy ourselves as those who remember that during the night also God is to be worshipped; we converse as those who know that the Lord hears them. After water for the hands and lights are brought, each one is called upon to praise God, either from the Holy Scriptures or of his own mind; hence it is proved how much he has drunken. As the feast began, so it is closed, with prayer. Thence we separate, not into bands for violence, nor for roaming the streets, but to take the same care of our modesty and chastity as if we had been at a place of instruction rather than at a banquet." Imagine such a religious service in its simplicity and youthful freshness, think of some church in times perhaps of persecution, expecting every moment that spies will betray them or a mob break in with yells and stones; yet hymns and psalms resound, the word of life is preached with plainness and holy earnestness, the congregation rise for prayer, the president leads, all join with him and solemnly repeat the Amen, all receive the body and blood of the Crucified One, whom perhaps they will soon follow in death, all unite in the feast of love, and with prayer and the kiss of peace they depart — verily, we can understand how the heathen who only once attended such a service should in many instances have been thereby won forever. In their temples dead ceremonial worship, here one of the living, life-giving Word; there a dumb, inactive mass of spectators, while the priest alone had intercourse with Deity, here a participating, singing, hearing, praying communion, all priests of the living God. Already, in 1 Cor. xiv. 24, 25, we read that unbelievers, who should see and hear this, would be deeply moved, fall on their faces, worship God, and confess that God was in them of a truth; and Eusebius, in his history, testifies explicitly: "The Holy Spirit wrought many wonders through them, so that vast crowds, at the first hearing of the Gospel, eagerly received it into their hearts." [14]

The Christians had what the heathen lacked, congregational life. Antiquity was not destitute of public spirit. On the contrary this existed to a special degree, as is proved by the numerous legacies and donations, and by the erection of public buildings, of which inscriptions give us information. In the domain of industrial life the impulse to association was very strongly developed. Colleges were instituted for the different branches of industry, and endowed with funds for the relief of the sick and the dying, and for burials. There were colleges also for religious purposes, associations for the service of special deities. The provincial assemblies (*Koinon*) were also united by religious festivals. But there was nothing like the Christian societies in pagan antiquity. Polytheism did not admit of it. Public spirit developed itself simply on the political side. But as political life declined it offered less and less room for activity. Freedom ceased to exist, all were slaves of one. Every act by which a man distinguished himself, every illustrious achievement was attended with the danger of exciting the jealousy of the sovereign power. Municipal life retained at first more freedom, but its offices, which had formerly been sought as positions of honor, became in time so burdensome on account of the heavy expenses connected with them, that every one, as far as possible, avoided them, so that it became necessary to enforce their acceptance by law. In the Christian communities, on the other hand, a circle was formed which, although small, was all the more active. Controlled by the spirit of fellowship, and united in fraternal affection by a common faith, all the members labored, prayed and suffered together. In such a society there was room for every kind of activity, and opportunity for the most varied talents. There freedom found a sanctuary, and there, in the midst of action and suffering, noble characters could unfold and grow strong.

III. CONDUCT OF THE CHRISTIANS.

And what testimony to the truth of Christianity was given by the conduct of its professors. "Among us," pleads Athenagoras,[15] addressing the heathen, "you can find uneducated persons, artisans, and old women, who, if they are unable in words to prove the benefit of the Christian doctrine, yet by their deeds exhibit the benefit arising from their choice." Times without number the defenders of Christianity appeal to the great and advantageous change wrought by the Gospel in all who embraced it, and continually set forth the contrast between the lives of men before and after conversion, to which St. Paul often refers in his Epistles. "We who formerly delighted in fornication," says Justin Martyr in his First Apology,[16] "now strive for purity. We who used magical arts, have dedicated ourselves to the good and eternal God. We who loved the acquisition of wealth more than all else, now bring what we have into a common stock, and give to every one in need. We who hated and destroyed one another, and on account of their different manners would not receive into our houses men of a different tribe, now, since the coming of Christ, live familiarly with them. We pray for our enemies, we endeavor to persuade those who hate us unjustly to live conformably to the beautiful precepts of Christ, to the end that they may become partakers with us of the same joyful hope of a reward from God, the Ruler of all." This distinction between Christians and heathen, this consciousness of a complete change in character and life, is nowhere more beautifully described than in the noble epistle of an unknown author to Diognetus.[17] "For Christians," it says, "are distinguished from other men neither by country, nor language, nor the customs which they observe; for they neither inhabit cities of their own, nor employ a peculiar form of speech, nor lead a singular life." And yet they are wholly different from the heathen. "They dwell in their own countries, but simply as sojourners. As citizens they share in all things with others, and yet endure all things as if they were foreigners. They marry as do all, and have children, but they destroy none of their offspring. They have a table common, but not unclean. They are in the flesh, but they do not live after the flesh. They pass their days on earth, but they are citizens of heaven. They obey the prescribed laws, and at the same time surpass the laws by their lives. They love all, and are persecuted by all; they are unknown and are condemned; they are put to death and yet live; they are poor yet make many rich; they are in want of all things, yet abound in all; they are dishonored, and yet in their very dishonor are glorified; they are reviled, and bless; they are insulted, and repay the insult with honor; they do good yet are punished as evil-doers; when punished they rejoice. They are assailed by the Jews as foreigners, and are persecuted by the Greeks, yet those who hate them are unable to assign any reason for their hatred." With confidence can Tertullian appeal to the transactions of the courts, in which no crime had ever been proved against Christians but that of their faith. "Daily," he addresses the heathen,[18] "you are presiding at the trials of prisoners, and passing sentence upon crimes. In your long lists of those accused of many and various atrocities, what assassin, what cutpurse, what plunderer of bathers' clothes is also entered as being a Christian? Or, when Christians are brought before you on the mere ground of their name, who among them is ever chargeable with such offences? It is always with your folk the prison is steaming, the mines are sighing, the wild beasts are fed; it is from you the exhibitors of gladiatorial shows always get their herds of criminals to feed up for the occasion. You find no Christian there, except for being such." Even the heathen themselves could not escape from this impression. The influence of Christian faith upon life and conduct was so powerful that heathen hatred itself could not but acknowledge it. Galen, the celebrated physician, certainly a cool observer and an unimpeachable witness, says, that most men must be taught by similes. In this way those who were called Christians had derived their faith from the parables of their Master. Yet they acted often as those who followed the true philosophy. "We are witnesses that they have learned to despise death, and that for shame they keep themselves from carnal pleasures. Among them are men and women who abstain from marriage; some, too, who in their endeavors to rule their spirits, and to live nobly, have made such progress that they come short in no respect of true philosophers."

Christianity as yet presented none of the external advantages which afterwards brought into the church so many spurious members. Instead of power, honor and wealth, it offered reproach, derision and constant peril. Nor did custom and tradition yet incline men to the mere outward profession of Christianity. Whoever adopted the new faith did so from personal conviction, and with the heart. Such an act was itself a sacrifice; for whoever became a Christian was compelled to renounce not only immemorial prejudices, but usually, also, father and mother, brothers and sisters, friends and relatives, perhaps office, place and employment. The turning-point between the pre-Christian and the Christian life stood out with great distinctness. It is characteristic of a period of conflict that sudden conversions are more frequent then than at other times, that the marvel inherent in every conversion becomes more evident, and, so to speak, more palpable. Not infrequently did it happen that the execution of a Christian occasioned the immediate conversion of some among the guards, soldiers, executioners and spectators. According to credible testimonies, yet more striking changes occurred. Under Diocletian, an actor in Rome, Genesius, appeared in a play in which the Christians were ridiculed. He performed his part without hesitation and to the delight of the people, until the moment when he was to ask for baptism. Seized by an irresistible power he suddenly stood still and silent, and then explained to the astonished audience, that he himself desired to become a Christian. Upon this he left the stage, received baptism, and soon sealed his faith with a martyr's death.[19]

With these extraordinary events may also be mentioned the frequent occurrence of conversions through wonderful dreams, as Origen[20] expressly testifies. Witnesses who are above suspicion leave no room for doubt that the miraculous powers of the Apostolic age continued to operate at least into the third century.[21] Yet the importance of these miracles should not be too highly estimated. It is true the Apologists appeal to them as a testimony to the truth of the Gospel. Yet there are no indications that they contributed, in any special degree, to gaining the people over to the faith.[22]

Even where conversion occurred less suddenly, there was the most definite consciousness of the change experienced, and as Christians were continually reminded by the heathen life around them of their peculiar calling, and their separation from this present evil world, so likewise were they ever sensible of their obligation to live differently from the heathen and to bring themselves into complete subjection to Christianity. This consciousness was expressed in customs and symbols. The Scriptures were read, and psalms were sung, in their homes. Not only was prayer offered before every meal, but also a piece of the consecrated bread which had been brought from the church was eaten. Whenever they went out and came in, when they put on their clothes and shoes, when they bathed, when they lighted the lamps, when they lay down and when they went to bed, Christians traced on their foreheads the sign of the Cross, and this was not then a dead sign but a living remembrance of the Crucified One, of baptism into His death, and of the obligations assumed in baptism.[23]

A calm and sacred earnestness pervaded the entire life of Christians. Knowing that Christ's followers are the salt of the earth and the light of the world, they endeavored to fulfill their calling. Their eyes turned to the future, to the Lord who had promised to come again, and in expectation of His speedy appearance they followed with zeal after that holiness without which no one shall stand before Him. Their life was a military service, under Christ their Captain. To Him they had taken in baptism the soldier's oath; and for Him they had renounced the devil, and all his works and ways. Their standard was the Cross, their watchword the confession of faith, their weapon, with which they stood on the watch night and day, and kept station and vigil, was prayer.[24] "Let us never walk unarmed," exhorts Tertullian; "by day let us remember our station, by night our watch. Under the arms of prayer let us guard the standard of our Commander; praying let us await the angel's trump." [25] Fasts also were frequently and strictly observed. Fasting was regarded as a specially important means of proving the earnestness of the Christian life, and of confirming one's self in it, but it was voluntary not prescribed. The fast in Easter-week, however, early became obligatory. Baptism, also, was prepared for by fasting.[26]

The Christian life was always uniform. "Nowhere," says Tertullian, whom we have just quoted, "is the Christian any thing but a Christian."[27] Not merely at church, but at home also, in their vocations and on the street, Christians desired to appear as Christians. They guarded with the greatest care against any connection with Heathenism; they avoided with the utmost conscientiousness every thing which could in any way be construed as a denial of their faith. Difficult indeed must have been the task, for their entire life was encompassed by a net-work of heathen customs which a Christian must every moment rend, if he would remain true to his God. Every step and turn necessitated a confession of faith, and every confession involved danger. The symbols, and still more the spirit of Heathenism were everywhere. If a Christian went upon the street, he saw the images of the gods standing there, and met processions in which they were solemnly carried about. All who passed by paid their homage; the Christian could not do this. If he entered the Senate, or a court of justice, there stood an altar with incense and wine. Custom required one in passing to offer a libation, and strew incense. If he stepped into a tavern, or stall, or shop to make a purchase or leave an order, he always found an altar and little idols, often no longer than the thumb. Or perhaps he was invited by heathen friends, or relatives, to a family festival. If he did not go, he gave offence; if he went, he still could not but incur their displeasure by declining to participate in the festal sacrifices and in the libations which were offered from beginning to end of the meal, especially to the Cæsar-god, and by refusing to partake of this or that article of food. Frequently on such occasions the heathen purposely tempted the Christians, by setting before them food prepared with blood, from which, according to Acts xv. 29, they were accustomed to abstain.[28] In such circumstances Christians esteemed it all the more their duty openly to acknowledge their faith. Not only custom and usage, but language also was thoroughly imbued with heathenism. The formulas of the oath, depositions, testimony before a tribunal, greetings and thanksgivings, all contained remembrances of the heathen gods. By Hercules! this and similar exclamations were often heard. The Christian must refrain from these, must at least protest by silence. He might give alms to a beggar on the street. Natually, in gratitude, the recipient would wish for his benefactor the blessing of some god. Christians who were strict in their deportment believed that it was not permitted them, in such a case, to remain silent, lest it should seem as if they accepted the blessing of an idol; they considered it incumbent upon them openly to avow that their charity had been given for the sake of the living God, and that He might be praised therefor. If a Christian had occasion to borrow money, the note which he must sign would contain an oath by the heathen gods. He could only refuse to execute the note.[29]

DIFFICULT POSITION OF CHRISTIANS.

Many special relations of life brought the Christians into still more difficult situations. A master would order a Christian slave to do something wholly unobjectionable from a heathen point of view, but sinful according to a Christian standard, and yet the slave was completely in the power of his master, who could have him, if disobedient, tortured and even killed. How should the Christian wife, who had a heathen husband, fulfill her Christian obligations, attend divine worship, visit the sick, entertain strangers, distribute alms, without offending her husband? How could the officer, or the soldier, perform his duties without denying his faith? For long the two callings were deemed incompatible, and the officer preferred to resign his position, the soldier to leave the ranks, rather than to give up his Christian profession.[30] Those who could not do this were often obliged to purchase fidelity to their Lord with their blood. Many a person also, in order to become and to remain a Christian must have relinquished the trade or the employment which procured him a livelihood. All who had obtained a support by the heathen cultus, servants and laborers in the temples, idol-makers, sellers of incense, as well as actors, fencing-masters in the gladiatorial schools, etc., were admitted by the church to baptism only on condition that they should abandon their occupations, and whoever as a Christian engaged in such employments was excluded from fellowship.[31]

Generally the churches maintained a strict discipline. The morals and conduct of church members were carefully watched over, and their faults earnestly reproved. Those who fell into gross sins, the so-called mortal sins,—idolatry, blasphemy, adultery, impurity, murder, fraud, false testimony, — were separated from the church. Only after a long probation, and after evidence of earnest repentance, could such offenders be re-admitted. And this restoration, in accordance with earlier usage, was possible but once. Whoever fell away a second time, could not again be taken back. Thus by strict discipline the church endeavored to keep itself free from impure elements, and at the same time to offer support to the weak. In spite of such effort it was not wholly free from corruption, and no little weakness comes to light. The primitive church was not a perfect communion of saints, but, like the church of all other times, a field in which the wheat and the tares grew together. Yet, notwithstanding these defects the Christian churches stood like far-shining lights in the midst of darkness, and proved themselves by their life and conduct new powers of life, powers of the world to come, capable of renewing from within the old and decaying world.

If human society was to be really regenerated, it was necessary that the foundations should be laid anew. These lie in marriage, and in the family. Married and domestic life had fallen into decay in the heathen world. Christianity re-established them by restoring freedom of marriage, by infusing into it a new spirit, by showing again to the wife her divinely-appointed position, and by making her once more her husband's helper instead of his slave.

In Antiquity marriage, like every thing else, centred in the State. Its end was to produce citizens. The individual, therefore, was under obligation to the State to marry, and the State, as already remarked, deemed itself constrained to enforce the fulfillment of this duty by penalties. Christianity made marriage free. It honored the liberty of the individual, and left it to him to decide whether he would marry or not. It honored also the unmarried state, and though we must concede that, in this respect, false and unevangelical opinions soon found acceptance, and an exaggerated estimate was put on the celibate life as peculiarly holy, a notion nowhere sanctioned in Scripture, yet it should not be overlooked that this regard for celibacy implies a conquest over the false and pagan conception of marriage.

For contempt of marriage in favor of celibacy did not prevail until long afterwards. On the contrary marriage then first received its due honor by being recognized and treated as a divine institution. Matrimony was contracted with the privity and sanction of the church. Intended marriages were notified to the bishop, and were entered upon with his blessing.[32] Marriages which were concluded without the co-operation of the church were not regarded by it as true marriages. A higher aim was now set than Heathenism had ever known. "Marriage," says Clement of Alexandria,[33] "is a school of virtue for those who are thus united, designed to educate them and their children for eternity. Every home, every family must be an image of the church, for, says our Lord, where two are gathered in my name there am I in their midst." A much closer and stronger tie now united husband and wife, the bond of a common faith. We find in Tertullian[34] a eulogy of Christian marriage in which he compares a complete union, where both parties, husband and wife, are Christians, with a mixed marriage where a Christian wife is joined to a pagan husband. From his noble words we see not only the high estimate put upon marriage, but also how it was elevated by being imbued with a Christian spirit. "How shall we fully describe that marriage which the church cements, the oblation confirms, and the benediction seals; of which angels carry back the tidings, and which the Father regards as ratified? What a union is that of two believers, who have one hope, one rule of life, and one service? They are brother and sister, two fellow-servants; there is no difference of spirit or of flesh. Nay, they are truly two in one flesh. Where the flesh is one, one also is the spirit. Together they pray, together they prostrate themselves, together they fast; each teaching the other, each exhorting the other, each sustaining the other. They go together to the church of God, and to the Supper of the Lord. They share each other's tribulations, persecutions and refreshments. Neither hides aught from the other, neither shuns the other, neither is a burden to the other. The sick are visited freely, the poor supported. Alms are given without constraint, sacrifices attended without scruple, the daily devotions held without hinderance; there is no stealthy signing with the cross, no trembling greeting, no mute benediction. In alternate song echo psalms and hymns; they vie with each other who best shall praise their God. When Christ sees and hears such things, He rejoices. To these He sends His own peace. Where two are, there also is He. Where He is, there the Evil One is not." In a house thus ordered, children could grow up in the fear and admonition of the Lord, and of such Christian families Clement of Alexandria justly says: "The children glory in their mother, the husband in his wife, and she in them, and all in God." [35]

As the whole life of the people was founded upon that of the family, so this in turn depended upon the position held by the wife. It is true that in marriage the husband is the head according to divine institution, yet the character of domestic and family life is more determined by the wife than by the husband. For this reason no sound family life could exist in the pagan world, because the wife did not occupy her true place. Among the Greeks, she was the slave of her husband. Among the Romans, she was more highly honored, yet was destitute of rights apart from him. Full and perfect worth as a human being Antiquity never conceded to woman. Man alone possessed this dignity. Christianity freed woman from this enslaved and unprotected state by making her the equal of man in that which is supreme, the relation to Christ and the kingdom of God. They are "heirs together of the grace of life." "The husband and wife," so Clement of Alexandria expresses this thought, "may share equally in the same perfection."[36] All the rest follows of itself. Though the wife remains, as respects the natural life, subordinate to her husband, she is no longer his servant, but his helper. "Thou didst not disdain that Thy only begotten Son should be born of a woman," says the consecrating prayer for deaconesses in the ancient church.[37] This fact, the birth of the Son of God from a woman, gave to woman a new position. It is true that as God created her to serve, so this remained her calling in the church. She should not teach publicly in the church, for that would invest her with an authority which is not her lot. But since all is service in the church, even the office of teacher and that of ruler, there is implied in this no degradation of woman, but only the assignment to her of a place corresponding to that divinely assigned her in creation. Women emancipated from this divine order were a product of Paganism, though even in Rome, in the time of its decline, in spite of the low estimate put upon their sex, women who caroused with men through the night and fought in gladiatorial armor, made themselves notorious. But as mothers who trained for the church its standard-bearers, as deaconesses in the service of mercy, as martyrs who vied with men for the immortal crown, serving everywhere, praying, toiling, enduring, women shared in the great conflict, and to them surely, in no small degree, was the victory due.

Esteeming service to be her calling, and the service of Christ as her highest honor, it followed of course that a Christian matron no longer indulged in the extravagant and unnatural luxury of dress which characterized the high-born women of the time. She renounced all such display when she became a Christian, and henceforth appeared, according to apostolic injunction, in neat and simple attire, gladly allowing it to be said: " She goes about in poorer garb since she became a Christian," [38] conscious that she was really much richer, and that modesty, purity, simplicity and naturalness were her most attractive ornaments. She had no further occasion for her former splendor. She no longer frequented the temples and the theatre, no longer observed the pagan festivals. She ruled in the quiet of home; labored there with her hands, cared for her husband and children, and cheerfully and heartily dispensed the rites of hospitality.[39] When she went out she visited the sick, or went to church to hear the word of God and to celebrate the Eucharist,—

SIMPLICITY OF CHRISTIAN WOMEN.

what need for finery there? And even if she called upon her heathen friends, or accepted an invitation to the homes of heathen relatives, she was not ashamed even there to appear with entire simplicity. Going thus, to use Tertullian's words, armed with her own weapons, she showed that there is a difference between the servants of God and the servants of the Devil, and she was an example to others for their profiting, that God, according to the word of the Apostle, might be glorified in her body."[40]

There appeared in the ancient church a strong opposition to the feminine luxury which had then reached so unexampled an excess. Tertullian[41] vehemently declaims, and not he alone but other church teachers as well, against dyeing the hair, and all artificial headgear! "The Lord has said: Which of you can make one hair white or black? They refute God! Behold! say they, instead of white or black hair we make it auburn" (then the fashionable color) "so that it is more attractive. Far from the daughters of Wisdom be such folly! What service does so much labor spent in arranging the hair render to salvation? Why is no rest allowed to your hair, which must now be bound, now loosed, now raised up, now pressed flat? Some are anxious to force their hair into curls, others, with seeming yet not commendable simplicity, to let it fall loose and flying. Beside which you affix I know not what enormities of false braids of hair, which now like a cap or helmet cover the head, now are massed backward toward the neck. I am very much mistaken if this is not contending against the precepts of the Lord. He has said that no man can add any thing to his stature. If the enormity does not cause you shame, let the impurity, lest you may be putting on a holy and Christian head the hair which has been taken from the head of some one else, perhaps of an unclean person, guilty perchance, and destined to hell. Nay rather, banish from your free head all this slavery of ornamentation. In that day of Christian exultation I shall see whether you will rise with your white and red and yellow pigments, and in all that parade of head-gear; whether the angels will carry women thus tricked out to meet Christ in the air. Keep yourselves now from those things which are condemned. To-day let God see you such as He will see you then."

Tertullian is zealous also, against the use of pigments. It is a sin, he says, for they who put on rouge desire to make themselves more beautiful than God has made them, and thus censure the Artificer of all things. He rejects purple garments, for if God had wished such to be worn, He would have created sheep with purple wool. Even garlands find no favor with Him. If God had wished for garlands, He would have caused not merely flowers but garlands to grow. This sounds strange to us, and it is unquestionably one-sided, yet it reveals a justifiable reaction against the unnaturalness of the luxury of that day. Tertullian contends for simplicity and naturalness, in opposition to unnaturalness and artificiality. "That which grows is the work of God, that which is artificial is the Devil's work," is a proposition which he is never weary of maintaining. Let us not forget all that among the heathen was connected with these arts of the toilet, and the horrors of licentiousness which they served. A severe reaction was needed in order to restore the simplicity and modesty of feminine life.

Lastly, let us consider the strenuousness of the times, and their demands upon a Christian wife. They were days of conflict, little suited to the cultivation of the beautiful, even to a legitimate extent. It was far more important to foster energy and courage. "Pleasures must be discarded whose softness may weaken the courage of faith. I know not whether the wrist, accustomed to a bracelet, will endure if the hard chain makes it stiff. I know not whether the leg will suffer itself to be fettered in the gyve, instead of by an anklet. I fear that the neck, hung with pearls and emeralds, will give no room to the broadsword. Wherefore, blessed of the Lord, let us meditate on hardships and we shall not feel them; let us relinquish pleasant things and we shall not desire them; let us stand ready to endure every violence, having nothing which we may fear to leave behind. The days of Christians are always, and now more than ever, not golden but iron. The robes of martyrs are preparing, they are held up by angel bearers. Go forth, then, amply supplied with the cosmetics and ornaments of prophets and apostles, taking your dazzling whiteness from simplicity, and your ruddy hue from modesty; painting your eyes with bashfulness, and your mouth with silence; inserting in your ears the words of God, and fastening on your necks the yoke of Christ. Submit your head to your husbands, and you will be sufficiently adorned. Busy your hands with spinning, and keep your feet at home, and hand and foot will please more than if arrayed in gold. Clothe yourselves with the silk of uprightness, the fine linen of holiness, the purple of modesty. Thus adorned you will have God for your lover." [42]

The heathen often sneered at the large number of women in the Christian churches. They called Christianity in contempt a religion for old women and children. But they were constrained to learn what Christianity made of these women, and to acknowledge, against their will, the difference between a heathen and a Christian woman. In the one case a passion for finery, vanity, coquetry beyond measure, in the other simplicity and naturalness; there immodesty and shamelessness, here chastity and propriety; there women who divided their time between making and displaying their toilet, and who shone at the theatre and the circus, at dinner-parties and festivals, here wives who dressed to please their husbands, mothers who lived for their children; there an enervated sex, painted, and spoiled by art, here heroines who paled not even at the sight of the lions in the amphitheatre, and calmly bent their necks to the sword. "What women there are among the Christians!" exclaimed the astonished pagan Libanius.

To children, also, the Gospel first gave their rights. They, too, in Antiquity were beyond the pale of the laws. A father could dispose of his children at will. If he did not wish to rear them, he could abandon or kill them. The law of the Twelve Tables expressly awarded to him this right. Plato and Aristotle approved of parents' abandoning weak and sickly children, whom they were unable to support, or who could not be of use to the State. Whoever picked up a child who had been deserted could dispose of it, and treat it as a slave. The father's power over his children was limitless; life and death were at his disposal. Christianity, on the contrary, taught parents that their children were a gift from God, a pledge intrusted to them for which they were responsible to Him. It spoke not merely of the duties of children, but also of the duties of parents, and since it invested these, as representatives of God, with something of His majesty and honor, it appointed to them the lofty task of educating their baptized offspring as children of God, and for His kingdom. The baptism of children soon became customary, and thus they shared from their earliest years in the blessings of Christianity. The exposition of children was looked upon by Christians as plainly unlawful, — it was regarded and treated as murder. And though paternal authority was highly esteemed, there could no longer be any claim to an unconditional right over children after men had learned to look upon them as God's property.

Every Christian home now became a temple of God, where His word was diligently read,[43] and prayer was offered with fidelity and fervor. "If thou hast a wife, pray with her," we read in one of the canons of the Egyptian Church, "let not marriage be a hinderance to prayer."[44] The singing of psalms and hymns was often heard. The day was opened with united reading of the Scriptures, and prayer, concluding with the Hallelujah. Then all the members of the family gave each other the kiss of peace, and went to their work. No meal was taken without a blessing. Each repast, however simple, had something of the character of the holy Supper, the Eucharist.[45] The day was closed by again joining in devotions. Under the name of "The Candle Hymn," an ancient hymn has been preserved[46] as it was heard in Christian homes: —

> "Joyful Light of holy Glory,
> Of the Father everlasting, Jesus Christ!
> Having come to the setting of the sun,
> And seeing the evening light,
> We praise the Father, and the Son,
> And the Holy Spirit of God.
> Thou art worthy to be praised
> At all times, with holy voices,
> Son of God, who hast given life;
> Therefore the world glorifieth Thee."

No less did Christianity transform the relation between masters and servants. It gave liberty to the slave. "The grace of God that bringeth salvation hath appeared to all men" — before this announcement slavery could not stand. Now it was proclaimed: "There is neither Jew nor Greek, there is neither bond nor free, there is neither male nor female, for ye are all one in Christ Jesus" (Gal. iii. 28). "Christian justice makes all equal who bear the name of man" is the explicit statement of an ancient teacher in the Church.[47] It is the Son who makes all free. As He delivered us from sin and the bondage of the law, so from Him also has come freedom for all the spheres of life. "Where the Spirit of the Lord is, there is liberty" (2 Cor. iii. 17). While the heathen valued a man according to his outward position, the Christian did not take this into account, a man's real worth was independent of it. Whether he was a slave, or a master, was merely accidental. The slave might be in truth, that is inwardly, free, and the master might be in reality, that is inwardly, a slave. There is only one real slavery, the bondage of sin, and only one true liberty, freedom in Christ.

For this reason the Christian Church did not in the

least entertain the thought of immediate emancipation. It recognized in this matter, as in others, the existing laws, and taught the slave to respect them according to the will of God. "Let every man abide in the same calling wherein he was called," is the rule laid down by the Apostle. Indeed spiritual freedom assumed such supreme importance to Christians, that they often wholly disregarded outward civil liberty. Tertullian, in his treatise "On the Crown," alluding to the custom of slaves' wearing chaplets at their manumission, addresses a Christian as follows: "The conferring of secular liberty is an occasion of crowning. But you have been already ransomed by Christ, and that at a great price. How shall the world set free the servant of another? Though it seems to be liberty, it will be found to be bondage. All things in the world are imaginary, nothing is real. For even then, as redeemed by Christ, you were free from man, and now, although liberated by man, you are Christ's servant." [48] Yet the Church did not leave every thing as it was. The new principle took effect, and wrought a moral transformation in the relation of master and slave. The treatment of slaves by their Christian masters, and the relation of Christian slaves to their masters, underwent an immediate change. They looked upon each other now as brethren, as Paul writes to Philemon of the slave Onesimus, "that thou shouldest receive him, not now as a servant, but above a servant, a brother beloved." As members of the church there was no difference between them. They came to the same house of God, adored one God, acknowledged one Lord, prayed and sang together, ate of the same bread, and drank from the same cup. This must have transformed the disposition of a master toward his slaves. He could not possibly continue to treat as a thing one who was his brother in Christ. The Church, it is true, would not receive a slave without a certificate of good conduct from his Christian master, but when this condition was complied with he became a full member without any limitations. He was even eligible to its offices, not excepting that of bishop. Not infrequently it occurred that a slave was an elder in the same church of which his master was only a member.

The church bestowed labor on both slaves and masters. It exhorted the slaves to obedience; they were not to make the knowledge that their masters were their brethren a pretext for disobedience, but only a reason for more faithful service. According to pagan conceptions slaves were incapable of morality. The church trained them for virtue, and not unsuccessfully. There were many slaves who, in extremely difficult circumstances, attested the reality of their Christian life with fidelity and great endurance. Even among the martyrs there was an unbroken line of slaves. The fairest crown fell to them, as well as to the free. Masters, on the other hand, were exhorted to love their slaves, to be just to them and gentle. "Thou shalt not issue orders with bitterness to thy man-servant nor thy maid-servant, who hope in the same God,"[50] is the injunction of the Epistle of Barnabas. Harsh treatment of slaves was considered a sufficient ground for excommunication.[51] The slave should not be urgent for manumission. "Am I a slave, I endure servitude. Am I free, I do not make a boast of my free birth." These words of Tatian[52] express the disposition which was cultivated in the slave. If he could not obtain his freedom, he was to bear his lot and be content, knowing that he possessed true liberty. The demand for redemption by the church was especially prohibited.[53] The church would not minister to the merely natural desires of the slaves for liberty. Yet it deemed it a praise-worthy act for a master to emancipate a slave.[54] It did not prescribe to any one the duty of enfranchisement; such an act should be voluntary. But it gladly recognized emancipation as a work of Christian love, and manumissions often occurred. Many, when they became Christians, set all their slaves at liberty on the day of their baptism, or on the feast days of the church, especially at Easter, that they might in this way testify their gratitude for the grace which they had received. It is narrated of a rich Roman, in the time of Trajan, that having become a Christian he presented their freedom, at an Easter festival, to all his slaves, of whom there were twelve hundred and fifty.[55] After the third century, it was customary to perform the act of manumission in the church, before the priest and the congregation. The master led his slaves by the hand to the altar; there the deed of emancipation was read aloud, and at the close the priest pronounced the benediction. Thus formal expression was given to the thought that they owed to the church their freedom. This appeared to be, as it was, the protectress and dispenser of liberty. The freedmen were truly free. While so many of those whom heathen vanity, or love of gain, had liberated, merely exchanged one kind of slavery for another, and, thrust without means of support into a society in which labor had no honor, and left to themselves and destitute of moral stamina, only swelled the *proletariat*, those who were set free in the

Christian community had a wholly different position. Their former masters esteemed it their duty to help and counsel them as Christian brethren, and thus they did not find themselves isolated, but in the midst of a communion which instructed them in the right use of their liberty, and trained them to be active and useful men.

For Christians now put a very different estimate upon labor. It no longer seemed to them, as to the heathen, a disgrace, but an honor; not an unworthy bondage, but something commanded by God for all men. Indeed the Lord Himself had been a carpenter, and the son of a carpenter. The Apostles, too, had been laborers, Peter a fisherman, Paul a tent-maker. The Fathers often emphasized the fact that manual laborers had a better knowledge of God than heathen philosophers.[56] "You will find artisans among us," says Athenagoras,[57] "who, if they cannot with words prove the benefit of our doctrine, yet prove it by deeds." The circumstance that Christians were shut out from so many employments — e.g. those of soldiers, public officers, assistants at services in the temples — by which the heathen gained a livelihood, contributed to increase the honor which they gave to manual labor. The so-called Apostolic Constitutions expressly refer to this kind of labor, and exhort all church members to industry: "For the Lord our God hates the slothful. For no one of those who worship God ought to be idle."[58] The Bishop was also enjoined to be solicitous to procure work for artisans who were without employment.[59] The greatest sages of Antiquity, Plato and Aristotle, declare labor degrading to a freeman; the Apostle exhorts that every one labor with quietness, and eat his own bread, and lays down categorically the principle: He who does not work, shall not eat. From this simple proposition has grown a new world that has wrought greater things than any Plato and Aristotle ever saw.

The correlate, among the heathen, to contempt of labor was the passion for shows. Bread and games! was the oft-heard signal. Men wished to be supported without labor by the State, and to be amused with games at the public expense. The watchword of the Christians was: Pray and labor. From this point of view we understand the decision with which the ancient church condemned the exhibitions in the theatre, the circus, and the arena. Labor performed "in quietness" presents a picture precisely opposite to that offered by the circus and the amphitheatre. *There* was no quietness, but passionate excitement. "God has enjoined on us," says Tertullian,[60] "to deal calmly and gently with the Holy Spirit, Whose nature is tender and sensitive, and not to disquiet Him with rage, or anger, or grief. How shall this be made to accord with the shows? For there is no show without vehement agitation of mind." "In the circus," he says, "excitement presides. See the people coming to it, already tumultuous, already passion-blind, already agitated about their bets. The prætor is too slow for them; their eyes are ever rolling with the lots in his urn. Then they wait anxiously for the signal, there is one shout of common madness. He has thrown it, they say, and announce to each other what was seen at once by all. I have evidence of their blindness, they do not see what is thrown. They think it a cloth, but it is the likeness of the devil cast headlong from on high. From thence therefore they go on to fury, and passions, and dissensions, and whatever is unlawful for priests of peace. Then there are curses without just cause of hatred; there are cries of applause with nothing to merit them." "Will one," he asks in another place, "at that time think upon God? He will have, I suppose, peace in his mind while contending for a charioteer." Besides, every thing there was purposeless, the opposite of earnest work; vain were the racings, still more vain the throwing and leaping. It was profitless, in Tertullian's eyes, to spend so much labor in training the body to the suppleness of a serpent, and for all the arts of the arena. Still more decidedly would the gladiatorial sports be condemned, the baiting of wild animals, the capital punishments in the amphitheatre. There "with murder they comfort themselves over death." In short, the amphitheatre was the temple of all evil spirits.

All such shows a Christian avoided. He had, as Cyprian represents, other and better spectacles. He had the beauty of the world to look upon and admire, the rising of the sun, the expanse of seas, the earth, the air, and all their tenants, the constant succession of sunshine and rain. He had in the Scriptures the great deeds of God, the lofty spectacle of the conflict between Christ and the devil, the devil and the whole power of the world lying prostrate under the feet of Christ. "This is an exhibition which is given by neither prætor nor consul, but by Him who is alone, and before all things, and above all things, and of whom are all things, the Father of our Lord Jesus Christ."

IV. BENEVOLENCE OF THE CHRISTIANS.

When St. Paul exhorts (Eph. iv. 28): "Let him that stole steal no more, but rather let him labor, working with his hands the thing which is good," he adds, "that he may have to give to him that needeth." The true end of labor was thus for the first time pointed out. It is not a mere selfish acquisition of one's own livelihood, still less the obtainment of riches and enjoyment. On the contrary we are to labor in order to serve our brethren, and to find the noblest reward of toil in the exercise of compassion. The primitive Christians adhered to this principle. Working with their hands they helped their brethren with the products of their labor. They, the poor, in this sense also, made many rich. The church in later years increased in wealth and dispensed more alms, its institutions for the care of the poor became more magnificent, but at no other time has its exercise of charity been relatively so large, and, all things considered, so pure, as in the period of conflict. Richly was the word of our Lord fulfilled: "By this shall all men know that ye are my disciples, if ye have love one to another." The heathen recognized this sign. With amazement they gazed upon this new strange life of love, and it is not too much to say that the victory of the church like that of her Lord was a victory of ministering love.

This was something wholly foreign to the heathen. "A new commandment I give unto you," thus does our Lord introduce the commandment of love. Pagan antiquity was thoroughly egoistic. Charity, compassionate love, was no virtue of the ancient world, says Boeckh, one of the highest authorities respecting it.

Every one sought his own interests regardless of others, and ignorant of any life but the present, knew no other aim than happiness which in its essence was only enjoyment, whether coarser or more refined. Self was the centre around which every thing revolved. A man of the ancient world despised whatever he drew into his service, and hated every thing which opposed him. This egoism was limited only by the egoism of the State. The individual, in order to be happy, needed the State. It was also essential to his happiness that he should live in a well-ordered State. The individual was of account only as a member of the whole body, as a citizen. Man was completely a ζῶον πολιτικόν, a political being, all virtues were only political. On the monument of Æschylus was inscribed merely that he had shared in the fight at Marathon, not a word about his having been a great poet. The State itself, moreover, was built upon thoroughly selfish foundations. Whoever was not a citizen of the State, was in reality not a man; he was a barbarian, against whom every thing was lawful. No bond united nations; each had before it an open course for its selfishness. It had the right to subject to itself other nations and to make them slaves. There were no duties to the conquered. Justice to the weak, compassion to the oppressed was unknown to Antiquity.

We are actually startled when we contemplate this consistent and thorough-going egoism. "A man is a wolf to a man whom he does not know," says Plautus,[61] and the whole life of Antiquity is a proof of this. The views even of Plato, the noblest of sages, respecting the State, were thoroughly egoistic. All beggars must be driven out. No one shall take an interest in the poor, when they are sick. If the constitution of a laboring man cannot withstand sickness, the physician may abandon him without scruple, he is good for nothing except to be experimented on. " Can you condescend so far that the poor do not disgust you?" asks Quinctilian. The aid bestowed — this was the thought — is of no help to the poor (i.e., it does not make them rich, the only happiness); it simply prolongs their wretchedness. " He deserves ill of a beggar," we read in Plautus,[62] "who gives him food and drink. For that which is given is thrown away, and the life of the beggar is protracted to his misery." We need at most do good to those who have done good to us; those who injure us we may hate, indeed it is our duty to hate them. According to Aristotle, anger and revenge are lawful passions. Without them men would lack powerful incentives to good. Even Cicero's ideal rises no higher. " The good man is to perform even to a stranger all the service that he can, and to harm no one even when provoked by injustice; but the helping whom he can is to be limited by this, that he shall not himself suffer injury thereby."[63] Of self-denial, of a love which gives more than it can deprive itself of without harm, of love even to one's enemies, Cicero has as little a presentiment as the rest of Antiquity. It discoursed indeed gladly and much of magnanimity, of generosity, of hospitality, but behind all these virtues there was still only egoism. Magnanimity and the much-praised mercy were at bottom only aristocratic pride, which looked down with contempt upon others, and seemed to itself far too great to be injured by them. Liberality was exercised toward friends and fellow-citizens, not toward all men; it was practised because it created fame and esteem, and was useful to the State. Hospitality was not a common virtue; it belonged exclusively to the rich, who entertained each other with careful regard to rank and position. We need only compare it with Christian hospitality in the earliest churches, where the poor man was as welcome as the rich, where the feet of all the saints were washed, and its splendor fades away. Even when Seneca speaks, as he often does, of benevolence, the egoism shines through. One must give without any prompting of the heart, with a perfectly tranquil spirit. Compassion is at bottom only weakness.[64]

Thus the ancient world had no knowledge of true benevolence. To be sure, as we have seen, it was not without public spirit, nor did it lack gifts and bequests for purposes of public utility. There was a distribution of corn; and not merely in Rome, but in the provinces as well, care was taken, and on the largest scale, that the people should have their gratifications and sports. But all this expenditure bore a different character from Christian benevolence. Love to man was not the impelling motive. It was an offering brought to vanity, to avarice, or to policy; it was a ransom which wealth paid to poverty in order not to be disturbed by it. We seek in vain for true regard for penury, and heart-felt compassion. The statesman, or the Emperor, who ordered the means of life to be distributed, acted from no such considerations, and the rich Roman who caused the *sportula* to be given to his clients had no genuine feeling of sympathy for them. They promoted the splendor of his house, and were paid for it. Consequently the extravagantly rich presents which were made brought no blessing. They degraded both those who gave, and those who received them. As love was wanting on the one side, so was gratitude on the other.

This judgment will not be changed by the fact that individual acts of charity to the poor and needy occurred in the pagan world. We ought not to imagine that the natural feeling of compassion was wholly wanting. When, during the reign of Tiberius, forty-six thousand persons were either killed or wounded by the fall of an amphitheatre at Fidenza, the Roman aristocracy sent physicians, medicines and food to the sufferers, and even received some of them into their own houses.[65] Titus exhibited a noble activity in aiding the unfortunate victims of the great calamities which befell his reign, the fearful outbreak of Vesuvius which destroyed Herculaneum and Pompeii, the fire at Rome and the pestilence which raged there. It need scarcely be mentioned, also, that many gifts were made to beggars who sat in the streets and especially before the temples. What, however, was wanting was a regulated and systematic benevolence. This did not exist where we should at first expect to meet with it, in the associations. Natural as it would seem to have been for the burial-clubs, whose object was to secure for their members a respectable interment with the appropriate religious rites, or for the confraternities of artisans, and many similar societies, to furnish assistance to their needy members, as was done by the guilds of the Middle Ages, we find in fact little or no such provision. Even the many bequests to the members of such clubs were not given for the benefit of the poor and needy in them, but on the contrary were gifts in which the officers of the society, or even all its members, shared in order that they might honor the memory of the donor. A real care of the poor, as now understood, was unknown. Hospitals existed only for soldiers, gladiators and slaves. The manual laborer who was without means, the poor man who was not a slave, found no place of refuge. Without consolation, without hope for the life to come, he was also without material help in sickness. Especially in time of epidemics did the ancient egoism appear without disguise. Men feared death, and took no interest in their own sick, but drove them out of the house, and left them to their fate. The ancient world was a world without love. There was much that was admirable in it; it produced great men and heroes, but this bond of perfectness was wanting. Whence should love have come? Religion taught none, and awakened none. It taught love to one's native country, obedience to the laws, bravery in war, sacrifice for the greatness and honor of the State — but not philanthropy. The ancient man was the natural man in his richest development. But the natural man is an egoist, and remains such until love from above transforms him.

It has done this. The life of the Christian Church is the actual proof. It was a life of love. Nothing more astonished the heathen, nothing was more incomprehensible to them. "Behold," they exclaimed, "how they love one another." [66] Among themselves Christians called each other brethren, and this fraternal name was no mere word. They lived as brothers. The kiss with which they greeted each other at the celebration of the Holy Supper, was no empty form; the church was in reality one family, all its members children of one Heavenly Father. Each served the other, each prayed for all the rest. They had all things in common. Even the stranger who came from far, if he but brought a letter of recommendation from his church which certified him as a Christian, was received and treated as a brother. "They love each other without knowing each other!" says a pagan in astonishment. This was indeed the most direct antithesis to the heathen saying: "Man is a wolf to a man whom he does not know." This fraternal love expanded to a universal love of man. The church, born of love, and living in love, was the appropriate organ for the practice of love. It interested itself first in those of its members who needed help in any way, then it went beyond them to embrace in its love those who stood without. For these were to be won for the church. Love worked in a missionary way. It excluded none, as the grace which kindled it excluded no one, not even enemies and persecutors.

Without doubt individual members of the churches performed by themselves many works of benevolence. Christians made earnest with the word of our Lord: "Give to him that asketh thee, and from him that would borrow of thee turn not thou away." One of the earliest of the Fathers, Barnabas, exhorts: "Thou shalt not hesitate to give, nor murmur when thou givest."[67] "Why do you select persons?" says Lactantius. "He is to be esteemed by you as a man, whoever implores you, because he considers you a man."[68] Tertullian shows us the obstacles which a Christian woman, living with a pagan husband, had to encounter in her acts of benevolence. "Who," he asks, "would allow his wife, for the sake of visiting the brethren, to go round from street to street to other men's, and indeed to all the poorer cottages? Who will suffer her to creep into a prison to kiss the chains of a martyr? If a stranger brother arrives, what hospitality for him in an alien's home? If bounty is to be distributed to any, the granary, the storehouses are closed against her." [69] Assuredly, this manifold and rich benevolence of the Christian woman was not exercised merely by direction of the church. It was expressly enunciated that the official benevolence of the deaconess should not exclude the private charity of the woman. Every woman should be in this respect a deaconess. "If any one of you would do good without being a presbyteress or deaconess, do it according to your inclination, for such deeds are the most precious treasures of the Lord." [70] That alms were also distributed in the freest way upon the streets is evident from a remark of Tertullian's, upbraiding the heathen: "our compassion gives more in the streets than your religion in the temples." [71]

Such personal charity withdraws itself from observation. The Lord alone knows what was then done by individuals, history has not preserved it. In her record appears only the charity practised by the church, and this, all things considered, is of incomparably greater importance. Precisely here is to be found what was new, what was higher — the existence of a communion whose vocation was to exercise compassion. From the beginning, from the days of the church of Jerusalem, the practice of charity was as necessary an activity of church life as the preaching of the Word and the administration of the sacraments; and for the one as well as for the others the church provided organs and ordinances. The means for its charities flowed to it from the free-will offerings of its members. The principle of entire voluntariness, which the Apostle (2 Cor. ix. 7) had already emphasized, was most rigidly adhered to. "Such as are prosperous and willing," says Justin, "give what they will, each according to his choice."[72] "Each of us," says Tertullian, "deposits a small gift when he likes, but only if it be his pleasure, and only if he be able, for no one is under compulsion."[73] And Irenæus rightly sees in this freedom the higher position of the New Testament. "There were," he says, "oblations among the Jewish people; there are such in the church: but with this difference, that there they were offered by slaves, here by freemen. The Jews were constrained to a regular payment of tithes; Christians, who have received liberty, assign all their possessions to the Lord, bestowing freely not the lesser portions of their property, since they have the hope of greater things."[74] So strictly was this principle carried out that, when the Gnostic Marcion separated from the church, the two hundred thousand sesterces which he had given at his baptism were returned to him.[75] When the children of a man who had bequeathed to the church in his will a certain sum, refused to pay it, Cyprian, though he reminded them of their duty to fulfil the purpose of their father, at the same time declared, as though it were a matter of course, that they were at perfect liberty to deliver the money or not. As the church would have no forced gifts, so it would have none from persons who did not in spirit belong to her, who did not give from love or from property rightly acquired. The Apostolic Constitutions contain upon this subject very definite directions.[76]

The usual form of giving was that of the offerings, or oblations, at the Lord's Supper. The communicants brought gifts, chiefly natural products. From these was taken what was necessary for the bread and wine of communion, and the remainder went to the support of the clergy and the poor. The names of the offerers were inscribed on tablets, the so-called diptychs, and were mentioned in the prayer. For deceased persons their relatives brought gifts on the anniversary of their death, a beautiful custom which vividly exhibited the connection between the church above and the church below.[77] Even those who had fallen asleep still continued, as it were, to serve the church. Giving was practised also in connection with special occasions, joyful occurrences, the day of christening. Cyprian sold his gardens, and made a present of the proceeds on the day of his baptism.[78] Beside this there stood in the place of meeting a box for the poor (called by Tertullian *arca*, by Cyprian *corban*), in which was placed every week a free-will offering. This was evidently an imitation of the custom which had grown up in the clubs, and was legally established. Every member paid monthly a regular tax. The Christians did likewise, only in their case the contribution was voluntary, and was not expended, as frequently by the associations, in feasting, but rather in providing for the poor.[79] Were larger means needed, a general collection was taken up, to which every one contributed from the avails of his labor. Poor persons, who had nothing, fasted in order to give what they saved. Sometimes a general fast was appointed in the church, and the proceeds expended for benevolent purposes.[80] "Blessed," says Origen, "is he who fasts to feed a poor person,"[81] and, indeed, no more beautiful way of giving alms can be imagined.

What the church received it immediately expended. Nothing was converted into capital. Present needs were great enough, and care for the future could be trustfully committed to love. The necessities of the times, also, compelled such a course. In the midst of the persecutions church property was insecure. The best mode of preserving it was to give it away. When the persecution under Decius broke out, Cyprian divided the entire sum which had been collected for the poor among the presbyters and deacons for distribution. When, afterwards, there was need, he directed that the deficit should be met from his private property.[82] When Bishop Sixtus II. was taken prisoner, his deacon, Laurentius, assembled the poor of the church, and distributed the whole of the church property among them. He even sold the holy vessels in order to give the proceeds to the poor.[83]

The Bishop superintended the care of the poor,[84] assisted by the deacons and deaconesses. The names of those who were to be regularly supported were enrolled in a register, after careful examination into their circumstances. When this had been done, they received aid.[85] To this class belonged those who could no longer earn a livelihood, or who by joining the church had lost their means of support because they had followed a trade or business which the church did not allow.[86] Yet it was strictly maintained that every one should labor to the extent of his ability. To those who had been obliged to relinquish their business, some other occupation was assigned, whenever possible, and they were not permitted to decline this, even if it was inferior to their former occupation. If they were unwilling to work, they received no aid. For conversion to the church was not to be made by idlers a source of worldly advantage.

A special class of beneficiaries consisted of widows,[87] for whose maintenance the Apostle gives particular directions. If their life was passed in reputable widowhood, they were highly honored in the church, and were cared for during life. In return they served the church, particularly in the education of children. Destitute orphans[88] were reared by widows or deaconesses, under the supervision of the bishop. The boys learned a trade, and when grown up received the tools necessary for its prosecution. The girls, unless they joined the number of those who remained unmarried, the deaconesses for instance, were married each to some Christian brother. Often children who had been abandoned by the heathen,[89] — and the number of such was large, — were received and given a Christian education together with the orphans. Even slaves[90] were also accepted, their freedom purchased with the church funds, and help afforded them to earn a living. Or, where captives had fallen into the hands of the barbarians, a ransom was paid for their liberation. Those who had been imprisoned on account of their faith needed special care. They were visited in their prisons, and provided for so far as possible. Cyprian, in his letters written while in exile, is unwearied in commending them again and again to the watchful attention of the deacons.[91]

This benevolence extended beyond the bounds of the particular church. One church helped another.[92] Thus, as early as the Apostles' day, the Gentile churches aided the impoverished church of Jerusalem. So the church at Rome, under Soter (A.D. 150), sent rich gifts into the provinces in order to alleviate there the misery of a famine.[93] At a time when the unity of the church was not manifested in outward organic forms, the church was held and bound together by its one faith and its one love. An active benevolence extended its net over the whole broad empire, and wherever a Christian went, even to the borders of barbarous tribes, and beyond these, too, he knew that he was near to brethren who were ready at any moment to minister to to his need.

The means that were available for this care of the poor must have been very considerable; and when we consider that the churches in the first centuries were recruited chiefly from the lower classes, it seems the more remarkable that such resources could have been accumulated. From the earliest age, it is true, we have no information as to the scope of the benevolence of individual churches, but judging by what we know of a later time, it was, even in respect to merely pecuniary gifts, very large. Cyprian easily collected in his church five thousand dollars, in order to help the Numidian bishop in ransoming prisoners.[94] Somewhat later, in the time of the Decian persecution, the Roman church supported fifteen hundred poor persons, widows, and children.[95] Still later, the church in Antioch, numbering, perhaps, one hundred thousand members, had three thousand beneficiaries.[96] Still more, worthy of admiration is the spirit in which this labor of love was prosecuted. Among the heathen the poor, the weak, the oppressed had been despised. The principle was established, that a man is to be valued according to his possessions. In the church it was said: Blessed are the poor, for theirs is the kingdom of heaven. In a certain sense every one must become poor in order to gain this kingdom. External wealth and outward poverty, are merely accidental. The godly poor are in truth rich; the godless rich in reality poor. "It is not the census," says one of the fathers, "that makes rich, but the soul." [97] Conscious of having become rich through the lowly Jesus, the church looked upon the poor as her treasures. In them she served the Lord. When, after the martyrdom of Bishop Sixtus, his deacon was required to point out and surrender the treasures of the church, he called all its poor together and showed them to the prefect of the city, with the words: "These are the treasures of the church." [98] A church which has such riches must conquer. In its benevolence it has the means of the purest *propaganda* — means which in the end must win even its opponents.

This benevolence made a deeper impression on the heathen because they were not excluded by the Christians from their love. "Our religion," says Justin,[99] "requires us to love not only our own, but also strangers and even those who hate us." "All men," says Tertullian,[100] "love their friends, Christians alone love their enemies." This was not mere words. When in the time of Cyprian a great pestilence raged in Carthage, and the heathen abandoned their sick, and, instead of burying their bodies, cast them out on the streets, the bishop convened the church and made these representations to them: "If we show kindness only to our own, we do no more than publicans and heathen. As Christians who would become perfect we must overcome evil with good, love our enemies, as the Lord exhorts, and pray for our persecutors. Since we are born of God we must show ourselves to be children of our Father who continually causes His sun to rise, and from time to time gives showers to nourish the seed, exhibiting all these kindnesses not only to His people, but to aliens also." Upon his summons the church engaged in the work. Some gave money, others shared in the labor, and soon the dead were buried.[101] So was it, also, at Alexandria, in connection with a pestilence in the time of the Emperor Gallienus. While the heathen fled, while the sick were thrust out of doors, and the half-dead thrown into the streets, the Christians cared for all, spared not themselves in the service of the sick and dying, and many brethren, even presbyters and deacons, sacrificed their lives in such ministry.[102] And they did this immediately after they had been most horribly persecuted by the heathen, and while the sword still hung daily over their heads.[103]

V. MARTYRDOM.

With love went sorrow hand in hand. The witness of word, of conduct, of love was perfected in the witness of blood, in martyrdom. The power of the martyr's death lay precisely in this fact, that this event was the completion of the testimony given by his life. For it is not suffering in itself considered, it is not merely the martyr's pangs and death-throes which give to martyrdom its value, but the disposition in which all this is endured. Not every martyrdom is a victory for the church, but only those which are genuine and pure.

It is first of all essential to genuineness and purity of martyrdom, that the disposition and demeanor of the martyr be free from insubordination toward the State, and the magistracy ordained by God. The Christian has to recognize at all times, and in every particular, the civil government which is over him, and to honor all its laws and ordinances as proceeding from his rulers, even when these laws and ordinances are contrary to God's Word. In such a case he cannot, indeed, honor them by obeying them, for he must obey God and not man, but by willingly and patiently submitting to whatever penalties for this reason the laws award to him. Then he honors the government and the laws by suffering, and in truth a man cannot more fully attest his regard for the law than by sacrificing to it his life. And every act of insubordination toward the government, every failure to show respect to the laws which it enacts, is to the Christian a sin. When he suffers not for evil doing, but for well doing (1 Pet. ii. 20, iii. 17), he suffers simply for Christ's sake. Then it may be said: "Who is he that will harm you if ye be followers of that which is good?" (1 Pet. iii. 13.)

The early Christians preserved this purity of martyrdom most solicitously. Always and everywhere they showed their readiness to honor the Emperor, and to obey him in all things as dutiful subjects, save when he commanded them to forsake Christ, and to worship idols. Nowhere is to be found a trace of disobedience, or even of want of respect toward the magistracy, and they suffered patiently the penalties awarded them by its authority on account of their confession, praying even in death for the welfare of the Emperor. Innumerable are the times when the martyrs, under the agonies of torture, testified before their judges, at the place of execution, that they were willing to obey the Emperor, but to worship him, to strew incense to him, that they could not do. The Apologists often protested that the Christians were obedient subjects who made it a matter of conscience not to break the laws of the State in the smallest particulars. "Therefore I will honor the Emperor," says Theophilus in his work addressed to Autolycus, "not worshipping him but praying for him. I worship the true God only, knowing that the Emperor is made by Him. You will say then to me: Why do you not worship the Emperor? Because he is not made to be worshipped, but to be reverenced with lawful honor. For he is not God, but a man, appointed by God, not to be worshipped, but to judge justly." [104] Tertullian calls the attention of the heathen to the fact,[105] that the Christians were in a condition to make resistance, and to acquire by violence liberty of faith, since their numbers were so great, constituting almost a majority in every city. Yet they obeyed the injunctions of patience taught in their divine religion, and lived in quietness and soberness, recognizable in no other way than by the amendment of their former lives. The Christians, he rightly points out, were truer and more obedient subjects of the Emperor than the heathen. In irony he exclaims: "We acknowledge the faithfulness of the Romans to the Cæsars! No conspiracy has ever broken out, no Emperor's blood has ever fixed a stain in the Senate or even in the palace; never has their majesty been dishonored in the provinces. And yet the soil of Syria still exhales the odor of their corpses, and Gaul has not yet washed away their blood in the waters of its Rhone." [106] Then he sets in contrast the fidelity and obedience of the Christians, who join in no intrigues nor riots, who pray for the Emperor whatever his character, who supplicate for him from God a long life, a peaceful reign, security in his palace, brave armies, loyalty in the Senate, virtue among the people, peace in the whole world. "So that," he concludes, "I might say on valid grounds that the Emperor is more ours than yours, for our God has appointed him."[107] Even in the midst of the excitement of a bloody persecution the most conscientious care was observed lest any thing should be done which might occasion the semblance of disobedience. Thus, for example, Cyprian[108] expressed disapproval in the strongest terms when some persons who had been banished on account of their Christian faith returned without the express permission of the authorities. "For how great a disgrace," he says, "is suffered by your name when one returns to that country whence he was banished, to perish when arrested, not now as being a Christian, but as being a criminal." Even to a persecuting government, even to its injustice and cruelty the Christian should oppose nothing but quiet and patient suffering.

This purity of martyrdom was most fittingly expressed by the martyrs' dying with praise and thanksgiving. "A Christian even when he is condemned gives thanks,"[109] — the truth of these words is often attested in the Acts of the Martyrs. "O Lord God Almighty," prayed Polycarp as he stood on the funeral pile, "Father of Thy beloved and blessed Son Jesus Christ by whom we have received the knowledge of Thee, the God of angels and powers, and of the whole creation and of all the race of the righteous who live before Thee, I bless Thee that Thou hast counted me worthy of this day and this hour, that I should have a part in the number of Thy witnesses, in the cup of Thy Christ."[110] When the Scillitan martyrs in Numidia (about 200 A. D.) received their sentence of death, they praised God, and when they reached the place of execution, falling on their knees, they gave thanks anew.[111] We often hear, also, that like the first martyr Stephen they prayed for their enemies. A Palestinian Christian named Paulus prayed, before he received the death-stroke, that God would lead all the heathen to faith and salvation, and he forgave the judge who had condemned him, and the executioner who carried the sentence into effect.[112] Pionius, a martyr in Smyrna, was heard supplicating, from the flames of the pyre, for the Emperor, for his judges, and for all the heathen. When an audible Amen was on his lips, the flames smote together above him, and ended his life.[113]

We hear no expressions of revenge, nor of anger, no maledictions, no curse. Even among the inscriptions of the Catacombs nothing of the sort appears. Nowhere is judgment invoked on their persecutors. Only one sigh is recorded, in the Catacomb of Callistus: "O sorrowful times, when we cannot even in caves escape our foes."[114] Even pictures of persecution (with but one exception, that of the trial of a Christian, in the cemetery of Prætextatus) are not to be found. Symbolic representations only are common, — Daniel in the lions' den, the Three Children in the fiery furnace, Elijah ascending to heaven in the chariot of fire.[115] When we consider the burning hatred with which the heathen persecuted the Christians, the inhuman cruelties which were allowed (enough concerning these will be said), we learn to admire the purity of a martyrdom which even in this respect followed the word of the apostle: "Recompense to no man evil for evil!" and the admonition of the Lord: "Pray for them which despitefully use you, and persecute you."

In this purity of martyrdom lay its power. If the Christians had allowed themselves to be tempted to offer open resistance to the persecuting State, they had been lost. The State would have ground them to pieces with its gigantic power. If they had been enticed into wrath and revenge their strength would have been broken, their consciences stained, and their martyrdom deprived of its power to act upon the conscience. For the might of true martyrdom lies in this, that it not merely turns the edge of opposition by its patience, but also, as a testimony, touches the conscience. Not infrequently it came to pass that the persecutors themselves, moved by this irresistible testimony, were converted at the place of execution, and became Christians.

The genuineness of Christian martyrdom was proved, secondly, by its freedom from enthusiasm and fanaticism. Enthusiasm is an impure flame which blazes up quickly and is as quickly extinguished. It could not have accomplished any thing in the conflict we are considering, it would have been quickly defeated by the power of the Roman State, and it could not have produced the moral effects which martyrdom did. Fanaticism has never yet built up the Church, and when it has had successes they have been merely momentary. Fanaticism is a heat which only scorches. The Christians allowed themselves no mockery of the heathen rites or idols, nor any use of cutting and insulting language. The case was wholly exceptional in which a Christian broke in pieces an image of a god.[116] It came to pass that individual Christians, excited to enthusiasm, pressed forward to martyrdom; the church always most decidedly disapproved of this. "We do not praise," writes the church in Smyrna in the letter in which it gives an account of the martyrdom of its bishop, Polycarp, "those who give themselves up, for the Gospel does not so teach."[117] Cyprian exhorted his people during a violent persecution: "Keep peace and tranquillity, as you have been so very often taught by me. Let no one stir up any tumult for the brethren, nor voluntarily offer himself to the Gentiles. For when apprehended and delivered up he ought to speak, inasmuch as God abiding in us speaks in that hour."[118] When, during a plague in Carthage, some Christians lamented that they should die on a sick-bed, instead of dying as martyrs, the Bishop reminded them: "In the first place martyrdom is not in your power, but depends upon the grace of God. Then, besides, God, the searcher of the reins and heart, sees you, and praises and approves you. It is one thing for the spirit to be wanting for martyrdom, and another for martyrdom to have been wanting for the spirit. For God does not ask for our blood, but for our faith. This sickness is sent to prove it."[119] The church teachers never failed to remind their people that persecution was at once a judgment on the church, and an earnest admonition to repentance.

With the same sobriety of judgment the Christians used all available means for escaping persecution. Opinions differed as to whether it was right to flee. Tertullian decided in the negative.[120] The majority took the affirmative, appealing to the well-known command of our Lord. Yet the flight should not imply denial. It must be merely a withdrawal, in which he who retires leaves every thing to the Lord, and holds himself in readiness when his hour comes. Thus Polycarp retired for a long time, as did Cyprian. But both showed by a martyr's death that their retreat was no flight, but only an act of self-preservation for the right moment. To purchase freedom in a time of persecution, to obtain safety by bribery, was generally regarded as denial. On the other hand, Christians were to avoid every thing which could attract to them the attention of the heathen, or excite them to greater violence. Cyprian, at the beginning of a persecution, prudently prescribed the arrangements which were thereby rendered necessary. The clergy in visiting the confessors in the prisons should take turns; the people should not press thither in crowds. "For," he writes, "meek and humble in all things, as becomes the servants of God, we ought to accommodate ourselves to the times, and to provide for quietness."[121] Calmly each awaited the moment when the hour of his persecution should arrive, and then stood the firmer, and with greater patience bore whatever came.

Out of such purity of martyrdom, out of a good conscience to suffer only for Christ's sake, on the one hand, out of such a spirit of sobriety and clearness on the other, were born the peace and joy with which those who witnessed for Christ met death, and endured what was worse than death. The worst, indeed, was not instantaneous death, nor the exquisite tortures which often preceded it. In order to measure completely the greatness of the contest, we must look into that inward conflict which preceded or accompanied that which was external. Great must have been the temptation to refine away the necessity of suffering, to represent death as a needless sacrifice which might as well be avoided, especially when it was so easy to escape suffering, when, as was actually the case, venal judges offered Christians for money a certificate, as though they had offered sacrifice, or when kindly disposed judges represented to the accused that it was only a question of a mere ceremony, that could be complied with without surrender of one's convictions. More painful than all the torments which iron and fire, hunger and thirst, prepared, must it have been to part from father and mother, wife and child, and to turn away from their entreaties, their lamentations, their tears. Harder than instantaneous death at the place of execution was banishment to the mines, where Christians were compelled to work among the offscouring of mankind, and like them have scanty fare, be clothed in rags, and be beaten by rough overseers, though at the price of a single word they could be free.[122] And yet worse than this some endured. Christian virgins (it is verily devilish) were condemned to be taken to the public brothels, to be abandoned there to the most horrible abuse.[123] The heathen knew how highly the Christians esteemed chastity, and that to them its loss was worse than death. And yet, when the Christian virgin Sabina, in Smyrna, was apprised of this sentence, she replied, "Whatever God wills!"[124] That was the heroism of martyrdom, that was to conquer all through Christ. A faith which so loved and suffered was invincible. Its victory was sure. And of it could the Apostle say, even before the conflict had begun: "Our faith is the victory which hath overcome the world."

BOOK SECOND.

THE CONFLICT.

"Think not that I am come to send peace on earth: I came not to send peace, but a sword." — MATT. x. 34.

CHAPTER I.

THE FIRST ENCOUNTER.

" Ye shall be hated of all men for my name's sake." — MATT. x. 22.

I. PRELIMINARY SURVEY.

"THINK not that I am come to send peace on earth: I came not to send peace, but a sword." Thus had our Lord spoken. He had not concealed from His disciples the conflict which awaited them, a conflict for life and death. "Ye shall be hated of all men for my name's sake. They shall lay their hands on you, and persecute you, delivering you up to the synagogues and into prisons, and whosoever killeth you will think that he doeth God service." It could not be otherwise. Never in human history have two opposing powers had a sharper encounter than Christianity and ancient Heathenism, the Christian Church and the Roman State. It is the antagonism between that which is from below and that which is from above, between natural development and the new creation, between that which is born of the flesh and that which is born of the Spirit, while behind all this, according to the Scriptures, is the conflict between the Prince of this world and the Lord from heaven.

Two such powers could not exist peaceably side by side. The conflict must come, and be for life or death. Every possibility of a compromise was excluded. This contest might be occasionally interrupted; but it could end only in the conquest of one or the other power. Christianity entered the conflict as the absolute religion, as a divine revelation, as unconditionally true, and claimed to be the religion for all nations, because it brought to all salvation. A religion co-existing with others the heathen could have tolerated, as they did so many religions. The absolute religion they could not tolerate. Diverging opinions about God and divine things could be allowed, but not the perfect truth, which, because it was the truth, excluded every thing else as false. A new religion for a single nation might have given no offence. It would have been recognized, as were so many heathen cults, and monotheistic Judaism as well. But a universal religion could not be thus allowed. The conflict was for nothing less than the dominion of the world. From its nature it could only end in the complete victory of one side or the other.

Christianity entered the field conscious, through the assurances of our Lord, that the world was its promised domain. Its messengers knew that they were sent on a mission of universal conquest for their Lord, and the youthful Christianity itself proved that it was a world-subduing power by the wonderful rapidity with which it spread. After it had passed beyond the boundaries of the land and the people of Judæa, after the great step was taken of carrying the Gospel to the heathen, and receiving them into the Christian Church without requiring circumcision or their becoming Jews, it secured in Syrian Antioch its first missionary centre; and from this point Paul, the great Apostle of the Gentiles, bore it from city to city through Asia Minor to Europe, through Greece to Rome, the metropolis of the world. His line of march was along the great roads, the highways of travel, which the Romans had built. Everywhere the Jewish communities served his purposes, like the magazines provided for soldiers. The synagogues were the points at which Christianity could be planted. There Paul and his co-laborers preached the risen Messiah, and proved from the prophets that Jesus is the Christ. The Jews, it is true, for the most part opposed, but the proselytes were a prepared field in which the scattered seed soon sprang up. The Jewish opposition resulted in a separation from the synagogue communities. Independent Christian societies were formed, under their own overseers. And in them the converts won from among the proselytes formed a means of connection with others who had hitherto belonged wholly to Heathenism. We know too little of this first period, apart from what is told us in the Book of Acts, to obtain an exact view of this diffusion of Christianity. Yet when we notice that Paul, even in his first journey to Rome, finds Christians in Italy, and this not merely in the capital, but also in little Puteoli, we are warranted in assuming that after a few decades there were in all the cities, large and small, Christian churches, or, if not perfectly organized societies, at least little bands of Christians. In the same way the church spread eastward and southward, and yet more vigorously, for the Jewish population was denser. We find Peter in Babylon. Edessa is already a missionary centre. Still more important was the church of Alexandria, whose founder is said to have been John Mark. Still others, even earlier, had carried the Gospel beyond the bounds of the Roman Empire; Thomas to Parthia, Andrew to Scythia, Bartholomew to India, that is, probably, to Yemen. From Rome, moreover, the church appears to have been transplanted on the one side into Africa, on the other into Gaul and as far as Germany and Britain. At least hardly a century had passed since the day of Pentecost before the entire Roman Empire was covered with a net-work of Christian churches. Although these may still have been small as respects the number of their members, yet, even in the time of Nero, Tacitus speaks of a great multitude of Christians in Rome, and other indications point to the conclusion that Christianity had gained an uncommonly rapid diffusion not only territorially, but also as respects the number of its professors.

How did this extension take place? Without doubt by means of missions. The church in Antioch was not the only one which esteemed it a duty to send forth messengers of the Gospel (Acts xiii. 2), and though Paul could say that he had labored more abundantly than they all, yet other laborers stood by his side. Though many things which are reported to us concerning the activity of the other Apostles are legendary, this much stands firm — they did not fold their hands. From a later time Origen informs us explicitly that the city churches sent out their own missionaries in order to preach the Gospel to the villages. Then we must recall our Lord's saying respecting the self-growing seed (Mark iv. 26–28): "So is the kingdom of God, as if a man should cast seed into the ground, and should sleep and rise night and day, and the seed should spring and grow up, he knoweth not how. For the earth bringeth forth fruit of herself; first the blade, then the ear; after that the full corn in the ear." Every Christian became a missionary, a witness to the Lord in whom he had found comfort and peace. Travelling craftsmen and traders (for example Aquila and Priscilla, who appear so often in the Epistles of Paul) told of the Messiah who had come, and brought tidings of what had occurred at Jerusalem. Others completed the narrations. A small company meet in private houses. Some one is found for a leader, and the little circle forms itself into a church. Public preaching on the streets or squares of the cities was not wanting, as for instance the Apostle's sermon in Athens. There was nothing unusual in this, inasmuch as at that age philosophers, or whoever had a new doctrine to proclaim, appeared in public and addressed the people. The private diffusion of Christianity was, perhaps, even more powerful and effective. One person told to another where he had found peace and comfort — one laborer to another, one slave to his fellow-slave. What was heard was interchanged, as was also what was received in writing, a Gospel, it may be, or an apostolical Epistle. The susceptibility of these Christian bands, on the one side, and on the other the kindling — we might say, the inflaming — power of Christianity, together with the activity of the Apostles and apostolic men, are the elements to be especially considered in this extension of Christianity.

These facts have also already indicated in what circles the preaching of the Crucified One first found acceptance. "See your calling," writes St. Paul (1 Cor. i. 26, 27), "how that not many wise men after the flesh, not many mighty, not many noble, are called, but God hath chosen the foolish things of the world, to confound the wise; and God hath chosen the weak things of the world, to confound the things which are mighty; and base things of the world, and things which are despised, hath God chosen, yea, and things which are not, to bring to nought things that are." "Not many"— some, however, from the higher classes were even thus early to be found. At least the recent investigations in the Catacombs at Rome, and the discovery of Christian burial-chambers whose rich artistic ornamentation belongs to the first, or the beginning of the second, century, have made it probable that Christianity must have found access earlier than has been believed, and to a greater degree, to the higher Roman families. De Rossi,[1] the explorer of the Roman Catacombs, has shown that in the oldest part of the Catacomb of Callistus, which is named for St. Lucina, members of the *gens Pomponia*, — from which Atticus, Cicero's friend, sprang, — and perhaps members of the Flavian house, were interred. So early had the Christian faith made its way into the old Roman families. Still, the great majority were people of inferior rank. Even toward the end of the second century Celsus scoffs that wool-dressers, cobblers, and tanners were the most zealous Christians. Above all it was the poor, who as the poor in spirit embraced the Gospel of the lowly Jesus who makes many rich. The oppressed and harassed, whom the spirit of Antiquity despised, the laboring classes, the slaves, were the ones who opened their hearts to the message of the kingdom of God as the realm of liberty and peace. Or wherever there were yearning souls, already at variance with the ancient views of the world, and whom neither the pagan religion nor the pagan philosophy could satisfy, souls weary and heavy laden, there were those who had an open ear for the preaching of the Gospel.

But while this attracted some, it excited in others — at first by far the larger part — opposition and hate. Every thing about it was too strange to the heathen, too repugnant to the views with which they had been familiar from childhood, for them to be able to understand it. To a cultivated and high-born Roman this whole fellowship of artisans and slaves was far too contemptible, and its superstition far too absurd, to admit of his at all busying himself with it and inquiring with any special care as to its precise character. Accurately as contemporary writers collect whatever else is worthy of note, Christianity is scarcely mentioned by them down to the middle of the second century. Pliny the Younger, and even Tacitus, although he relates the persecution by Nero, evidently do not regard it as worth while to concern themselves about this generally despised mass of men. That such persons, on the whole, deserved nothing better than to be thus persecuted, even without investigation, passed with them as something settled. Precisely where something of the genuine Roman spirit prevailed was the opposition the most powerful, for the Christian spirit and the Roman stood in sharpest antagonism. The circles of the aristocracy were the most difficult in which the church could make conquests. They were for the most part morally too corrupt to have any feeling for what is higher. And where a better spirit prevailed, where the endeavor was to maintain the old Roman character and to re-invigorate it, this effort in itself involved ill-will toward an oriental religion which was numbered without examination with "the detestable and senseless" that flowed to Rome, and with the innovations which must be set aside in order to restore the State and the national life to the old traditional basis.

The sentiment of the middle classes is made known to us in the ingenious colloquy which Minucius Felix wrote in defence of Christianity under the title *Octavius*. Cæcilius, who defends Heathenism, represents in his views a class of persons large then as always, persons having a certain measure of culture yet incapable of any profound knowledge, and touching the subject of religion only on the surface. Conservative in their disposition they adhere to the faith in which they are born neither from choice, nor from inclination, but from decorum and love of quiet. They regard it as a mark of good breeding not to dispute much upon such a topic. They are no dreamers, nor mystics. On the contrary they are somewhat sceptical, and inclined it may be to ridicule religious beliefs. Yet they are unwilling to see the old traditions disturbed, and they are easily inflamed against religious innovators, and are credulous of every absurdity which is reported about them. Nothing in Christianity more excites the anger of Cæcilius than its claim to be in possession of assured truth. Often enough does he repeat that one can know nothing with certainty.[2] "Human mediocrity is so inadequate to the exploration of things divine that it is not granted us to know, nor is it permitted to search, nor is it religious to force the things which are upheld suspended in the heavens above us, nor those which are sunk deep in subterranean abysses." Yet in spite of his scepticism he adheres to what has been handed down. "Since then either chance is certain, or nature is uncertain," this is his last word, "is not the tradition of the fathers the most venerable and the best guide to truth? Let us follow the religion which they have handed down to us, let us adore the gods whom we have been trained from childhood to fear rather than to know with familiarity, and let us beware of disputing about them."[3] This seemed to him the surest and most useful method. He clings to the utility of the old religion inasmuch as its truth cannot be determined. "Since all nations agree to recognize the immortal gods, although their nature or their origin may be uncertain, I cannot endure that any one swelling with audacity and such irreligious knowledge should strive to dissolve or weaken a religion so old, so useful, so salutary."[4] Without doubt many held the same position. They had no longer any heart for the old religion, yet they did not venture directly to break with it. They doubted, they reckoned it a sign of culture no longer to hold the ancient creed with exactness, they occasionally scoffed at it, — this was a mark of being well bred; yet at last they held fast to the old faith. They lacked the energy which was necessary to seize a new one.

Besides this there was the depressed condition of the Christians — an offence to all. Much was involved in attaching one's self to these despised, persecuted men. What we call public opinion is for the most part determined by success. The God of the Christians had so far shown few successes. The Roman deities had made Rome great, had given her the victory in countless battles, had laid at the feet of the city on the Tiber the dominion of the world. But this God of the Christians, why did He not interest Himself in those who believed in Him? Why allow them to be so despised and trodden under foot? Did the Christians appeal to the future, did they point to the day of final redemption and completion of the kingdom of God, to the resurrection and the coming blessedness, this was to the heathen of no importance, since the present was so troubled. "Where is the God?" asks Cæcilius, "that can help those who come to life again, while He does nothing for the living? Do not the Romans govern and reign without your God? Do they not enjoy the whole world and rule over you? The greatest and best portion of you are the prey of want and cold, are naked and hungry. Your God suffers this, and seems not to know it. Either He can not, or will not, help His own: thus He is either weak, or unjust."[5] A mode of reasoning which must certainly have struck home to the heathen, to whom the present was all, and whose worship had this ultimate aim — the attainment of something from their gods as a reward for their zealous veneration.

The less Christianity was understood, and the more foreign and contradictory every thing about it was to the opinions which hitherto had been accepted, the more easy was it for misunderstanding and hatred to excite the strangest reports; and the more absurd these were, the more readily did they obtain currency, not only among the masses who are always credulous, but even more widely and in select circles.

The spiritual worship of the Christians was something

utterly unintelligible to the heathen. No pagan could conceive of a religious service without temples and images, without altars and sacrifices. Since the Christians had none of these they could not have a God. It is true they talked of an invisible, omnipresent God, but such a Deity was to the heathen inconceivable. "What absurdities," exclaims Cæcilius,[6] "do these Christians invent! Of the God whom they can neither show nor see they recount that He is everywhere present, that He comes and goes, that He knows and judges the actions of men, their words, and even their secret thoughts. They make Him out to be a spy, a troublesome policeman, who is always in motion.[7] How can He attend to every particular, when He is occupied with the whole? Or how can He be sufficient for the whole, when He is engaged with particulars?"[8] Therefore the Christians appeared to them to be godless, to be atheists. Away with the atheists! was the customary cry of popular rage in the persecutions. Or, since the Christians according to pagan thought must have some sort of a deity, the slander circulated about the Jews was transferred to them — they adored the head of an ass. Thus in Tertullian's day, there was circulated a picture of a figure with the ears of an ass, clothed with a toga, holding a book in its hands, and with these words inscribed beneath: "The God of the Christians."[9] So likewise, among the ruins of the Palace of the Cæsars in Rome, there has recently been found a sketch, roughly drawn with charcoal on the wall, representing a man with an ass's head hanging on a cross, and below, in rude Greek letters: "Alexamenos adores his god." Evidently a scoff of the soldiers at some Christian comrade.[10]

Even worse accusations were made. The close connection of Christians with each other, their brotherly love, their firm union even to death, it was believed, could only be explained by the fact that they were united in a secret sacrilegious covenant by horrid oaths and yet more horrible practices. Men shuddered as they related that in the Christian assemblies, at the *Agapæ*, human flesh was eaten, and human blood drunk. "The story about the initiation of novices," Cæcilius narrates, "is as much to be detested as it is well known. An infant covered over with meal, that it may deceive the unwary, is placed before the neophytes. This infant is slain by the young pupil, with dark and secret wounds, he being urged on as if to harmless blows on the surface of the meal. Thirstily — O horror! — they lick up its blood; eagerly they divide its limbs; by this victim they are pledged together; with this consciousness of wickedness they are covenanted to mutual silence." After the feast, it is further related, when they are intoxicated, a dog that has been tied to the chandelier is provoked by throwing a morsel to jump, and by the leap he extinguishes the light, and in the darkness thus occasioned, deeds of the most abominable lust are committed and the wildest orgies are celebrated. Even cultivated and thoughtful heathen like the Orator Fronto under Marcus Aurelius, and even, it appears, the Emperor himself credited such reports; and those who did not wholly accept them were of the opinion that things so utterly impious, and only to be mentioned with apology, would not be reported unless there were some foundation in truth.

But apart from such stories, — which with the lapse of time must have been seen to be wholly baseless, though believed through many a decade and often enough kindling the rage of the populace and influencing even the measures of the government, — the Christians passed with the heathen as a race averse to all that is great, fair and noble in our humanity, as even hostile to it, and haters of mankind. In its origin their religion was barbarian : they despised all science. This is the rule laid down by them," writes Celsus : [12] " Let no one come to us who has been educated, or who is wise or prudent, for such qualifications are deemed evil by us; but if there be any ignorant, or uncultivated, or unintelligent, or foolish person, let him come with confidence." Their teachers, he affirms, say : " See that none of you lay hold of knowledge ! Knowledge is an evil. Knowledge causes men to lose their soundness of mind; they perish through wisdom." [13] Since the Christians were obliged to withdraw from public life, since they took no part in the pleasures of the heathen nor shared in their interests, they were regarded as useless, as a gloomy and light-shunning race. Their life seemed to the heathen joyless and dismal. " We," says one of their number, " worship the gods with cheerfulness, with feasts, songs and games, but you worship a crucified man who cannot be pleased by those who have all this enjoyment, who despises joy and condemns pleasures." [14] Even what the Christians said of a judgment for the godless, of eternal punishments in hell, was deemed a proof of their hatred of men. To the pagan Cæcilius [15] they are a " reprobate, unlawful, desperate faction," who had conspired against all that is good and beautiful, a " people skulking and shunning the light, silent in public, but garrulous in corners. They despise the temples as charnel-houses, they abhor the gods, they laugh at sacred things; wretched, they pity, if they are allowed, the priests; half naked themselves, they disdain honors and purple robes. In their wondrous folly and incredible audacity they despise present torments, though they dread those which are uncertain and future; and, while they fear to die after death, they do not fear to die for the present. So does a deceitful hope, the consolations of a revival, soothe their fear." The solicitude of the Christians for their salvation was to the heathen something wholly unintelligible and even absurd, and they regarded the Christians as the most irrational and wretched of men because they renounced the sure, substantial blessings and enjoyments of this world for the sake of things future and wholly uncertain in order to escape an imaginary evil and attain to an imaginary blessedness. "You in the mean time, in suspense and anxiety," says Cæcilius,[16] "are abstaining from respectable enjoyments. You do not visit the shows; you are not present in solemn processions; you do not appear at public banquets; you abhor the sacred contests, and the meats and drinks a portion of which has been offered and poured out upon the altars. You do not wreathe your heads with flowers; you do not honor your bodies with odors; you reserve unguents for funeral-rites, you even refuse garlands to your sepulchres — pale, trembling beings, worthy of pity, even the pity of our gods. Thus, wretched ones, you neither rise again, nor meanwhile do you live." Surely if Cæcilius was correct in this last statement, he was altogether right in calling the Christians the most wretched of human beings. For if in this life only we have hope in Christ, if we are not born again by the resurrection of Christ to a living hope, we are indeed of all men the most miserable (1 Cor. xv. 19).

The greatest peril for the Christians lay in this, that these reproaches had a political side, or that they could so easily be turned in this direction. Just because public life was wholly interwoven with Heathenism, were Christians compelled to withdraw from it. Their demeanor towards the State was, it is true, everywhere determined by the command: "Submit yourselves to every ordinance of man for the Lord's sake," "Let every soul be subject unto the higher powers," but while the State was thoroughly pagan their relation to it could only be a negative one. Their interests lay elsewhere than in the Roman State, and in its grandeur and honor. "Nothing," Tertullian acknowledges with perfect frankness, "is more foreign to us than public affairs." [17] They avoided military service and public offices, for the soldier was obliged to assist at sacrifices, and civil officers to superintend the performance of religious rites. Therefore it was said: "You are a lazy race, useless and indolent in public affairs, for it behooves a man to live for his native land and the State." [18] While the heathen religions were thoroughly national, Christianity (and this was to pagan thought something wholly absurd) appeared as a universal religion, as a religion for all nations. Even those who were not Romans, even the barbarians, who confessed Christ, were to the Christians brothers. The reproach was close at hand: You yourselves are not Romans, you are enemies to the State. Christianity seemed to the heathen anti-national, and the church, firmly united in its faith and separate from all other men, was looked upon as a dangerous faction in the State. Was the Emperor's birthday celebrated, the houses of the Christians remained dark in the illuminated cities, and their doors were not garlanded. Were games given in honor of some triumph, no Christian allowed himself to be seen in the circus, or in the amphitheatre. To strew incense to the Emperor, to do homage to the image of the Emperor, to swear by his Genius, was accounted by the Christians a fall into idolatry. Of course they were deemed guilty of high treason, enemies of the Emperor. To Romans the eternal duration of Rome was an indisputable truth. How often Rome appears on coins as "the eternal city." "To them," says Jupiter in Virgil, "I set neither limit, nor times; I have given them dominion without end." [19] The Christians spoke of a destruction of the whole world, therefore of Rome. They even expected this speedily, and rejoiced in it as in a redemption. They hoped for another, better country, and regarded this earthly one only as a foreign land. Thus they were a people without a fatherland. It was even charged that they plotted the destruction of Rome. Let them protest as often as they might that they were obedient, peaceable subjects, that in their congregations and in their houses they prayed assiduously for the Emperor, that they paid punctually their taxes, what did it all avail? Here, in truth, was an antagonism which necessarily led to bloody conflicts.

All the States of Antiquity had a theocratic foundation, Rome not less than any other. As national life was everywhere interwoven with religion, so the religious life was a part of the political. It was the duty of a citizen to honor the national gods, and to obey the laws of the State in religious things as in all others.

Human life was on all sides absorbed in civil life, the State embraced and regulated all its departments. A pagan could not conceive the possibility of there being any sphere of human life which was not reached by the power of the State. It was to him wholly incomprehensible that a man could believe himself constrained from regard to his conscience, for the sake of God, and in order to obey God, to refuse obedience to any law or ordinance of the State whatsoever. The State itself was to him, so to speak, God, and its laws divine. In Rome this theocratic tendency culminated in the worship of the Emperors. What other gods a man might worship, was his private concern, — in this respect the State was exceedingly tolerant, — but he must honor the divine Emperor, this was his duty as a citizen. The *crimen læsæ majestatis*, the crime of violating the majesty of the Emperor, and the *crimen læsæ publicæ religionis*, the crime of violating the established religion, were most intimately connected. From this point of view all the charges above mentioned were true. Christianity was for Romans anti-national, hostile to State and Emperor, un-Roman, an opposition to the State religion, and therefore to the State itself. And so long as the State was built on such foundations it could not act otherwise than it did, it must treat and persecute Christianity as a prohibited religion. *Non licet esse vos*,[20] you have no right to exist, this was the constantly repeated cry against Christianity. "Your associations are contrary to law," thus Celsus begins his book against the Christians, passing, as it were, sentence of death before the trial. The judicial proceedings against the Christians, as these fall under our notice in numerous Acts of the Martyrs, always become decisive at this point, — the refusal of the accused to pay divine honor to the Emperor. "You ought to love our princes," said the Proconsul to the martyr Achatius, — to give merely a single instance of thousands, — "as behooves a man who lives under the laws of the Roman Empire." Achatius answered: "By whom is the Emperor more loved than by the Christians? We supplicate for him unceasingly a long life, a just government of his peoples, a peaceful reign, prosperity for the army and the whole world."— " Good," replied the Proconsul, "but in order to prove your obedience, sacrifice with us to his honor." Upon this Achatius explained: "I pray to God for my Emperor, but a sacrifice neither he should require nor we pay. Who may offer divine honor to a man?" Upon this declaration he was sentenced to death. This one transaction is typical for all. The pagan-Roman State, so long as it bore this character could not do otherwise than persecute the Christians. In refusing divine honors to the Emperor, they denied the State in its profoundest principles. Conversely, if the Christians had obeyed in this particular, they would have renounced Christianity in its inmost essence. Here was a conflict which could be settled by no compromise, which could only be gotten rid of by a battle for life or death. Not until the Emperor bowed before the Supreme God, not until Christianity became the foundation of the State, could the era of persecution come to an end.

Let us not unjustly censure the Emperors who persecuted the Christians, nor the judges who sentenced them to death. Let us not make of them, as did the later legends of the martyrs (not the ancient and genuine *martyria* so many of which have been pre-

CHARACTER OF THE CONFLICT.

served), fanatical and bloodthirsty tyrants. The judges decided simply in accordance with the laws, and, in the great majority of cases, did so coolly, calmly, without passion, as men who were simply discharging their duty. Among the Emperors there were some, who like Nero and Domitian, that "piece of Nero in cruelty,"[22] as Tertullian says, were persecutors from cruelty and thirst for blood, but most of them were actuated by nobler motives. Those of the second century recognized more as by instinct, those of the third clearly, the danger which threatened the Roman State in the new spirit of Christianity, and they strove to protect it. We must concede that in this matter they were not deceived. Christianity was, in fact, a power hostile to the Roman State as it had hitherto existed. The new spirit which inspired the Christians would inevitably destroy the old political organization. The Emperors could not as yet perceive what renewing and rejuvenating powers for the State were possessed by Christianity. It would be unjust to expect from the Emperors of the second century the act of Constantine. It would have been in all respects premature.

Let us avoid forming a wrong conception of the whole conflict. It was not, as later times have thought in an entirely unhistorical way, a fanatical war waged with uninterrupted fury by the old faith on the new. It was a religious contest on the part of the Christians alone, who suffered and died for their faith. Only in its last stages at most did it assume this character to the heathen. In this fact lay, from the beginning, the weakness of Heathenism, and the strength of Christianity. Not the priests, but the Emperors led the attack, and the Emperors did not fight for their faith —

indeed the most zealous persecutors were pre-eminently sceptical as to the heathen religions, while those who were believers in them often left the Christians unmolested, — they fought for the existing order of the State, and the object of their endeavors was, not to convert the Christians again to the pagan faith, but to compel them to submit to the established laws. It is true the Christians never rebelled against the State. They cannot be reproached with even the appearance of a revolutionary spirit. Despised, persecuted, abused, they still never revolted, but showed themselves everywhere obedient to the laws, and ready to pay to the Emperors the honor which was their due. Yet in one particular they could not obey, the worship of idols, the strewing of incense to the Cæsar-god. And in this one thing it was made evident that in Christianity lay the germ of a wholly new political and social order. This is the character of the conflict which we are now to review. It is a contest of the spirit of Antiquity against that of Christianity, of the ancient heathen order of the world against the new Christian order.

Ten persecutions are commonly enumerated, viz., under Nero, Domitian, Trajan, Hadrian, Marcus Aurelius, Septimius Severus, Maximinus the Thracian, Decius, Valerian, and Diocletian.[23] This traditional enumeration is, however, very superficial, and leaves entirely unrecognized the real course of the struggle. The persecutions are made by it to appear as arbitrary acts of particular Emperors, as though some persecuted, while others recognized, Christianity. Though times of relative tranquillity occurred, Christianity remained, notwithstanding, a prohibited religion. This being the case, the simple arrangement of the persecutions in a series makes the impression that they were all of the same character, while in fact the persecution under Nero was wholly different from that under Trajan and his successors, and this again varied essentially from those under Decius and Diocletian. The first persecution which was really general and systematically aimed at the suppression of the Church, was the Decian. That under Trajan and his successors consisted merely of more or less frequent processes against individual Christians, in which the established methods of trial were employed, and the existing laws were more or less sharply used against them.[24] Finally, the persecutions under Nero and Domitian were mere outbreaks of personal cruelty and tyrannical caprice.

In what has preceded I have indicated the three periods which mark the course of the conflict.

The strictness of the Roman laws against foreign religions has been already noticed. Christianity belonged to this class. It was therefore from the outset a prohibited religion. The Christian churches were illegal societies (*collegia illicita*). Participation in forbidden associations was severely punished. The penalty for membership was the same as for appearing at public places or temples with weapons in the hand, the punishment of treason; that is, the guilty party could, according to the decision of the judge, be either beheaded, or cast to the wild beasts, or burned. If these severe laws had been at once rigidly employed against the youthful Christianity, it must have immediately succumbed to the attack. But, apart from the fact already noticed that the Romans were somewhat timid about strictly enforcing these laws, two circumstances came to the help of Christianity, and secured to it at least sufficient protection to enable it to gain strength until it could withstand open assault. One of these was the protection which the Christians could obtain under the laws concerning the *collegia*. To these legally sanctioned *collegia* belonged the burial clubs, — associations, mostly, of the poorer class of people, who joined together to secure to their members, by regular contributions, suitable burial upon their decease, and the due observance of the usual religious solemnities at their interment and on anniversary days. The extensive catacombs in Rome and elsewhere prove that the Christians enjoyed legal protection for their graves. There are also many other indications that they endeavored in every possible way to avail themselves of the shelter afforded by the laws and usages respecting associations for burial purposes. In this way they could not only bury their dead in safety without molestation from the heathen, they were also able to meet together under the protection of law, to arrange collections for the poor, and above all to hold their services of religious worship at the cemeteries.[25]

Of greater importance than this means of protection — which, indeed, was of more avail for the dead than the living — was the other fact to which I have referred, that the heathen at first were unable to distinguish the Christians from the Jews. The Christian brotherhoods passed continually with the Romans for Jewish associations, and thus they remained unmolested; and more than once it was the Roman law which afforded protection to the nascent Christianity against the fanatical hatred of the unbelieving Jews. Paul appealed successfully to his rights as a Roman citizen, and in Corinth the Proconsul Gallio drove the Jews with their accusation against Paul from his judgment-seat, with the declaration that he was not disposed to be a judge of their disputes.[26]

On the other hand the Christians inherited all the hatred which so heavily oppressed the Jews; and this hatred did not diminish, but only augmented as the heathen ere long discovered, especially in the large cities, that there was a difference between Jews and Christians. The Jews themselves, who everywhere persecuted the Christians most violently, took care to make it plain that the latter did not belong to them. At first the Christians appeared to the heathen only as a faction of the Jews, and, indeed, as the most dangerous and objectionable faction of these despisable and irrational beings, and therefore when the cruelty and murderous passion of an Emperor like Nero seized upon these Christians in order to make them atone for a crime of which they were guiltless, he could be sure of the assent of the great mass of the people. In other respects, though the zeal of a governor who thought in this way to recommend himself to the Emperor, or some outburst of popular rage demanded here and there a victim, no systematic persecution of the Christians occurred in this period. They were still protected by the pagan ignorance of the true character of their religion. They were, besides, too insignificant to make it possible for them to be regarded as an important opponent by the heathen world in the fullness of its power.

The situation changed when, with the destruction of Jerusalem and the complete overthrow of the Jewish State, the protecting sheath fell off from Christianity; when it could no longer remain concealed from the heathen that Christianity was a *tertium genus*, a third religion by the side of Heathenism and Judaism; and when at the same time, about the beginning of the second century, this religion spread with such power that for the first time the thought occurred to Roman statesmen that it might become dangerous to the State. Now a definite position in regard to it could no longer be avoided; and this was taken in the rescript of Trajan to Pliny, in which the Emperor communicated exact directions respecting legal proceedings against the Christians. This introduces the second period of the contest, for the edict of Trajan remained substantially the law for the following century and a half. The effort was to limit the growth of the church by the use of the established laws in the ordinary methods of judicial transactions. Meanwhile, however, Christianity kept on growing; and as early as the reign of Marcus Aurelius it had become evident that these means for its suppression were inadequate. Already they had to be employed on so large a scale that the persecution, in many places at least, was universal.

Yet all this was only preparatory to the decisive conflict. This was first kindled when the question arose, on what should the State be founded, on a restored Heathenism with annihilation of Christianity, or on Christianity with an abandonment of Heathenism. On the one side, the revolution maturing within Heathenism itself, which we have characterized above as its restoration, on the other, the magnificent development of the Christian church, first brought the opposing parties into a position in which the decisive battle could be fought. The general persecutions began with Decius. They aimed at a complete suppression of Christianity. All previous conflicts had been, as it were, single combats. Now the contest raged along the whole line of battle. On both sides all the forces at command were brought into action. Heathenism, now become fanatical, put forth its last strenuous exertions, and the contest ended only with the full victory of the Cross.

II. THE PERSECUTION UNDER NERO.

Not much more than three decades had passed away since Pentecost, the birthday of the Christian Church, when there occurred its first bloody encounter with the Roman State. It took place, characteristically enough, in Rome, in the world's chief city, and no less a person than the Emperor gave the signal for a contest which was to bring grave anxieties to many of his successors on the throne of the Cæsars, until, again before the gates of Rome, at the Milvian bridge, the legions of the first Christian Emperor won, under the sign of the long-persecuted Cross, the decisive and final victory.

We do not know when the Gospel was first preached in Rome. It was certainly at an early date. The intercourse between Rome and the East was very active. Numerous vessels came from Antioch and the coast of Asia Minor. And on one of them, perhaps, came the first converted, and for us nameless, Jew who bore to the large Jewish communion there the tidings of the Messiah who had appeared, the crucified and risen Jesus. The earliest, indistinct trace of this introduction of Christianity into Rome is to be found in Suetonius's report of the expulsion of the Jews, which is mentioned also in Acts xviii. 1. Suetonius alleges as the cause of this expulsion that the Jews had excited constant disturbance at the instigation of a certain Chrestus. This Chrestus, whom Suetonius appears to regard as a leader of the Jews at that time, can only be Christ, as the verbal form Chrestus not unfrequently appears instead of Christus.[27] It was the controversy whether the Messiah had already appeared, or was still to be expected, which excited the Jews. The Roman Jewish community shared in the disquiet which now disturbed more and more the whole Jewish world. Rejecting the true Messiah they looked all the more enthusiastically for a Messiah who should correspond to their own expectations, a Messiah who should break in pieces the Roman yoke. Incited by the Pharisaic party fanaticism flamed higher and higher. Already in the Holy Land the clouds were gathering for the fearful tempest which was soon to break upon that unhappy country, and the expulsion of the Jews from Rome was a sign of the approaching storm. Although they soon returned, they were henceforth increasingly suspected by the Romans, and whereas, down to this time, it had been one of the traditions of the Julian house to show them especial favor, they now met from the government many tokens of displeasure.

Meanwhile the number of the Christians increased perceptibly. It may have happened that many, like Aquila and Priscilla, departed as Jews and returned as Christians. Doubtless the two persons just named, to whom Paul in the Epistle to the Romans gives the first place in his greetings, largely contributed to the founding and enlargement of the Roman church. Paul, on his arrival in the city, found an important church already in existence, and through his efforts, while he lived as a prisoner two years in a hired house, it considerably increased. It could no longer remain wholly concealed from the heathen as a distinct community, and although it may still have been regarded as a fraction of Judaism, yet as such it now became of note. The consequence, indeed, was only greater hatred and profounder contempt. The Christians appeared to the heathen to be the most dangerous fraction of Judaism, more unreasonable than the rest of the Jews, more hostile to the whole Roman State, to all that in their eyes was great, noble and good. Judaism was still a national religion, Christianity wholly anti-national, and this anti-national religion was rapidly diffusing itself with its superstition among the lower orders. It contradicted every thing which hitherto had been esteemed sacred, and it could only be explained by assuming that it originated in hatred to all that is human. The Jews who were hostile to Christianity stirred up, so far as they were able, the ill-will and hatred of the heathen towards the Christians, and it is not improbable that they, above all others, diffused and kept alive the horrible reports about the Christians which even thus early appeared and were only too readily credited, the stories of the abominations which the Christians were said to practise in their secret assemblies, their eating human flesh, and their licentiousness.

The hostile feeling of the people toward the Christians which was thus excited forms the background of the First, the Neronian Persecution, which, as before remarked, was no persecution in the later meaning of the word, but only a sudden, fierce outburst of hate, though for this reason all the more bloody and horrible.[28]

On the night of the eighteenth of July, A.D. 64 (the

same day of the year on which the Gauls had once set fire to the city, a fact to which the superstitious ascribed especial importance), a great conflagration broke out in Rome. The fire originated in the stalls near the Circus Maximus, in which many of the Jews carried on their traffic, and there, where combustibles of different kinds were accumulated, it found its first supply of fuel. Then it seized the Circus with its wooden stagings and seats, and lashed by the wind spread with astonishing rapidity. All efforts of the firemen and soldiers, who tore down houses with engines of war, to arrest the flames, proved abortive. The fire raged six days and nights, until it was finally conquered far away from where it began, at the wall of Servius Tullius near the gardens of Mæcenas. Nor did this suffice. The fire broke out anew in another quarter of the city, and raged three days more. Of the fourteen "regions" of the city only four entirely escaped. The metropolis of the world was a vast heap of ruins. The calamity was immeasurable.

As always happens at such times, the origin of the fire was the object of the most eager and excited inquiry; and among the people the suspicion arose, that Nero himself had instigated the conflagration. It was asserted that men had been seen to hurl firebrands into the houses, and to hinder the extinction of the flames. Moreover they were said to have declared that they thus acted by order of the Emperor. Others believed that they had recognized these incendiaries as his servants. Yet others narrated that Nero himself had exulted in the splendor of the sea of fire; that from the tower of Mæcenas, he had been a spectator of the conflagration, and in his well-known stage costume had declaimed over it a poem on the burning of Troy.

It is, to-day, hardly possible to discover whether there was any truth in these reports. The impartial verdict of history must be that it is at least very improbable that Nero was really the incendiary, since he was not in Rome at all, but at Antium, and did not return till the fire threatened to attack his palace. But this at least is certain, the reports found credence. Nero was accused of having set fire to the world's capital for his own pleasure. It made no difference that, during the conflagration, he hurried to and fro directing and urging on the efforts for its extinction, or that after the fire he cared for the people and promoted the rebuilding of the city in the most munificent manner. The sacrifices too which he offered and the services of atonement and consecration which he instituted, were in vain, The rumor held its ground in spite of all. The rage of the people demanded a victim, and for the sacrifice the Christians were chosen. Nero, says Tacitus, falsely charged the Christians with the crime.

It need not be wondered at that, when a crime had been committed, these were selected to expiate it, though they were the farthest of all from perpetrating the crime. They were hated for deeds of shame imputed to them, and so seemed equally capable of the crime and worthy of the punishment. Besides, as already indicated, suspicion might easily be made to fall on the Jews, and the Christians were still considered as Jews. The conflagration had begun near the circus where the Jews had their shops, and the quarters inhabited by them were among the few parts of the city, which the fire spared. But, the Christians were regarded as the worst and the most dangerous among the Jews, because their numbers constantly increased. By making them suffer death, an additional advantage would be gained in getting rid of them. It is possible, also, that the Jews, being enemies of the Christians, managed to divert suspicion from themselves, to those whom they so much hated. Whether Poppæa Sabina, Nero's consort, and the friend of the Jews, had a part in it or not, cannot be decided. We have no information on the subject, and the story told by French historians of an intrigue of Poppæa against Nero's mistress Acte, whom they suppose to have been a Christian, is a romance spun from sparse and wholly inadequate materials.

However, some Christians were arrested and confessed — what and how, we are not told. Perhaps only that they were Christians, but if also that they took part in kindling the fire, then those who confessed it were no Christians, or torture forced untrue confessions from their weakness. In the narrative of Tacitus there is a veil over this matter, and this veil was not thrown over it by the historian, but before him by those who examined the accused. The prefect, Tigellinus, who was at no loss for the witnesses necessary to convict Nero's innocent wife Octavia, of all sorts of infamous deeds, would not feel any embarrassment in this case. From the testimony of those first arrested, a more searching inquisition was instituted for the Christians. A multitude of arrests were made, and if the prisoners could not be convicted of kindling the conflagration, yet as Tacitus reports with icy coldness, they could be condemned for hating the human race. That was sufficient; of such people the worst was probable, and they might be treated as incendiaries even though proof of the deed was not to be had.

There followed a carnival of bloodshed such as Rome,

thoroughly accustomed as it then was to murder, had never yet seen. It was not enough simply to put the supposed criminals to death, for of course the more cruelly they were treated, the more guilty would they be made to appear. And so the most horrible torments were employed, and new modes of execution were invented to torture them. Those who were crucified and thus imitated their Lord in their death, could consider themselves favored. Others were sewn up in the skins of wild beasts and torn to pieces by dogs. Still others were used in tragic spectacles in the manner before mentioned. We have a scene from this persecution recalled by the words of Clement of Rome in his Epistle to the Corinthians:[29] "By reason of jealousy, women, Danaids and Dirces, being persecuted, after that they had suffered cruel and unholy insults, safely reached the goal in the race of faith, and received a noble reward, feeble though they were in body." Christian women personating the Danaids and Dirce were brought upon the stage, and there certainly happened to the one who represented Dirce, what, according to the legend, befell her, namely that she was bound to a raging bull, and dragged to death. But the evening was the climax of the carnival. The populace assembled in Nero's garden to behold a magnificent display. All around, huge torches were blazing to dispel the darkness. They were Christians who, covered with tow and coated with pitch, and then bound to stakes of pine, were lighted and burned as torches. Juvenal, who probably was an eye witness, describes [30] how

"At the stake they shine,
Who stand with throat transfixed and smoke and burn."

Among them Nero drove about, fantastically attired as a charioteer, and the people shouted with delight.

This was the first of the persecutions, as it were the fiery portal, through which the Christians entered the arena in which they were now called to strive, to bleed, to die for their faith during two and a half centuries. This first persecution was no carefully-planned attempt to suppress Christianity, founded upon civil or religious policy, but only a cruel outburst of hatred, which Nero turned to account in his own interest. Heathenism had not as yet learned to understand Christianity at all. It appeared to the heathen only as something entirely strange, utterly opposed to every existing and traditional belief. And the Christians were regarded as men who, since they hated every thing human, deserved nothing but hatred, in dealing with whom therefore any thing was permissible, and all considerations of humanity might be set aside. Now Christians might learn what awaited them. Heathenism had openly declared by action, that Christianity was not to be tolerated, that it was to be annihilated as inhuman, hostile to the human race. Now, too, might the heathen know what they had to expect from the Christians. In patient silence they endured all. The Heroic Age of the Christian Church had begun, a heroism not of action, but of a suffering mightier than all deeds.

It is certainly significant that Nero, the most bloodthirsty and cruel of all the Emperors, was the one who heads the list of the persecutors of the Christians. It is not difficult to understand why the defenders of Christianity in later times have often referred to the fact that a Nero began the persecutions, nor to see how the legend arose that Nero was Antichrist, and would return in that character at the end of the world. Indeed here Christianity and Anti-Christianity stood confronting one another more directly than they will again antagonize till the end of time. Here we see the Christian church still in its original simplicity and purity, still under the guidance of apostles, full of living faith and active love and (in all the weakness and imperfection, which even then were not absent) as yet in truth composed of saints who sought holiness, who included all in their brotherly love and who were prepared to endure all things for their faith. Opposed to these stood the Emperor, stained with the blood of many innocent victims, with the blood of his brother, of his wife, of his mother, wallowing in licentiousness and the indulgence of every lust; and a degenerate people, a populace clamoring only for "bread and games." And while the Christians, innocent, but accused of the most disgraceful crimes, writhed in mortal agony and blazed as torches at the stake, the Emperor made his vanity as an actor conspicuous, paraded his skill as a charioteer, and a rabble drunk with sensual pleasure saluted him with shouts of applause.

In the metropolis of the world Heathenism and Christianity then for the first time came into collision. The conflict had begun, and the way in which it began left no doubt on which side the victory would be. Of those who fell at that time we know only two by name, the great apostles, St. Peter and St. Paul. The apostle of the Jews and the apostle of the Gentiles, whose paths often led them far apart in life, in death united their praises to the one Lord who "wrought effectually in Peter to the apostleship of the circumcision and was mighty in Paul toward the Gentiles" (Gal. ii. 8). The rest, whose charred and mangled remains were thrown into a common pit, after the carnival of murder was past, were probably from the lower classes, artisans and slaves, nameless in life and nameless in death. But the seer beheld their souls " under the altar, resting for a little season until their fellow-servants also and their brethren, that should be killed, as they were, should be fulfilled" (Rev. vi. 10, 11). And throughout the book of Revelation sounds the Hallelujah over the victory these nameless ones gained by their death, the sure pledge of the final triumph.

CHAPTER II.

THE CHRISTIANS BEFORE THE TRIBUNALS.

" They will deliver you up to the councils, and they will scourge you in their synagogues; and ye shall be brought before governors and kings for my sake, for a testimony against them and the Gentiles." — MATT. x. 17, 18.

I. TRAJAN'S LEGISLATION AGAINST THE CHRISTIANS.

FEARFULLY as the Neronian persecution raged in Rome itself, it seems to have been principally confined to the capital.[1] Yet it is not improbable that the manner in which the Emperor himself attacked the confessors of the new faith, drew attention to them where they were prominent in the provinces, and that in a few cases the local officials may have proceeded against them. At least we hear of a martyr Antipas in Pergamum (Rev. ii. 13), whose martyrdom probably belongs to this period. The persecution was like a sudden storm which soon spent its fury. Those who escaped the clutches of Nero's minions probably remained in hiding for a time and then went back to their former positions, while some who had fled the city were permitted to return without molestation. Tacitus indeed expressly tells us that the fate of the Christians slain by Nero awakened sympathy for them (though they deserved to suffer the worst of punishments), on the ground that they were destroyed not for the public good, but to glut the cruelty of a single man. The only results of Nero's action were that the heroism of the martyrs strengthened the faith of the survivors, and the example of the dead stimulated the zeal of the living. The spread of Christianity was not hindered but rather helped by this event.

Not until the reign of Domitian do we again hear of persecutions. Primarily, of course, these had the Jews for their object. After the destruction of Jerusalem and of the Temple, they were obliged to pay their former temple-dues, the Didrachma, to the Capitoline Jupiter, and this poll-tax was often collected in a harsh and cruel manner, because some Jews refused to pay a tribute to a heathen deity.[2] In the conflicts which thus arose, the Christians, especially the Jewish Christians, were often involved, for the heathen had not yet learned to distinguish definitely between Jews and Christians. We learn also that some were condemned for defection from the religion of the State to Judaism, or, as the accusation sometimes reads, for atheism.[3] The Emperor condemned even his own cousin, Flavius Clemens and his wife Flavia Domitilla. Flavius Clemens was executed soon after the close of A. D. 96, the year of his consulate, and Flavia Domitilla was banished to the island Pandateria. The historian Suetonius calls Clemens a man "of the most despicable indolence."[4] Many to-day regard it as clear that the accusation of being a Christian is covered by this expression, and therefore that Clemens is to be regarded as a martyr. But the ancient authorities show no knowledge of this, and it must appear very doubtful, that, if the Church could really count among the martyrs of that day a man of consular rank, it could have passed so completely out of remembrance.[5] In any case we here find the very earliest traces that Christianity had begun to gain a foothold among the higher classes.

For the first time also there seems to have sprung up in the ruling circles a certain anxiety on account of Christianity. Hegesippus[6] informs us, that Domitian had heard there were still living in Palestine relatives of Jesus, descendants of the royal house of David. He was terrified at the news, and summoned them — two grandsons of Judas, the brother of Jesus — before him. But, when they told him, that, together, they possessed only an estate of the value of nine thousand *denarii* (about $1,800) and cultivated it themselves, as they proved by showing their horny hands; when they testified on his asking about the kingdom of Christ, that it was not of this world, and would not come till the end of all things, the Emperor dismissed them without doing them any harm.

The persecutions under Domitian were very short, and Nerva his successor recalled those who had been banished and restored to them their confiscated possessions, in part from his private purse.

With the beginning of the second century there came a great change in the situation of the Christians. The separation of Christianity from Judaism was completed so as to be recognized even by heathen eyes. The destruction of Jerusalem put an end to the outward existence of the Jewish nationality. The temple fell, the sacrifices ceased. And yet, without a temple, without a daily sacrifice, without a visible centre, Judaism, the most hardy of national religions, managed to preserve its existence, even after the insurrection under Bar Cocheba had been quenched in blood, and, thereby, the Jews' last hope of regaining their old position had been destroyed. Their religion now became consolidated into the real Judaism, in essentials such as we see it to-day. Spread abroad over the earth, without a local centre, or the bond which had existed hitherto in the temple service, Judaism henceforth was united only by the common Law, and by the common doctrine contained in the newly collected Talmud. Thus it became completely separated from Christianity. Talmudic Judaism severed all the connections which had hitherto bound it to Christianity. Henceforth three times every day in the synagogues was invoked the awful curse on the renegades, the Christians. It came to be a rare exception for a Jew to go over to Christianity, while the heathen thronged into the Church in ever increasing numbers. The remainder of the Jewish Christians dwindled away or disappeared entirely in the churches of heathen Christians, or turned heretics and were cut off from the Church. The Church now found the field for its work and growth almost exclusively in the heathen world, and became composed entirely of Gentile Christians. It was therefore no longer possible to confound the Christians with the Jews. Henceforth they were recognized by the heathen as a *genus tertium*, as they were often called — a third party beside Heathenism and Judaism.

Thus Christianity lost the protection which it had hitherto enjoyed as a supposed Jewish sect. Like a young plant, it now showed itself, free from the sheath which had shielded it, and exposed to every storm. From the moment when Christianity was recognized as a separate religion, it became an illegal religion, and was attacked by the severe Roman laws against illicit societies. And though the change did not at first produce its full effect, this was because the State had not yet proclaimed its attitude towards the new religion, and so the method of procedure lay entirely within the arbitration of the several governors, some of whom were already beginning judicial action against the Christians, while others ignored them. The treatment the Christians experienced was more or less severe according to the personal leanings of the judge, no general rule having been made. But it soon became necessary that one should be given. Christianity hitherto little known, daily gained in prominence. In some provinces the defection from the religion of the State was so visible, that the temples were deserted and the meat of the sacrifices found no buyers. During Trajan's reign the rage of the people broke out against the Christians in some places. Spurred on by the priests or roused to fanaticism by some special occurrence, the mob demanded severer penalties against the hated race, or threatened to administer them with its own hand. Mob violence could not be tolerated, and thus it became necessary to make rules for the treatment of the Christians.

The immediate occasion was supplied by a letter which Pliny the Younger, Proconsul of Bithynia, addressed to the Emperor in the year A.D. 111 or 112.[7] When Pliny came into the province, he was in great perplexity how to treat the Christians, who were especially numerous there. Christians of both sexes, and of all ages and ranks, appeared before his tribunal. Was he to take into account age, sex, and rank, or to treat all alike? Was he to pardon those who recanted, or should the renunciation of the faith be of no avail to one who had been a Christian? Was the name of Christian, the mere fact that a man was a Christian, enough ground for condemnation, even when no crimes could be proved against him, or should only any crimes, that might be connected with the Christian name, receive punishment? At first Pliny made a practice of asking the accused, if they were Christians. When they confessed it, he repeated his question, adding the threat of punishment with death. If they remained stubborn, he had them executed; for their stubbornness alone, without regard to other considerations, seemed to him to merit punishment. But soon other cases came up, and brought him into still greater perplexity. Anonymous accusations against the Christians were sent to him. Ought he to receive them? Some of those whom he arrested and questioned, denied that they were Christians, others said they had been Christians, but were now no longer such. In order to demonstrate the truth of this assertion, he had images of the Emperor and of the Gods brought in, and commanded the accused to offer incense and to curse Christ, for he had heard that nothing could persuade real Christians to do so. When the accused obeyed the command he set them at liberty. The result of his further inquiries as well as what he learned about the new religion from some deaconesses, questioned under torture, did not satisfy him. He discovered only a boundless superstition: that they came together on an appointed day, to sing hymns to Christ as a God, and that they bound themselves by an oath, to do no evil, but to avoid evil, theft and adultery, and to deceive no man.

Then it had been their custom to separate, and to reassemble in the evening at a meal, but an entirely innocent meal. Yet they had discontinued this latter, since the promulgation of the imperial edict forbidding nocturnal assemblies. Plainly the Christians in order to show their obedience to law, had given up the Love-Feast, hitherto held in the evening. Thus Pliny was at a loss what to do, yet something must be done, for the superstition spread like a conflagration, and had already penetrated from the towns into the country, while on the other side there seemed to be hope that, if with firmness mildness were combined, and pardon extended to those who recanted, the superstition might be extirpated.

The Emperor in his answer approved in the main the conduct of Pliny thus far, and without attempting to give directions for all cases, issued the following orders for the future. The Christians were not to be sought out, yet when accused and convicted, they must be punished. Those however who denied that they were Christians, and proved it by sacrificing to the gods were to be pardoned by reason of their recantation, even though there might be suspicion that they had been Christians in the past. Trajan closes by saying that anonymous accusations were not to be received at all, because that would set a bad example and be unworthy of the age.

This imperial edict regulated the treatment of the Christians for more than a century. We cannot deny that, considered from the Roman's point of view, it does not belie the clemency and love of justice generally attributed to Trajan. Christianity seemed to him a stubborn opposition to the laws of the Empire, and as such it could not be left unpunished. Yet he not only ordered the strict observance of the forms of law in dealing with it, but also insisted that all unnecessary harshness and cruelty be avoided. He treated the Christians as men who had been led astray and whom he was trying by merciful measures to induce to return. Trajan indulged the hope that by such means it would be possible to put an end to the pernicious error, if not at once yet gradually at least. But sagacious as this decision and action might appear from the statesman's point of view, they were none the less mistaken. The political and judicial point of view is entirely insufficient for the consideration of this subject. His edict contained a hidden contradiction, which in time must come to light and necessitate additional legislation. Further — and this was the principal mistake — the Emperor had formed no adequate idea of the strength of the faith with which he had thus begun a contest before his tribunals.

Even in the ancient Church the opinions expressed concerning the Emperor Trajan differed widely. Some regarded him as the persecutor and some as the protector of the Church; his edict was by the one party viewed as a sword, by the other as a shield. In truth it was both. It was an edict of persecution, for here for the first time it was distinctly laid down that to be a Christian was in itself a capital crime. Henceforth if any Christian were accused before the tribunal of being such, capital punishment was executed upon him solely on account of his Christianity, though no other misdeeds could be proved against him; and this punishment could be avoided only by denying his faith. But on the other hand the Christian was by no means an outlaw, a regular indictment and a judicial process were necessary for his condemnation. The edict was thus a protection, to the extent that Christians could be punished only by way of a legal trial, so that the law gave to them the same protection as it did to criminals. More, indeed, for the governors were forbidden to admit anonymous accusations or to seek out the Christians by means of the police. Thus Christians might remain in peace so long as no accuser came forward.

But here an internal contradiction appears in the edict itself. Tertullian indeed had a right to exclaim:[8] "What a self-contradictory sentence! He forbids their being sought out, as if they were innocent, and commands that they be punished as if they were guilty." There was a yet greater contradiction in punishing those who confessed that they were Christians, while those who denied their faith by bringing a sacrifice to the heathen gods were to be set at liberty. For if it was a crime to be a Christian, it was also a crime to have been a Christian. Would a thief, for instance, be liberated on his mere promise to steal no more? Yet the Emperor cannot be reproached with this inconsistency. His aim was to suppress Christianity. On that point the edict betrays no vacillation, and contains no contradiction. The being a Christian was clearly designated as a crime which was to be suppressed. But he cherished the hope of succeeding by milder measures, and of reaching thereby with all the more certainty his object, the suppression of Christianity. Because a few had shown themselves ready for recantation, it was supposed that the majority could be persuaded to it in like manner, while the few who remained stubborn could be put out of the way. The calculation was mistaken.

because the self-sacrificing heroism of the Christians was not taken into account; because it was not known that "the blood of the martyrs is the seed of the church."⁹

In spite of the leniency of the edict the position of the Christians was still one of great difficulty. It is true that wholesale executions did not take place. The legends of such executions *are* legends, and transfer to this period what really belonged to a later age. We have even reason to believe that the number who in those times died for their faith was comparatively small. But the sword hung, so to speak, every moment over their heads. They could not hide their faith without denying it. Every occasion called for a confession, and out of every confession an accusation might grow. Nothing more was needed to bring a Christian to trial, than that some one from religious zeal or private spite should inform against him. Instances are given which show that the conduct of the Christians towards the images of the gods, or at public festivals gave occasion for accusation; that workmen informed against their fellows, and men against their wives.

A heathen woman had become converted, and, as a Christian, renounced her former voluptuous life. After trying in vain to win her husband over to the faith, and since on the other hand he used every means to draw her back into his godless life, no course was open to her, but to separate herself from him. Then her husband accused her of being a Christian. She confessed and suffered for her faith.¹⁰ Well-disposed governors exercised extreme leniency, but with definite accusations they could not do otherwise than carry out the existing laws. And when the Christians had enjoyed tranquillity for a time, any day might bring a governor of a different disposition who would act with the greatest severity. In some places the rage of the multitude was kindled against the Christians. At the festivals of their gods, and at the games, incited by the priests or by wandering magicians, and intoxicated with sensual pleasure, the heathen would demand the death of the Christians. In great calamities the Christians were said to have aroused the anger of the gods. "The Christians to the lions!" was then the cry. For indeed the decree of the Emperor had opened the way for the popular fury, though on the other hand it did not satisfy the people's hatred of the Christians, nourished as that was by the most horrible rumors. The Christians were branded by the decree as those who had no right to exist, as enemies of the State and of the gods; and it was difficult to deny to the people, when they earnestly demanded it, the death of these enemies of the gods and of the State. Such was the state of things under Trajan and his successors. Persecution blazed up frequently in different places, sometimes more sometimes less severe, sometimes fanned by the severity of the governor, at others by the rage of the people, sometimes confined within the fixed forms of judicial procedure, while elsewhere these forms gave way to the pressure exerted by an excited mob.

Two facts stand out clearly from the history of this period. First, that persecution had not the power to stop the growth of the Church. Though a few were driven back by fear, though weaklings became deserters, yet on the whole, the Christians showed themselves (to borrow Tertullian's expression [11]) "a people always prepared to die." Among the prominent persons who suffered martyrdom during this period, the names of two, Simeon, bishop of Jerusalem, and Ignatius, bishop of Antioch, have been handed down, who met their death in the reign of Trajan. The former is said to have been a relative of Jesus, a son of Mary the wife of Cleophas (John xix. 25), and to have been crucified when one hundred and twenty years old; the latter was sent to Rome and exposed to the wild beasts. Several martyrs are also mentioned who suffered in the reign of Hadrian. The sinister spirit which overshadowed the Emperor towards the end of his stormy life, and instigated him to deeds of cruelty in his last years, seems to have led him into some isolated acts of persecution, though he appears to have been, apart from these, indifferent to the Christians, whom he regarded as equally foolish and ridiculous with other fanatics. In his reign, Telesphorus, bishop of Rome, suffered martyrdom; the first time, so far as we know, that a Roman bishop fell a victim.[12]

History narrates also the martyrdom of a mother called Symphorosa, which resembles that of the mother of the Maccabees. Her husband Getulius, and her brother Amatius had already been executed as martyrs, when to her and to her seven sons was given the choice: to sacrifice, or to die. She remained firm and answered: "You think then to turn me by fear, but I desire only to rest in peace with my husband Getulius, whom you have put to death for Christ's name's sake." She was drowned, and then her seven sons one after the other suffered death in various ways.[13] In Asia the proconsul Arrius Antoninus (afterwards the Emperor Antoninus Pius) had already condemned many Christians, when one day the Christians appeared in such numbers before his judgment-seat, that he recognized the impossibility of punishing them all. He arrested some from among them and dismissed the rest with the words: "Miserable men, if ye desire to die, have ye not ropes and precipices!"[14] During the reign of Antoninus Pius also, the Christians were now and then molested.

Secondly, it is plain that this judicial action against the Christians became more and more insufficient. As the number of the Christians increased, the fury of the people increased also, and the well-meant attempts of the several governors, and even of the Emperor himself, to confine the persecution strictly within the limits of judicial action were unsuccessful. There is extant a rescript of Hadrian addressed to the Proconsul of Asia, in which he condemns a tumultuous rising against the Christians, which had taken place, and insists upon a regular judicial process for the future. When those in the provinces brought an accusation against the Christians, they must themselves appear before the judgment seat and prove their accusation, but no attention was to be paid to mere petitions and popular clamor, lest the innocent should be punished and informers should have opportunities for extortion.[15] Conscientious governors acted henceforth on this rescript. Vespronius Candidus set a Christian at liberty, saying. that it was illegal to yield to the clamor of the masses. Another governor, Pudens, acted in the same way when he saw from the protocol transmitted to him, that the accused had been set upon with tumult and threats, and explained that he could not legally hear the case without a special accuser. And yet Antoninus Pius had to issue new rescripts of like tenor. There arose in Greece a severe persecution in which Publius, the bishop of

Athens, lost his life.[16] The Emperor sent rescripts to Larissa and to Thessalonica, in which he forbade the introduction of new measures in the treatment of the Christians, and ordered that the limits prescribed by Trajan's edict should be strictly observed.[17] And in all probability this was generally done in the time of Antoninus Pius. His reign was peaceful and happy, and there were no special events to stir up the anger of the people. But the case was different under Marcus Aurelius. Though it has been truly said that under the Antonines the stream of Roman history appears yet once more as a calm and peaceful lake, and then swiftly shoots towards the precipice, yet in the time of Marcus Aurelius we become aware that the waters begin to flow more rapidly. We are come to an epoch in Roman history, which also marks an epoch in the conflict of Christianity.

II. THE INCREASING INFLUENCE OF CHRISTIANITY.

If we glance at the position of Christianity, we shall soon realize what progress it had made. It is true that all trustworthy data for even an approximate estimate of the number of Christians are wanting. Estimates like those of Tertullian — that the Christians of a single province were more numerous than the whole Roman army, which would make a total of about nine million Christians in the Empire, or that Carthage would have to be decimated if all the Christians were to be punished [18] — are worthless, being mere rhetoric. The Christians were certainly not nearly so numerous at that time, and their numbers probably varied a great deal in different countries. In the East the Church had made much greater progress than in the West. By this time it had almost become the national church in Eastern Syria. There Christianity first won a throne in Abgar Bar Manu (A.D. 152–187) whose coins first bore the sign of the cross. It need scarcely be said that elsewhere the Christians formed a decided minority, decreasing towards the West. But never again were they such a despised handful of the uneducated lower classes, as they had been at the beginning of the century. They could already count the illustrious, the rich, and the well-educated among their associates. In the time of Hadrian, Aristides and Quadratus the philosophers went over to Christianity. Later followed Justin, who had studied the heathen philosophy of all the schools, the orator Miltiades, the Roman lawyer Minucius Felix, the learned and eloquent Athenagoras and the Stoic Pantænus "famous for erudition."

The conflict with Heathenism now began in literature also. Christianity had hitherto spread mainly in obscurity, and its adherents, — "a dumb folk babbling only in corners,"[19] as the heathen mockingly called them, — had defended themselves simply by silence and endurance. But now men schooled in classic learning and mighty in eloquence come forward in their writings as the champions of Christianity. The first apologetic essays belong to the reign of Hadrian, and there is extant from the time of the Antonines a rich apologetic literature, which shows what advances Christianity had made in that direction. Justin appeals to the pious Emperor Antoninus and to the truth-loving Marcus Aurelius, his adopted son, in order to demand from the rulers' piety and love of truth justice for "the unjustly hated and persecuted."[20] His second Apology was addressed to the senate and to the whole Roman people, with a boldness regardless of consequences, although he knew and foretold that this defence of a just cause would bring death upon him. Others, like Athenagoras, appeal in a similar manner to the Emperors or directly to the public, for the Apologies addressed to the rulers were intended for a larger audience. To the latter class belong the treatise addressed to Autolycus by Theophilus of Antioch, and the beautiful dialogue *Octavius* by Minucius Felix, in which Christianity was for the first time defended in the Latin language.[21] The former aimed at altering the attitude of the rulers, the latter rather at the conversion of their heathen readers.

The first task of the Apologists was to refute the charges which were made against Christianity; to prove that the Christians were not atheists as they were accused of being, nor guilty of such abominations as the rumors of Thyestean banquets and Œdipodean alliances imputed to them, nor finally enemies of the Emperor and the State. Next in importance was the removal of the general prejudice which the heathen entertained against the new faith. This could be accomplished only by making the heathen acquainted with the nature of Christianity, for most of their prejudices arose from ignorance. Therefore the Apologists clearly explain the doctrines and principles, the customs and usages, and the whole moral aspect of Christianity. They urge in support of its truth the fulfillment of prophecy, the excellence of its doctrines, the influence of the faith on the lives of its adherents, their purity of conduct, their activity in works of love, their silent endurance and the heroism with which they met death.

At this point they assume the offensive; apology

becomes polemic. They put clearly and sharply before the heathen the foolishness of idolatry, the immodest character of the images which were fashioned by depraved artists and cared for by dissolute guardians; the immorality of the myths which constituted the reading of the heathen; the immorality of art which exhibited most shameless displays; finally the fruit of all this as shown in heathen life which was a stagnant pool of immorality — these things were held up before the heathen with the greatest clearness and directness.

But the Apologists did not stop there. They recognized not only that side of Heathenism which is opposed to Christianity, but also that which is favorable to it. Their endeavor was not to make the gulf between Christianity and Heathenism as wide and impassable as they could, but to bring Christianity as near as possible to Heathenism. Therefore they sought out foreshadowings of Christianity in Heathenism, parallels between the teachings of the philosophers and those of Christianity, types and prophecies of it in the heathen world. It may sound strangely to us when Justin Martyr[22] reminds the heathen that they have the figure of the cross, which they so despise, before them everywhere, in their tools, in their windows and doors, in the erect form of man and even in their banners and emblems of victory. But in all this play of fancy by which Justin seeks to present the cross to the heathen as something long known and typically prefigured everywhere in nature and life, there is a deeper meaning. Justin is really following in the path marked out by Paul at Athens, when he took occasion from the inscription of a heathen altar To an unknown God to preach this unknown God to the heathen. But Justin brings forward still another cause for the original destination of man for Christianity, from which spring all these unconscious intimations of Christianity in Heathenism. It is found in the doctrine of the *Logos* (the *word*, John i. 1), of which he makes this application. The Logos was made flesh in Christ, but while the Christians possess as it were the entire Logos, the Lord Jesus Christ, yet fragments of the Logos, sporadic manifestations of it are scattered through the heathen world. There the activity of the Logos has been displayed in the philosophers, poets, and lawgivers. Hence the echoes of Christian truth found in heathen treatises and poems, and the manifold excellences of heathen legislation! Moreover the great men among the heathen, their men of heroic virtue, became what they were through the Logos. All these are as it were fragments of Christianity in Heathenism which should attract the heathen to embrace the perfect whole.[23] Still more definitely is the age of Heathenism recognized as a time of preparation for Christianity in the Epistle to Diognetus.[24] In order to answer the question so often put by the heathen, why God had sent His Son so late, the author explains that the world had first to grow ripe for the mission of Christ. There are indeed Apologists whose writings contain scarcely any thing but polemics; Tatian for instance, who can see in Heathenism only folly and wickedness, and who can discern no good thing in all its products.[25] But such are exceptions.

Speaking generally, there is audible in all the Apologetic writings of the period a tone of winning love, which finds its most beautiful rendering in the noble epistle to Diognetus, to which reference has often been made. The Apologists aimed not to repel but to attract, and for this purpose they made use of every point of contact with Christianity which they could find in Heathenism or in the souls of the heathen. Christianity was viewed by the heathen as something antagonistic to human nature; the Apologists showed that it was the realization of true humanity, for as Tertullian later so beautifully said, "the human soul is naturally Christian." [26]

It would be very interesting to know what impression these Apologies made upon the heathen; but this is denied to us, for a direct trace of their influence is nowhere to be found. Even Celsus, in whose time a number of Apologetic writings were in existence, gives them so little attention that we cannot even tell whether he had read them or not. But this at least is clear, that it was no longer possible to ignore a religion which entered the arena in such a manner. The policy of ignoring Christianity was forever at an end. In the former half of the century the educated heathen had considered it beneath their dignity to concern themselves with the "barbarian superstition." But now this had changed. The philosopher Crescens disputed in Rome concerning the Christian faith with Justin. But, of course, when he could not conquer by argument he resorted to denunciation and sought to confute his antagonist by means of the death sentence from the judge. Fronto, the rhetorician, the teacher of the Emperor Marcus Aurelius, one of the most celebrated men of his time, who was regarded by his contemporaries as an unsurpassed master of eloquence, and worthy of disputing Cicero's pre-eminence, — Fronto felt the necessity of employing his skill in an attack upon Christianity. This was the first heathen controversial work of which we know, but it was soon cast into the shade by the treatise of Celsus, which was far more comprehensive in its scope and based upon actual study of Christianity. Lucian, the popular scoffer, scoffed at Christianity, and even the Emperor could not forbear making occasional mention of it in his *Meditations*. Although the opinions expressed were all unfavorable, some of them full of bitter hatred, yet they bear witness to the fact that Christianity had come to be felt as a force in the mental life of the period.

It was impossible that communities like the Christian churches of that time, possessing such an energy of faith and love, should exist in the midst of the heathen world, without exercising an influence outside their own sphere on the views and lives of those who continued heathen. There was, so to speak, a Christian atmosphere which was diffused around the Church and penetrated ever deeper into the atmosphere of Heathenism so that gradually even there the air of Christianity began to be breathed. But, certain as the assumption is that this diffusion, which resulted from the nature of the case, really took place; yet it is impossible, at least in this period when it had but just begun, to prove its existence, much less to gauge its progress. The process was of too spiritual, intangible a nature to be measured, or to permit the assertion that this or that change in the heathen world took place under the influence of Christianity. There was as yet no outward sign of it. Even in Tertullian's time, several decades later, the towns still wore quite their old heathen aspect, images of the gods were still displayed everywhere in the streets and squares, the shops and houses. But the outward signs of Christianity could not appear until it had become the ruling power. On the other hand we may discover even at this time a series of phenomena in the heathen world which are foreign to the antique spirit, but remarkably akin to the spirit of Christianity.

Let us dwell for a moment on this most interesting fact. According to the spirit of the ancient world a man was not the object of his own life, but served only as a means in realizing the ideal, which was political — the State. Hence a man was worth just so much as he contributed to this ideal. He was nothing in and of himself, but only with reference to his earthly destiny did he count for any thing. For this reason, woman, child, and slave counted for nothing, since they contributed nothing to the ideal of the State. Only the citizen was of any value, he alone had rights. Under Christianity every human being as such is of value entirely apart from his particular destiny on earth. The Holy Spirit seeks the salvation of every soul, and though He establishes a kingdom, the kingdom of God, it is composed of sanctified and blessed individuals. The temple which God is building consists of living stones, and each single stone is also itself a temple. Each individual becomes an end in the common end and goal, God's kingdom. But now — the interesting fact referred to — Heathenism made an approach to Christianity in precisely this characteristic. In contradiction to the genuine and uniform spirit of the ancient world, the individual came more and more to have rights even in the view of the heathen; a human being began with them to have a value as such.

This is seen in the case of woman. The claims of woman gained greater recognition, in respect to the property of married women and in other matters. A husband could now be arraigned by his wife for adultery, no longer only the wife by the husband. The change showed still more plainly in the treatment of children. The Roman of the ancient stamp showed little love and tenderness to his children. Cicero says: "When a child dies young, it is easy to be consoled; if it dies in the cradle no concern is felt about it;" and when a child of his daughter dies he speaks of the event with entire equanimity.[27] How tender, on the other hand, was the feeling of Marcus Aurelius towards his grandchildren! How he grieves when they happen to be sick, and with what anxiety does he speak in his letters of the cough which his dear little Antoninus has. The "little nestling" occupied his thoughts amid all his solicitude about the Empire, and his friend the orator Fronto does not fail to present his greetings to the "little ladies," and to ask Marcus Aurelius "to kiss for him their fat little feet and dainty hands."[28]

Hitherto children had possessed no rights. They were completely in the power of the father, who might do what he pleased with them, even kill or expose them. But at this time the paternal power underwent increasing limitations. Exposed children might according to the ancient law be treated as slaves by those who brought them up. Trajan decreed that they should be free. Alexander Severus allowed to the father the right of reclaiming his child, provided that he repaid the expense of its maintenance. Children began to be the objects of much more care in all respects. Famous philosophers recommended mothers to nurse their children themselves, a practice which had for some time entirely ceased among the higher classes.[29] We find inscriptions in which a mother boasts of having nursed her children herself, or a son eulogizes his mother by inscribing on her tomb that she was also his nurse.[30] The training of children became a favorite theme with authors in this period. Seldom has so much been said and written on this subject as in the age of the Antonines. Poor children too, for the first time, received attention. Hitherto children had been given nothing in the distribution of corn, but now five thousand children received their *tesserœ*. This became the rule in the time of Trajan, but it seems to have occurred before in exceptional cases.

But most remarkable of all were the institutions for bringing up poor children, commenced by Nerva, and greatly extended by Trajan and his successors.[31] The Emperor provided for the care of five thousand children in Rome, and also for a considerable number in other Italian towns and in Africa. From monuments fortunately preserved we gain a tolerably definite idea of this arrangement. The Emperor had lent to the town of Veleia near Placentia funds (1,116,000 *sesterces* = about $55,800) for the improvement of its land. In return a rent of 55,800 *sesterces* (about $2,790) was levied on the land. From this sum 263 boys were to receive 16 *sesterces* each per month (about $9.60 per annum), and 35 girls 12 *sesterces* each per month (about $7.20 per annum), and also two illegitimate children were to be supported. The boys received this support until they were eighteen, when they could take service in the legions; the girls until they were fourteen. Hadrian and the Antonines enlarged these institutions, Commodus and Pertinax abolished them, but they were re-established by Alexander Severus. This charity had, it is true, a prominent political object, as is plain from the fact that the number of boys supported so greatly preponderates. The intention was to furnish a valuable contingent to the army: "nourished by thee they enter thy service," says Pliny in his panegyric on Trajan.[32] Yet this was not simply a political institution, humanity had also a share in it. When Antoninus lost his wife Faustina, he thought that the best way to honor her memory was to found an institution for the support of poor girls (the *puellæ Faustinianæ*); and Alexander Severus established a similar institution in honor of his mother Mammæa (the *pueri Mammæani*).[33]

Persons in private stations began also to found charities of this kind. Pliny, for instance, endowed one in Como with 30,000 *sesterces* per annum (about $1,500).[34] A rich lady provided for the support of one hundred children in Terracina, and gave for that purpose 1,000,000 *sesterces* (about $50,000).[35] All such institutions were hitherto unheard of in the ancient world, and the change in the spiritual atmosphere of the period is most clearly illustrated in a relief on the column of Trajan, which represents the Emperor in the act of distributing gifts to poor children.

From this time the instances of such manifestations of mercy and love become everywhere more numerous, even among the heathen. Pliny gave his nurse an estate which had cost him 100,000 *sesterces* (about $5,000), and provided a dowry for the daughter of one of his friends.[36] He founded libraries or schools for the towns which had claims upon him, since he thought them a greater benefit than gladiatorial shows.[37] Such deeds of philanthropy are also mentioned in inscriptions. A dealer in healing herbs (*aromatarius*), in a little Italian town, left by will to the town 300 jars of drugs and 6,000 *sesterces* (about $300), in order that medicine might be gratuitously dispensed to the poor. Inscribed on a tomb we find these words: "Do good, and thou wilt carry it with thee."[38] Yet such sentiments were far from being general, as may be gathered from the casual remark of Pliny, when he calls the good works we have mentioned "useful but not very popular." The people doubtless still preferred gladiatorial shows.

The condition of the slaves also began to improve. How different was Pliny's treatment of his slaves, from Cato's. While Cato's slaves were compelled to work in chains, and find a sleeping-place among the stalls of the oxen, on Pliny's estates no slave ever worked in chains, but their master permitted them to acquire property, and even ate at the same table with his freedmen. Pliny was not ashamed to give expression to his sorrow over the death of a slave, nor did he restrain his tears, but he takes occasion to say, "I know that not all think as I do, that many see in the death of a slave only a pecuniary loss, and that they think themselves greater and wiser by reason of this lack of feeling."[39] More significant than such utterances of an individual is the fact that the law now began to take the slaves under its protection. Hadrian forbade the arbitrary killing of slaves; they were to be brought to trial, and condemned, if guilty. He prohibited the sale of slaves, male or female, for disgraceful purposes. The *ergastula* were abolished, and the law which had destroyed so many innocent persons, even as late as the time of Nero — namely, that when a master was murdered, and the assassin was not discovered, all slaves under the same roof with the murdered man forfeited their lives — was restricted so that only those were to be executed who were so near their master, that they might have been witnesses of the deed. Further, slaves could in certain cases be admitted as witnesses; they could use their property for the purchase of their freedom, and public slaves were permitted to bequeath by will more than half of their possessions. All this is novel, and when we remember what were the views of Plato and Aristotle and even Cicero, concerning slavery, we recognize the great difference in tone of these words written by Ulpian, the great jurist of the age of the Antonines: "According to natural law, all men are born free; in civil law, it is true, slaves are treated as having no rights; not so, however, by natural law, for by this all men are equal." [40] We often meet, in this period, with similar assertions of the equality of all men, that they are all brothers, all fellow-citizens. Such assertions begin to be common property, and no one gives them more definite expression than the Emperor Marcus Aurelius. "If our intellectual part is common," he says in his *Meditations*, "the reason also, in respect of which we are rational beings, is common: and if this is so, common also is the reason which commands us what to do, and what not to do: if this is so, there is a common law also; if this is so, we are fellow-citizens; if this is so, we are members of some political community; if this is so the world is in a manner a state." [41]

Free labor, too, began gradually to gain ground, and to receive its due honor. This was largely due to the guilds of artisans which were given their freedom by Severus and Caracalla, and soon attained a most flourishing condition. In this direction, also, legislation had become more liberal and humane.

But all this was foreign to the spirit of the classic world. These were the first breathings of a new world, — a new social order. Was this development under the influence of the Christian spirit? and, if so, to what degree? — these are questions as difficult as they are interesting.

Some[42] have believed that we may recognize the fruit of Christianity in this gradual change, which, from this time forward, became ever more perceptible. They place it all to the credit of the Christian Church, and weave from it a wreath of very doubtful glory. Doubtful, because if the Church could then exercise so pervading an influence on heathen life and Roman legislation, it becomes impossible to understand why the complete transformation of the heathen state into a Christian government was so slowly brought to pass. And it is especially worthy of notice that the Christians of that day viewed the matter otherwise. The reforms we have described within Heathenism, in the interests of humanity, did not escape the sharp eye of Tertullian, for he speaks of them in his *Apologeticus.* Yet he does not use them as a proof of the influence of Christianity, but, assuming their independent heathen origin, adduces them to show, according to his favorite argument, that in this direction, no less than in others, there is, in the natural order of development, a current which sets towards Christianity; that, to use his own expression, "the soul is Christian by nature." If we remember that this whole change in the views of the heathen commenced before any influence from the spirit of Christianity could be thought of, that it may be traced back even to Augustus; if we note that its source is clearly to be recognized in the then prevalent Stoic philosophy; and if we realize, as is implied in the statement just made, that there was a great difference between this humane reform and the new life infused by Christianity; then we can no longer remain in doubt of the real nature of this reform. It was an independent development in which the heathen world took a step to meet Christianity, just as we have seen that in Heathenism a Universalism sprang up which prepared the way for the universal claims of Christianity. In this also we see the way in which God led the heathen towards His Son, and here too we recognize that "the fulness of the time was come."

But if this was a movement entirely apart from the influence, and parallel to the course of Christianity, the further question arises: at what point is the confluence of the two currents, where does the course of Heathenism come under the control of the progress of Christianity and coalesce with it? Of course the exact point cannot be determined with certainty; for such spiritual currents make a hidden, a subterranean course, so to speak, long before they become visible and traceable. The influence of Christianity on Heathenism cannot be traced in the time of Marcus Aurelius. We find no evidence of it in Celsus, in whom if anywhere it would show itself. Celsus, though he is forced against his will to recognize the power of Christianity, yet occupies a position of unqualified opposition to it. But only a few decades later the influence of Christianity on Heathenism gives most striking proofs of its existence. In the receptions of Julia Domna, the talented consort of the Emperor, Septimius Severus, who drew around her a circle of philosophers, rhetoricians and jurists, it was recognized that Christianity contained many elements in which Heathenism was deficient, and the question was discussed how these advantages of Christianity could be transferred to Heathenism. This circle produced the remarkable book of Philostratus, the biography of Apollonius of Tyana, in which characteristics drawn from the portrait of the despised Jesus are transferred to the heathen Prophet, — not to call him the heathen Messiah. But if the influence of Christianity on heathen modes of thought can from this time no longer be denied, then, in my view at least, it is not rash to assume that even in the time of Marcus Aurelius a silent, intangible and yet really existing influence was at work.

But even if the existence of such an influence be utterly denied in this period, there are not wanting other signs of the extent to which Christianity had become a power. The heathen world trembled for the first time with the fear that this Christianity hitherto so thoroughly despised might gain the ascendancy. It is only necessary to read Celsus in order to perceive the anxiety with which he already viewed the numbers of the Christians to which he often alludes. He even imagines the possibility of their controlling affairs, and can then see in the future nothing but a frightful catastrophe in which the Empire would be wrecked. The Barbarians would conquer the Emperor deserted by his subjects, and usurp the supremacy, and no smallest vestige of the Christian worship or of the true wisdom would remain.[43] It was this anxiety which arose spontaneously among the heathen, the half-felt consciousness that they were already under the ban of the new faith, which at this time roused to the utmost the rage of the people against the Christians. Great calamities came upon the Empire in the reign of Marcus Aurelius. In the East the Parthians crossed the frontier, and laid waste the country. When the Emperor had been successful in driving back the foe, and even regaining Mesopotamia, which had been given up by Hadrian, the army brought back with it from the East a terrible plague, which traversed the entire Empire, carried off countless multitudes, and left whole districts completely desolate. To this succeeded a not less terrible famine, and when the strength and courage of the people had been enfeebled by the united pestilence and famine, war broke out along the Danube with the Marcomanni, a war which proved one of the severest in which Rome ever engaged. These were the first waves of the migration of the nations, which, threatening the destruction of the Empire, were beating against its frontiers. In this time of distress the heathen sought help from their gods, and the Emperor himself instituted expiatory sacrifices and offerings. The people, excited to fanaticism, saw in their misfortunes the anger of the gods, which the Christians were supposed to have incurred. More zealously than ever before were spread the rumors of the revolting crimes of the Christians, which found an apparent confirmation in occasional confessions wrung from them by torture, and which even to a man like Fronto were the most weighty charge against them. Such godless men must be utterly destroyed in order to appease the anger of the gods.

The Christians on their part made their appeal to the Emperors' love of justice. The object of their entreaties and demands was not as yet recognition, not yet complete religious freedom. The thought of these was yet in the background and was first made prominent by the Apologists of the third century. Before this the Christians asked only that the justice of the Emperors would put an end to the unjust persecutions and condemnations. "In behalf of those men of all nations who are unjustly hated and oppressed, I, Justin, . . . being one of them, have composed this address and petition. . . . Since then you are universally termed pious and philosophers and guardians of justice and lovers of learning, it shall now be seen whether you are indeed such. For we have not come to flatter you by these writings of ours, nor to seek to please by our address; but to make our claim to be judged after a strict and searching inquiry; so that neither by prejudice nor desire of popularity from the superstitious, nor by any unthinking impulse of zeal, nor by that evil report which has so long kept possession of your minds, you may be urged to give a decision against yourselves. For it is our maxim that we can suffer harm from none, unless we be convicted as doers of evil, or proved to be wicked. You may, indeed, slay us, but hurt us you cannot. But, lest any should say that this is a senseless and rash assertion, I entreat that the charges against us may be examined; and, if they be substantiated, let us be punished as is right. But if no man can convict us of any crime, true reason does not allow you through a wicked report to wrong the innocent, or rather yourselves, who are disposed to direct affairs not by judgment but by passion."[44] This plea was well founded; and the Christians were too fully persuaded of the justice of their cause, not to expect justice from an Emperor like Marcus Aurelius. They were mistaken. It was under Marcus Aurelius that the persecution grew more severe than ever before. They asked for peace, and the Emperor by reason both of his personal attitude and of the situation of the Empire could not give them any other answer than war.

III. THE PERSECUTION UNDER MARCUS AURELIUS.

Marcus Aurelius was one of the best Emperors who ever ascended the Roman throne. Great earnestness and an almost excessive conscientiousness are the principal traits of his character. He was Emperor from a sense of duty, because the Gods had placed him at that post, and he must therefore occupy it. The imperial dignity was for him an office which he must administer, and this he did gratuitously, for his personal wants were supplied from his private purse. To preserve peace of soul amid all the vicissitudes of life, and his life contained many; to be true to himself, just and merciful towards others; to be moderate in all things, and to follow the voice of conscience regardless of men's praise or blame, — such were the duties he required from himself. Till the end of his life he toiled at the elevation of his own moral character. His *Meditations*, twelve books "addressed to himself," a kind of diary which he wrote in part amid the turmoil of war "in the land of the Quadi," bear witness to this. In them he sets before himself a lofty ideal, and it must be allowed that he earnestly strove to realize it. Man is in his view a being created for disinterested activity, and lies under an obligation to labor unweariedly for the good of his fellows, regardless of gratitude or reward. " When thou hast done a good act, and another has received it, why dost thou still look for a third thing besides these, as fools do, either to have the reputation of having done a good act or to obtain a return?" "Art thou not content that thou hast done something conformable to thy nature, and dost thou seek to be paid for it? Just as if the eye demanded a recompense for seeing or the feet for walking." All men, he often emphatically lays down, are brothers; even wicked men are only erring ones, who act in opposition to their better selves. " Men exist for the sake of one another. Teach them, then, or bear with them."[45] And this very Emperor who would have men tolerate the wicked as erring brethren, and whose administration of justice was so painfully conscientious, that he would spend whole days in the investigation of a single case, in order to be certain of not wronging any one, — this Emperor was destined to be one of the most determined persecutors of the Christians, that is, do the greatest of wrongs to the best of men.

Marcus Aurelius was a Stoic, and though the virtue of humility was foreign to the entire antique world, of the Stoic philosophy we may say that its very life was pride. The Emperor's religion was a fatalistic Pantheism; Nature was his God. "Every thing harmonizes with me, which is harmonious to thee, O Universe! Nothing for me is too early or too late, which is in due time for thee. Every thing is fruit to me which thy seasons bring, O Nature! from thee are all things, in thee are all things, to thee all things return." In proud resignation to the decisions of fate he sought his peace. " Willingly give thyself up to Clotho, allowing her to spin thy thread into whatever things she pleases." Marcus Aurelius believed that he could realize his moral ideal by his own power. He believed in himself and at bottom in himself only. "It is sufficient to attend to the dæmon (good Genius) within, and to reverence him sincerely." The sage holds intimate communion with him who is enshrined within. "Bear it constantly in mind that thou must exhibit the steadfast character which becomes a man." "And further let the deity which is in thee be the guardian of a living being, manly and of ripe age, and engaged in matter political, and a Roman, and a ruler, who has taken his post like a man waiting for the signal which summons him from life, and ready to go, having need neither of oath nor of any man's testimony." We can distinctly hear in this the Pharisaical tone: "God, I thank thee that I am not as other men are." "Call to recollection," he soliloquizes, "that the history of thy life is now complete, and thy service is ended: and how many beautiful things thou hast seen; and how many pleasures and pains thou hast despised; and how many things called honorable thou hast spurned; and to how many ill-minded folks thou hast shown a kind disposition." [46]

A man who took this attitude could only reject the story of the cross, the gospel of grace for sinners. Marcus Aurelius was far too much of a slave to his philosophic theories, far too thoroughly steeped in the prejudices of the schools, to be able to give a hearing to the artless message of salvation. He was far too proud and cold to receive from the Christians' joy in their faith, any other impression than that of fanaticism. And in his *Meditations* he thus speaks of Christianity: "What a soul that is which is ready, if at any moment it must be separated from the body, and ready either to be extinguished or dispersed or continue to exist; but so that this readiness comes from a man's own judgment, not from mere obstinacy, as with the Christians, but considerately and with dignity and in a way to persuade another, without tragic show."[47] How far above the Christian martyrs, the Emperor evidently thought himself! Of what led them to death, he had no conception. He can hardly have known more of Christianity than what was conveyed to him by hearsay, and what Fronto, his teacher and friend, may have told him of it.

It is significant for the position of Marcus Aurelius, that Fronto, the first literary antagonist of Christianity, was so intimate with him. Fronto was a learned man, an advocate of the then fashionable Renaissance. The revival of the antique was the fashion. Ennius was rated above Virgil, Cato's style preferred to that of Cicero. Fronto was a rhetorician. He was better supplied with words than with ideas. The form of what he had to say was finished to the last degree; the less there was to be said, the more energy was spent in declamation. Yet Fronto was a thoroughly honorable man, humane, a willing servant, faithful to his friends even in misfortune, not lacking in feeling, so far as his rhetoric left room for it. He was no zealot; he held tenaciously but with a certain coldness and tranquillity to a belief in the gods, in providence, and in a joyful life after death. Predominant in his character is the proud self-consciousness of the Stoic. When aged and sickly, deeply sorrowing over the death of his wife, and afflicted by the loss of five children, he yet could write these words:[48] "That which consoles me is that my life is near its end and goal. When death comes I will freely display my conscience, and give to myself the testimony that in all my life I have done nothing for which I needed to blush, or reproach myself, as being a blemish or a cause of shame. No trace of avarice or unfaithfulness has been discoverable in me, but on the contrary numerous acts of liberality, of affection, of fidelity, and of courage often with peril of my life. I have lived in the most intimate union with the best of my brethren. The honors which I have attained have not been sought by evil ways. I have put care for my soul before carefulness for the body, and the pursuit of knowledge before that of my own interests. I have been poor rather than ask the help of others, I have suffered want rather than beg. I have not spent my superfluous possessions with prodigality, but at times I have freely bestowed that which was necessary to me. I have sought truth conscientiously, and have heard it gladly. I have preferred to be forgotten rather than to flatter, to be silent rather than to dissemble, to be a slack friend rather than a zealous courtier. I have put forward few claims, but not few nor small have been my merits. I have been zealous to help those who deserved help, and not slow to help those who did not deserve it, and the scant gratitude which I have received has not made me unwilling to do others as much good as I could." A man who at the end of his life made such a confession as this, must naturally find the gospel of the Saviour of sinners incomprehensible. He felt no need of a Saviour, and when he came in contact with Him, it could be only to oppose Him. But Fronto is only a type of the age. Many more held the same views, especially among those who stood nearest to the Emperor. Philosophy, long looked upon with suspicion and often persecuted by earlier Emperors, had now come into power. A philosopher sat upon the imperial throne, philosophers filled the highest offices of the State and governed the provinces. For the Church such a condition of affairs could only mean not peace but war.

But entirely aside from his personal sympathies or antipathies, the political views and aims of the Emperor must have made him the enemy of Christianity. For him the State was supreme. "The end of rational animals," he asserts, "is to follow the reason and the law of the most ancient city and polity." "That which is not good for the swarm, neither is it good for the bee." It is a law of the universe to sacrifice the part to the whole, so too in the State. Those who disturbed the union of the citizens were rebels, in the eyes of the Emperor. He had no conception of an individual conscience, nor of what it demands. He was a Roman; the restoration of Roman virtue and thus of the Roman State, this was his chief ambition. "Every moment think steadily as a Roman and a man to do what thou hast in hand . . . ,"[49] he exhorts himself. Thus Christianity presented itself to him as nothing but an anti-Roman superstition, which must be done away with, in order to make room for the true Roman spirit.

During the first years of the reign of Marcus Aurelius the Christians' position remained the same as before. Trajan's regulations were still the standard for all proceedings against them, except that the many calamities which had come upon the Empire had excited the fanaticism of the heathen to greater fierceness, and the authorities opposed less resistance to the demands of the people. A persecution flamed up with peculiar fury in Asia Minor, and in it Polycarp, the last of those who had been taught by the apostles, suffered martyrdom. The Proconsul had already yielded to the popular clamor so far as to execute a number of Christians by torture, or by exposure to the wild beasts, or by burning at the stake, when the multitude assembled in the amphitheatre demanded in addition the death of Polycarp. "Away with the Atheists! Search for Polycarp!" with shouts like these they besieged the Proconsul. Polycarp had withdrawn to an estate near the city, and, when he was sought there, escaped to another; yet two slaves were captured, one of whom under torture betrayed the retreat of the bishop. When the soldiers sent to take him prisoner approached the villa, Polycarp was in the upper story, and might easily have fled from there to the roof of the next house. But when urged to do this, he refused, and quietly went down to deliver himself up to the soldiers. He asked only a single hour for prayer. But he remained two hours in rapt devotion, so that even the heathen were moved by it.

Then the aged bishop was conveyed to the city on an ass. On the way he was met by the chief of the police, who took him up into his carriage, and said in a friendly manner: "What harm can there be in saying: 'The Emperor, our Lord!' and in sacrificing?" Polycarp at first was silent; but when they urged him, he quietly answered: "I shall not do as you advise." Then with abuse they thrust him so violently out of the carriage, as to injure one of his legs. But he went onward cheerfully as if nothing had happened. In the circus the Proconsul was awaiting him, surrounded by an immense multitude of people who had flocked thither at the news that Polycarp was captured. The Proconsul at first reminded him of his great age, and urged him to regard it, and show his penitence by swearing by the Genius of the Emperor, and joining in the cry: "Away with the Atheists!" The bishop looked with a steadfast countenance on the tumultuous crowd, and pointing to them with his finger, raised his eyes to heaven, and said: "Away with the Atheists!" Then the Proconsul urged him further: "Swear, and I release thee, revile Christ!" Then Polycarp answered: "Eighty and six years have I served him, and he has never done me a wrong; how can I blaspheme him, my King, who has saved me?" When the Proconsul yet again pressed him: "Swear by the Genius of the Emperor!" Polycarp replied: "If thou cherishest the vain thought that I will swear by the Genius of the Emperor, as thou sayest, and pretendest not to know who I am, hear it plainly: I am a Christian!" This was the decisive word, and the trial was properly at an end. Nevertheless the Proconsul still sought to save him, if he would only persuade the people to desist from their demands. But Polycarp refused: "To thee I owed an answer, for we are taught to pay due honor to the powers ordained of God, but those men I do not think the proper persons to hear my defence." In vain the Proconsul now threatened him with the wild beasts and the stake. Polycarp remained true to his confession, and so the Proconsul caused it to be proclaimed: "Polycarp has confessed himself to be a Christian." Hardly had the herald made the proclamation, when the whole multitude cried out: "This is the teacher of impiety,[50] the father of the Christians, the enemy of our gods, who teaches so many not to sacrifice, nor to worship the gods." They rushed in a body to Philip, the Asiarch, who had charge of the public games, and demanded that he should let loose a lion upon Polycarp. When he refused, because the games were already finished, they clamored for him to be burned. With all speed they collected wood from the workshops and baths near by, and made a pile. Polycarp was unwilling to be fastened to the stake. "Leave me thus," he said: "He who strengthens me to endure the fire will also enable me to stand firm at the stake without being fastened with nails." Then after he had prayed with a loud voice: "Lord God Almighty, Father of our Lord Jesus Christ, I praise Thee that Thou hast judged me worthy of this day and of this hour, to participate in the number of Thy witnesses and in the cup of Thy Christ," he was consumed by the flames. This took place on the 6th of April, A. D. 166.[51]

About the same time Justin sealed the testimony given in his Apology by his martyrdom.[52] When he wrote the second Apology, he was already aware of what awaited him. He narrates the executions of several Christians, which had given the occasion for the Apology, and then adds: "I too expect to be taken in their snares, and impaled."[53] He knew that the philosopher Crescens longed to be revenged upon him and had daily before his eyes proofs of how easy it was to procure the death of a Christian. Crescens denounced him, and with several other Christians he was brought before Junius Rusticus, the Prefect of the city. Justin quietly explained who he was, and what was his occupation, that he had himself sought and found the truth, and that now when any one came to him he communicated to him the teachings of the truth. "Art thou not then a Christian?" asked the Prefect, and Justin replied: "Yes; I am a Christian." After the rest had made the same confession, the Prefect turned again to Justin, and asked mockingly: "Listen, thou who art called learned, and believest that thou knowest the true doctrines, art thou persuaded that when thou shalt have been scourged and beheaded, thou wilt then ascend into heaven?" — "I hope," replied Justin, "to receive Christ's gracious gift, when I shall have endured all those things." — "Thou really thinkest, then, that thou wilt ascend into heaven, and there receive a recompense?" asked the Prefect yet more scornfully. "I not merely think so, but I know and am thoroughly convinced of it," answered Justin. This must have seemed perfect madness to the Prefect. He did not think it worth while to parley with such people. "To come to the point, advance together, and unite in sacrificing to the gods!" — "No right-minded man will leave the worship of God for its opposite," was the answer. "If ye do not obey, ye must suffer punishment without mercy," threatened the Prefect, but the Christians responded with cheerful courage: "Do what you will, we are Christians, and do not sacrifice to idols." Then the Prefect pronounced the sentence: "Since they are such as do not sacrifice to the gods, nor obey the command of the Emperor, let them be scourged and executed according to the laws." Giving praise to God, the martyrs went to the place of execution, where, after being scourged, they were beheaded with the axe.

When we bear in mind that we have detailed accounts of the persecution only so far as it dealt with prominent men like Polycarp and Justin, but that besides these, as may be inferred from many scattered indications, a large number of nameless victims suffered for their Lord, the position of the Christians will appear to have been distressing enough, even in the first years of the reign of Marcus Aurelius. But it was destined to become much worse. We can easily guess what induced the Emperor, for the first time, to go beyond the regulations of Trajan. The situation of the Empire grew more and more gloomy. True, the Parthians were subdued, but pestilence and famine devastated the Empire, while the war along the Danube was carried on with varying success, and demanded the greatest exertions. That the Romans suffered severe defeats may be gathered from the fact that later, when the war was ended, the Iazyges restored one hundred thousand Roman prisoners. Once the Emperor and his whole army came near being taken prisoners by the Quadi. The rescue is said to have come in answer to the prayer of the XIIth. Legion, which was almost entirely composed of Christians. When all seemed lost, the Christians prayed to their God. Then came a terrible storm, the rain refreshed the legions, which were perishing with thirst, and, amid thunder, lightning, and hail, which fell upon the enemy, the Quadi were routed. The story, in this form, is only a legend; for it can be proved that the XIIth. Legion bore the name *Fulminata* (which was said to have come from this event) as far back as the times of Nerva and Trajan. The historical part of it is only that the army of the Emperor, in great straits, in danger of perishing from thirst, was saved by a sudden and heavy rain-storm. Heathen accounts and contemporaneous monuments ascribe the rescue to heathen gods, specially to Jupiter Pluvius. On the part of the Christians, no doubt the above legend sprang up at the same time, since it is mentioned even by Tertullian.[54]

While this war was still undecided, a new danger threatened the Emperor, from the East. Avidius Cassius, the conqueror of the Parthians, rebelled, and was proclaimed Emperor. As he was unquestionably superior to the Emperor as a general, and possessed an energetic character, he might, at the head of the Oriental army, have proved a dangerous rival. Marcus Aurelius accordingly concluded a rather unfavorable peace with the Danubian tribes as speedily as possible, and hastened eastward. Avidius Cassius was assassinated when the Emperor was still a long way off, and thus that danger was removed; but the Emperor nevertheless considered it necessary to pursue his march, in order to re-establish his authority in the East. The impressions there received do not seem to have been cheering; at all events, the Emperor's melancholy disposition grew upon him from this time, and, in particular, he became peculiarly zealous in heathen rites, a trait which had not previously characterized him to such a degree. He instituted great lustrations and sacrifices everywhere, and, in Greece, was initiated into the mysteries. But in Greece the hunt after Christians was just then most vigorously prosecuted. "For what reason, men of Greece," Tatian complains, "do you wish to bring the civil powers, as in a pugilistic encounter, into collision with us? And why . . . am I to be abhorred as a vile miscreant?"[55] From the writings of Celsus, we can see what aspect of the case was probably laid before the Emperor. The Christians were responsible for the distress of the Empire; they alone refused the State their assistance at a time when all sources of strength must be drawn upon, in order to resist the foe. The rapid growth of the Church was pointed out, and the large numbers who already were Christians. If this were to proceed at the same rate (it was stated), the Emperor would soon stand alone, and the Empire become the prey of the barbarians. Such words would find a ready acceptance with the Emperor, whose antipathy to the Christians would not fail to be fostered by his teachers and friends, Fronto and the city prefect Junius Rusticus who is so often named in connection with the persecution of the Christians. The restoration of Roman virtue, and of the Roman Empire, still floated before him as the supreme object of his life; but, if that goal was to be reached, these false Romans must be extirpated.

Therefore Marcus Aurelius issued a rescript [56] which went far beyond the regulations of Trajan. We do not know its exact tenor, but Melito calls it barbarously cruel. Though a general persecution was not directly ordered, yet the decree that the accusers of the Christians should come into possession of their property practically instigated an almost universal persecution. For not only were accusations multiplied by persons in private life who coveted the property of the Christians, but the officials themselves made haste to earn the reward of Judas. Now, as never before, the Christians were sought out everywhere, brought to trial, often executed with the greatest cruelty, and their property confiscated.

We gain an idea of how much more severe this was than all previous persecutions, when we read the letter in which the churches of Lugdunum (Lyons) and Vienne narrate the story of their sufferings.[57] The people began by insulting the Christians, throwing stones at them, and plundering their houses. Next a number were imprisoned, and the attempt was made to extort confessions from them by means of various tortures and torments. Most of them held out; but a few apostatized, to the great sorrow of the Church. Worse than this, slaves of Christian masters stated on the rack that the stories of atrocities practised by the Christians in secret were true. Thus the proofs of impiety were secured, and the rage of the heathen rose to the highest pitch. They sought by the most horrible tortures to extract the same disclosures from the Christians. They were tormented the whole day long, till the executioners were weary, but they remained true to their faith. Blandina, a delicate maiden, to all the questions answered only: "I am a Christian! Among us no wickedness is committed," and still repeated this response when every species of torture had been tried on her, and, bleeding and mangled, she scarcely continued to breathe. Ponticus, a boy, notwithstanding his youth (he was but fifteen), bore all the tortures unflinchingly. His own sister stood by his side, and exhorted him to steadfastness. Pothinus, the bishop of Lyons, a man over ninety years old, in reply to the legate's question, "Who is the God of the Christians?" hurled back the bold answer, "If thou art worthy thou shalt know." He was tortured so severely that he died in prison two days afterwards. Even those who had at first recanted were so inspired by these examples, that they summoned courage to re-affirm their faith. Since there were Roman citizens among the accused, the legate sent for orders from Rome; and, by command of the Emperor, the Roman citizens died by the sword, while the rest were thrown to the wild beasts. From far and near the heathen flocked together to this spectacle. All the condemned met their death with great joy; and the last to suffer was Blandina, who had been a spectator of the deaths of all the rest, and had encouraged and exhorted the brethren. With joy and thanksgiving she entered the arena as though she were going to her nuptials instead of to be thrown to the wild beasts. Enclosed in a net she was exposed to the fury of a wild bull, and, after being several times tossed into the air from its horns, was put to death. Even the heathen conceded that never woman among them had shown such endurance, and the Church added, "Thus the Lord glorified himself in those who seemed weak and insignificant in the eyes of the world." The bodies of the martyrs were burned, and their ashes thrown into the Rhone. "Now we shall see if they will rise again," said the heathen mockingly.

The picture here spread before us was only a single scene of this terrible drama. In vain did the Apologists, Melito, Miltiades, and Athenagoras lift up their voices. The persecution extended throughout the entire empire, an early prelude of the subsequent general persecutions. "The demon" (of the Christians), Celsus exultingly asserts, "is not only reviled, but banished from every land and sea, and those who like images are consecrated to him are bound and led to punishment and impaled (*or* crucified), whilst the demon — or, as you call him, the Son of God — takes no vengeance on the evil doer." Celsus saw in this the fulfilment of the saying of Apollo's priest: "The mills of the gods grind late," and he scornfully points to the fate of the worshippers of the one God. "They (the Jews), instead of being masters of the whole world, are left with not so much as a patch of ground or a hearth; and of you (the Christians) one or two may be wandering in secret, but they are being sought out to be punished with death."[58]

IV. THE FIRST SIGNS OF VICTORY.

In all his exultation over the destruction of the Christians, Celsus must still have felt that this persecution had not exterminated them, and would not do so. Otherwise why did he choose just this time to make a literary attack on them? For, in all probability, the famous, or rather infamous, treatise which he published under the title, "A True Discourse," belongs to this very time. It is no longer extant in a perfect form (in later times Christian zeal considered its destruction a duty), but yet we can reconstruct it with tolerable completeness from the reply of Origen. In reading it we are filled with astonishment; not simply because Celsus evidently has so accurate a knowledge of Christianity, and is well read in both the Old and New Testaments; nor yet because of the almost unequalled measure of venomous hatred which he displays, chiefly against Christ himself: but principally because of the acuteness with which this heathen philosopher hit upon the really decisive issue; and yet more, because in this, the oldest polemical writing against the Christian faith whose contents we know, every argument is to be found which has been brought against it up to the present time.

According to a carefully laid plan, Celsus begins by representing Christianity as combated by a Jew, and then afterwards himself comes forward to attack both Judaism and Christianity. In this way he is enabled not only to make capital out of the Jewish hatred of Christ, and all the lies concerning him promulgated by it, but also to use Judaism as a foil to Christianity, in order to make the latter appear still worse and more worthless. Judaism indeed was an apostasy from the religion of the fathers, but it was at least a national faith, it contained an element of patriotism; but Christianity, on the contrary, which arose out of another apostasy, from Judaism, and thus capped the climax of folly, was sheer sedition, open rebellion.

As we have already indicated, the hatred of Celsus was chiefly displayed against our Lord Himself. He found in Him nothing that is good. He regarded Him as merely a common swindler and charlatan. Born of a poor peasant-woman, who had to spin for her living, and who lived in adultery with a soldier, Panthera by name, He learnt the magic art in Egypt, and by means of it gained some adherents from the lowest classes, publicans and fishermen. He deceived them into the belief that He was the Son of God and born of a virgin, led with them the life of a wretched outcast; finally (so small was His power even over His own adherents) He was betrayed by one of His disciples, denied by another, and came to a cowardly and shameful end. This "pestilent fellow," "boaster," "magician," never did any thing great, but only practised a few magic arts, and even in these was inferior to others. He did many evil and wicked actions, only Celsus is unable to say just what they were. The stories told of Him in the Gospels are founded partly on His own lies, partly on those of His disciples. It is true He is said to have predicted His suffering, and also the betrayal and the denial, but (Celsus explains) the very fact that it so came to pass is itself a proof that it could not have been predicted. For, how could those to whom it had been predicted out of His own mouth, yet betray and deny Him? If He as God predicted it, then it must so happen, and those who did it were led into this impiety by Himself, the God. And if it was necessary that it should so happen, and He obediently submitted Himself to the will of His Father, why then did He so lament and ask for help in Gethsemane? It may be true that He told His disciples He would rise again, but others have made similar vain boasts. Besides we learn, from the myths, of men who have risen again. All such stories are pure myths. " Or do you suppose the statements of others both are myths and are so regarded, while you have invented a becoming and credible catastrophe to your drama in the voice from the cross when He expired and in the earthquake and the darkness? That while alive He was of no assistance to Himself, but that when dead He rose again and showed the marks of His punishment, and how His hands were pierced with nails: who beheld this? A half-crazy woman, as you state, and some other one perhaps of those who were engaged in the system of delusion, who had either dreamed so, owing to a peculiar state of mind, or under the influence of a wandering imagination had formed to himself an appearance according to his own wishes, which has been the case with numberless individuals; or, which is most probable, one who desired to impress others with this portent and by such a falsehood to furnish an occasion to impostors like himself." [59] If He had really risen, Celsus asserts, He would certainly have appeared before His judges and the public in general; and he finds it very strange that Jesus during His life preached to all, and found no acceptance, but that when He had risen, and could so easily have induced all to believe on Him, He appeared only to one insignificant woman and to His associates, and that secretly and timidly.[60] We hardly need to point out that here we have the very same things which are promulgated at the present day as the surest results of the most recent science. Here we have Renan's "*femme hallucinée*," the hypothesis of visions most completely developed; and besides, in order that the other theory, which boasts that it is the properly spiritual conception, may not be omitted, Celsus in other places concedes that the dead Christ may have truly appeared, not as one risen in bodily form, but as a ghost.

We have seen that the hatred which Celsus cherished against Christianity had its root in the fact that the God of the Christians is a sinners' God, and that Christianity was a religion of the poor, the slaves, the miserable. A God who takes pity upon sinners, and on the other hand turns away from proud and self-reliant souls, seemed to the heathen to reverse all conceptions of God. The gods of the heathen neither give nor receive love, and the strict justice attributed to them makes forgiveness impossible. Therefore Celsus directs his polemic principally against this God, who takes the part of the wretched, who stretches out His arms towards those who suffer and weep, and who does not repulse even the guilty.

He regards as the central point of all Christianity (and rightly) the belief that God has really come down from heaven to redeem men. In the eyes of the philosopher this belief is the most absurd thing conceivable.

"'What is the meaning of such a descent on the part of God unless in order to learn what goes on among men? Does He then not know all?' Then as if we (the Christians) answered, 'He does know all,' he raises a new question, saying, 'Then He does know all things, but does not improve their condition, nor is it possible for Him by divine power to do so ... without sending some one in bodily form for that purpose.'"[61] If He descended then He must have left His place in heaven empty, and His coming into the world would bring a revolution, "for if thou shouldest change a single thing, even the smallest on earth, all would be overturned and go to ruin."

But Celsus attempts a yet more serious attack on this principal article of the Christian faith. It is founded on the belief of the Christians that the world was made for the sake of men, and they are special objects of God's care. This seems to him so ridiculous that he compares the whole tribe of Jews and Christians to frogs and worms who hold an assembly by a puddle, and quarrel. The frogs say, "God first reveals every thing to us, and tells it beforehand, and He forsakes the whole earth and the celestial sphere, and dwells only in our midst." Then the worms rejoin: "There is one God, and next to Him we come, who have derived our being from Him, and are in all respects like Him, and every thing is subject to us, earth, water, air, and stars; all things exist for our sake, and were arranged to accommodate us! And now, since some of us transgress, God will come or send His Son to burn the unjust and to give the rest of us eternal life with Him."[62] Celsus declares that it is pride to suppose that God made all things for man's sake. From natural history, from the acute faculties of many animals, it may be shown that all things were created as much for them as for man. Celsus even labors to show that animals in many respects stand higher than men, and that men are in subjection to animals. The bees have a ruler and build towns, the ants lay up for the winter and bury their dead, the snakes and the eagles understand magic arts. The birds foresee the future and give signs of it in their flight. Not even is piety a prerogative of man. No beings are more faithful to an oath than the elephants, and the storks surpass men in piety.

In fine — and this is the culmination of his argument — Celsus denies that the world has any purpose at all. "Therefore all things accordingly were not made for man any more than they were made for lions or eagles or dolphins, but that this world, as being God's work, might be perfect and entire in all respects. For this reason all things have been adjusted not with reference to each other, but with regard to their bearing upon the whole. And God takes care of the whole, and his providence will never forsake it; and it does not become worse; nor does God after a time bring it back to himself; nor is he angry on account of men any more than on account of apes and flies. Nor does he threaten these beings, each one of whom has received its appointed lot in its proper place." The world, he explains in another place, remains ever the same. "There neither were formerly, nor are there now, nor will there be again, more or fewer evils in the world. For the nature of all things is one and the same, and the generation of evils is always the same."[63] Indeed, if Celsus had been right Christianity would have been refuted in its very foundation, for that is nothing other than the belief in this divine deed, that God has taken the part of the human race, and has redeemed and restored a sinful world by the sending of his Son.

There is a very striking coincidence here between the most ancient antagonist of Christianity and Strauss, its most modern foe. Just as with Celsus, so with Strauss, the principal argument against Christianity is the impenetrable connection of the order of nature; and like the former, so the latter finally arrives at denying any design in the world. Its purpose is that it is. There will come, he explains, a time when the earth will no longer be inhabited, yea, when the very planet will no longer exist, and when not only all earthly things, all human occupations and achievements, all nationalities, works of art and science, shall have vanished, but not even a recollection of it all shall endure in any spirit, since with this earth, its history must naturally perish. Then either the earth has failed to accomplish its purpose, since nothing has been evolved in its existence, or that purpose did not consist in any thing which should endure, but was accomplished at every moment of the world's development. Like Celsus, Strauss denies any improvement or deterioration in the world. The same statement which we have just read in Celsus, we read again in "The Old Faith and the New" by Strauss.[64] "The universe is in no succeeding moment more perfect than in the preceding, nor *vice versa.*" So exactly indeed do these two antagonists of Christianity agree, that, like Celsus, Strauss endeavors to obliterate the distinction between man and animal. "The chasm between man and animal," he says, "was first opened by Judaism which is hostile to the gods of nature, and by Christianity which is dualistic;" and it sounds like the voice of Celsus when we read: "the more carefully the life and habits of any species of animals are observed, the more does the observer find reason to speak of their understanding. . . . A kind of sense of honor, a sort of conscience, is hardly to be ignored in the better bred and cared-for horses and dogs." Strauss discovers even "the rudiments of the higher moral faculties" in animals, and bees, ants, and elephants play the same parts in his argument, as with Celsus.[65]

It has seemed of interest for once to bring out the parallel between this time of the Church's conflict and the present day, which I have elsewhere purposely refrained from doing. Do the modern enemies of our faith know of no objections to bring forward, except those which were advanced by our first antagonist seventeen hundred years ago? If so, then they are refuted before they write. For Celsus is refuted, I do not mean by Origen's answer, though this presses him very hard, but by the fact that the faith he scorned has triumphed.

Even Celsus seems to have trembled with a foreboding of this coming triumph. He was unable to deny that among the Christians "there are some men, sensible, well-disposed, intelligent, and skilled in allegorical interpretation." [66] And while on the one hand he proclaimed that the Founder of Christianity was only a swindler, yet on the other hand he considered the religion as a kind of philosophy, and thus at least compared it to the grandest thing known to the ancient world. Also his oft-expressed fear of the magic arts of the Christians shows that he could not deny the existence of a power in Christianity, though, in consistency with his other views, he regarded it as only magical. The most important fact is that Celsus shows he is not quite secure in his own belief. He defends Polytheism with the air of being ashamed of it, and introduces considerable modifications into it. He expressly warns men against excessive zeal in serving the gods. "The more correct view is that the demons (subordinate deities) desire nothing and have need of nothing, but that they take pleasure in those who discharge towards them offices of piety." The principal thing is "never in any way to lose our hold upon God whether by day or by night, whether in public or in secret, whether in word or in deed, but in whatever we do or abstain from doing ... to let the soul be constantly fixed upon God."[67] Here Polytheism is completely abandoned. Celsus himself has already lost faith in it, and has evidently a suspicion that he is the champion of a lost cause. His whole book is indeed a prediction of victory for Christianity.

Thus we can understand how Celsus, with all his bitter hatred of Christianity, yet finally proposed a kind of compromise to the Christians. They were to have toleration, even freedom to serve the one supreme God, if they would also worship the demons, the subordinate gods which are set over particular departments in this world, and if they would make up their minds to honor the Emperor and to help him in this time of difficulty by participating in the efforts and burdens of the Roman Empire. Celsus took great pains to render this compromise acceptable to the Christians. He set himself to work to bring philosophy and the Christian faith nearer together. It was not much that he asked,

They might remain Christians in all else, worship the supreme God as before, if they would only also pay to the demons the honors which were their due. It was not as if they were required to do any thing disgraceful. What impiety could there be in singing a beautiful hymn to Athene? In her the supreme God was really worshipped. Or, what impiety was there in swearing by the Genius of the Emperor? Had not God given him his power? Did he not issue his commands by God's permission, and under His authority? But in case the Christians should resist these advances, Celsus threatened them with force — they were to be utterly exterminated. The Christians might take their choice: Peace or war?[68]

To the Christians there was of course no choice. They could not accept the compromise. The worship of the supreme God excluded the worship of the demons, and Christianity must be more than a religion tolerated side by side with others. The deification of the powers of nature and of the Emperor would have made Christianity into a new Heathenism. Yet the Christians would one day share the efforts and burdens of the Empire; yea, they were one day to become its strongest support. A time was to come, when the old and tottering Empire would seek and find in the youthful strength of Christianity the basis of a new life. But that time was yet distant. For the present the Christians could do nothing but suffer. The persecution under Marcus Aurelius was, it is true, as brief as it was severe. The terrible war on the Danube began again. The Emperor marched thither never to return, and his successor Commodus was entirely different from him. The persecution ceased again. But it had become clear that the Christians had been mistaken in basing their hopes of tranquillity on the gentleness and justice of the Emperor's personal character. Even if the Emperor of himself were favorably disposed, the time was not yet come. Heathenism must yet pass through further developments before it would bow before the Cross. Christianity must pass through other conflicts before the victory could be won. All the conflicts of the past had been only isolated skirmishes. They were not enough. The great battle was still to be fought. The Church must enter upon the terrors and distresses of a general persecution.

We are filled with sorrow when we think of the rivers of blood which were still to flow. But this was God's plan, and it was good. Christianity must go through the whole conflict, and owe its victory not to any fortunate circumstance nor to the personal favor of any Emperor, but solely and wholly to its own indwelling powers. Thus only could the victory be a real victory; thus only could the Church reap for all time the full benefit of this conflict and of this victory.

But the great battle, as I called it, came not yet. Next after the stormy reign of Marcus Aurelius came a period of comparative quiet. In this period the internal development of Heathenism and of Christianity was accomplished, and not until then were the antagonists in a position to summon all their powers, and measure their strength against each other.

CHAPTER III.

THE RE-ACTION.

"*Professing themselves to be wise, they became fools.*" — Rom. i. 22.
"*The Spirit of truth . . . will guide you into all truth.*" — John xvi. 3.

I. THE INTERNAL RE-ACTION IN HEATHENISM.

We should have an entirely false idea of the Titanic struggle between Christianity and Heathenism if we were to imagine the two antagonists as remaining in the same positions throughout. The conflict endured too long for that, for it lasted three centuries. In this time both Christianity and Heathenism underwent a great development, and when the last decisive battle was fought they had both become entirely different from what they were when the struggle began. Only when this is taken into account, is it possible to understand and to appreciate the victory of Christianity. For this victory was by no means a mere outward displacement of Heathenism, but an inward conquest. Hence before we go further we must try to gain a view of the great re-action which, in both Heathenism and Christianity, was prepared in the second century and showed itself in the third; and which first puts the antagonists into such a position as to bring the crisis of the conflict. On the part of Heathenism the re-action may be briefly designated as a restoration; or, to indicate in general the real nature of this restoration, the change that now took place consisted in the substitution of superstition for scepticism. This was a perfectly natural development. The restoration was only a necessary stage in the fall of Heathenism, a symptom of its waning power. Once more the heathen State summoned all its forces in order to withstand the antagonist who was growing stronger and stronger. Scepticism necessarily brings forth superstition as its complement. Neither an individual nor a people can long endure the emptiness of unbelief. It is impossible to live in a vacuum. And so the space emptied by scepticism fills up with superstition. The denial of the true leads by an internal necessity to the affirmation of the false. This change, which must come in the course of development, was greatly hastened by the position of affairs. When Marcus Aurelius, attacked by the plague, lay upon his death-bed, and his friends stood round him weeping: "Weep not for me," said the Emperor, "weep over the plague and the general misery."[1] In the time of Commodus the rottenness of the Empire, hitherto hardly concealed, and unremedied even by the best of the Emperors, came to light with an awful suddenness. A reign of terror set in, from the time when the son of Marcus Aurelius was seized with the frenzy of despotism. This imperial madness attacked almost all whom chance or fortune placed on the dizzy height of the imperial throne, and endowed with such an unlimited range of power as only the strongest souls could possess without inward ruin —

until it finally culminated in the production of monsters like Elagabalus and Caracalla. In bloodthirsty cruelty and unlimited debauchery the Emperors endeavored to exhaust the joys of that uncertain possession, the throne. The last vestiges which seemed to perpetuate the Republic were obliterated, while no real monarchy took its place, but a Cæsarism of the worst description. Not only was there no dynasty in which the throne was hereditary, but worse still, there was not even any settled rule as to who should have the right to nominate the Emperor. The Senate had in a certain sense the historical right on its side, but the Prætorian guard usurped the position, and its power increased with the wickedness of the Emperors. For, the worse the Emperor's character, the more he needed the protection of the Prætorian body-guard, and hence the greater the favors shown to it. Then the legions in the provinces also took their turn at electing Emperors; and, since each new usurper tried to keep the soldiers on his side by bribes greater than those of his rival, they soon found that their best advantage lay in having the reigns as brief as possible, till finally the position of Emperor was sold at public auction to the highest bidder.

The last words of Septimius Severus were: "Enrich the soldiers, and ignore the rest."[2] With him began the military monarchy, which, with a few intervals when the old imperial madness re-appeared, produced a succession of great soldiers under whose rule the State was saved from ruin. But it was an age of iron, the whole Empire stood to its arms, everywhere there was war. Sometimes it seemed as if all order was about to give place to chaos. Whole provinces detached themselves from the Empire, and chose Emperors of their own.

Often there were so many usurpers that we do not even know all their names. The barbarians were beating against the frontier like a storm, the Goths had already reached Northern Italy, Gaul remained for some time in the possession of Teutonic tribes, till the great generals by continuous campaigns brought the Roman world back to order. Times such as these, in which all is wavering and uncertain, in which the highest to-day are to-morrow the lowest, in which the whole world becomes a camp, and mighty men raise themselves from the ranks to the throne, only ere long to yield to more fortunate usurpers, — such times are exactly adapted for the growth and maturity of superstition. It is a general rule, that times of success chiefly bring forth doubt and scepticism from their luxury and license. Not less, on the other hand, do times of distress stimulate superstition as well as faith, for, the more uncertain the things of earth become, the more earnestly does man seek that which is supernatural and miraculous.

Besides superstition, corruption spread below the surface. That the world was growing old, was an ever-deepening conviction after the time of Marcus Aurelius. The heathen themselves were conscious of it. They often complained that the course of things tended downwards. Since the advent of Christianity, they said, all blessings had taken flight. War, pestilence, drought, locusts, famine, everywhere prevailed. The Roman Empire grew poorer and poorer. Even in its best days the financial situation of the Empire had been bad, as is evident from the two facts that the rate of interest did not decrease, nor did the population increase. But now the State was hurrying onward to the precipice of financial ruin. The cause of its bankruptcy is easily comprehended. It lay in the ancient contempt for labor, in the practice of slaveholding, and worse than all in the fact that idleness and indolence were privileged. The cities where no work was done had little or nothing required of them, the Roman idlers were fed by the State. All things, "bread and games," came from the State and were expected from it. Great cities in our day consume the produce of the country, but they pay it back in the products of manufacturing industry. But the commerce and industry of the ancient cities were essentially unproductive. Rome paid its debts with the taxes collected from the provinces, that is, it did not really pay them at all. It lived on the resources of the provinces, but these were not inexhaustible. In the peaceful reigns of the great Emperors in the second century, this waste was not noticed, but now when troublous times had come, when one civil war succeeded another, when Emperor fought with Emperor, and the provinces were devastated again and again — then the financial ruin declared itself. The world was poverty-stricken, because free labor, the one thing which creates and preserves true prosperity, was unknown.

But the degeneracy of the time was not merely material, it had also a spiritual side. Freedom and beauty, the two foci of the ancient world's life, had vanished. The Emperors of the second century had permitted at least a shadow and semblance of freedom, so that men still might dream that it existed, but now even that disappeared. The wretches who now occupied the throne, or the subsequent Soldier-Emperors, who had reached greatness in the camp and put their whole trust in their swords — what did they care about the freedom of the Roman people? Beauty also faded away; art rapidly degenerated. Art no longer created, it did not even reproduce, at its best it only multiplied repetitions. Size took the place of beauty. Alexander Severus set up a number of gigantic statues in Rome, and Gallienus wished to place on the highest site in the city a statue two hundred feet high, representing himself as the god of the sun. The spear in its hand was to be so massive that a child could go up on a spiral staircase constructed inside of it. The beautiful statues of the ancient gods now gave place to horrid monstrosities. Images of the Ephesian Diana with innumerable arms, caricatures, representations of the universal god, called Pantheus, took the place of the splendid forms which Greek art had created. Poetry also ceased. The Romance displaced the Epic and the Drama. Centos from Virgil, that is, poems put together out of Virgil's verses, poems of various shapes (for instance, one which when written had the form of a shepherd's pipe), and similar trifles, now won the popular favor. Philosophy gave way to rhetoric. With the reign of Septimius Severus the ancient philosophy came to an end. Men degenerated even physically; at least, one cannot help noticing that the portrait busts and statues of that period still extant display an increasing ugliness. Their forms look unhealthy, either bloated or shrunken.

In short, the world was growing old, and in old age became pious. Men began again to speak of the gods with all seriousness. Ælian in the third century devoted a whole book to instances of the dreadful fate of the gods' enemies, and he narrates with other edifying legends that even the elephants kneel each morning and pray. Apuleius, the most popular novelist of the time, rhapsodizes in the most enthusiastic manner on things divine, and is full to the brim of superstition; but his tales have a sensual tone, while his piety, and the piety of his time, is rather like that of a man who, after a youth spent in profligacy, becomes religious in old age. The temples were again diligently attended, and it became fashionable to show great zeal in all that pertained to the service of the numerous deities.

Of course this zeal was shown more towards foreign gods than for those of Rome. The religious syncretism, which had already begun, now reached its climax, and foreign rites almost entirely displaced the native cultus. Now the festival of the great mother was celebrated with the greatest splendor in Rome, and her priests appeared in proud state, who in Juvenal's time were to be found only in corner taverns among sailors and runaway slaves. The lamentations for the lost Attys resounded by the Tiber as loudly as ever formerly by the Orontes; and the day of the Hilaria, the re-discovery of Attys, was a gala-day for the whole of Rome. The shrines of the Egyptian gods had formerly found a place only in a nook outside the walls, but before this time Domitian had built a splendid temple to Isis and Serapis, and there were particular stations (*pausæ*) for the processions of these gods in the streets of Rome. The Emperor Commodus, shorn like a priest of Isis, himself walked in the procession, and carried the image of the dog-headed Anubis. Even the Persian Mithras, the last in the series of the gods who constantly migrated to Rome from farther and farther east, now had numerous worshippers. He was a god of light, a sun-god; as god of the setting sun, he was also god of the nether world; also as the invincible god (the "invincible companion" as he was often called) he became the patron of warriors, and as such thoroughly fitted for those times in which the whole world was filled with war. His worship was always held in a cave. In Rome the cave penetrated deep into the Capitoline Hill. Emperors were numbered among his adorers, and everywhere where Roman armies came (on the Rhine, for instance) there images and caves of Mithras have been found. This religious syncretism reached its culmination when Elagabalus, a Syrian priest of the sun, becoming Emperor, had the sun-god after whom he was named brought from Emesa to Rome, in the form of a conical black stone. In Rome a costly temple was built, and great sacrifices were offered to him. Then the image and the treasures of the celestial goddess were brought from Carthage, and she was solemnly united to the god Elagabalus. Rome and Italy celebrated in a most splendid festival the marriage of the gods. The fire of Vesta and the Palladium, those holy things of ancient Rome, were placed in the temple of the new god.

The consequences of this confusion of religions in the select circle of the learned were different from its effect upon the common people. With the learned the whole ritual was only a veiled pantheism. Each god was to them a symbol of the universal deity. The same is indicated by many inscriptions from this period, such as "To all the Celestials," or "To all Gods and Goddesses." All the gods were even compressed into one; and a figure, in which as many attributes as possible of the several gods were combined, was called *deus pantheus*, god of the universal deity. For the most part they believed in one supreme god, who, immutable and inaccessible himself, governed the world through an innumerable multitude of subordinate powers, lesser gods, his intermediaries, his messengers, who brought to him the thanksgivings and votive offerings of the faithful. With the multitude, on the other hand, this worshipping of foreign gods was only a veiled fetichism. These gods had no connections with the people and the State; their worship had no historical roots, and was pure fetichism. Therefore they were no longer joyously honored as the beneficent gods, but they were regarded as demons, which men feared, and strove by every kind of service and gift to render friendly. Heathenism became demon-worship: the rites acquired a dark and dread element which was foreign to the ancient Heathenism. The gods were now only dreaded, no longer trusted.

In close connection with this change was the great influence attained by magic. That too was a characteristic of the demon-worshipping, corrupt Heathenism, which became more and more prominent. Heathenism and the magic art are inseparably connected. Heathenism as a whole is permeated with magic. Everywhere we find a belief in magicians who bring storms, and bewitch fields, a belief in love-philtres, in the transformation of men into beasts, in the conjuration of the dead, and the like. The heathen lived in perpetual dread. They feared all sorts of sounds, omens, evil eye, charms, and the spectral shapes of the bloodsucking *Lamiæ* and *Empusæ*. But against these there were all kinds of charms, with which men protected themselves, a regular system of means of defence.

Especially were amulets valued, and the heathen covered themselves with them from head to foot.

All this had long existed. The Emperors in the first century had often consulted seers, astrologers, and Chaldeans. Was not the noble Germanicus encircled and hunted to death with murderous magic; his enemies sparing no crime however horrible, which had to be committed in order to furnish the charms, pieces of human bodies and such other things as were necessary! But now this magic art increased fearfully. The oracles, which had never become absolutely silent, were now more consulted than ever. The augury by the inspection of entrails, for a time neglected, though it was the old Roman way to inquire into the future, now came into frequent use. Alexander Severus paid teachers to give lectures on the subject. Not only the entrails of animals but also of men were examined, in order to discover what the future would bring. The general insecurity of the time, the dread of what might be coming, or the ambition which was waiting for the death of the Emperor, with the hope of taking his place — all led to it. The last heathen Emperors were particularly and passionately addicted to this magic art. Women and children were cut open alive in the palace of Diocletian's co-regent, in order to inspect their entrails. Numerous amulets were worn to protect from magic. Omens and signs were diligently observed. Of almost every Emperor portents which predicted his reigning are narrated by his contemporaries. In the life of Diocletian one of the most important events was the prophecy of a Druidess, who foretold that he would be Emperor, when he was only a subaltern in the army near Lutetia (Paris). Maximinus Daza never made any change without an omen; he did not even go out without consulting his Chaldean book of hours. The interpretation of dreams was pursued with especial zeal. Artemidorus of Ephesus spent his whole life in investigating all that had been written on dreams, and even took long journeys to collect experiences and materials. The result was his book *Oneirocritica*, the interpretation of dreams. In it, dreams are divided, with a semblance of science, into definite classes, and then their meaning is given. If one has a dream of a great head, that signifies riches and honors to such as have them not, otherwise it portends care. Long and smooth hair signifies happiness, short hair misfortune; wool instead of hair, sickness; a shorn head, misery. If a man dreams that ants creep into his ear, that signifies many hearers to an orator, but death to other men, for ants come out of the earth.

Wandering magicians made a paying business out of this nonsense. They wandered about in fantastic costume, and offered their charms for sale. They sold oracles, amulets, talismans, ointments, chains and bands, which were said to keep off all kinds of evil, and to heal certain diseases. Magicians and charmers enjoyed great consideration. People crowded into the chambers of mystery in which they made known the future and conjured the shades of the dead, and exhibited table-moving and spirit-rapping; and though perhaps the great satirist Lucian, in order to scoff at his contemporaries, drew a caricature in his Alexander of Abonoteichos, by combining too many swindles in that one person, yet similar characters must have existed at that time. In partnership with a comedy-writer from Byzantium, Alexander bought a huge serpent in Pella.

Then they hid in the temple of Apollo at Chalcedon two brazen tablets on which was written that Æsculapius, with his father Apollo, would soon come to Abonoteichos in Pontus. The discovery of the tablets made the desired excitement, and Alexander went to Abonoteichos to build the god a temple and to prepare all things for his reception. Fantastically dressed in a purple garment with white stripes, he appeared among the people, and raised their expectations to the highest pitch by various artifices. Meanwhile he had hidden in the foundation of the temple an egg with a little serpent in it, and now he appeared in the market-place to announce to the people the advent of their god. By occasional phrases of Hebrew and Chaldee he gave to his speech the proper magical stamp, and when the excitement had reached its climax he ran to the temple, brought the egg, and showed the infant god to the astonished multitude. After a few days Alexander solemnly presented their god to the people. Clad in rich garments the prophet reclined upon costly cushions in a dimly-lighted chamber, and about him coiled the serpent which he had bought and trained for the purpose; this was the god already grown up. From all quarters the people flocked thither; the new god dispensed oracles, and became a fountain of riches and honor to his prophet. Alexander received gifts in abundance, and even coins were struck in his honor, representing himself with his god Glykon. Nor was this all romance. In truth Alexander had worshippers enough even among the higher classes. In Rome Publius Rutilianus, a man of consular rank, was his zealous disciple. Marcus Aurelius asked counsel from him when affairs went badly on the Danube, and by his advice instituted a great expiatory sacrifice. Near Carlsburg an inscription has recently been discovered, which mentions Alexander and his serpent-god side by side with Jupiter and Juno. Even as late as the time when Athenagorus wrote his Apology, the statues of Alexander were still publicly worshipped.[3] There were also other cases in which men were worshipped as gods by the people. There was a half-wild man who wandered about in the plain of Marathon, and who was venerated by the inhabitants as a demi-god under the name of Agathion.[4] In Troas a certain Neryllis was regarded as a prophet and a worker of miracles. His statue stood in Troas, and was frequently crowned with flowers; sacrifices were offered, and cures attributed to it.[5] All these things show the hopeless confusion in which the religious consciousness of the time was involved.

Another characteristic of this time was its love for all kinds of stories about ghosts and apparitions. Phlegon wrote whole books teeming with ghosts and monsters. And the *Golden Ass*, the popular romance written by Apuleius of Madaura, is really nothing but a series of tales of ghosts and magic, the product of an unrestrained and impure imagination. Such books were enjoyed with secret terror by his contemporaries. There was a general belief that the dead might be summoned and would appear, and such as understood the art were much sought after. When Caracalla had murdered his brother Geta, and in his remorse believed that he was perpetually pursued by his dead brother, armed with a sword, he was driven by terror to conjurations. Commodus and Severus appeared to him, but with Severus came Geta uncalled, and uttered terrible threats. Apuleius in the *Golden Ass* describes a conjuration of this kind. He narrates the manner in which an Egyptian conjured a corpse in the marketplace of Larissa. He stood before it clothed in a linen robe, laid herbs three times on its mouth and breast, and murmured prayers, turning towards the rising sun. Such arts were now cultivated with a fanatical zeal entirely foreign to earlier times. Heathenism became fanatical in its demon-worship (we must bear this in mind, as it will supply the key to many events to which we shall come), and by this fanatical Heathenism the conflict with Christianity was conducted in a far more cruel and bloodthirsty manner than it had been carried on by the earlier, more natural phase of Heathenism.

The attraction of the hereafter, which we noticed under the early Empire, had now become much stronger. If we look at the epitaphs of the third century, we find indications of a heathen heaven. We read: " Ye hapless survivors, lament this death; ye gods and goddesses, rejoice over your new fellow-citizen;" or: "Now art thou happy for the first time, far from every earthly event; high in heaven thou delightest in ambrosia and nectar with the blessed gods;" or again: " Gods of the nether world, open to my father the groves where shines the rosy light of an eternal day."[6] Consecration is needed for entrance to this heaven. Redemption is necessary, the heathen too now realize that; but each must be his own redeemer, and must accomplish his redemption by all kinds of trials and sufferings.

Here was the root of the strong tendency to asceticism which dominated this period. The orgy of pleasure was past, the treasures of the conquered world had been squandered; with returning soberness the world felt its misery, and sought to gain peace and salvation by every kind of penance, self-chastisement, and self-torture. This was also the cause of the widespread popularity of the various Mysteries. The earlier Mysteries had a local stamp. He who came to Eleusis would doubtless, from traditional reverence, seek initiation into the Eleusinian Mysteries, but they were not widely known. At this time however an entirely new order of Mysteries appeared, which spread through the whole Empire, and all of which made the attainment of purification, regeneration, immortality, and blessedness their object. Of many of these we know but little, because they were secret rites; of others we possess more particular information. There were the Mysteries of Sabazius, of which we know only a few formulas. There were also the dread Taurobolium and Kriobolium. The novice was dressed in symbolic garments, and placed at midnight in a vault covered with boards. Above him a bullock or a ram was then sacrificed, and he was to receive on his face and hands as much as possible of the blood, that dripped through the holes and cracks of the boards, for this was the *vires æternæ*, the blood of eternal consecration. Then he had to go about in the bloody garments for a certain period, and considered himself, as the votive inscriptions testify, *in æternum renatus*, regenerated forever.[7] Besides these there were the highly venerated Mysteries of Isis which were much more complex. A long preparation preceded them, including abstinence from meat, baths, and sprinkling with water of consecration. The initiated and their friends brought votive offerings. On the consecration-night indicated by a dream, the novice watched in the temple, first in a harsh linen robe, then changing twelve times his robes, all of which had symbolic meanings, he went through a number of scenes and visions which signified death and resurrection through the favor of Isis.

A certain Lucius tells us concerning these rites: "I traversed the portals of death, I crossed the threshold of Proserpine, and after passing through all the elements I returned. In the middle of the night I saw the sun in its brightness, I approached the presence of the gods, and drawing near unto them I offered my petitions." At dawn Lucius found himself clad in a figured robe, with a crown of palm-leaves on his head and a torch in his hand, standing on a raised platform in front of the image of Isis. Suddenly a curtain was drawn away, and the multitude assembled in the body of the temple saw in him a living image of the sun. All kinds of apparatus for producing these appearances belonged to the necessary furnishings of the temple, and mirrors were principally used for this purpose. In the doorway which leads to the inner temple of Demeter at Eleusis, there are still visible grooves in the stones which make it probable that by means of ingenious machinery the initiated were conveyed into the inner court of the temple, so that they seemed to descend into the realm of shades. Hippolytus gives [8] a long list of these artifices, of the way the priests so contrived, that the doors of the temple opened of themselves, that at the moment when the flame of the sacrifice blazed up on the altar a mysterious music was heard, that majestic forms appeared in the altar-flames, and the like. Thus the novices really believed themselves perpetually surrounded with miracles.

The mysteries of Mithras were more awe-inspiring, and they best show how much the heathen were willing to undergo in order to attain the expiation of their sins. There were different degrees of consecration, the *raven*, the *warrior*, the *lion*, and so on. Novices had to undergo many tests, called disciplines. There were eighty such disciplines: fasting, standing and lying in ice and snow, even for twenty days at a time, the rack, horrors, flagellations, &c. They were so severe, that many lost their lives in them. Yet great numbers including nobles, and even Emperors, pressed forward for the privilege of becoming warriors of Mithras.

This period presents a strange picture. One might feel inclined at the first glance to make it a subject of laughter and mockery, and yet it cannot be contemplated without sadness. Must the splendor of the ancient world end in such a Witches'-Sabbath! The world which has listened to a Socrates and a Plato, produced a Sophocles, and seen so much beauty, which once shone with the glory of those works of art whose heroic proportions still inspire our youth,—*this* world as it comes to an end prays to a thousand wondrous gods, dog-headed idols, and cone-shaped stones, creeps into the caves of Mithras, and seeks regeneration in the expiatory blood of the Taurobolia, trembles before ghosts and magic charms, and becomes the prey of every charlatan who plays off miracles upon it!

It is not difficult to understand why the greatest scoffer that ever lived should be born at this time. All this superstition was to Lucian of Samosata, only a merry comedy which supplied him with inexhaustible subjects for laughter. "Be sober and incredulous!"

With this motto he confronts the men of his age like a solitary clear-headed man before a company of drunken revellers. He mocks at all things, gods and men. In his dialogues of the gods, we witness a domestic squabble between Jupiter and Juno; then we find all Olympus in despair when the cause of the gods is ill sustained in a disputation between Stoic and Epicurean philosophers; and again we learn what kind of a reception is given to all the queer new gods who crowd into Olympus. With the most biting satire he attacks superstition, magic, and the wandering jugglers; but then Plato and Socrates also are objects of his mockery, and in Christianity he sees only one of the many follies of the time. The worshippers of "the crucified sophist" are to him just such superstitious fools as the devotees of Alexander's serpent-god. He recognizes the benevolence of the Christians. They show, he concedes, an unsurpassed activity in helping, defending, or consoling one of their number, and they are utterly regardless of expense in matters affecting their common good. But he only laughs at the fiction which their first lawgiver inculcated, that they are all brethren. He sees how they despise death, but this too is ridiculous to him; for the hapless beings (according to him), have persuaded themselves that they are entirely immortal and will live for all time. There is indeed no more terrible spectacle than such a man, to whom every thing is ridiculous; for this proves that there is for him no longer any thing holy. Accurately as Lucian pictured his age, he yet did not understand it. He saw only the peculiarities and monstrosities, but the earnest striving which pervaded it, the yearning which produced such strange developments, he never suspected. To a thorough-going materialist such as Lucian, no age is so incomprehensible as one like his.

After the orgies of the earlier Empire, a fast-day penitential feeling had taken possession of the world, and far and wide the question moved all hearts: "What must I do to be saved?" Such times are always of great importance for the kingdom of God. The anxiety about their souls' salvation, which impelled men to resort to the Mysteries, might show them the way to the true and unique mystery of redemption. The longing for forgiveness, which did not shrink from severe discipline and penance, was fitted to open their hearts to the preaching of that forgiveness which is freely offered to all through grace.

At first, of course, Heathenism attempted to deliver itself, to satisfy from its own resources the deficiencies which could no longer be ignored. Once more the Greek spirit bestirred itself, and framed a new and final system of philosophy, — Neoplatonism.

Ammonius the porter, of Alexandria, is said to have been the father of Neoplatonism, but his pupil Plotinus first developed it into a regular system. It was in all respects a medley such as times of ferment are wont to produce. It was a philosophy, a revival of Platonism, but in such fashion as to incorporate with Platonism many other elements. Plotinus actually endeavored to show that all philosophic systems had but one aim, and attempted to unite Aristotle and the Stoics with Plato. But Neoplatonism was at the same time a theology, or more correctly a theosophy. The whole system was pervaded by a moral and religious way of looking at things, corresponding to the strong religious tendency of the age. Thus the knowledge of the Supreme Being was to be gained not by philosophic speculation, but by contemplation, by immediate intuition. Indeed, Neoplatonism appeared in the character of a new revelation. Ammonius was called "the inspired of God,"[9] and Plotinus believed himself accompanied by not merely a demon, but a god of superior rank. When he was invited to a sacrifice he answered: "It is the part of the gods to come to me, not mine to go in search of them."[10]

Plotinus designates as the object of his teachings " to lead the soul from the state of dishonor, in which it is estranged from its father and its source, in which it ignores its true being and grovels among transitory things, to a condition the reverse of the former, up to the supreme good."[11] The original and supreme being, the first cause of all things, was, according to Plotinus, the One, the Good, who is exalted so high above all, that definition and distinction and relation to any thing else are excluded from his being. Yet although the One dwells in an absolute isolation, from him proceeds a communication of force, descending step by step. The gradations are the thinking mind, the creative soul, and matter. Matter is the last product of the descending series of emanations from the First. It is the negation of being, and while the One, the First, is the Good and the source of good, matter is the last, in which no element of good remains, the source of evil. It is the darkness over against the light. Now it is the office of the soul to enlighten matter, since its sphere borders on matter. But matter re-acts on the soul. By mixing with darkness the soul's light becomes dimmer. This is the fall of the soul. It is true the soul itself still remains pure, good, and rational, but its being is obscured with matter, like one plunged in the mire. Man's duty then is to purify himself from matter, to win his way back from the material world to the higher sphere. This duty may be accomplished through virtue; that is, the soul liberates itself from material elements by asceticism, and concentrates itself upon the One. Thus the soul comes to the contemplation of the Supreme Being, and though these moments of mystic union are only rare glimpses of light during this earthly life (Plotinus himself attained to this contemplation only a few times), yet, when the soul is freed from the fetters of the body, it will enjoy the uninterrupted contemplation of the Supreme Being.

The similarity of this system to Christianity is as easy to discern, as their radical difference. In both, redemption is the object, but Plotinus recognized neither the depth of sin nor the height of grace. His Supreme Being is not the living God, who is love, the Creator and Father of all, but an abstract unity. It was only the "unknown God" whom Plotinus recognized. And therefore matter was regarded as evil in itself, and redemption as consisting in the withdrawal of the soul from the material world. And this redemption man could accomplish for himself by asceticism, and the practice of virtue. As Plotinus was entirely shut in by the heathen horizon of thought, he naturally brought the heathen mythology into his system. The myths were, in his view, nothing but the drapery clothing speculative ideas. His whole system had convenient points of connection with the popular faith of the heathen, and his pupils followed out the hints he gave. The idea that God works and reveals himself in various emanations was expanded into a regular hierarchy of superior and inferior gods. Next to the supernal gods came those inhabiting the earth, and below these the demons good and bad. In this way the entire popular creed could be philosophically justified. The people addressed as their gods those who inhabited the earth, while the sage elevated his thoughts to the Supreme One.

The idea that soul permeates the entire world, and that therefore every thing therein was instinct with life and soul, even things apparently destitute of them, that one life animates the whole, and that therefore there exists a secret sympathy in all things — this idea gave a philosophic basis for magic and soothsaying, so that the whole business of sorcery could now be retained and even zealously cultivated. Thus Neoplatonism developed into the theology of restored Heathenism, which was in this way made to rest on a scientific foundation for the educated. The Neoplatonists, however, purposed not only restoration, but reform. In giving a new foundation for the heathen religion, they purposed also to purify it from the grossest objections, and to communicate to it some elements which Christianity already possessed. For instance, bloody sacrifices were to be abolished, and bloodless offerings and prayers were to take their place. Worship also was no longer to consist only of dead ceremonies, but teaching and preaching were to be included in it, according to the example of the Christian Church.

This fact clearly shows that Christianity, although still decidedly in the minority, had already become the dominant power in the world. Strange indeed had seemed to the heathen the spiritual worship of the Christians, and much scoffing was directed against 'their practice of instructing artisans and old women in religious matters.' But now, that which had been derided was recognized as a want which the heathen strove to satisfy on the basis of Heathenism. Their worship, too, was to be spiritualized, the gross materialism of animal sacrifices removed, and provision made for the instruction of the people. Consciously, or unconsciously, the reformation of Heathenism was evidently guided by the influence of Christianity, and the latter became to such a degree the mainspring of the movement, that reformed Heathenism adopted features borrowed from Christianity and even grew to be an imitation of it.

We used a borrowed expression in speaking of "a heathen heaven," to indicate the similarity to the Christian heaven which the heathen idea of the next world assumed. In like manner a heathen Bible might be spoken of. Porphyry, one of the leaders of the Neoplatonist school, made a collection of heathen oracles and divine utterances, in the preface to which he says: "Those will best recognize the usefulness of this collection, who in their longing for truth have prayed that they might enjoy a vision of the Gods, in order that they might find rest from their doubts in teachings which emanated from trustworthy authority." [12] What is this but a heathen Bible! All the Christian conceptions—expiation, purification from sin, regeneration—were now to be met with among the heathen, and the goal of their Mysteries was redemption, that is, a heathen redemption. The heathen colleges of priests, also, had entirely changed their organization; indeed, in Diocletian's time, they had become a sort of hierarchy, a kind of teaching order. In this, also, the approximation to the Christian Church is sufficiently perceptible. A heathen Church organized itself in opposition to the Christian Church, and, to push the parallel to the utmost, there was put forward a heathen Christ, or, rather, several.

Long before, Seneca had said that man must have a guide in order to attain peace, and this desire for a guide to the soul had grown ever stronger. Some sought this guide among the gods, and Mithras, "the invincible companion," was among those selected. Others took for a guide one among the sages of the past, yet then it was not a historic, but an idealized image of the sage which was set forth. Thus were Plato and Pythagoras treated. The greatest celebrity of this kind, however, was accorded to Apollonius of Tyana, for we find him exhibited as a veritable heathen Christ. The historical Apollonius was a magician and necromancer, who spent his life in journeying about and plying his magic arts, and who also asserted that visions were vouchsafed to him. In the reign of Septimius Severus, Flavius Philostratus wrote a biography of this Apollonius, in which, by the most fanciful idealization, he is set forth as a counterpart and rival of Christ. His mother bore him to the god Proteus; swans sang sweet lullabies over the cradle of the new-born child. Even in childhood he gave indications of marvellous powers, and in early life he withdrew into solitude, and took long journeys. He acquired the wisdom of India in that land, and then began his progress through the world in order to reform Heathenism. He drew disciples round him, preached in the principal cities of the Roman Empire, and performed numerous miracles. "His mouth was a brimming cup, and every one was free to come and slake his thirst."[13] The miracles which Philostratus relates are often very similar to Christ's miracles. In Rome, for instance, Apollonius met a funeral procession; a young girl lay upon the bier; her bridegroom followed weeping, accompanied by many friends. Apollonius stopped the procession, asked the name of the dead, then touched the corpse, and spoke a few words. Immediately the young girl arose, as if she had awaked from sleep.[14] His preaching inculcated the reform of Heathenism. He rejected bloody sacrifices, and offered only incense. He approved the erection of temples and altars to the gods, but not statues; it ought to be left open to every one to form his own inward imagination of the deity.[15] It is peculiarly significant that Apollonius urged men to love their neighbors and to do good. Standing on the steps of the temple at Ephesus — so Philostratus narrates[16] — he was preaching, and with vivid illustrations was exhorting men to be helpful one to another. Near him were some sparrows quietly perched on a tree. There came another sparrow, and uttered a cry, as if to communicate some tidings. Then they all flew away, and followed the messenger. Apollonius, seeing it, interrupted his preaching, and said: "A child was carrying some corn in a basket. The child fell down, and then went on, after partially collecting the corn, but left some of it scattered in the street. The sparrow saw it, and sought his fellows, in order that all might have a share in what he had found." Some of those present immediately went, and found that it was indeed just as he had said. Then said Apollonius to the people: "You see how much interest the sparrows manifest in each other's welfare, and how willing they are to divide their possessions one with another; but you, on the other hand, when you see that a man is sharing his property with others, call him a spendthrift." Apollonius also suffered persecution on account of his reformatory work. In vain did his friends endeavor to hold him back from going to Rome, where Domitian was gratifying his savage passions. "I dare not flee from my enemies," answered Apollonius, "I must fight for my friends." Domitian threw him into prison, but Apollonius suddenly disappeared from the sight of his judges, and in the evening re-appeared to his friends at Pozzuoli.[17] These refused to believe that it was indeed himself, but he permitted them to touch him to convince them that it was no phantom which they beheld. Later in the island of Crete he disappeared, when a voice was heard, "Leave the earth, and ascend to heaven!"[18]

There can be no doubt that we have here a representation drawn with the full intention of constructing a heathen counterpart of Christ. Philostratus was not, like Lucian, merely writing a satire, but he was seriously making the attempt to set up a heathen Christ in opposition to the Christian Christ. And this is the more significant since we have here not simply the personal views and intentions of Philostratus. He was an honored member of the coterie of learned men which gathered around the intellectual women at the court of the Emperor Septimius Severus, Julia Domna his wife, her sister Julia Mæsa, and their niece Julia Mammæa. In this circle religious questions were much discussed, and without any prepossession in favor of the religion of the Roman state. Julia Domna indeed was the daughter of a priest of the sun in Emesa. The predominant tendency in this circle was thoroughly syncretic, and this syncretism was not averse to Christianity. The Christian religion, too, was not without adherents at the court; a chamberlain of Commodus was a Christian,[19] and another Christian called Proculus belonged (according to Tertullian[20]) to the household of Severus. It was recognized that there was something in the new religion. The spotless morality of the Christians and the steadfastness of the martyrs made a profound impression. The idea was no longer repudiated that the Christians possessed something which the heathen lacked. Was it not possible, then, for Heathenism to appropriate this? Could there not as a rival to the Christ of the Christians be set up a heathen Christ, in whose portrait the excellence which belonged to Christianity might be combined with Heathenism? Such was the school of thought from which sprang the book of Philostratus.

Indeed there was at this time a general and perceptible desire for a harmonious agreement with Christianity. Even Celsus had proposed a kind of treaty with the Christians. But now the thought of the age was still more definitely directed towards it. Elagabalus made room for a chapel for Christianity in his universal temple; Alexander Severus openly showed his sympathy with the new faith. Christianity was to be received among the religions of the Roman Empire, but of course only, on condition that it would seek for nothing more than to be a religion amongst many others, and that it would itself recognize the heathen religions. But this was impossible, and therefore there was no alternative but to renew the conflict. Indeed even this idea of an agreement which would concede to Christ a place in the Roman Pantheon, by the side of Jupiter, Isis, and

Mithras, would contribute, since the plan proved impracticable, to hasten the real decisive struggle.

It would show but little knowledge of human nature, to found on the fact that Heathenism had come considerably nearer to Christianity the hope that it would henceforth occupy a more friendly attitude towards the Christian faith. These advances on the part of Heathenism may perhaps have made a bridge on which an individual here and there passed over into the Church; but, on the whole, they would only intensify the antagonism, when it was recognized that Christianity would enter into no compromise. For the heathen now believed that they possessed, and that in a much purer form, the excellences which Christianity was conceded to contain. Hence this Christianity which utterly repudiated union had now the less right to exist. The earlier form of Heathenism would not have had the strength to fight a decisive battle with Christianity. It cannot be denied that this restoration put new strength into Heathenism, though the strength was not of the right kind. And further, the purpose could now be formed of making restored Heathenism serve as a religious foundation for the restoration of political and national life, and thus of accomplishing the restoration of the ancient world as a whole. But the first step towards this consummation must be the annihilation of Christianity. The unnaturalness of the restoration became the measure of its fanaticism, and it was restored Heathenism which first, with all the ardor of a fanatic, began a war of extermination against Christianity. The combatants approached each other, not to join hands, but only to grasp each other the more firmly for the last desperate struggle.

II. THE INTERNAL RE-ACTION IN CHRISTIANITY.

We may say of Christianity, that it likewise had in a certain sense drawn nearer to Heathenism. Christianity had passed through a comprehensive development, which may be concisely described as its naturalization in the world.

The early Christians had many of the characteristics of men who have just entered on a new life. While vividly conscious of having forced their way into an entirely new existence, they were no less aware that they were cut off from their former life and separated from all those who were left behind in it. Their new and youthful enthusiasm made them ready for sacrifice, rejoicing to suffer; but the tendency towards the renunciation of the world was stronger than the zeal for its conquest. They lived in constant fear of losing their new-found treasure, and were very wary of risking it by any proximity to the world. They could not as yet summon courage for the endeavor to make the new life permeate the world around; but showed an inclination to withdraw into solitude, in order to rejoice by themselves in the grace they had received. They preferred simply to have the enjoyment of it, rather than to put it out at interest and work with it. They associated freely with those of like views, but only to cut themselves off the more strictly from the rest of the world. They feared to do many things lest they might fall into sin, and thus an element of legalism easily mingled with the earnestness and zeal of their consecration. The whole horizon of their life was a narrow one, and if they might choose, it would be that man might speedily leave this world and be at home with his Lord. From this came the tendency so characteristic of the Christian life of this period, to be chiefly intent on the next world, to the comparative neglect of the Christian's duties here; from this, the predilection for occupying the thoughts with eschatology and the coming of Christ.

All this gave to the earliest Christianity — let me say it without seeming to apply modern party-names to that period — an almost pietistic character, and to the Church a trace of the conventicle. The coming of the Lord was then believed to be quite near, and this hope dominated the whole life. No provision was made for a long continuance of the Church on earth, and all efforts were exclusively directed towards remaining in the world without spot, till the day of Christ's coming. The mission of Christianity to conquer the world, to permeate it with the Christian spirit, and thereby to shape it anew, had scarcely received any attention.

Not thus could Christianity conquer the world! It must become larger-hearted, must go to meet the world, condescend to it, in order in this way to conquer. The Church must not remain as it was, it must strip off the guise of the conventicle, and become the Church of the people.

Of course every step in this direction was fraught with the greatest danger. If the strict exclusion of the world were discarded, how easy would it be to descend to the level of the world, and so become entirely unable to subdue it! For he who puts himself on a level with the world is so far from being able to conquer it, that rather he is conquered by it. Instead of becoming the Church of the people in the true sense, the Church might have become any and every body's Church, and thus have sacrificed to the world its essential character. There was imminent danger that if the Church did not remain in seclusion and silence, it would become so liberal that the dividing line between Christianity and Heathenism would be obliterated, and that the former would be wholly absorbed by the latter.

Under the guidance of its Lord, the Church was victorious over these dangers, and indeed it was in the great conflicts with Montanism and Gnosticism that the changes were occasioned which brought into existence the Church of the people, and so prepared Christianity for the decisive battle with Heathenism.

The exclusiveness above referred to seemed indeed about to disappear naturally. The fearful storm of persecution under Marcus Aurelius had resulted in the opposite of its object: instead of annihilating the Church, it promoted the Church's growth. In the comparatively tranquil times which followed, the number of the Christians increased with special rapidity, and we learn in particular of an extraordinary number of conversions among the higher classes. So that even Tertullian could say: "We are of yesterday, and yet have filled every place belonging to you, — cities, islands, castles, towns, assemblies, your very camp, your tribes, companies, senate and forum;"[21] and Eusebius observes that since the time of Commodus "the saving word has brought the souls of men of every race to the devout veneration of the God of the universe, so that already in Rome many of those distinguished by descent and wealth have sought salvation with their whole house and family."[22] The natural result of this was a relaxation, with many, of the rigid strictures hitherto maintained. Christians in the higher classes, who had numerous family connections among the heathen, did not scruple even to attend family festivals in heathen households, and of course, also, to be present at the customary heathen rites, to wear garlands, and join in the festal banquet. It is true they always made it a point not to participate in heathen worship, yet the range of that which was considered permissible was gradually though imperceptibly enlarged. Some even ventured to accompany their heathen relatives to the games and to the theatre.[23] In the long run it became impossible for the Christians to refuse military service and public offices, and thus new ties were necessarily, though unwillingly, formed with the world. Opinions differed very much in Carthage, when a soldier on the Emperor's birthday held his garland in his hand, and refused to wear it. When he was condemned to death for his refusal, he was regarded by some as a martyr, a steadfast witness, while others saw in him a fanatic, who had given unnecessary offence by his conduct.[24] In many places it was openly said to be Christian wisdom not to oppose the world with too great strenuousness. Christians ought not, it was said, to provoke the heathen; and Titus ii. 5 became a favorite verse to excuse various courses of conduct, by saying that they were adopted in order that the name of God and of Christ might not be blasphemed by the heathen.[25] Under this pretext, it was asserted to be permissible, not only to flee from persecution, but even to avert it by bribing soldiers and magistrates. They were only, so they said, rendering to Cæsar the things that were Cæsar's,—namely, money; and by means of a pecuniary sacrifice providing that the Church might assemble in tranquillity, and keep the Lord's day without being molested.[26] The discipline of the churches also began to be more lax. Those who had actually apostatized were received back into the Church on easier terms than before. Even when they were refused by the proper authorities, the members often took the exercise of discipline into their own hands. For those who had been in prison, or had suffered torture for the faith, soon began to claim as a right what had been conceded to them as a mark of honor; namely, that every one whom they admitted to fellowship should be regarded as thereby re-admitted to the fellowship of the Church. And they exercised this right in the most arbitrary manner, so that the discipline of the Church in many places became completely disorganized from this cause.

It must be admitted that weakness was not the only cause of this relaxation from the original stringency, and that there was some truth in the frequent prominence given to Christian wisdom and prudence. Of course what was feasible so long as the churches were small, and the Christians almost without exception belonged to the lower classes, became impossible when the churches grew large and numbered some members among the nobility. It was easy for an artisan to retire from the world, but how could a knight, a senator, or a member of some distinguished family, break with all his previous connections when he became a Christian? And was such a course likely to prove advantageous for the Church? Did not the hope of the further spread of Christianity among the educated classes depend mainly upon those very connections? And, further, was it possible permanently to withdraw from military service? If a soldier was converted, must he not remain a soldier?

Rome was the earthly fatherland of the Christians, no less than others: did not their duty as citizens require them to share in its defence? Was it right for Christians to continue to decline all public offices? Would they not, as officials, enjoy special opportunities for serving their Lord? But if they served as soldiers, if they held public offices, they must be permitted to do many things which it had formerly been held duty to avoid as bringing them into contact with Heathenism. And was it possible to continue the former severity of discipline, when the churches were no longer little conventicles, but, many of them, large congregations in the great cities? If the multitude were to be received into the Church, the standard of holy living must not be set too high; or to speak more correctly (since this standard is not under the control of the Church) it became necessary to help the weak by not making the way to reconciliation with the Church too difficult for such as stumbled and fell.

Yet it cannot be denied that the relaxation of former stringency betrayed much real weakness, which was only hidden under the pretext of Christian wisdom and foresight. The difficult problem of the relations between the Church and the world was not to be solved by retaining the former strictness in theory, and making one concession after another to the weakness of individual members; for this would have led to an inclined plane, by which the Church might have descended to complete identification with the world. And so it was well for the Church, that against this wide-spread laxity there arose an energetic re-action, which, of course, like all re-actions, not merely strove to maintain the previous practice, but went beyond it, and so impelled the Church, in vanquishing the extreme party, to an intelligent search for the true position.

This re-action took the form of what was called Montanism, the doctrine of a sect which obtained its name from its supposed founder, Montanus. It arose about the middle of the second century in Phrygia, and by the beginning of the third it had become prevalent and to some extent predominant in Asia Minor and Africa, also in Rome and the West in general. The prime object of Montanism was to preserve the early strictness of conduct and discipline, and to restore it where it had been relaxed. Yet it did not stop there, but sought to increase stringency beyond the former limits. With this object its prophets and prophetesses re-awakened the expectation of the speedy advent of Christ, which had already become weakened. The Montanists proclaimed that the end of the world was at hand, and that the Church had entered upon the last period of its existence; the period of the Paraclete, of the Holy Spirit, who was giving to the Church by the mouth of his prophets a new law, new precepts for conduct and discipline. These precepts without exception inculcated an increase of strictness. The former rule had been: what is not forbidden is permitted. But now the rule was: what is not expressly allowed is forbidden. The Church was bidden to sunder itself more sharply from the world. Montanism took a position directly opposed to all worldly culture, art, science, and pleasure. All these were sinful, and the Christian must not become involved in them. Great stress was laid upon the duty of martyrdom, and every evasion of it, even an escape by flight, was punished as a denial of the faith. The fasts were made more strict, and enforced with the severity of a law. Much importance was attached to many little things, such as that virgins were not to come to church without being veiled. But above all, the discipline of the Church was made much more strict, and in this the essential character of Montanism is most clearly seen. Montanism absolutely and forever refused to receive again into the Church all who had fallen into mortal sin, even after their repentance. God might receive them again (that possibility was not denied), but the Church, never.

If this sect had gained the upper hand in the Church, the Church could never have become a factor in the world's history. It would have shrivelled up to a conventicle, condemned to immobility, and possessing no influence upon the life of the people. If it had shut up the doors between itself and the world, it would have become incapable of conquering the world. By taking a position opposed to science and art, the Church would never have had the power to bring forth a Christian science, a Christian art. It might thus have fostered within its walls a heroic renunciation of the world, it might have produced characters of intense devotion, saints and sufferers, but it could never have become the teacher of the people. For it is a necessary condition of education, that the teacher should be able to come down to the level of the taught, and that was impossible to such a community of saints. They were acquainted with only a discipline which excludes, not an education which wins and gathers in. And in this way the Church could never have laid the foundation for the reconstruction of the State, since a Christian State is inconceivable from the Montanistic point of view. But the Church succeeded in conquering Montanism, though only after a severe struggle, and that, without itself being led into the opposite extreme; a fact which must be taken into account in order to appreciate the real value of the victory. The Church did not disregard the warning against laxity, which was contained in Montanism, but it realized no less the necessity of becoming naturalized in the world, and deserves the recognition of the fact that it long held, on the whole, to the golden mean. Without letting go the hope of the final advent of the Lord, the Church entered upon its historical development and its citizenship on earth. Without renouncing the high standard of sanctification in its members, the Church learned condescension to the weak. While sustaining discipline with all energy, the Church also held open to the fallen a way of return. Though conscious that it was not of this world, yet the Church gave scope to all that is great and beautiful in man, according to the apostolic word, "all things are yours." The purely negative renunciation of the world gave place to the victory over it, which indeed is the end, to which renunciation is only a means; and henceforth the Church more and more recognized its mission to permeate all things, including science, art, and the life of the people, with the spirit of Christianity.

The antipode of Montanism is Gnosticism. It is difficult in a few lines to sketch this Gnosticism, whose first germs appeared in the apostolic age, and which grew into a great danger for the Church in the second century. *Gnosis* means *knowledge*, and the essence of this movement lies in the word which furnished its name; since it put *Gnosis*, that is *knowledge*, into the place of *faith*. To the Gnostic the great question was not, "What must I do to be saved?" but his inquiries concerned the genesis and development of the world, the origin of evil, and the restoration of the primitive order of things in the world. In the very knowledge of these was redemption as the Gnostic understood it. Thus, by combining with the ideas original to Christianity the most various elements, such as Greek philosophy, Jewish theology, and ancient Oriental theosophy, great systems of speculative thought were constructed, all with the object of displaying the process of the world's development. According to this development, from a pantheistic First Cause emanates a series of beings called Æons, beings of Light, of which each in succession as it recedes from the First Cause is also less perfect than the preceding. Finally the last and lowest comes into contact with Matter, which from all eternity has stood opposed to the divine Light — as Darkness, Non-existence, and all that is the reverse of divine. From this contact, from the mingling of the Light with Matter, the visible world comes into being, in which a portion of spiritual being, of Light, is held captive by Matter and combined with it. Redemption is the liberation of this captive Light from the fetters of Matter, the dissolution of this union, and the restoration of the original order of things. This redemption has been accomplished by Christ. This last tenet bears testimony to the connection of Gnosticism with Christianity, in contrast to many similar heathen systems, but of course what the Gnostics call redemption is something entirely different from that to which the Scriptures give the same name. Gnostic redemption is not deliverance from sin, but the restoration of cosmic order, and so Christ is to them, not the Saviour who brings salvation, forgiveness of sin; his sphere is not saving, but the ordering of the universe. There is no place in the Gnostic system for the creation, or for the incarnation. The view that Matter in itself is evil, excludes the possibility of Christ's having really assumed a human nature. Only in appearance did he become man, and his whole life on earth, especially his passion and death, were all an illusion. The Gnostics were thorough Docetists, that is, they treated the whole manifestation of Christ as only a semblance. The events which brought salvation were not facts to them, but remained only as symbols, and the substance of Christianity was evaporated into speculative ideas.

I have already called Gnosticism the antipode of Montanism. Such indeed it was. If Montanism was over-narrow, here we find an all-embracing breadth. Gnosticism knew how to utilize every mental product of the age. Elements, oriental and occidental, in a curious medley, philosophy and popular superstition, all were collected and used as materials for the building of Gnostic systems. The myths of the heathen may be found side by side with the Gospel histories, which were only myths to the Gnostic. One proof-text is taken from the Bible, and the next from Homer or Hesiod, and both alike are used by an allegorical exegesis to support the ready-made creations of the author's fancy. Breadth enough too, in morality; no trembling fear of pollution, no anxious care to exclude the influence of Heathenism. It was no fiction inspired by the hatred of heresy, when the Gnostics were said to be very lax in their adhesion to the laws of morality. Many of them expressly permitted flight from persecution.

Gnosticism extended far and wide in the second

century. There was something very imposing in those mighty systems, which embraced heaven and earth. How plain and meagre in comparison seemed simple Christianity! There was something remarkably attractive in the breadth and liberality of Gnosticism. It seemed completely to have reconciled Christianity with culture. How narrow the Christian Church appeared! Even noble souls might be captivated by the hope of winning the world over to Christianity in this way; while the multitude was attracted by the dealing in mysteries with which the Gnostic sects fortified themselves, by offering mighty spells and amulets, thus pandering to the popular taste. Finally, some were no doubt drawn in by the fact that less strictness of life was required, and that they could thus be Christians without suffering martyrdom.

But the victory of Gnosticism would have been the ruin of Christianity. Christianity would have split into a hundred sects, its line of division from Heathenism would have been erased, its inmost essence would have been lost, and instead of producing something really new, it would have become only an element of the melting mass, an additional ingredient in the fermenting chaos of religions which characterized the age.

And the Church fought as for its life with all the forms of the false Gnosis. Over against the mighty systems of the Gnostics, the Church stood, in sober earnestness and childlike faith, on the simple Christian doctrine of the apostles. This was to be sought in the churches founded by the apostles themselves, where they had defined the faith in their preaching. Tradition was appealed to against the heretics, but in truth with the same end in view which the Reformers had in going back to the Scriptures, in order to oppose a corrupted tradition. For then the Church was in direct possession of an unadulterated tradition, from which the doctrine preached by the apostles could be known with certainty. At this time the Church began to make a trustworthy collection of the apostolic writings, and, on the basis of both scripture and tradition, held with the greatest tenacity to the historical facts as the basis of true Christianity, parrying every attempt to transform them into semblances or symbols. These facts were condensed, on the basis of scripture, into a short rule of faith, and this, whose perfected expression in the "Apostles' Creed" is still our rule of faith, was set up as a firm breakwater against the flood of Gnostic speculation. In it, over against the Gnostic scheme of æons emanating from the First Cause, the Church acknowledged with clear simplicity God the Father, Maker of heaven and earth. In opposition to Gnostic idealism, the Church avowed its faith in the real historical facts, that the Son of God truly became man, was born of the Virgin Mary, was truly crucified and died, truly rose again. Thus the Church rescued Christianity, and also began the framing of a confession of faith, created the elements of a catechism, and so supplied the necessary basis for the Church of the people. Neither Gnosticism nor Montanism could have produced a Church of the people. Montanism would only have gathered a conventicle of select saints, while Gnosticism would indeed have brought together a great multitude, but without any definite boundary on the side of Heathenism, so that no one would have known whether the members of the Church were Christians or heathen.

But the Church, by the conquest of both Montanism and Gnosticism, really took the form of a Church for the people.

Finally, in the midst of these struggles, there grew up something not less important to the development of the Church than its victories, namely, the form of its polity.

From the first, the Church had had a polity; church-offices had always existed. To imagine the churches as at any time without administration and organization would be entirely unhistorical. Where the apostles founded churches, they also appointed officials. These were called *Presbyters*, that is, *Elders;* or, what had then the same meaning, *Bishops*, that is, *Overseers.*[27] Every church had several of these officials; no single person stood at the head of the church, but a college of equal elders held sway. Yet their office was not primarily that of teaching. Teaching was the prerogative of the apostles; and, in a broader sense, any member of the church might come forward as a teacher, if he had a gift for the work. Only the women were excluded by Paul. The duty of the elders was rather to preside over the church, to guide and govern it. Their office was primarily to rule. But of course it naturally came to pass that the duty of building up the church in doctrine was committed to them, since they, as the most prominent members, were best fitted for the task. Beside the Eldership, but subordinate to it, was the office of *Deacon*, that is, *Servant*, not principally, still less exclusively (as some represent it nowadays), an office of almsgiving, but of service generally, auxiliary to the Presbyterate, and so, of course, largely connected with the work of charity in the church.

The Eldership, however, was only a local, not an ecclesiastical office; that is, it related only to the local church, not to the Church at large. The local churches, apart from the bond of sharing the labors of the apostles, who belonged to no local church, were only united by the connection of one common faith, and by the tie of love which embraced all.[28] An organic connection through an ecclesiastical office, which should rule over several local churches, had not then come into being.

The organization of the churches remained in this simple condition after the apostolic age and into the second century. Few forms were needed, because the Spirit was still present in fulness of life and power, while the churches were small, and all their relations very simple. But with the first decade of the second century, an important change came about. Not at one time in all the local churches, still less by any common decision, but by an inward necessity, which made itself felt simultaneously in different localities, one of the presbyter-bishops was raised from among his peers to be the leader, and to him, with the thenceforth restricted title of bishop, the government of the church was confided; so that there were offices of three grades: a single bishop and a plurality of elders and of deacons.

In this new form the episcopal office was still only over the local church, and the difference between the rulers and the ruled was regarded as only a difference of office, not yet as the difference of two distinct orders. Bishops and elders were not contrasted as priests with the laity, but all Christians were priests.

In the conflict, however, with Montanism and Gnosticism, a further development appeared. From a simple local office, the episcopacy became an ecclesiastical office. When, in the struggle against Gnosticism, it became important to insure the purity of the faith, the transmission of the rule of faith connected itself with the episcopal office. To the bishop was confided the task of preserving the purity of the doctrine handed down. When in the struggle against Montanism, it became important to re-organize the discipline of the churches, it was the bishop again to whom the exercise of discipline was assigned. He who was in fellowship with the bishop was in fellowship with the local church and with the Church at large. The bishop represented the local church, and the bishops collectively the whole Church. Then the clergy began to be more sharply distinguished from the *Laos*, the people, the *laity*. The clergy alone were invested with the priestly character, and on the basis of the name *priest*, the comparison with the Old Testament priesthood secured to them place and power. Thus we come to find a firm and orderly hierarchy, and the more the Church showed its need of strong leaders in its mighty conflicts within and without, the more did this hierarchy develop in power.

If now we for a moment compare the Church soon after the death of the apostles, let us say about at the time the first century gave place to the second, with the Church at the middle of the third century in the time of Cyprian, bishop of Carthage, in whom for the first time the episcopal office meets us in its full maturity as an ecclesiastical office; what a development has come about! The Church has grown outwardly, the whole Empire is occupied by it; no longer do only artisans and women confess Christ, but the churches can count their members in all ranks. The Church is also strengthened within, and has naturalized itself in the world. It is true, the first new radiance, or rather the supernatural glory, which signalized the entrance of the Church into the world, is disappearing: the Christian life is now calmer and more sober. The hope of the speedy advent of Christ, which shone so brightly in the early days, has now become dimmed. The Church has reconciled itself to the destiny of a longer continuance in this world, of a longer progress through history. And the Church has armed for it also. A clear consciousness of the facts on which the Church's being rests has been attained. Its polity is firmly settled, the great multitude of churches are one in faith, and form a compact organization with distinct grades of office. The prospect has widened, there has awaked among Christians a sympathy with all things great and beautiful among men, including art and letters. Already Christianity can show adherents who defend their faith by their writings. Already men like Irenæus and Origen have drawn the first plans of a Christian theology; already have appeared the beginnings of Christian art, which like a young scion on an old stock, will bring forth new blossoms. The Church is no longer a conventicle of recluses who shun the world, but appears in the character of the Church of the people, able and zealous in educating the masses by instruction and doctrine, and a discipline as wise as it is strict.

Such a Church must also view the world from a different point, and estimate its own mission differently from the earlier Church. The heathen world is growing old, and after the manner of the aged, it turns its gaze backwards, for there is the golden age now lost and gone. The present age is one of iron, and more and more dawns upon Heathenism the consciousness that it is the waning power. Christianity is the growing might; with the energy of youth it looks the future in the face, and there sees victory beckoning onward. And how changed are now its ideas of that triumph! The earlier period had no thought of any victory but that which Christ was to bring at his coming. The Roman Empire and the heathen world were to endure till the coming of the Lord. "The persecutions," says Justin Martyr, "will continue till the Lord comes and sets all free."[29] Even with Tertullian the continuance of this world is to coincide with that of the Roman Empire. The moment of the collapse of the Roman Empire is also for him the moment of Christ's return. Therefore the Christians pray for the Empire, and give their aid in prolonging its existence, since they thus pray and work for a *mora finis*, a delay of the end. Tertullian thinks it foolish and absurd to expect that Roman Emperors will ever be Christians.[30] But in the time of Cyprian the hopes of the Christians are directed towards another victory: they begin to grasp the idea that Christianity will vanquish Heathenism from within, and become the dominant religion in the Roman Empire. Celsus had said to the Christians: "If all men were to act like you . . . the affairs of the earth would fall into the hands of the wildest and most lawless barbarians; and then there would no longer remain among men any of the glory of your religion or of the true wisdom." Origen answers: "If all do as I do, then it is evident that even the barbarians when they yield obedience to the word of God will become most obedient to the law, and most humane. And every form of worship will be destroyed except the religion of Christ, which will alone prevail. And indeed it will one day triumph, as its principles take possession of the minds of men more and more every day." [31]

This is a presentiment, nay more, it is the certainty, of victory. But in order to lay hold upon the victory much blood must yet be shed, far more than has already flowed. The severest stress of the conflict still lies before the Church now confirmed in its strength. Restored Heathenism first made the attempt to annihilate Christianity by general persecutions. But it will be seen that restored Heathenism is only a galvanized corpse, unable to inspire the declining State with a new life; and then not by the favor or freak of an Emperor, but by an inward necessity the victory will fall to Christianity, which has remained faithful even under the severest persecutions.

CHAPTER IV.

THE GENERAL PERSECUTIONS.

" We are accounted as sheep for the slaughter." — ROM. viii. 36.

I. FROM MARCUS AURELIUS TO DECIUS.

THE fearful storm of persecution under Marcus Aurelius was succeeded by a time of comparative quiet: as if the Church was given a respite in which to build up and strengthen itself in peace, before the coming of the most terrible storms. Commodus, the degenerate son of Marcus Aurelius, left the Christians unmolested. Marcia, his favorite, even contrived to influence him in their favor. She obtained from the Roman bishop a list of the Christians who were languishing in the mines of Sardinia, and influenced Commodus to set them free.[1] Commodus was more attached to his foreign gods, particularly to those of Egypt, than to the religion of the Roman State, and if he promoted one, he might also permit the existence of another foreign religion of the East, namely, Christianity. Yet the laws enacted hitherto remained, though, when Christians were accused, recourse was had to the earlier procedure under

Trajan. It created a stir when in Rome Apollonius, a senator, was denounced as a Christian by his own slaves, as is narrated. He made his defence before the Senate itself, and was condemned to death by his peers. And thus the highest corporate body in the Empire listened to the confession of Christ.[2]

Under Septimius Severus the indictments and executions became more numerous. The Emperor seems to have been at first favorably disposed towards Christianity. It is said that Proculus, a Christian slave, cured him of a severe sickness by means of anointing with oil.[3] Perhaps it was the vigorous propagation of Christianity at this time which led to a change in his views. The laws against Christianity as a prohibited religion were renewed in the year A.D. 202, and embracing it was forbidden with greater strictness than before.[4] And so the judicial persecution of the Christians began once more. Where the governors were unfavorable, executions ensued, while other governors were less severe or used the occasion only to enrich themselves by extorting money from the Christians.[5]

The persecution raged for a time with great violence in Egypt and Africa, in Egypt to such a degree that the Christians believed that the end of the world was near. In Alexandria Leonides, the father of that great teacher of the Church, Origen, suffered death, and the son, who was still young, was only with difficulty restrained by his mother from following his father. Next we learn the names of a number of Origen's pupils who likewise won the martyr-crown. Of women, too, many died for their Lord, among them the maiden Potamiæna, who was burned together with her mother Marcella. Basilides, one of the lictors who conducted her to the place of execution, protected the maiden from the insults and violence of the rabble. She thanked him and promised him in return that he should shortly attain the crown. That which he had seen and heard became indeed to Basilides a call to Christ. He was converted on the spot, openly confessed his faith, and speedily followed in death those whom he had conducted to execution.[6]

In the city of Scillita in Numidia a number of Christians, both men and women, were brought before the tribunal of the Proconsul. He offered them mercy if they would return to the worship of the gods and swear by the Genius of the Emperor. One of them, Speratus, replied: "I know of no Genius of the ruler of this earth, but I serve my God who is in heaven, whom no man hath seen nor can see.. I render what is due from me, for I acknowledge the Emperor as my sovereign; but I can worship none but my Lord, the King of all kings and Ruler of all nations." The Proconsul remanded them to prison, and the next day attempted once more to bring them to terms. But they remained firm in their confession, "We are Christians!" And when the Proconsul asked them: "Do you refuse all mercy and pardon, then?" one answered in the name of all, "In an honorable contest there is no mercy. Do as thou wilt. We will die joyfully for Christ our Lord." At the place of execution they once more knelt in prayer together, and then were beheaded.[7]

A few years later a number of martyrs suffered in Carthage, amongst whom were two young women, Perpetua and Felicitas, who were only catechumens, and received baptism in the prison.[8] Perpetua had recently become a mother, but neither her love for her child, which she took with her to the prison, nor the entreaties of her aged father, could make her waver. When her father urged her not to bring such disgrace upon the family, she answered: "Thou seest this vessel, a pitcher. Can we call it other than what it is?" And when the father said "No!" she continued, "So I too cannot call myself other than what I am, a Christian." In the prison, whose darkness at first frightened her, since she had never experienced such a thing, she had a vision. She saw a golden ladder stretching up to heaven, on either side of it swords, spears, and knives, and at its foot lay a dragon. Being commanded to mount the ladder, she courageously set her foot on the dragon's head, with the words, "He will not harm me in the name of Jesus Christ," and mounted the ladder. At the top she entered a large garden, and found there the Good Shepherd, who gave her refreshment.

The prisoners now knew what awaited them, and prepared for their farewell to this world. At the final public hearing the Procurator made one more attempt to persuade Perpetua to recant. In the presence of her father, he appealed to her: "Spare thine aged father, offer sacrifice for the welfare of the Emperor." Her father himself assailed her, and reminded her of her child: "Have pity on thy child!" But Perpetua quietly answered, "I cannot, I am a Christian." All were condemned to fight with the wild beasts on the birthday of the Cæsar, Geta. On the evening before the spectacle they held one last meal together, which they celebrated as an Agape with prayer and hymns of praise. As was frequently the case, they were even in their death to play parts in a tragedy. It was intended to clothe the men as priests of Saturn, and the women as priestesses of Ceres. But they refused. "We have come here," they said, "of our own free will, that we might not be deprived of our freedom. We have forfeited our lives in order to be delivered from doing such things." The heathen themselves recognized the justice of the demand, and yielded. One of the martyrs, Saturus, found a speedy release, for a leopard killed him with a single bite. Perpetua and Felicitas were put into a net, and exposed to a wild cow. When the hair and dress of Perpetua became disordered, she carefully re-arranged them, mindful even then of womanly modesty. When finally they were all to receive the death-blow, Perpetua called to the soldier, Pudens: "Be strong, and think of my faith, and let not all this make thee waver, but strengthen thee." Then they greeted one another with the kiss of peace, and were slain with daggers. When the young gladiator approached who was to kill Perpetua, his hand trembled. Then she laid her hand on his, and guided it to her throat for the death-blow.

Under Caracalla the persecutions gradually ceased, and the Church rejoiced in a perfect peace which the sun-priest Elagabalus did not disturb. Alexander Severus and his mother Julia Mammæa even showed signs of favor towards the Church. In the private chapel of the Emperor, among the statues of other great men, stood that of Christ. He was fond of repeating the words of Christ, and when in Rome the guild of the cooks had a dispute with the Christian Church concerning a building-site, he decided in favor of the Church, for he held, "it was better that God should be worshipped there in any way whatever, than that the space should be given up to the cooks."[9] This was of course nothing more than practical toleration, and indeed the succeeding reign soon showed itself unfavorable to the Christians.[10] Maximinus the Thracian, a rude barbarian, who plundered even the heathen temples,[11] recommenced the persecution of the Christians, less from religious or political reasons, than because they had been favored by his predecessor. Eusebius says,[12] he ordered that the officers of the Christian churches should be executed. The order does not appear to have been literally carried out, yet in many places the Christians had to suffer. The Roman bishop Pontianus was banished to Sardinia, and died there from ill treatment in the mines.[13] Origen had to remain concealed for a time in the house of a Christian virgin named Juliana.[14] The presbyter Protoctetus of Cæsarea and his servant Ambrosius shared a worse fate. They were hurried from prison to prison, and underwent many sufferings, but escaped with life. Yet Ambrosius was robbed of his property, showing that the avarice of the judge played a part in the case. The worst of the persecution was in Cappadocia, where the fanatical passions of the rabble participated in it, and a number of Christians sealed their faith by death.[15] Philip the Arabian is said to have showed the Christians so much favor, that the legend arose that he himself was secretly a Christian.[16]

With the exception of the attack made on the Christians by Maximinus the Thracian, it may be said that they had thirty years of rest. The Emperors of this period were thoroughly un-Roman, even in their religious lives. They were syncretists, and their syncretism, whether it appeared in a ruder form, as in Elagabalus, or in a nobler, as in Alexander Severus, brought with it all kinds of compromises, which, though Christianity of course could not accept them, yet, for the first time, put Roman Emperors into a really friendly relation to the Christian Church. Naturally it was not an enduring peace, but only a slackening of the conflict. As soon as the ancient Roman spirit began to re-act against this un-Roman state of affairs, there would necessarily begin a sterner method of dealing with Christianity. The rest was only the prelude to yet fiercer struggles. They commenced with Decius, whose reign marked the dawn of a period of re-action, ending only with Constantine. The ancient Roman spirit once more arose in its might, and attempted a restoration of the fallen Empire. Closely connected with, indeed springing from, this attempt, were the general persecutions of the Christians which now began. In order to understand this we need to recall the situation of the Empire.

The frenzy of despotism had brought the State to the brink of ruin. The Empire was in imminent danger of destruction from the utter absence of all restraint. Confusion the most complete prevailed everywhere. In Rome itself, senate, people, and soldiery formed opposing factions. Day after day regular battles were fought in the streets, and, as a consequence, part of the city was laid waste by fire. The state of things was similar in the provinces. No respect was paid to the laws, because no one felt an inward bond of union with the law. Usurpers arose here and there, and attempted to seize the throne, or were compelled by their followers to make the attempt. Meanwhile the barbarians were storming at the frontiers; in the North the German tribes, in the South-east the Persians, were already threatening to overwhelm the empire. The Franks were pouring across the Pyrenees, the Alemanni were at the gates of Milan, the Goths had destroyed the celebrated Temple of Diana at Ephesus, the Persians had advanced as far as Antioch in Syria. In this universal distress the genius of Rome arose once more from the only place where it still dwelt, the army. A series of Soldier-Emperors saved the Empire from almost certain destruction. It was God's purpose that the Empire should not fall into the hands of the Germans, until it had become Christianized, and was thus capable of instructing its conquerors in the Christian religion.

These Emperors, were, it is true, not Romans by birth: they were provincials, for the most part Illyrians, but the city of Rome began at this time to lose its importance as the metropolis. The centre was rotten, while the circumference still preserved a comparatively healthy life. These Emperors, brought up in the camps of the legions where the ancient Roman courage, discipline, and virtue were still to be found, and trained in the traditions of Rome, were indeed more truly Romans than the inhabitants of the city. While Rome was revelling, the armies had been guarding the frontier by strenuous efforts, and in the uninterrupted succession of campaigns there grew up a race of able generals. They now took the control of things, and chose, usually from among themselves, the bravest and ablest men for the throne. These were men who had served from the ranks up, without much education, but severely moral and strict in discipline, exactly the opposite of those dissolute debauchees who had so often polluted the imperial throne. They were soldiers through and through, yet they almost all showed a strong tendency to be idealists, one may even say fanatics. Brought up amid war, perpetually in the camp, they yet longed for peace. Their favorite expression was, that war was only waged for the sake of peace; their dream was, that soon there would dawn an era of peace, in which soldiers would be no longer needed; they even attempted, in the person of Probus, one of the most powerful of these Soldier-Emperors, to accustom their armies to the arts of peace. Whenever a short respite between the campaigns allowed, Probus would set his legions to digging canals and planting vineyards. They sought to realize the ideal of peace to which they aspired, by means of a restoration of the ancient Roman order of things. Roman manners and morals were to be revived — that was now the solution of the problem. Some of these Soldier-Emperors addressed the Senate and the people of Rome as reverently as if they were still the Senate and people of the time of the Republic; they spoke of the eternal *Roma* and her power just as a fanatical Republican in the best days of the ancient city might have done.

For the restoration of the Roman order of things, however, the restoration of the religion of the Roman State was of course essential. All these Emperors (this too was a characteristic common to them) were pious heathen; more than that, they were excessively superstitious. In their broken, changeful lives, perpetually surrounded by perils, they had learned to heed omens and predictions. They ascribed the greatest value to the favor of the gods, and, well knowing the instability of a throne which is supported by power only, they sought to attach their followers and to bind them to themselves by all kinds of superstitions. It was restored Heathenism, fanatical and demon-worshipping, which now came into power, and was represented even by the Emperors.

When we bear this in mind it becomes easy to understand why just these Emperors were persecutors of the Christians, above all their predecessors. They had to be: indeed there could be nothing more false, than to imagine that these persecutions arose from mere arbitrary choice, or from cruelty and personal hostility. They were rather the result of the entire political situation, and were a necessary product thereof. To the schemes of restoration which ruled this period, there was nothing so antagonistic as Christianity. If ancient Rome was to arise in renewed glory, Christianity, which utterly opposed the ancient Roman order of things, must be put out of the way. But by this time the Church had acquired such strength, that methods such as Trajan had employed a century before were no longer adequate. There could no longer be a hope, such as Trajan had indulged, of subduing Christianity slowly and gradually; the only alternative was the recognition of Christianity or its annihilation. The former was impossible without entirely renouncing the whole project of restoration; so the latter was determined upon. And thus the persecution assumed an entirely new character. It was now no longer an outbreak of popular rage, to which the officials yielded in some places, no longer a judicial process against individuals expressly accused according to the ordinary methods of Roman law, but a general persecution, based on the deliberate policy of the State, which affected all Christians alike, and had for its express object the annihilation of the Church.

II. FROM DECIUS TO GALLIENUS.

Decius was the first to order a general persecution. His reason for so doing was certainly not a personal one, his antagonism to Philip the Arabian, for instance, whom he conquered, and who was favorable to the Christians. The cause was rather that purpose of restoration which has been described, and which was embodied in Decius. Great were the plans made by Decius. Like a second Trajan (whose name he assumed), he purposed to re-establish the ancient glory of Rome. Ancient institutions were revived, the Senate regained its honors, the office of Censor was renewed, Rome was fortified once more and adorned with buildings. It was impossible that an Emperor with such aims could behold unmoved a religion, illicit according to Roman ideas, extending its sway, the ancient shrines deserted and the temples standing empty. As a second Trajan, he was bound, like the first, to undertake the conflict with the religion which was the enemy of the State. Soon after ascending the throne (A. D. 249), he issued an edict in the year 250, that all Christians without exception should be required to perform the rites of the religion of the Roman State. If they refused they were to be compelled thereto with threats and tortures. In fulfilment of this edict the local magistrates in every place fixed a term, before which the Christians were to appear before them, and to sacrifice to the gods. Those who left their native land before this term were not further molested, but their property was confiscated, and they were forbidden to return on pain of death. Those who remained, and up to the fixed term had not given proof that they had sacrificed, were summoned before a commission of investigation, composed of the magistrates and five of the principal citizens. Then they were dealt with, not as in the former judicial process, with a view to their conviction and sentence, but with the object of persuading them to recant. At first they were only threatened and given a further respite. If this did not succeed, recourse was had to tortures, and if these failed of the desired result, the stubborn recusants were thrown into prison, in order there to shake their determination by continued tortures joined to hunger and thirst. Capital punishment at first was rare, and only resorted to against bishops; but many were killed by the tortures or died in the prisons. The persecution became gradually more stern. The endurance of the Christians provoked greater severity. Because in some places the local magistrates made exceptions, and urged the matter with too little diligence in the Emperor's view, he directed the prefects to interfere personally, and where they seemed too merciful they were replaced by others more strict.

Men of acute minds had foreboded the storm. Origen predicted its coming, and Cyprian foresaw it in a vision.[17] He seemed to see a father standing between his two sons. The one on the right sat in sorrow and deep grief; the one on the left carried a net in readiness to catch those who stood near. When Cyprian in wonder asked who they were, the explanation was given, that the one on the right (Christ) sorrowed because his commands were not obeyed; the one on the left (the Devil) rejoiced because he would soon be permitted by the Father to vent his rage on the people. Thus Cyprian foresaw the persecution in the shape of a distinct judgment on the laxity which had been allowed to enter the life of the Christians. But on the majority of the Christians it came with an utter suddenness. Some churches had enjoyed uninterrupted quiet for thirty years, and many Christians no doubt believed that the peace was to be lasting. This made the panic all the greater. In the times of tranquillity some impure elements had found an entrance into the Church, and even the best of the members were unaccustomed to conflict. So it is not to be wondered at, that much weakness was brought to light. Many did not wait for the fixed term to come. Such as held public offices, and respectable citizens who feared for their business, made haste to renounce Christianity by offering sacrifices. "Before the battle," Cyprian complains, "many were conquered, and, without having met the enemy, were cut down; they did not even seek to gain the reputation of having sacrificed against their will." [18] It appeared as if some had only awaited this opportunity to break loose from Christianity. When the commission could not get through in a single day, and remanded the rest to the next day, they entreated to be allowed to present themselves, as if they could not assure their safety quickly enough. Even children were brought and made to offer incense with their little hands. Others were persuaded by their relatives, or induced by their heathen friends to go. Pale and trembling they approached the altar as if they were about, not to sacrifice, but to be sacrificed. The bystanders mocked them, saying that they were too cowardly either to sacrifice or to die. There were dreadful scenes. Some who had denied were suddenly seized with horror, which rose to madness. A Christian woman in Carthage, after she had pronounced the word by which she renounced Christ, became dumb, and could not utter another word. Another went directly from the sacrifice to the bath, and when she returned had become insane. The venality of the officials made it possible in many ways to evade the law. For money they provided the Christians with a certificate that they had sacrificed, or, without coming and having such certificate made out, they could obtain the privilege of having their names inserted in the protocol among the number of those who had complied with the edict. They quieted their consciences by saying that they had done nothing themselves which was a denial of their faith. The Church did not allow itself to be deceived by these practices, but declared with clear decision that such a way of escaping persecution was a denial of the faith.[19]

Thus there was no lack of weakness, and the persecution became a sifting which removed the chaff out of the churches. But Christian heroism also was not wanting. The church in Rome led all the rest in this. First the bishop Fabianus suffered martyrdom.[20] At the risk of his life Cornelius succeeded him in the episcopate, and not long after in death too. He was first banished, then executed. Lucius, who had the courage to carry on the succession, likewise shortly went to receive his crown. In the Catacombs may be seen to-day the simple gravestones of the martyr-bishops near together, each marked only with the name.[21] The bishop Fabianus was accompanied in death by Moses, one of the presbyters. Besides these the virgins Victoria, Anatolia, Agatha, and a great multitude of other martyrs, died under fearful tortures. In Alexandria the number who were sacrificed was not less than in

Rome.[22] Even before the regular process began, the rabble attacked individual Christians. They tried to compel an old man named Metras to speak blasphemous words. When he refused he was stoned to death. They brought a woman named Quinta into a temple, and demanded that she should worship the idols. When she remained firm they dragged her by the feet through the city, and killed her. They broke the teeth of Apollonia, a virgin, because she would not repeat the blasphemous words which were dictated to her, and finally burnt her at the stake. After this the regular process of persecution began, and many more suffered death for their steadfastness. Especial mention is made of a boy, Dioscurus, who, though only fifteen, by his apt replies and his firmness under all tortures extorted the admiration of even the Prefect himself, so that he finally released him in order, as he said, that he might come to a better state of mind. Even in the smaller towns and villages of Egypt many were numbered among the martyrs. In the Thebaïd the Prefect had a Christian husband and wife crucified side by side. They lived for days upon the cross, and encouraged one another.[23] In Jerusalem the bishop Alexander, in Antioch the bishop Babylas, died under tortures endured with steadfastness.[24] In Toulouse the bishop Saturninus was bound to a wild bull, and dragged to death.[25]

Cyprian, the bishop of Carthage, had withdrawn to a safe place at the beginning of the persecution. He was blamed by some for this, but his subsequent martyrdom proved that no lack of courage was his reason for hiding. From his place of exile he consoled and encouraged the members of his church, and gave directions for their conduct during the persecution.

The alms for the poor, which were usually managed by one person, were now to be divided among the presbyters and deacons, so that, if one of them were taken prisoner, the others would still be able to carry on the work, and, besides, the poor would be cared for all the more easily. The presbyters were to be diligent in their pastoral care of the prisoners in the dungeons, and to carry them the holy communion, and yet to do all with caution in order to give no provocation to the heathen. The poor were to be helped with greater care than usual, but they must be on their guard against such as put themselves forward, and sought — as was sometimes the case — to cover a disgraceful life by a seeming martyrdom.[26] The Carthaginian church had no lack of confessors and martyrs.[27] Many of them lay in the dungeons while the heathen attempted to bring them to denial by means of hunger and thirst. Fifteen of them are mentioned who died of starvation in the prison. Others died by the pangs of the torture, and yet others were executed. One of the members of the church, Numidicus by name, was especially prominent. He had inspired many with courage for martyrdom, and had seen his own wife die at the stake. He was condemned to the same death, and left lying half burnt and covered with stones. His daughter sought out her father's body in order to bury it. Great was her joy at finding signs of life still in him. In haste she carried him home, and really succeeded by her careful nursing in completely restoring him. Cyprian afterwards made him a presbyter.[28]

The most dreadful thing about this persecution was that the heathen did not aim at the death of the Christians, but only at compelling them by means of torture to recant. "Tortures overtook them," thus Cyprian [29] speaks of the persecution, "tortures wherein the torturer ceases not, without escape of condemnation, without the consolation of death; tortures which do not dismiss them speedily to their crown, but rack them until they overthrow their faith; except perhaps that God in his mercy removed one here and there in the midst of his torments, and so he attained his crown not by the full ending of his torture, but by the suddenness of death." They were not only thrown into prison, laden with chains, their arms and legs stretched on the rack; not only were the ordinary tortures employed, the crushing of the fingers, the dislocation of the limbs, the tearing of the flesh with nails and hooks, but the most refined and novel tortures were invented. The prisoners were exposed to the most intense heat, and left to thirst for days; they were burned with fire, with charcoal and red-hot iron. We are told that some were stripped, smeared all over with honey, and exposed to the stings of the insects. In all this the fury of the fanatical heathen rabble rose higher than ever before. Great was their rejoicing when they had succeeded in torturing a Christian until he finally stretched out his hand to scatter the incense on the idol's altar! How they gloated over the torments of the poor victim! The Christians were now outlaws. They were attacked in their houses, robbed of whatever was worth taking, and the remainder of their household goods was broken or burned. No Christian dared to be seen in public. In the streets they were insulted, stoned, and beaten, or a mob collected, and tried to induce them to pronounce blasphemous words.

Those were the times in which the Christians, beset

on every side, often betrayed and attacked in their assemblies, fled to the deserts and the woods, or descended to the dead in the Catacombs. There in little assemblies they held their services, listened to the Word, and partook of the sacrament by the light of the *terracotta* lamps such as are often found there now. Those who gathered there did not know but that a fate might soon overtake them like that of those whose names were called over at the Lord's Supper as confessors and martyrs, or whose unadorned graves with their simple inscriptions were all around them there. How solemn and earnest such a service must have been, truly fitted to strengthen their faith for a joyful confession! Some had fallen away, but those who remained faithful were all the more closely united in the distress of the time. How strongly did they support each other by prayer! Times without number Cyprian exhorted the church to prayer for the tempted and persecuted, and they in turn from their prison asked the intercession of the church. How willingly they served each other, though often enough they had to pay for the privilege with their lives! What honor was shown to the martyrs and confessors! — the Christians embraced them on their way to the place of execution, and kissed their chains in the prisons. They were given as honorable a burial as was possible, and no heed was paid to the danger incurred in procuring this for them. With diligent care their names and the story of their martyrdom were recorded for a memorial. And if perchance the persecution ceased for a while, and some returned from the prisons or from exile, how jubilantly they were greeted! The Christians hastened to meet them, crowded round them, embraced them with heartfelt affection, and hung on their necks with kisses.[30]

Like a storm which lulls indeed for a while to return again with redoubled fury, the persecution continued for a decade. The endurance of the Christians wearied the heathen, or the zeal of the Emperor was turned into other channels by campaigns and revolts. Thus there came times of tranquillity in which the Christians could breathe once more, and collect their scattered forces. And then the persecution would break out anew, and with twofold zeal and new measures the heathen would toil at the annihilation of the Church.

When Decius had fallen (A. D. 251), in the war against the Goths, the change of rule brought a short breathing-space; but in the following year, when the Empire was suffering from plagues of different kinds, drought and famine, the absence of the Christians from the great sacrifices instituted everywhere to appease the gods, gave the impulse for new persecutions.[31] At that time many Christians were punished by being sent to the mines. This was an exceedingly hard lot, for there the Christians were worse treated than galley-slaves.

When Gallus was murdered by his own soldiers another short pause ensued; but Valerian took up again the interrupted work of persecution. He used different tactics. The fearful bloodshed under Decius had failed. Valerian hoped to attain the object without shedding blood. To this end the Emperor gave orders that the bishops be separated from their churches, and prohibited all assemblies of the Christians, all gatherings for worship, and all visits to the cemeteries where the Christians were wont to pray by the graves of the martyrs.[32]

These regulations soon proved without effect. The

bishops were banished; for instance, Cyprian to Curubis, Dionysius of Alexandria to Kephro: but in their banishment they maintained their connection with their churches. From the places of their exile they still guided their flocks by letters and by means of travelling clergy. They only became dearer to their churches, inwardly more united with them; and the word of the exile for the faith was more effectual than that of the bishop present in person. In the places to which they were banished, they gathered new churches about them, and the seeds of the gospel were thus carried to some places whither they had never come before.

So the Emperor advanced to severer measures. In A. D. 258, he issued an edict [33] which ordered that the bishops, presbyters, and deacons should immediately be slain with the sword; that senators and magistrates were to lose their property, and if they still remained Christians they were to be executed in like manner; that women of rank should be banished after their property had been confiscated; and that Christians in the service of the imperial court should be put in chains, and divided among the imperial estates to labor there.

Thus the bloody work began again. The shepherds of the flock were particularly the objects against which the full force of this persecution was directed, and a large number of them sealed their faith with death. In Rome the bishop Sixtus suffered Aug. 6, A. D. 258. He was arrested in the Catacombs while holding divine service. After receiving his sentence he was conducted by the executioner back again, and beheaded on the spot where he had just been celebrating the Lord's Supper. His episcopal chair was sprinkled with his blood.[34] On the way to death his deacon Laurentius met him. "Whither goest thou, father, without thy son? whither, priest, without thy deacon?" said Laurentius. "Cease weeping, thou wilt soon follow me," replied the bishop. And on the fourth day after, the 10th of August, the deacon did follow him in death. Laurentius is said to have been roasted on an iron chair.

In Carthage, Cyprian received the martyr's crown. Some of his principal friends wished to aid him in escaping; but, though he had previously thought it his duty to his church to save himself, yet now he refused. He only remained in hiding a short time in order not to be taken to Utica, where the Proconsul was at that time staying, because it was fitting that the shepherd should meet his death before the eyes of his church. As soon as the Proconsul returned to Carthage, Cyprian was taken prisoner, and brought before him. An immense crowd had collected in the prætorium. The hearing was short. "Thou art Thascius Cyprianus?"—"I am."—"Thou hast permitted thyself to be made an official in a sacrilegious sect?"—"Yes."—"The sacred Emperors have commanded thee to sacrifice."—"That I will not do."—"Consider it well."—"Do what is commanded thee; in a cause so just no reflection is needed." The Proconsul consulted his counsellors and immediately pronounced the sentence: "Thascius Cyprianus shall be executed with the sword." Cyprian answered only: "Thanks be to God!" and the sentence was immediately executed. The bishop disrobed himself, knelt, and prayed. With trembling hands the executioner gave the fatal blow (Sept. 14, A. D. 258). Cyprian was not the only martyr in Carthage. Beside him several presbyters and deacons met their death.

When one of them, named Montanus, was being led to execution, he tore the cloth with which his eyes were to be bound, in two, and asked that one-half of it might be kept for his friend and fellow-presbyter, Flavianus, who would soon follow him. A few days afterwards they bound the eyes of Flavianus with the half of the cloth, and he too received the deadly stroke.

From Egypt, Spain, and other countries of the Empire we have the names of a large number of martyrs, for the most part bishops and presbyters. But the churches were not spared. Their assemblies for worship were attacked, they were dispossessed of their churches and cemeteries. In Rome the heathen surprised a Christian congregation which was holding divine service in one of the catacombs, and walled up the entrance of it, so that the Christians perished within.[35] In Africa a multitude of Christians were thrown into a lime-kiln, and burned.

As little was accomplished by this persecution as by those which preceded it. In A. D. 260, Valerian was taken prisoner in a campaign against the Persians; and with the close of his reign the persecution also ended. His successor, Gallienus, restored to the Christians the buildings and land, the cemeteries and holy places, which had been taken from them. He even wrote friendly letters to several of the bishops, and expressly declared that it was his will that they should henceforth exercise their office in peace.[36] This was, of course, not a regular legal recognition of Christianity. It still remained a prohibited religion. Indeed, even under Gallienus, Marinus, a captain, suffered martyrdom, though only as the result of an indictment brought against him; and when Aurelian decided to order a new persecution, he had no need to revoke the so-called edict of toleration of Gallienus. After Gallienus, as before him, it was a penal offence to be a Christian, only no one of the Emperors, in the unspeakable confusion of these years, was sufficiently lord of the Empire to think of persecuting the Christians. Thus the Church enjoyed for forty years a tranquillity which in general was uninterrupted.[37]

And the Church needed rest. It was like a fortress which had repulsed an enemy, who had tried every means of attack. The enemy had not been able to conquer it, but yet the walls and towers lay in ruins at some points, and the appearance of the citadel showed what it had suffered. That which had fallen must be rebuilt, and the damages repaired. The Church did not remain uninjured in the time of persecution, and the suffering afterwards was often worse than the storm. Such times arouse the powers of the Church, but they also bring great dangers with them. The life of the Church is forced out of its quiet grooves, and, with a kind of one-sidedness, all energies are concentrated on one point. Those who had heroically held out under persecution, the confessors who had lain in prison, and could still show the stripes and wounds of their torturers, were now held exclusively in honor. They became a peculiar kind of ecclesiastical aristocracy. Earnestly and vehemently as the faithful teachers warned them against pride, it was natural that some of the highly venerated confessors should not withstand the temptation to misuse their authority in the Church by all kinds of arbitrary interference with the regular order of things.[38] And this was the more dangerous, because in many places this order had already suffered so much from the pressure of the times, and because the Church had now to face the exceedingly difficult question of the treatment of those who had fallen away in the persecution. There were many such, and of different kinds: some who had voluntarily sacrificed, others who had been driven to do so by torture, yet others who had bought a certificate, or had procured the insertion of their names in the lists. The confessors directly interfered in this matter. They gave to many of the lapsed, who asked for them, certificates of peace, on the ground of which these then demanded reception into the Church, and in some places were re-admitted to the Lord's Supper even without penitence or confession.[39] The confessors did not confine themselves to giving certificates to particular individuals, but wrote them quite indefinitely, in favor of a number of persons.[40] They even meddled in the affairs of churches to which they were strangers. Celerinus, a Roman, asked of a Carthaginian confessor a certificate for his two apostate sisters.[41] Some indeed came forward with the assertion that they had been commissioned by this or that martyr before his death to give reconciliation to all who should ask for it.

In opposition to such dealings, some earnest Christians insisted on the greatest strictness. It seemed to them unjust, that the lapsed should so easily find acceptance, and thus be put on an entire equality with those who had remained steadfast. They did not believe in any reception of the lapsed at all. Those who had denied their Lord should be commended to God's grace, but the Church ought not to be polluted by their reception. In some places, these differences led not only to scandalous scenes, but even to lasting schisms. The strict divided themselves from the lenient, and formed separate churches, which claimed to be the only undefiled ones.

In this difficult situation the Church strove to keep the wholesome middle way. It was impossible to shut her doors to all the lapsed. Nor could she view them as those in whom she had no concern, but was earnestly solicitous in their behalf, in order to lead them back to a genuine repentance. Very wisely their re-admission was postponed until the time after the persecution. He who could not wait so long was free to reverse his previous denial of being a Christian, and suffer for it; for the Church always regarded those who did this as fully received back into fellowship. The matter could not be exhaustively settled amid the disturbance of a time of persecution. A most minute examination was necessary (and this was another wise rule) in order that each case might be decided according to its peculiar features. It was plain that those who had yielded only to the severest tortures deserved a different treatment from those who had voluntarily sacrificed; that those who had really sacrificed stood on a different footing from those who had believed, though by a sinful mistake, that they might shield themselves from persecution by buying a certificate of sacrifice. To each one was assigned, according to the measure of his guilt, a time of probation, during which he was to show the genuineness of his repentance, and only at the expiration of that time were they received, some sooner, some later; and those who had most grievously sinned, only on their death-beds. Strictness and leniency worked together to repair the injuries of the time of persecution, and gradually to re-establish order in the churches.

Another comparison may be applied to the Church after the persecution. It was like a field after a thunder-storm. Many a blade is broken, many a bough torn off, the water has made deep furrows here and there; but the storm has also purified the air, and the rain has fertilized the land, and now when all is quiet again and the sun once more shines out, all things are growing with greater freshness and gladness than before. So in the Church there followed the persecution a time of new and stronger growth. Many elements of impurity had been eliminated, the word of God had displayed its power, the testimony of the martyrs had penetrated many a heart. Everywhere the number of believers was increasing. The Christians' places of meeting had to be enlarged, or new ones built. In the cities there were already large churches. There were Christians everywhere, in town and country, among the rich and the poor, Christian officers in the army, Christian officials in the government as high as the Prefects, Christian chamberlains and officials of the court about the person of the Emperor. It must have seemed to many as if the victory were already won, but it was not. This was only a practical toleration, not as yet one really sustained by law. Emperor and Empire were still heathen. It had not yet been decided on what basis the purpose of a restoration of the Empire, which inspired all the able Emperors, should be realized; whether on the basis of restored Heathenism and the Neoplatonic philosophy, or on the basis of Christianity and God's word. In reality the cause of the tranquillity was only this, that no one of the successive Emperors was sufficiently master of the confusion prevailing throughout the Empire, to be able to commence the restoration. The first Emperor who really succeeded in carrying forward the plan which all had followed, made the last attempt to annihilate Christianity.

Thus the time of tranquillity was indeed not yet the victory longed for, but only an interval for recuperation before the decisive battle.

BOOK THIRD.

THE VICTORY.

"This is the victory that overcometh the world, even our faith." —
1 JOHN v. 4.

CHAPTER I.

THE DECISIVE BATTLE.

" Look up, and lift up your heads: for your redemption draweth nigh."
— LUKE xxi. 28.

I. THE WORK OF THE CHURCH AMONG THE HEATHEN.

THE Church owed its victory not only to the steadfastness of the martyrs in times of persecution, but at least as much to the faithful work of its members in times of peace. For the victory was indeed no mere outward triumph, but the defeat of Heathenism in its inner principles. Hearts were won, consciences convinced, the heathen were made Christian in disposition, the views, life, conduct, and customs of the people were changed from within. The whole of this great transformation is of course hidden from our eyes by its internal nature, to the degree that we are not now in a position to follow it step by step, to discover its course and to distinguish its stages in the different periods. But we may gain a glimpse of the mighty work of development in the Church, which was the preliminary stage. And this is the place for such a glimpse, because only thereby can we come to comprehend and appreciate that the victory of the Church in the last decisive battle was more than a lucky stroke of fortune, and had causes far deeper than any momentary combination of favorable circumstances. For the sake of this preparation, God let the Church remain at rest for a considerable period before the last and severest struggle. He designed that the work among the heathen should have so extended, that even the utmost efforts of its enemies could no longer avail for its annihilation.

The early Christians made no special provisions for drawing the heathen into the Church. The Christian worship, so far as services of prayer and preaching were concerned, was open to the heathen, and only the separate celebration of the Lord's Supper, with which the love-feast was connected, was closed to them. To this, the Holy of Holies, only those who had received baptism and joined the Church had access. Thus Christian worship exerted a missionary influence upon the heathen world beside that of missionary preaching proper; and when individuals had become interested by such means, they sought further instruction from one of the officers or other principal members of the Church. In this way they gained a more particular knowledge of Christianity, and, for the most part, soon entered into the actual membership of the Church by baptism. This process was personal and private in character. Christians who possessed peculiar gifts for teaching probably gathered the proselytes around them, but there was as yet no regular provision made for catechumens.

In the times of persecution all this was changed. The celebration of the Lord's Supper, which hitherto had been separated from the preaching service and held in the evening, was joined to the other service in order to avoid the appearance of transgressing the laws against secret assemblies; and the dangers of the time soon obliged the Christians to exclude the heathen altogether from their worship. The Church was compelled to withdraw into concealment in order to worship God in peace. Only thus could disturbances of the service be avoided, and the ridicule and blasphemy of any heathen, who might intrude into the meetings, be escaped. And by the same change the occasion for persecution was removed, so far as possible. In this period we find also the first steps towards a regular catechumenate. The position of the Christians necessitated it, for there was need of caution in two directions in receiving those who sought admittance into the Church. On the one hand, it could not be known whether they were to be trusted, or some enemy and traitor was effecting an entrance under the pretext of wishing to become a Christian. And on the other hand those who were about to join the Church now lacked the preparation which had previously been supplied by their attendance at the preaching services, since all were now excluded from these except the actual members of the Church. There was felt to be a need of something to mediate the transition from a position entirely outside of the Church to full membership in it This was provided by the catechumens receiving a course of instruction by this time fully arranged, without participating in the worship of the Church; and then, after vows of renunciation, being admitted to the church services so far as they consisted of preaching and prayer. Thus the preaching supplemented the instruction already received, and so baptism followed comparatively soon.

The time of rest after the persecution brought a new danger with it, a danger in some respects more nearly affecting the life of the Church than the persecution itself. Great multitudes of the heathen crowded into the Church. How easily might these multitudes bring elements of impurity in with them! The cessation of the state of war had itself an enervating influence. The Church could not venture to throw open its shrine to all without probation. Yet, on the other hand, it was a subject for rejoicing that the heathen were coming in, and access must not be denied to any. With the sagacity of a great teacher the Church united the two. The Sacrament, that Holy of Holies, was withdrawn into yet deeper retirement, and while the outer doors were thrown open to all, there was, so to speak, a long and narrow way which led from the outer court to the inmost shrine. This way was the now developed catechumenate. The preaching service was once more thrown open to all, even the heathen; but, before they could receive the sacrament, a long, carefully arranged and graded process of preparation must be passed through. Let us take a survey of this path from the first impulse towards Christianity to the full reception into the Church.

When the desire to become a Christian inspired a heathen, he made it known generally to some church-member, and he in turn conducted him to the bishop or to a presbyter or deacon, in order that his purpose might be put to the test. From these he received some brief and condensed instruction; and if he persisted in his desire, he was received into the number of the catechumens by a simple ceremony. This gave him the right, and also the duty, of attending the preaching services.

"Go to the temple of God, forsake the idols," was the command. Hence those who belonged to this class were called *audientes*, "the hearers." If he made use of his opportunities of learning the truths of Christianity from the preaching, he was, after a time, admitted to the second class of the catechumens, *orantes*, "the praying ones," or *genuflectentes*, "the kneelers." The distinguishing mark of this class was, that they took part in the Church prayers. While after the preaching the *audientes* were dismissed with the unbelievers, the *orantes* were permitted to join in the prayer for the strength and growth of the Church, which was offered to God every Sunday. Those who by the length of their probation, and in other respects, seemed fit, were required to declare expressly once more their desire for baptism, and to hand in their names. Thereby they entered the last stage of the catechumenate, and were called *competentes*, "seekers," that is, real candidates for baptism. And now began the regular course of instruction to the catechumens, which was given during Lent, since Easter Sunday was the usual day for baptism. They were now initiated into the real mysteries of the Christian faith, particularly into the mystery of the sacraments, which had hitherto been carefully hidden from them; and at the close they were taught the confession of faith, the real *symbolum*, the mark of the Christian, and with it the Lord's Prayer, the prayer of the children of God. Finally the reading of Psalm xlii., "As the hart panteth after the water-brooks, so panteth my soul after thee, O God," introduced the rite of baptism.

Two things were aimed at and attained by the Church through this long probation: on the one side, for the sake of the Church, the most thorough test which could be applied to those who sought to become members; and on the other side, no less important, an entire freedom of choice on the part of the candidates. Those who came were to come voluntarily, and to take the step with a full consciousness of what it involved. No persuasion was attempted, nor do we find a trace of proselytizing, and all the arts which are wont to be connected with it. The first declaration of his purpose, by which a heathen acquired the privilege of listening to the preaching, was only preliminary. It was open to him to recede from his position, and as yet there were no bonds uniting him to the Church from which he could not liberate himself at any moment. Opportunity was given him to become more intimately acquainted with the Church, its belief, and its life, and only then, when he had advanced so far in knowledge as to be fully conscious of what he was doing, was he allowed to hand in his name and thus fix his choice. But, although the candidate was thus left in perfect freedom, yet he remained under the influence of the prayers and the pastoral care of the Church, which in that day were more prominent than the specific instruction.

The Church showed a wonderful sagacity in this whole matter. Its mission to instruct the heathen was fulfilled with great wisdom and prudence, and it was owing to this good judgment that the times of tranquillity did not cause more injury than the seasons of persecution, and that the friendship of the world did not prove more disastrous than its enmity. Though elements of impurity could not be wholly prevented from finding their way into the Church, which thus, the more it began to be the Church of the people, became more and more like the field in which the wheat and the tares grow together promiscuously, yet this much was attained, that the accession of the masses did not deprive the Church of that measure of purity and power, which was necessary for sustaining the severe and final conflict.

Another part of the word of instruction undertaken by the Church is to be found in the Apologetic literature of the time. We have already noticed its beginnings. A richer development was attained amid the struggles of the third century. The Church was now the object of literary attacks on the part of rhetoricians and philosophers, and therefore was compelled to defend itself in literature, as indeed it did. Several of the greatest Apologists belong to this period; above all, Origen and Tertullian. With quiet superiority and vast learning Origen refutes the slanders of the heathen, lays open the emptiness of Heathenism, and yet everywhere seeks to gain points of connection with Christianity. With incisive keenness and biting wit, Tertullian supports the cause of the Christians, often in the style of an advocate, not shunning even sophistry, but ever burning with zeal and full of sturdy conviction. And though he, as no other, has laid bare the weakness of Heathenism, and held it up to mockery and scorn, yet it was he who wrote that exquisite little treatise to prove " The Soul by Nature Christian,"[1] and showed the heathen that they were all created for Christianity, and that in every one of them there was implanted, even if unconsciously, an inclination towards Christ, a longing for Him.

The earlier Apologists had asked only toleration, only justice for Christians as well as other men, but the Apologists of this period go a step further: they demand freedom. Religious freedom, that mighty word, was now first openly pronounced. Strongly does Origen emphasize the fact that belief is a matter of entire freedom. "Jesus Christ," he says, "did not wish to win men like a despot, who draws them into the revolt which he leads, nor like a robber, who puts arms into the hands of his comrades, nor like a rich man, who buys adherents by his liberality, nor by any blamable means, but by means of his wisdom, which was so fitted to unite to God in fear and holiness those who yield themselves to his laws."[2] "It is irreligious to use compulsion in religion," cries Tertullian. "Man has a right, and it belongs to the natural power of every individual, to worship what he thinks best; and one man's religion does not profit or injure another." "Allow one," he demands, "to worship God, another Jupiter. Let one raise his suppliant hands to heaven, another to the altar of Fides. Let one in his prayer (if ye think this of us) tell the clouds, another the ornaments of the ceiling: let one devote his own life to his God, another that of a goat. For beware that you do not give a further ground for the charge of irreligion, by taking away *religious liberty* and prohibiting a choice of deity, so that I may not worship whom I will, but am constrained to worship whom I will not. No one, not even a mortal, would desire to be worshipped by any against their will. . . . Every province also, and state, hath its own god. . . . But we alone are forbidden to have a religion of our own."[3] "Religious liberty!" Tertullian created for the new idea this new name, which here for the first time appears. In later days the Church itself threw away this jewel, and put compulsion again into freedom's place; it even proceeded so far as to vanquish heretics by shedding their blood; but it cannot be denied that the Church has the honor of emphasizing, in the midst of a heathen world which had no knowledge of true religious liberty, the fact that it did not intend to owe its victory to any outward means, but simply and solely to the might of truth. To win this victory the Church must of course again enter the furnace of persecution. Not all the powers of Heathenism had been exhausted, not all its resources expended. An increasing severity of persecution was still possible, and this too was to spend itself before the dawn of victory.

II. THE RESTORATION OF THE EMPIRE.

When our Lord predicted the persecutions to his disciples, he represented them as a necessity. "Ye shall be hated of all men for my sake," said he (Matt. x. 22), and in John xv. 19 he disclosed the ultimate cause of that hatred: "If ye were of the world, the world would love his own; but because ye are not of the world, but I have chosen you out of the world, therefore the world hateth you." And so the persecution increased by an inward necessity until the final outbreak under Diocletian brought its culmination and its end. This gradual growth is clearly marked. Under Nero a general blind hatred raged against the Christians without even knowing them. From the time of Trajan this hatred clothed itself in a legal form: *Non licet vos esse!* "Ye have no right to exist!" was the expression of it. With Decius the persecution became a political principle, and it belonged to the policy of the Emperors who purposed the revival of ancient Rome, to destroy the Church. But, while there the political motives outweighed the religious, with Diocletian the latter preponderated. It was the heathen priests and philosophers who urged him to a persecution which as a statesman he would fain have avoided, and it was the superstitious nature of the Emperor which gave the party of persecution a foothold. Heathen fanaticism here nakedly and openly appeared as the antagonist of Christianity, and the word of Christ in characterizing the supreme climax of persecution: "Whosoever killeth you will think that he doeth God service:" was now fulfilled among the heathen, as it had been formerly among the Jews. Hence this persecution was the most cruel of all. But in it Heathenism spent all its strength, and then collapsed. It had no further powers to summon against Christianity, and so the latter, after enduring all, remained victor on the field, and speedily took the place of Heathenism as the religion of the State.

It has already been hinted that I do not find the persecution under Diocletian so enigmatical and incomprehensible as some seem recently to have found it. They have even thought it necessary to have recourse to all kinds of suppositions in order to solve this so-called riddle.[4] The Christians are supposed to have attempted revolt, to have cherished the plan of capturing the throne, and are thus themselves made to bear the blame of the persecution. Now there is no kind of support for such hypotheses in the historical sources, and also no need of them. It is only necessary to follow the development of history, and to recall the situation of Diocletian, and not only does the enigma disappear, but it even becomes clear that the policy which Diocletian pursued would, necessarily and against his own will, lead to the persecution of the Christians.

A time of unspeakable confusion immediately succeeded the capture of Valerian by the Persians. The perpetually changing plurality of generals (the so-called Thirty Tyrants) did not permit the Empire to settle down into peace and harmony. Time proved that the attempt to revive the ancient Roman spirit, and to restore the Empire on the old basis of the Roman government with its Senate, consuls, and censors, was a failure. The aspiration after the Roman ideal, which inspired the, in some respects, able Emperors, showed itself too weak for the difficult task, and from the time when Diocletian, by the choice of the generals, ascended the throne in A. D. 284, we are conscious of having entered quite a different atmosphere.

Diocletian's predecessors — those of them who had sought to restore the Roman Empire — had turned their gaze back, and had endeavored to assist the fallen Empire by means of the Senate, and the office of censor, by the revival of the ancient Roman spirit. Diocletian turned his thoughts forward to something wholly new. Indeed the Empire, still called Roman, was no longer Roman, and it was more than mockery when Galerius asserted in his blunt way that the Empire ought to be called no longer Roman, but Dacian.[5] The army had ceased to be Roman; it was a motley mixture of all nations under heaven. Probus had in one day received sixteen thousand Germans into the Roman army.[6] Goths and Persians fought under the Roman eagles. Rome itself was now only nominally the capital and the centre of government. This was really where the Emperor had his camp. An Emperor now rarely lived any length of time in Rome. Aurelian was an exception. And he could not feel at home in the imperial palaces, whose walls reeked with so much blood. He occupied a simple villa, and there he might be seen practising gymnastics and exercising his horses in the court-yard. This was still in the ancient Roman style. With Diocletian, Rome entirely ceased to be the imperial residence. The Emperor lived in the East, in Nicomedia, where he had a magnificent palace, and was surrounded by court officials of many different grades. He assumed the title of *Dominus*, Lord, which no Emperor hitherto had borne. He rarely appeared in public, and then only in resplendent Oriental costume. A painfully complicated court etiquette barred access from without. It was difficult to approach his presence, and possible only amid endless formalities. All this was not personal vanity; but Diocletian knew the power exercised by ceremony, and how necessary it was to surround the imperial throne with this dignity, after its authority had suffered from so many insurrections and rebellions, and by the buying and selling of the crown. But this was of course no longer Roman, but already the beginning of what was afterwards called the Byzantine style.

Diocletian also threw aside the ancient forms of government, like useless ballast, and replaced them with new ones of his own creation. The greatest danger to the Empire lay in the fact that, in the absence of a ruling dynasty, ambitious men were perpetually aspiring to the crown, and one usurper deposed another. Diocletian understood this, but also realized that it was not possible to establish a dynasty. He therefore sought other means of meeting this danger. He associated co-regents with himself, and raised this arrangement to the rank of a settled institution. There were now to be always two *Augusti* and two *Cæsars* simultaneously, who, without dividing the Empire itself, shared the labor of ruling it, while one of the *Augusti* had the superintendence of the whole as supreme Emperor. This indeed reduced considerably the danger of rebellion. A single emperor was too much exposed. But now, if a rebellion arose against one of the princes, the others were there to rescue him, and even a usurper who was at first successful stood little chance of attaining the throne. Another still more important advantage was, that this arrangement opened to ambition and ability the possibility of reaching the throne without usurpation. For the choice of the *Cæsars* was to be made only with reference to ability, apart from all considerations of relationship, and those chosen were adopted by the Emperors into an artificial filial relation. Finally, it was, as it appears, from the beginning, intended, that the reign of each one should not exceed a fixed time, twenty years. At the expiration of this time the Emperors were to retire to private life, and give place to the *Cæsars*, to whose office new *Cæsars* were then to be elected. Thereby Diocletian hoped to secure two things: first, that, as the situation of the Empire really demanded, only men at the zenith of their powers would bear rule; and, second, that a premature usurpation of the throne on the part of the Cæsars would be prevented, since they knew beforehand that time would bring them to the imperial office.

This organization of Diocletian was a strange construction, the like of which would be hard to find anywhere in history, — a monarchy, but without a **dynasty**, its place being supplied by choice and adoption; an absolute and unlimited despotism, not for life, but restricted to a definite time; four rulers, and yet no partition of the Empire, but indeed a strict guarantee for its unity, since two of the four were subordinate to the others, as one of these was to his fellow. But every thing clearly depended on the preservation of this subordination by the voluntary obedience of the Cæsars to the Emperors, and of all to the supreme Emperor. Without this subordination and obedience the unity of Empire aimed at must fall to pieces. By what means, then, did Diocletian hope to attain and insure this subordination, and with it harmony among the rulers? This question leads to the religious aspect of the system, and thus to its first foundation.

Diocletian was a genuine champion of restored Heathenism. His whole life was interwoven with credulity and superstition. Even his accession to the throne was connected therewith. A Druid priestess had predicted to him, years before, that he would become Emperor. Diocletian was the son of a Dalmatian slave, and served in the army from the ranks upward. At the time when he was a subaltern in the camp at Lutetia, a Druid priestess mockingly laughed at him for his stinginess. "I will be more liberal when I am Emperor," he replied, also in jest. Then the woman responded, raising her voice with a solemn tone, "Jest not: thou shalt be Emperor after thou hast killed the wild boar."[7] Many years went by, and the former subaltern, who in the mean time had been passing from one military rank to another, had killed many a wild boar in hunting. He could not yet have met with the right one, but the prophecy of the Druidess was never forgotten. After the death of the Emperor Numerianus, Aper, the Prefect of the guard, was summoned before a court-martial on the charge of having killed him. Diocletian was one of the generals who assembled to hold the trial; and, directly Aper was brought before them, Diocletian rushed at him, and cut him down. He had found the right wild boar (*Aper* means *wild boar*), and he was chosen Emperor immediately afterwards. Having thus come to the throne, Diocletian, as Emperor, was perpetually involved in heathen superstition. He was "ever devoted to the sacred customs," "a seeker after the things of the future."[8] He sought omens and oracles for every important political move. The haruspices had the freedom of the palace; every day the entrails of the sacrifices were inspected; lightning and dreams aroused the Emperor to the greatest excitement.[9] By such signs he chose his fellow-rulers, and then regarded them as persons designated to him by the gods. He strove to attach them to himself by religious bonds through sacrifices and consecration. The imperial government was in every point deliberately connected with the gods and their sway. Diocletian regarded himself as standing specially under the influence of divine Providence. He gave himself the epithet Jovius, and called his co-regent Maximian, Herculius. Jupiter was in a peculiar sense his patron. By Jupiter he believed his imperial power was bestowed, and to the hands of that god he confided it, when he abdicated the throne.[10] In his palace at Salona, the temple of Jupiter towered above all the rest, and his imperial mantle was the mantle of Zeus himself.[11] The Emperors were to hold the position of representatives of the gods, executing their will, and also to be regarded as armed with the power of the gods and supported by them. Thus Diocletian, who was well aware that only religion can control the conscience, hoped to establish a bond of conscience between rulers and subjects, to create an obedience to authority for conscience' sake, and thus gain the true and firm foundation for his dominion.

But here we come upon the weak point of the system, which in other respects was undeniably planned and followed out with great political wisdom. A dangerous contradiction lurked in it. On the one hand Diocletian had thrown aside the ancient Roman order of things as mere ballast, on the other he strove to retain a portion of that ancient order, the old religion, and even to make it the foundation of the whole structure. But was religion at all exempt from the general ruin? was it the only healthy part of the life of that former period, while all else was sickly? On the contrary, religion too was in a dying condition, and that condition was in a sense the ultimate cause of the ruin of the whole. Could it now be made the foundation of the new structure? It is true the priests and the Neoplatonist philosophers must have said a great deal to Diocletian about a restoration of the ancient religion; but the error of this statesman, in other respects so acute, lay in his mistaking the restored Heathenism of his fanatical priests and Neoplatonists for a religion endowed with new life, and in his planning to make it the foundation of his new structure. For indeed it was only a spectre restored to the appearance of life, and, being itself doomed to inevitable death, would necessarily carry the whole skilfully planned system of the Emperor to destruction

CHAP. I.] DIOCLETIAN FORCED TO PERSECUTE. 401

with it, until finally Constantine repaired the mistake, and in a sense brought Diocletian's work to perfection. He abandoned the last relic of the ancient Roman State, which Diocletian had preserved, namely its religion, and gave the new Empire, which began politically with Diocletian, a new religious foundation, — Christianity.

This was a position in which Diocletian would be driven to persecute the Christians, whether he would or not. Was it possible really to carry out his plan so long as Christianity and the Church existed? This is a question which Diocletian seems not to have considered at all in the beginning, but which was not thereby eliminated, and which would necessarily come up in a most unavoidable form, when the realization of the Emperor's schemes had made some progress. Their aim was to insure the unity of the Empire. But the Christians were an element which it was utterly impossible to incorporate into this Empire as Diocletian planned it, and which threatened to divide its unity like a wedge perpetually growing larger and penetrating deeper. Restored Heathenism was to be the cement which should hold the Empire together, but this restored Heathenism could attain no strength so long as Christianity lived.

It is narrated[12] that one day a solemn sacrifice was to be offered in the Emperor's presence, in order to investigate the future by inspecting the entrails. The officials of the court were standing round about, and among them some Christians. When the sacrifice was offered, these last crossed themselves as they were wont to do, in order thereby to show that they did not take part in the worship of idols. But to the terror of

Tagis, the chief priest, the hoped-for signs did not show themselves in the entrails of the sacrifice. He ordered the repetition of the offering, and when the signs again were wanting, he cried: "The gods refuse to appear at our sacrifice, because profane men are present, and hinder the revelation, by means of the sign which the gods hate." This is said to have determined Diocletian to persecute the Christians. Whether this story be true, or not, in any case it shows with the greatest accuracy the condition of affairs. And indeed the truth was, as Tagis stated; the cross lay like a spell upon Heathenism.

It is true that the Christians were still greatly in the minority. It is generally assumed that they formed about one-twelfth of the whole population in the East, and in the West about one-fifteenth. Even this is perhaps too high an estimate. But there were two things which gave a great importance to this minority. First, that no single religion of the much divided Heathenism had so many adherents as the Christian. Over against the scattered forces of Heathenism, the Christians formed a close phalanx; the Church was a compact and strongly framed organization. Second, the Christians were massed in the towns, while the rural population was almost exclusively devoted to Heathenism. There existed in Antioch, for instance, a Christian church of fifty thousand souls. Finally, the fact of chief importance was that they were already spiritually the predominant power. They possessed the word of the living God, the forces of a new life; and although the rapid growth of the churches had permitted some elements of impurity to force their way in, yet how great was the contrast between these churches with their assurance of faith, their ardor of love, their graces of Christian virtue, their strict and earnest morality, and the heathen world in its darkness, superstition, and hopeless ruin! It was impossible for the heathen to ignore the impression conveyed by the testimony thus given. The certainty of belief in their own gods had received a mortal blow from the proclamation of the true God, and a renewal of the strength of Heathenism was not possible so long as this spell of Christianity still rested upon it.

Diocletian does not seem to have comprehended this clearly, at least in the beginning. He tolerated the Christians, not only in the army and in the administration, but was himself surrounded by Christians who filled high positions at the court. To them, as those whom he had found the most faithful, he specially confided his personal safety.[13] And the new faith had penetrated his own household, even his own family. His wife Prisca, and his daughter Valeria, the unfortunate wife of Galerius, stood at least in an intimate relation to the Church.[14] But there was at the court a party which saw the truth clearly enough, and worked with entire consistency for their object, the annihilation of Christianity. This party was chiefly composed of the heathen priests, who frequented the imperial palace. They fought for their influential position. If Diocletian's system of government could be permanently established, their supremacy also was assured; for, if the decision for every imperial act was determined according to omens and oracles, then the power lay in truth in the hands of those who interpreted the omens, and imparted the oracles. Besides the priests, there were distinguished statesmen, men of learning, and philosophers belonging to this party. Neoplatonism was at this time the prevalent philosophy; and while with Plotinus the antagonism to Christianity was for the most part unexpressed, yet in his successors an irreconcilable hostility plainly appears. They would allow the Christians to worship the supreme God, but only on the condition that they also worshipped the subordinate gods. It could be only stubbornness and self-will which hindered their doing so, and this obstinacy must be broken down. It was pretended that this would be really doing nothing but bringing Christianity back to its original purity. For the Christianity of Christ, the Neoplatonists asserted, was quite a different thing from that of the time then present. Christ did not give himself out for a God, but appeared only in the character of a wise teacher, and without showing any opposition to the religions of the nations. It was the apostles, who first made him a God. If the religions of the heathen nations were reformed according to Neoplatonic ideas, and Christianity brought back to its original state, then there would really exist no more antagonism between the two. In harmonious unity all the nations of the Empire would worship the one supreme God, and subordinate to him the national gods. The unity of belief, so necessary for the unity of the State, was easily to be established in this way. It was only necessary to take the heads of the Church seriously in hand: the multitude, which was only led astray, would yield, and the majority of them would pass over peacefully into the Neoplatonic State-Church. Hierocles, Prefect of Bithynia, was conspicuous in advocating these views at the imperial court; and he also upheld them in literature by writing a "Truth-loving

Discourse" to the Christians, which sought to win them, apparently in the interest of peace, but bloody persecution loomed up in the background.[15] If they did not hearken to such words of peace, then there would be the better ground for denouncing them to the Emperor as stubborn disturbers of the peace.

This party, which had long been secretly at work, found a head in the *Cæsar* Galerius. This man had risen from a shepherd's crook to a sceptre by his military talents; but his was an uncultivated nature, brought up in the blindness of heathen superstition, and he lacked the keen political insight for which Diocletian was distinguished. That which cannot be said of Diocletian may be predicated of Galerius in the highest degree, — he was a fanatic for Heathenism.

The party at first strove in vain to move the Emperor to another persecution of the Christians; Diocletian was too well aware of the power of the Christians, he saw too clearly the danger of such a step to the system he had created. To those who urged forcible measures, he recalled the fact that already a number of unsuccessful attempts had been made to crush the Church, and thus so much blood had been uselessly shed. Now too, nothing would be accomplished except to set the Empire in confusion and uproar.[16] Yet Galerius succeeded in carrying through the purification of the army as a preliminary measure. In A. D. 295 the order was given that all the soldiers should take part in the sacrifices. Many preferred to part with their military rank; men left the higher as well as the lower grades of the service, in order to remain faithful to their faith. Even in this case, there were some condemnations and executions. In Tangiers, Marcellus, a centurion, was condemned to death, because, when the order was issued to sacrifice, he threw down his belt and staff, the insignia of his military rank, and exclaimed: " From this moment I cease to serve your generals. I scorn to worship your gods of wood and stone, which are only dumb idols. If military service brings with it the obligation to sacrifice to the gods and to the Emperor, I throw down my belt and staff, I desert the standards, and cease to be a soldier." [17]

For a long time Diocletian would not be persuaded to take any further steps. But the heathen party urged him unceasingly, and the consistency of the system was on their side. It is certain that Diocletian would never have become a persecutor of the Christians of his own motion, and without being incited to it by Galerius; but Galerius would never have succeeded in bringing him to that point, if the political system and the religious views of Diocletian had not supplied arguments for his purpose.[18] The Emperor was already growing old: should his life-work remain unfinished? Yet unfinished it must remain, so long as the power of Christianity remained unbroken. The time approached at which Diocletian had determined to abdicate: would not that moment prove perilous to the whole system which he had created, if it were not firmly settled on the religious foundation, which, as we have seen, was so important? And who was to succeed him? This very Cæsar, Galerius, the fanatical foe of the Christians, would then be raised to the rank of Augustus, and he was destined to be the supreme Emperor. Galerius also did not urge on the persecution simply from personal hatred. He intended to establish and inaugurate his imperial rule with the great achievement, the destruction of the

Christian Church. Then he would be the restorer of the Empire, and his power would stand securely.

III. THE PERSECUTION UNDER DIOCLETIAN.

Galerius spent the winter of A. D. 302–3 in Nicomedia. Diocletian was becoming sickly, his powers were failing. There was noticeable in him a certain lack of decision, which had never before been one of his characteristics. Now or never was the moment for the heathen party to carry through their plans. Without any stir, in secret assemblies whose object no one suspected, they worked on the Emperor. He yielded so far as to permit the matter to be submitted to a council of the higher officers and members of the administration. By this move the heathen party had the game in their own hands. In the council next to Galerius (whose mother, Romula, a fanatical heathen, stood behind him to incite and urge him on), sat Hierocles the governor of Bithynia, the chief of the Neoplatonists, a religious zealot, who believed that he would do his god service, if he brought those stubborn disturbers of the peace, the Christians, to reason by force.[19] Diocletian became more and more wavering and undecided. He could not hold his own against the headlong fanaticism of Galerius, allied with the dexterous skill of Hierocles. He decided to seek advice from the gods, instead of men. There could be no doubt, what counsel they would impart. An oracle of the Milesian Apollo gave the decisive word. The Emperor determined to follow it; but he insisted on one condition, no blood must be shed.[20] Of course the heathen party were not disturbed by this condition. It would be entirely unnecessary, they said, to shed blood. As soon as the Christians were seriously taken in hand, the Church, which owed its growth only to laxity, would cease to exist. The Christians would not be willing to become martyrs, but would come over in a body. The heathen were well aware of what they were doing. If they could only bring the Emperor to make a beginning, he would have to continue, whether he would or not; and they would not need to urge him, since the obstinacy of the Christians would do that for them. Thus the ominous decision was made. At one of the principal festivals of the heathen, the Terminalia, which was celebrated on the 23d of February, the floodgates of the last and most terrible persecution were to be opened.

Early in the morning, when it was only half light, the Prefect of the guard, with a detachment of soldiers, marched up to the large and beautiful church in the city of the imperial residence. The doors were beaten in, all the sacred books discovered were burned, the church gutted and razed to the ground. On the city walls an imperial edict might be read: that all Christian churches were to be torn down, and all sacred books burned. The Christians were entirely prohibited from coming together; if they did not abjure Christianity, the men of rank among them were to be degraded and deprived of all rights (*infames*), all others were to be reduced to slavery.[21] The purpose of this edict was plainly to cut off Christianity from the sources of its life. For this reason provision was made for preventing worship by destroying the churches and depriving the Christians of the Scriptures. Thus they hoped to crush the Church without shedding blood; for the Emperor did not wish any blood shed. Yet it was soon to come to that. A Christian of high rank ventured, not with a pure zeal, it must be confessed, to tear down the edict with the scornful remark that it seemed to proclaim some more of the Emperor's victories over the Sarmatians. He was cruelly tortured and executed.[22] The heathen party made a most skilful use of circumstances, if we are not to attribute much graver blame to them. In the eastern provinces there broke out several insurrections insignificant in themselves; but they were expanded into dangerous rebellions, and the Emperor, already full of anxiety, was made to believe that the Orient was in flames, and that the Christians had stirred up the disturbances. On two occasions near together, fires broke out in the imperial palace at Nicomedia. It is impossible to say who set them. The Christians said Galerius had them kindled in order to ascribe the guilt to the Christians. At all events, this last came about. The Emperor was urged on by such means. The Empire was represented as endangered; terrible pictures were painted of a conspiracy among the Christians, which was said to have accomplices in his own palace, and to be already threatening his life. The Emperor's anger flamed up. He ordered his whole household to present themselves before him, and to clear themselves from the suspicion resting upon them by participation in a sacrifice. His wife and daughter, who, though they may perhaps not have formally gone over to Christianity, yet in heart favored it, gave way and sacrificed. The Christian officials of the court refused. Then torture was used. Peter, an official of high rank, was beaten, his stripes rubbed with vinegar and salt, and then his limbs burned one after the other. Nevertheless he joyfully confessed his faith. Finally, all who would not sacrifice were strangled.

In the provinces also the edict was carried out with greater or less severity, according to the disposition of the governors. The churches were torn down, the sacred books, when not voluntarily given up (as, alas! happened often enough), were seized by force, and publicly burned, the worship of the Christians was hindered, and they were reduced to slavery, and employed in public works. In some places they already went so far as to torture and execute the Christians. Though the edict contained no such orders, yet it commanded the surrender of the sacred books, and the abandonment of worship. Christians who refused to give up the books, or held their services in spite of the law, were punished according to the will of the respective governors. Thus, for instance, in Abitina, a town in Proconsular Africa, forty-nine Christians who had assembled to read the Scriptures and for the communion, were taken prisoners, and, when they would not renounce their faith, were executed. Among them was a boy named Hilarianus. The Proconsul thought he should frighten him easily. "I will cut off all thy long hair," he said to him, "and thy nose and ears." But the boy replied: "Do what thou wilt, I am a Christian." And when he too received the sentence, his answer was, "Thank God!"[23]

Meanwhile the Emperor had issued a second edict,[24] which commanded that all the clergy should be imprisoned; and, after a few months, a third,[25] in which it was ordered that all who denied by sacrificing should be set free, but the others compelled by torture. Many yielded, but many remained steadfast. For years they endured the imprisonment and the tortures applied from time to time, without wavering; and in the time after the persecution, many a servant of the Church bore visible marks of the torments then suffered.

But it was impossible to stop even with this. The heathen people themselves urged the matter on. In the circus in Rome the Emperor was greeted with the shout, "Away with the Christians! O Augustus! No more Christians!" So the fourth edict appeared, extending to all Christians. All without distinction were to be forced to sacrifice to the idols.[26]

Then began a persecution which surpassed even that under Decius in extent and cruelty. Everywhere the Christians were summoned on an appointed day. The towns were surrounded with guards in order that no one might escape. Then those who had been summoned were called by name, and ordered to sacrifice. Those who refused went straight to prison, and the attempt was made to induce them to recant by means of the most refined tortures. The wishes of those who showed signs of yielding were met in every possible way; every device by which they might try to conceal the fact of denial from themselves or others was readily accepted, so long as they only denied. A grain of salt, a pinch of incense was sufficient, if they only participated in the sacrifice. Of those who remained steadfast, some died under the tortures, others were executed. Blood flowed in streams throughout the Empire.

How large a share in this fourth edict Diocletian had, is not clear. It was, it is true, issued in his name, but when it went forth he was lying sick. He had become a broken man generally, in body and soul. What had come of his schemes? An Empire in which peace and unity prevailed was what he had striven for, and it at one time appeared as if he had succeeded in realizing this aim. When, shortly before the ominous winter of A. D. 302–3, he celebrated his triumph, the whole Empire was at peace, as it had not been for decades. And now this single step, to which he had allowed himself to be persuaded, yet which was well-nigh inevitable, since it was the consequence of his mistaken system, must destroy the whole! The union among the rulers was broken. In Gaul the *Cæsar* Constantius Chlorus had already begun to act independently. It is true, that, for the sake of appearances, he had caused some churches to be destroyed, but in other respects he left the Christians undisturbed. The peace of the Empire had fled, for fire and sword were busier than in the civil war; the Emperor himself was at war with a large part of his people. And what was gained by the persecution? His heathen counsellors must have tried to convince him that Christianity was now annihilated. Diocletian cannot have made himself believe this.[27] The fearful massacre which he had instigated had broken down, not the strength of the Christians, but the Emperor himself. Sick in body and in soul, living in anxiety, terrified by evil omens, trembling at every flash of lightning, he hid himself in the privacy of his palace. His day was over. It weighed heavily upon his heart at this time, when his whole life-work was in danger, to have to confide the government to other hands, and such hands! We can understand that at the last moment he still hesitated. But the same Galerius who had urged him to persecute, now urged his abdication; and Diocletian could not resist the second demand, because he had not resisted the first. On the 1st of May, A. D. 305, in Nicomedia, in the presence of the army, and before an image of Jupiter, he consummated his abdication, and departed to Salona, where he had built himself a palace in the hope of there passing his last years in peace. This hope was not to be fulfilled. That which he already feared, he was destined to see, — the complete collapse of the system of government created by himself.

With Diocletian, his Co-Emperor Maximian resigned the imperial dignity; and though Constantius Chlorus could not be passed by, but must be allowed to move up from the rank of *Cæsar* to that of *Augustus*, yet Galerius not only received the supreme power, but in nominating the *Cæsars* he passed over both Constantine the son of Constantius Chlorus, and Maxentius the son of Maximian, and chose instead two men who decidedly shared his hatred of the Christians, Severus and Maximinus Daza. Then Constantine fled from Nicomedia, where he no longer believed himself safe, to his father; and when the latter died, not long after, the army elected the son by acclamation to succeed him. Galerius, seeing that Constantine, who was supported by the army and greatly beloved in his father's realm, could not be got rid of, yielded so far as to recognize him as second *Cæsar*, at the same time raising Severus to the rank of *Augustus*, and Maximinus Daza to that of first *Cæsar*. Thus the system of Diocletian received another dangerous shock. It rested upon the idea of adoption, but the adoption was here broken through in one instance by inheritance. The consequences of this soon showed themselves. When Maxentius the son of Maximian, who had been passed over at the same time with Constantine, heard that the latter had attained the rank of *Cæsar* on the ground of inheritance, he did not delay bringing forward his own similar claim, but made himself *Cæsar*, and was immediately recognized as such in Italy, where the arbitrary government of Severus had become odious. And then, to bring the confusion to a climax, Maximian revoked his unwilling abdication, and re-assumed the imperial purple. Diocletian must have been most deeply pained to see the system he had constructed with so much toil falling apart and crumbling piece by piece. In vain did he once more appear upon the scene, and attempt to restore the shattered union; but the conviction was soon forced upon him that all was lost; he even found his own life threatened; and, anticipating what he feared, he took poison, and himself brought his life to an end.

But let us return to Galerius. He had chosen his Cæsars so that they would be supporters and auxiliaries to him in his principal task, the annihilation of Christianity. Maximinus Daza indeed was a thoroughly superstitious, fanatical heathen, full of rough strength, but utterly without education. So the persecution, which had somewhat slackened so long as Constantius wielded an influence as *Augustus*, flamed up again with redoubled violence. It is true, the western part of the Empire enjoyed perfect tranquillity. Constantius Chlorus, when he became *Augustus*, no longer needed even to destroy churches for the sake of appearances; and after Severus had attacked the Christians in Italy with such fury that the heathen themselves became indignant, leaving the Christians in peace was one of the measures by which Maxentius won the people over to himself. In the East, on the contrary, the persecution endured for six years more, and for the first time assumed a character truly fanatical. Murder was perpetrated by wholesale. There were instances in which ten, twenty, even a hundred, were put to death in a single day. Occasionally they went to work in a summary manner, and burnt the whole local church with their place of meeting. In Phrygia a whole town was surrounded with soldiers, and, like a town in an enemy's country, was burned with its inhabitants, who were all Christians.[28] Still more characteristic of the heathen fanaticism, which now reached its culmination, was the refinement of cruelty with which murder was carried on. Galerius issued an edict in which he ordered that the Christians should be put to death with slow fire. At first a little flame was placed under the feet of the victim till the flesh gradually calcining fell from the bones, then the other parts of the body were burned one after another with torches. At intervals cold water was dashed into the faces of the tortured, in order that death might not come too soon. Only at the end was the whole body burned on the pyre, and the ashes cast into the sea or into a river, in order to prevent the veneration even of the martyrs' ashes.[29] When the Emperor's express orders were of such a nature, we need not wonder that the governors also vied with one another in the invention of novel torments. They hung up the Christians by the feet, and kindled fires beneath them, they cut off their noses and ears, tore out their tongues, thrust out their eyes, and maimed their hands and feet by cutting through the sinews. For a time it would seem that mutilation was systematically practised, and was regarded as a mitigation of punishment compared with death.[30] They poured melted lead over the Christians, and cut them in pieces. The corpses of those who had been executed were not allowed to be buried, they were left lying till the dogs and the vultures consumed them.³¹ This was also the time when Roman governors condemned Christian maidens, still wearing the fillet, the sign of their unsullied honor, to be flogged with rods, half-naked, up and down the streets; when it happened not infrequently that matrons and maidens of noble rank were sentenced to be taken to the brothel, and exposed to the lust of the heathen. It was precisely the philosophically cultured officials, the Neoplatonists proud of their wisdom and virtue, who thus made themselves sadly conspicuous. More than once matrons and maidens preferred death to dishonor, and took their own lives in order to escape a worse fate. Their contemporaries counted such too into the number of the martyrs who died for their faith; but a later, colder age cast doubts upon their claim to be considered martyrs.³²

Yet the persecution, in the six years during which it still went on, did not continue with steady pressure, but after a fierce outburst it slackened a little while, and then broke out more violently than before. The patience of the Christians wearied the heathen; but when in the times of tranquillity the Christians reassembled, and the heathen were forced to see that all their rage had failed to annihilate Christianity and the Church, then their wrath flamed up anew, and the persecution began once more, frequently more terribly than before, till weariness again followed the second outbreak. About the sixth year of the persecution, in A. D. 308, peace seemed to settle down everywhere. The prisoners in the mines, of whom there was a large number, were treated more leniently. The Christians were already breathing more freely, and gave way to the hope that the storm was over. Then it broke out again with greater violence than before. An imperial edict appeared, addressed to all the military and civil authorities, ordering them to resume the persecution with all the powers at their command. The ruined temples were to be rebuilt; all, men, women, freemen, slaves, and even the youngest children, were to be compelled to sacrifice, and to partake of the meat of the offering. The bloodshed began again, and they now went so far as to sprinkle all the provisions in the markets with sacrificial wine, or with the water used in the offerings to idols, in order by this means to bring the Christians, who would not sacrifice of their own accord, into contact with the offerings to idols, against their will. And after this storm had subsided, a short outbreak of rage came in the year A. D. 310, occasioned by the circumstance that the prisoners in the mines had assembled for worship. But this very speedily passed over.

The fire of persecution burned itself out. The brute force and the raging fanaticism which characterized these last outbursts could accomplish nothing against the silent endurance of the Christians. Heathenism had exhausted all its powers. Even the executioners were wearied. The heathen themselves began to denounce the useless effusion of blood, and to take the part of the persecuted Christians. Galerius lay on his deathbed; a dreadful disease, the consequence of his debaucheries, had attacked him; he suffered the greatest agony while corruption spread in his living body. From his deathbed he issued, in A. D. 311, the remarkable edict which entirely put an end to the persecution.[83] In it the Emperor, with his colleagues, proclaimed that it had been his purpose to bring every thing back to the ancient laws and political system of the Romans, and therefore to take care that the Christians who had forsaken the religion of their forefathers should return to a proper attitude of mind. But since the majority of them had obstinately adhered to their purpose, and he had seen that they neither paid due honor to the heathen gods, nor even worshipped the God of the Christians, therefore of his favor he would grant that they might again be Christians, and hold their assemblies once more, on condition that they did not violate the existing order of affairs. It would be well that they should pray to their God in behalf of the welfare of the Emperor and of the State, in order that the State might remain uninjured in all respects, and that they themselves might live in security.

This edict contains a plain confession of the impotence of Heathenism. It does not speak of recognizing or favoring Christianity. The Emperor still regards it only as a defection from the ancestral religion: he does not conceal his desire that the Christians would return to it. But he renounces the attempt to accomplish this desire by force, because he has come to see that it is impracticable, and that which he can no longer refuse to Christianity, he allows to appear as a gift of his favor, in order to cover up his impotence to some extent. Did the pangs of conscience have a voice in this edict? Did the streams of blood which he had shed leave to him, as to Diocletian, no peace upon his bed of pain? The wish so earnestly expressed at the close of the edict, that the Christians would pray for him, perhaps discloses some such feeling. The schemes of Galerius, like those of Diocletian, now lay in ruins.

On him, too, crime revenged itself. He died soon after in unspeakable torments.

The real conflict thus came to an end. It is true, Maximinus did not recognize the edict, or at least executed it in a very ambiguous manner. Soon after its promulgation, he began again to limit the freedom of the Christians, and to forbid their assemblies in the cemeteries. He also strove to strengthen Heathenism by various measures, and even commenced persecution once more.[34] But these were only the last convulsive movements of expiring Heathenism. It had really given up the contest.

But, of course, that which Christianity had won was at first only an unwilling toleration. It had need of more than that to fulfil its mission in the world: it needed recognition. It was necessary that it should come into connection with the State, that, though in a different manner, it should occupy the place of Heathenism, and form, as Heathenism had hitherto done, the basis of the life of the people. All this was still lacking. The edict of Galerius was not the complete victory. But the complete victory was close at hand. The man had come upon the scene, to whom the historical task fell, to close the period of conflict, and, by cementing the relations which were to bind State and Church together for the future, to bring a new era to the nations, — Constantine the Great.

CHAPTER II.

THE VICTORY.

" By this sign conquer."

RARELY is a man so differently judged as Constantine the Great. Opinion still is unsettled about him. Our own day generally regards him with little favor. Indeed, many forces are at work to-day in destroying what he achieved. Many even regard it as a chief duty of the present age to undo the deed of Constantine, the connection of Church and State. But not only to those whose object, whether they avow it or not, is the removal of Christianity from the State and from the national life, even to some who estimate Christianity at its true value, his action appears dubious, at least of doubtful worth, and this judgment is easily transferred from the deed to the doer.

In order to judge Constantine fairly, two prejudices must be guarded against. First, the idea that a man to whom Christianity owes such an entire change of position in the world must necessarily have been himself a peculiarly pure, spiritual, and active Christian. With this idea, we may feel repelled by not finding what we anticipated, and so fail to see what Constantine really was. Of course the inner development of the Church, an advance in its spiritual life, requires for its promoters men who have experienced this advance in their own souls. But where a change in the external situation of the Church is concerned, — and such was the nature of the revolution which we are now to consider, — it may naturally be brought about by a person who for his own part has little or no share in Christianity. Many render services to Christianity and to the Church, whose hearts are not Christian; but it may often be observed that these services bring to such men the blessing of gradually drawing them near to the Church in heart, though at first only outwardly active in its behalf. Such a man, in my opinion, was Constantine. When he took the first steps toward making Christianity the predominant religion, his relation to it was little more than outward, more like superstition than faith. But he afterwards came nearer and nearer to Christianity, and it cannot be ignored that later he recognized and embraced its truth in his soul.

Second, it is not just to ascribe to direct hypocrisy every case where the conduct does not square with the profession. That is a false alternative, which is often put as decisive in judging Constantine: either a Christian through and through, or not a Christian at all, and therefore a liar and a hypocrite: either Constantine acted from purely Christian or from purely political motives, and in the latter case his Christianity was only a mask. Constantine was no saint, and it is not my purpose to make him out a saint; but those who jump to the conclusion that he must have been a hypocrite do not realize how many things may exist together in the heart of a man. Even the blood-guiltiness with which he burdened his soul, and which I have no disposition to excuse or extenuate, does not prove that what wears the aspect of Christian piety in his life was pure hypocrisy. A service of very questionable value is done to Constantine by those who, by way of compensation, exalt the statesman as much as they depreciate the Christian in him. For political wisdom whose ultimate root is hypocrisy can hardly lay claim to be called genuine political wisdom at all. The very fact that Constantine undoubtedly achieved a great and lasting success, should be a warning against regarding him as a mere hypocrite. For where was ever in the world a great achievement made without inward participation in it? Those who deny this to Constantine, who view him as a cold and calculating politician, without any heart in the work he did, without any inward longing for the Christianity which he made the basis of his political career, fundamentally fail in comprehending both the man and his work.

The time immediately after the death of Galerius was one of those moments of great suspense which occasionally come in history. Every thing was prepared for a great revolution; the actors who were destined to take part in it had already come upon the stage, but no one could forecast the way in which the drama would unfold. Every one was conscious that things could not remain as they were; but it was just this consciousness which restrained all concerned from taking the first step. Thus there came a moment of tranquillity; but it was the calm before the storm. It could not last long; and when once it was broken, the revolution everywhere prepared was accomplished with startling rapidity.

In the East, Maximinus Daza and Licinius (who had succeeded to the position of Galerius), after arraying themselves against each other, made peace again, and divided the Orient between them. The West was ruled by Constantine and Maxentius. Thus the situation had become similar to that which Diocletian had in view. And yet how great was the difference from the time before the persecution. There was no thought of an undivided dominion such as Diocletian had planned, nor even of harmony among the four rulers. Each governed independently of the others in his own territory, and silently prepared for the war which must come. No one of them trusted another, and each was conscious that he must either conquer the rest, or fall. In truth war was inevitable; an Empire with four independent rulers was an impossibility. Nor was it the question of supremacy alone which brought on the war; a deeper cause was the still undecided question of the State's attitude towards Christianity. In this direction, also, the position of affairs was untenable. The State now tolerated Christianity, but only because it could not do otherwise. The Church was no longer persecuted, but efforts were made to hinder its growth by oppressive limitations. The State had defined its attitude in the edict of toleration of A. D. 311, and in the directions for carrying it out, which were sent to the governors; but both Maximinus Daza and Maxentius at least did their best to make the execution of the edict bring as little as possible of good to the Christians. That such limitations could not long continue was to be foreseen, for the Church had already become too powerful, and even the mere unwilling tolerance conceded to it was sufficient to bring in numbers of the heathen. Everywhere multitudes were coming forward to join the Christians. And what a contradiction lay in this toleration. If Heathenism was still the religion of the State, even toleration was too much. How could the State harbor two such antagonistic religions for any length of time, without being itself split in two? For a moment the scale might remain in equilibrium, but it must shortly turn in favor of one side or the other. The two questions of supremacy and religion thus naturally combined. The struggle for supremacy, as indeed it had originated in the persecution under Diocletian, assumed more and more the character of a conflict between Christianity and Heathenism, and the triumph of Constantine over his rivals resulted also in the victory of Christianity over Heathenism.

The very first act of the great war, the conflict between Constantine and Maxentius, was decisive. Maxentius, who ruled Italy and Africa, was a profligate and a tyrant. He assumed an increasingly hostile attitude towards Constantine. His command that all statues of Constantine in Italy were to be thrown down, showed what was to be looked for from that quarter. Therefore Constantine determined to be beforehand with him. Before his antagonist had seriously thought of war, he crossed the Alps with his army, and descended on Northern Italy. Constantine's attack was exceedingly venturesome. His army numbered about forty thousand men, while that of Maxentius was at least three times that number, and included the Prætorian Guard, the flower of the Roman army, and eighteen thousand horse, of special importance in the plains of Northern Italy. Besides, the fortresses round about greatly strengthened the position of Maxentius, and the great resources of Italy and Africa were at his disposal. Indeed, some in Constantine's army denounced the undertaking as rash. Constantine himself was well aware what risks he was running, what a venture it was to start on this campaign with an army comparatively small, and that (a weighty consideration) against Rome itself. For Rome was still, at least in name, the centre of the Empire; a nimbus of sacredness still encircled the city which ruled the world, and it was no light thing to lead Roman troops to battle against the very Rome in whose name they took the field, and whose symbol they bore upon their standards. We can understand that Constantine in such a situation sought other, higher help. According to his own account, at that time he long considered to which god he should turn for help, and prayed to the supreme God, whom his father had worshipped as god of the sun, to reveal to him who he was. Then there appeared to him one day a wondrous sign. When the sun was declining in the west, he saw a bright cross upon the sun, and over it the inscription in letters of light: *TOYTΩ NIKA* (*in this, by this sign, conquer*). He was disturbed by the vision, and not clear what its meaning might be; but in the night Christ appeared to him, and commanded him to make this cross his banner, and then to go into battle with the certainty of victory. In fulfilment of this direction, Constantine had a banner (the *Labarum*) prepared, bearing the cross and the monogram of Christ. He himself set a cross on his helmet, and his soldiers painted it upon their shields.

Then he led his army from victory to victory, under the banner of the cross, until, in the bloody battle at the Milvian Bridge, the power of Maxentius was entirely broken. Constantine entered Rome in triumph, and soon the whole West acknowledged his sway. In token of his gratitude for this result, the Emperor had a statue of himself set up in Rome, carrying a cross in his hand, and bearing the inscription: "By this salutary sign, the true proof of valor, I have freed your city, and saved it from the yoke of the tyrant."[1]

I can not and will not pass over the question of the estimate to be put upon this narrative. Let us examine it without prejudice, particularly without the prejudice (for it is nothing more) that there are no such things as miracles, and that therefore the story, however strongly supported, cannot be true. Beyond the limits of the New Testament, we must certainly be very cautious in accepting miracles which are narrated, but we must not, we can not, deny the possibility that the Lord may at peculiarly critical moments in the history of his Church interpose by miracles. The story is given in the greatest detail by Eusebius, who claims to have received it from the Emperor's own lips.[2] Constantine in his old age had narrated it to the historian, and confirmed it with an oath. The story cannot therefore be wholly rejected as pure fiction, unless one is willing to consider either Eusebius or Constantine guilty of deliberate falsehood. It is true that Eusebius is no impartial historian, at least in his life of Constantine, yet a partisan coloring or conception of the facts is a long way from the fabrication of events which never happened. Eusebius too would hardly have ventured to invent such a story about the Emperor. If there be any falsehood in it, Constantine unquestionably is the guilty party. Now I hold Constantine to be capable of a falsehood, even his oath I should not consider binding without other reasons, since he did not respect it himself, where political advantage was concerned; but I cannot comprehend the motives for such a strange falsehood as this, nor what could induce him to invent such a story in his old age, and to tell it to Eusebius in a moment of confidence. There might have been some advantage in having the story circulated earlier, but then when he told it, all those things were long gone by; they belonged to history, and had no longer any value for the present.

And it is impossible on other grounds to relegate the whole story to the realm of fiction. It is a fact that in Constantine's attitude to Christianity a complete change took place between A. D. 311 and 313, and that suddenly. At the beginning of A. D. 312 he seemed, to say the least, cool and non-committal. He had issued the edict of Galerius, and the orders concerning its execution, which as we have seen were but little favorable to Christianity. He was, no doubt, even then a monotheist; but the one God whom he worshipped was rather the Sun-god, the "Unconquered Sun," than the Father of our Lord Jesus Christ. But at the beginning of A. D. 313, he issued the edict of Milan, which was extraordinarily favorable to the Christians, and took the first decisive steps towards raising Christianity to the position of the dominant religion.

These innovations are commonly attributed by recent writers to purely political considerations. It is said that the Emperor, convinced of the impotence of Heathenism and of the power of Christianity, conceived the great political purpose of gaining Christianity over to his side and thus making its strength serviceable to him. He recognized with statesman-like keenness to which religion the future belonged, and that the State could be built up anew only on the basis of Christianity, strong in the strength of its youth. In my view this explanation does not correspond to the situation of affairs at the time, nor does it find any support in those facts which are indubitably certain in Constantine's own testimony.[3] Constantine did not need to gain over the Christians: they had been on his side from the time of his father, so far as the Christians can be said to have taken sides at all in these conflicts. His own army was mainly composed of barbarians, and among these the Christians were certainly not in the majority. Indeed, in all the West they were only a small minority as yet, and in Rome Heathenism still greatly preponderated, so that in that city favor to the Christians was the last thing to win popularity for him who showed it. Purely political considerations would necessarily have rather counselled against the step he took, for, while he gained nothing by it which he did not already possess, he was likely to render the heathen hostile to him. The edict of Milan, without doubt the best original document on the subject, indicates motives quite other than those which modern historians have attributed to the Emperor from their own circle of ideas. In the edict Constantine himself gives as the motive of the favor he was showing to the Christians, the benefits which he had received from the Supreme God and the wish that these divine benefits might remain henceforth assured to him.[4] Constantine therefore believed that he owed the brilliant victory which he had gained over a force much stronger than his own, to a special interposition of the Supreme God on his side; and wherever we look, among Christians or heathen, we come upon just this view, everywhere the unexpected victory is attributed to the special protection of the Supreme God. More than this, the special protection was distinctly connected with the banner of the cross. With all the labor that has been spent on the task, it has proved impossible to make away with the fact that first in the war with Maxentius, and after that more and more prominently, the cross was the banner under which Constantine fought and conquered. At this date the heathen emblems disappeared from the imperial standard, and were supplanted by the cross and the monogram of Christ. On the helmets, on the shields, on the very coins, we find from that date, in hundreds of examples, the cross and the two sacred letters *X. P.*, the Greek initials of the name *Christ*. And if we could still cherish any doubts as to the significance of this, the equally undoubted fact, above mentioned, that Constantine allowed himself to be represented in a statue, holding the cross, and expressly declared it to be the banner under which he had conquered, should banish all doubt.[5]

So much, then, is certain, Constantine himself believed that he owed his victory to the cross. But this fact would be wholly isolated, if we were to obliterate that story of the vision as a pure fabrication. The question then would be, What brought about this sudden change in the views of the Emperor? Something must have happened which induced Constantine to make the cross his standard. It may be conceded that Eusebius has somewhat, perhaps greatly, embellished the story, or, with still greater probability, that (as often happens with just such stories as have afterwards come to a significance and fulfillment beyond all anticipation), it was painted in vivid colors by the recollections of the Emperor; but that it was a simple fabrication is impossible in view of the facts. Further, we have no right to twist it round after the rationalistic method, — to assume, for example, that Constantine saw only a chance shaping of the clouds in the figure of a cross, and held it to be a sign, because it responded to the state of his emotions; for thus we place at the foundation of what the original documents relate an element foreign to them of our own devising, and which finds no support whatever in those documents. And then the whole course of events in one of the greatest crises of history would rest upon a chance, and on a superstitious illusion on the part of Constantine. This I at least cannot accept. To me the history of Christ's Church is something other than an aggregation of chances and human illusions. I hold firmly that the exalted Saviour, as He promised, rules and guides His Church. And in this decisive moment He interposed. It pleased Him to condescend to Constantine, and to answer his questions, as God condescended to the wise men from the East, and, by means of their astrological superstitions, led them to Bethlehem with a star. Constantine hitherto had reverenced the Sun as the supreme God, and the cross placed upon the Sun was to show him that the God who has revealed himself in the crucified One is the supreme God; and when Constantine did not immediately understand, it was explained more particularly to him in a dream. From henceforth this was the banner under which he and his army fought, and the victories which he gained confirmed him in the belief that the god who gave him this sign was the supreme God. But I do not at all suppose that Constantine was completely converted by this vision, and forthwith became a faithful Christian in the full meaning of the words. The sign of the cross was to him at first rather an object of superstitious reverence than a symbol of salvation. Not until later did it become more to him. For the present he only thought of winning the favor of the supreme God by taking the part of Christianity, though in his own heart he had not yet completely broken with Heathenism, and his personal convictions contained a medley of heathen and Christian elements. Not until the conflict assumed more and more the character of a struggle between Heathenism and Christianity, was Constantine compelled to take the Christian side; and only when the war was ended by the victory over Licinius, did the Emperor personally confess himself unreservedly a Christian.[6]

The revolution now went on with surprising rapidity. On Oct. 27, A. D. 312, Maxentius and his army had been cut to pieces at the Milvian Bridge. His Prætorian guard had fought with the valor of veterans; no one of them had yielded a foot; they lay in ranks, as they had stood, on the field of battle. The rest of the army, and the tyrant, had been ingulfed by the waters of the Tiber. Rome, Italy, the Islands and Africa immediately fell to the victor. Constantine held this to be a gift from the Christians' God, and hastened to render his thanks for it. In the early part of A. D. 313 he met Licinius in Milan, and thence issued the edict of toleration.[7] Directly afterwards the war which had been threatening between Licinius and Maximinus broke out. In this case, too, the victory of Licinius, who was then friendly to the Christians, over their persecutor Maximinus, was a wonderfully rapid one. On June 13 the edict of Milan was published in Nicomedia, the city from which ten years before the persecution had gone out. This edict was now in force throughout the Empire.

In this edict, which marks the beginning of a new era, full religious freedom was given. Every one in the Empire was henceforth to have entire liberty to embrace whatever religion he thought the best. The great principle was thus for the first time promulgated, that religion is the most personal affair of every man, and about it no other man has a right to legislate; that it is not the office of the powers that be to coerce or compel any one to embrace a religion. Thus was won at length that which the Christians had so long demanded, that for which they had struggled and shed their blood. The edict of Milan marks the great moment when the truth obtained recognition, that no one could be forced into a religion, because forced religion ceases to be religion at all. These fundamental principles of religious freedom have often again been obscured, for long enough, for centuries they have almost been lost sight of; but they have always again worked their way to the surface, and he who denies them denies in its essence the Christianity to which they belong.

It was simply a consequence of these principles, when Constantine ordered that all the property confiscated during the time of persecution should be restored to the Christians. This indeed only made good the transgressions of the previous years against the principle of toleration. But the Emperor added, with great wisdom, that those who had bought the confiscated estates of churches should give them back indeed, but should receive compensation from the imperial treasury. Thus the Christians received their rights, and yet harshness and discontent were avoided.

The edict itself did not go further than this, but the urgency with which Constantine enjoined on the officials its prompt and careful fulfillment, fosters the suspicion that Constantine did not intend to stop there. His attitude towards Christianity was no longer merely neutral, but already one of positive friendliness and favor. It could not be otherwise: it is impossible for the State to occupy a purely neutral attitude towards the religions which prevail in it. A State without a religion is a mere figment of the imagination, which can only be cherished by those who have no idea what religion is. Religion controls the whole life of man. Must it not also control the lives of those who govern the State? As soon as Constantine had become favorably disposed towards Christianity, the change in him would necessarily influence the policy of his government, and that in an increasing degree, the nearer he himself approached to becoming a Christian. Already Christianity stood in his estimate higher than Heathenism, for his favorite name for it was "the most devout religion." He came to see clearly that fallen Heathenism was drawing the State into its ruin, and that if the State was really to renew its life, it must be on a new religious basis, which only Christianity could offer. The more distinctly he recognized this, the more zealously did he seek to make a place for Christianity, and to establish a connection between the Church and the State. Christianity was to be the salt to preserve the State from the corruption of Heathenism.

A series of measures was the fruit of this endeavor. As early as March, A. D. 313, the clergy were released from the duty of filling municipal offices, at that time a great and costly burden.[8] Thus one of the privileges of the heathen priests was extended to the clergy, who were thus put on an equality with the priests. About the same time the Emperor gave considerable sums of money for the support of the clergy.[9] The Church also received the right of having wills drawn in its favor.[10] Then several statutes in the laws, which were contrary to Christianity and its principles, were repealed. The punishments of crucifixion and of breaking the legs were done away with.[11] The cross, now the sign of salvation, the highly venerated symbol of Christianity itself, could no longer be used in a disgraceful punishment. Criminals were no longer to be branded on the forehead, that the majesty of the human countenance, which is fashioned in the image of heavenly beauty, might not be dishonored.[12] This was a seemingly unimportant, but really very significant regulation, for it is founded on the recognition of the dignity of man, of which Heathenism knew nothing, and which Christianity first brought to light. Limitations were also imposed on the gladiatoral contests. They were, of course, not expressly forbidden, but it was decreed that in future no criminal was to be condemned to the Games. Those who had deserved such a sentence should rather be sent to labor in the mines, that they might expiate their crimes without bloodshed.[13] Thus the State withdrew from the Games, and no longer co-operated to promote them. Attention was directed towards the prisons, and the merciful treatment of prisoners was made the duty of the officials.[14] The laws concerning marriage were in several particulars accommodated to the views of the Christians. The laws against the unmarried and the childless were abrogated, and, on the other hand, laws were enacted punishing adultery and seduction.[15] The exposure of children was forbidden.[16] If a father declared that he was not in a condition to support his child, provision was made for its care.[17] When on the occasion of a severe famine in A. D. 321 many parents sold their children, this practice too was prohibited. If parents were in want, the public treasury would provide for their relief; "for it is against our customs, that, under our rule, any one should be compelled by hunger to commit a crime."[18] The manumission of slaves was facilitated, and at the same time it was provided that it should take place in the church and in presence of the priest.[19] The Church thus received the great office of continuing the emancipation of slaves, already begun by it, with the support of the State. Of peculiar importance, finally, were the laws which commanded the general observance of Sunday. On "the venerable Day of the Sun" no labor was to be performed excepting pressing agricultural work; the courts and administrative offices were to be closed, and no legal business transacted except the manumission of slaves.[20] The soldiers were conducted into the open country, and there held a service of a peculiar kind, but one entirely characteristic of this time of transition. It was not heathen, but it was also not as yet thoroughly Christian. It consisted mainly in the invocation of the one supreme God, at this time recognized by most of the heathen, that He might bless the Emperor and the Empire.[21]

The heathen worship indeed was not forbidden. Not

till later did Constantine shut up certain temples in which the rites were connected with gross licentiousness, and forbid the celebration in private houses of sacrifices which included the inspection of the entrails.[22] Those who felt the need of sacrifices were to go to the temples. "We do not forbid," the Emperor declares, "the ceremonies of the old cultus" (by this time the official name for Heathenism), "but they must be celebrated in broad daylight."[23] Now, as formerly, the Emperor exercised the office of *Pontifex Maximus*, which was joined to the imperial dignity. Not only in Rome were ancient temples restored, but even in the new Rome on the Bosphorus, in Constantinople, although the town from the first was predominantly Christian, temples were still erected to the gods. While on the one hand the bishops enjoyed constant access at court, yet on the other hand the Emperor held frequent intercourse with heathen, and had some of them constantly near his own person. The forcible suppression of Heathenism in any way was never thought of. The State respected the religious freedom of the citizen, and did not regard it as its duty to convert him, but gave the Church a place, and left it free scope. The State did not esteem itself able, or in duty bound for its part, to uproot every thing un-Christian with excessive zeal, but it withdrew from partnership with Heathenism. Christian ideas were permitted to influence the legislation of the State, and the general observance of Sunday wove a very firm bond between the life of the people and Christianity; but beyond this the new religion was left to work itself out.

Constantine's conduct, especially in these first years, has been called ambiguous, and certainly not without reason. The Emperor himself indeed confessed it, when, on his death-bed, he accompanied his request for baptism with the words, "Now all ambiguity vanishes."[24] But in order to be just to Constantine, two things must not be forgotten. First, how difficult it was to be a Roman Emperor and at the same time a Christian. Constantine indeed often felt it deeply enough, and finally gave expression to this consciousness by never again assuming the imperial purple after his baptism.[25] Secondly, it must be conceded, that the attitude of Constantine in his difficult position, and considering the magnitude of his task, was in many respects wise and prudent. Without violence, State and Church approached each other, step by step, Heathenism was thrust back, and the influence of Christianity on the life of the State and of the people steadily increased. The State was not yet Christian, but it was near the point of becoming so, and drew every year nearer. Even without the express removal of Heathenism from being the religion of the State, and the substitution of Christianity for it, there could be no doubt that no longer heathen but Christian ideas influenced the measures of the State to an increasing extent; and while in public matters, such as documents, inscriptions, coins, neutral formulas and symbols were favored, — for instance, the now very common expression, *deity*, — yet it is easy to see that these neutral formulas were intended to pave the way for others specifically Christian. Indeed, this was a time of transition for Constantine, as well as for his Empire. In this period many things not germane to Christianity, many plainly heathenish, existed side by side with Christianity. But, instead of reproaching the Emperor with this fact, we ought rather to admire the statesmanlike wisdom with which, although his own purposes were certainly settled at that time, he yet did not rashly grasp at their fulfillment, but waited tranquilly until the right moment came, and that which he sought dropped like ripened fruit into his hand.

This was particularly the case in his attitude towards the East, which still remained under the rule of Licinius. The union of the whole Empire was certainly from the first the object of Constantine's ambition, but alluring as was the scheme of attaining this object in a single campaign after his brilliant victories, yet the Emperor checked himself, and bided his time. Even after the war had broken out with Licinius, and Constantine had won the first battle, he made peace again with him. Enduring, of course, the peace could not be. The Empire could not continue divided, either in government or religion. Indeed, as in this period all political questions were at bottom religious, and in every conflict the real issue was the conflict between Christianity and Heathenism, so was in this case the division of the Empire no less religious than political, and became so increasingly from day to day, in the natural course of things. While Constantine was more and more taking the side of Christianity, rivalry to him made Licinius the firm ally of Heathenism. His political suspicion made him mistrust Christianity. In every Christian he saw an adherent, in every bishop a secret agent of his rival, Constantine. Without resorting to bloodshed, he endeavored to hem in Christianity as much as possible, and to promote Heathenism.[26] Assemblies of the bishops were forbidden, Christian instruction was hindered under all kinds of pretexts, in some places the services of the Christians were banished from the churches in the towns to the open country; and to this last order Licinius mockingly added that the fresh air would be more wholesome for such numerous assemblies.[27] In Pontus a number of churches were permanently closed. The Christians were accused of having prayed for Constantine, instead of for Licinius. From the Emperor's vicinity, from the chief offices civil and military, all Christians were removed, and the entire administration, including the command of the army, was put into the hands of stanch heathen.[28] Still worse things came about, but without our being able to see how far Licinius was to blame, how far his officials were guilty, whom their master's feeling against Christianity might easily have incited to acts of open persecution. Christians were condemned to the confiscation of their property, on account of their fidelity to their religion; they were deprived of their rank and their freedom, sent to the mines, and ill treated in other ways.[29] Indeed, even at this time some Christians sealed their faith with death; namely, among the soldiers, in whose case both military discipline and the severity of martial law came into play. Such were the famous Forty Martyrs of Sebaste. The governor of Armenia Minor, so we are told, gave orders that forty soldiers, who refused to deny their faith, should be exposed, completely naked, on the ice, to the fierce cold of a winter night. For those who made up their minds to renounce Christ, a warm bath and every means of restoration were provided on the bank. Only one yielded and came to the shore. But in his place one of the guard immediately went out as a martyr, so that forty came to their death.[30] The result of all such measures was, that the Christians really began to look to Constantine as their deliverer, while the heathen set their hopes on Licinius. And when the long suspense finally gave place to open war again, it necessarily assumed the character of a conflict of religions.

Licinius for his part openly proclaimed it. Before beginning the campaign, he assembled the chiefs of the army and the principal nobles of the court in a sacred grove. After the sacrifices had been offered, he pointed to the statues of the gods, as those which had come down from the forefathers, and accused Constantine of having deserted the ancestral shrines, of worshipping a foreign god, and of putting the army of the Romans to shame by means of the disgraceful banner of the cross. Then he expressly demanded a judgment of God. "The present crisis," he said, "will prove which of us errs in judgment, by deciding between our gods and those revered by our adversaries. . . . And, indeed if the stranger (god) whom we now laugh at, prove victorious, we too must recognize and honor him, and bid a long farewell to those for whom we burn tapers in vain. But if our own gods conquer, as is no wise doubtful, then, after this victory, we will prosecute the war against the impious."[31] On the other side, Constantine carried into the field the banner of the cross, and in more than one fierce and bloody battle he and his army believed that they owed their victory to this banner. Licinius was completely vanquished; Constantine remained sole lord of the re-united empire.

The judgment of God which they had invoked fell heavily upon the heathen. Heathenism seemed to be annihilated at one blow, and now the heathen crowded in multitudes into the Church. Everywhere in the towns and villages the white robes of the baptized were to be seen; the temples of the ancient gods were deserted; the churches of the victorious God of the Christians could not contain the multitude of His worshippers. And the course of events must have exerted a great influence upon Constantine. He now showed quite a different spirit from that of his utterances after the victory over Maxentius. He openly confessed his belief in the true God, and condemned Heathenism as error and sin. He distinctly declared that he was now called as a servant of God to lead the world from the setting to the rising sun, out of darkness into light, into the service due to the true God. Yet he expressly disavowed any purpose of trying to suppress Heathenism by force: the erring should enjoy the same tranquillity as the faithful, though his counsel to all men would be to embrace Christianity. "Let every one do what his soul desires.... Those who hold themselves aloof may have, as they desire, the temples of lies. But we have the most glorious house of Thy truth, which Thou hast given us for our own. And we ask the same blessing for them that they too may attain this joy through the universal peace and concord." [32]

Now appeared in swift succession a series of laws all calculated to allow of the gradual extinction of Heathenism, and on the other hand to promote Christianity and to make it the sole religion of the Empire. Old and ruined temples were not to be restored. Officials were forbidden to participate in sacrifices, and it would seem that later the attempt was made to do away with sacrifices everywhere. In some places the people went further than this. Avarice put its hand to the work, temples were plundered, despoiled of their statues, and their columns, timbers, and stones used for other buildings. On the other hand a general enlargement of the churches was instituted, and Constantine himself erected a number of splendid basilicas in the great cities, in Antioch and Nicomedia. In Jerusalem, on the spot where the Lord was buried and rose again, was built the magnificent Church of the Holy Sepulchre and of the Resurrection; and Helena, the mother of the Emperor, adorned the Mount of Olives and Bethlehem with shrines. Finally Constantine gave to the Empire a new metropolis, Christian from its beginning. Since old Rome held strongly to the heathen religion, he created a new Rome on the Bosphorus. There Christian churches rose, chief of all the large and stately Church of the Apostles, built of marble and colored stones; there the city was full of Christian signs and symbols. There, were not to be seen, as in the squares of the ancient towns, the statues of the gods, but in the market-place stood a statue of the Good Shepherd;[33] and at the entrance of the imperial palace there attracted the gaze of all who went out and in, an immense picture representing Constantine himself with the *Labarum*, the banner of the cross, in his hand, and under his feet, pierced with arrows, a dragon, the dragon of Heathenism.[34]

In truth that dragon was conquered, after having vented his rage upon Christianity for almost three centuries. The victory was complete and lasting, for the final attempt of the Emperor Julian to restore Heathenism to power could only result in completely laying bare its impotence and hastening its utter destruction. Constantine's work was not without its great and serious defects; we shall learn more about them later. From the new situation there arose new dangers and new injuries to the Church. Yet it was no "Adonis garden blooming for a single day,"[35] as his nephew Julian scornfully called it, that the great Emperor planted; but it had a destiny of centuries, and every day we enjoy its fruits. Constantine could not, of course, save the Roman Empire. Its life ran out, for it had fulfilled its mission of gathering for Christ. Its destiny was to die by the hand of Christianity, because its chief end was to prepare for Christianity its first sphere in the world. Afterwards the Christian age was to bring new forms of national and political life. Constantine the Great was succeeded — though it was centuries later — by Charlemagne. Out of the ruins of the Christianized Roman Empire, the Roman Empire of the German nation arose, and in this the achievement of Constantine was really completed. The whole succeeding history of the Teutonic peoples was defined and determined by the deed of Constantine, and we need only to be reminded of the significance of the "Christian Magistracy" for the Reformation, in order to see how the blessing of this action of the first Christian Emperor flows down through the Reformation to ourselves. From the days of Constantine there existed a Christian magistracy — in those words the whole result is summed up to every one who can comprehend their meaning.

Our own age is the first which has commenced to batter at Constantine's work, and many hold it necessary to demand the exact reversal of the step he took, as the prerequisite of a step forward in the development of civilization. Those who make this their endeavor would do well to consider, that it was the State which in its distress sought the alliance with Christianity, because it needed a new bond with the conscience of the citizen, because it was in want of a new moral salt to preserve the national life from complete corruption. If it should really come to pass that the bond, which Constantine created between Christianity and political and national life, should be ruptured, it would soon become evident that the State cannot do without Christianity, and the national life would necessarily become hopelessly corrupt without the salt of the Christian religion. Retrograding beyond Constantine the world would adopt Diocletian's policy, the attempt would have to be made once more to suppress Christianity by force, and then, either our entire national life and civilization would go to ruin, as Diocletian's schemes and the whole antique civilization went, or it would be necessary to decide upon doing Constantine's deed a second time, if that were still a possible thing.

One thing, however, I do not intend to assert. I do not mean to say that Constantine took the right method in all respects to create this bond between Christianity and the life of the people, or that the attitude which the State and Church then assumed towards one another was one really appropriate to their respective natures and ends. If — God grant it! — the struggles of to-day result in confirming the bond which Constantine created, but also in bringing it to perfection, in causing State and Church to maintain their alliance, but to preserve it in a purer form, then the benefits of Constantine's achievement would accrue in richer measure to us and our children, and in every sphere of life the promise given to Constantine would be anew confirmed: "In this sign conquer!"

CHAPTER III.

THE LAST EFFORT OF HEATHENISM.

"*Nubecula est, transibit!*" *It is only a little cloud. It will pass.*
ATHANASIUS.

IN the reign of Decius, so runs the legend, seven youths in Ephesus who had confessed their Christian faith in the persecution, but afterwards escaped their persecutors, fell asleep in a cave in which they took refuge. When they awoke again, the next morning as they supposed, they sent one of their number to the town to fetch food, and he was greatly astounded to find there every thing completely changed. Heathenism had disappeared, the idol statues and temples were gone, in their place were splendid churches; and over the city gates, on the houses, and above the churches, everywhere, shone victorious that cross, for whose sake they had, as they thought, been persecuted but yesterday. They had slept two hundred years in the cave. This legend of the Seven Sleepers well represents the impression which must have been made on the contemporaries of Constantine, by the gigantic revolution which they had experienced. The history of the world had taken an immense stride forwards, such as seldom comes so suddenly. On the imperial throne sat a Christian; from that quarter the Church was no longer persecuted, but favored; the power which the Emperor possessed, his personal influence, the resources at his command, stood at the disposal of Christianity. The Church for the first time learned what it meant to have the magnates of the earth as friends — what advantages, but also what dangers, lay therein.

How suddenly all this had come! It is true that if we follow out the conflict carried on by Christianity for three centuries past, the victory seems completely accounted for. We see that in proportion as Christianity became inwardly more and more the ruling power, the moment drew ever nearer when it must become so outwardly. And yet the moment when, by the decision of an Emperor, it came into power, must have thrilled the whole Empire with a mighty shock, and its effect was plainly perceptible in the revolution sustained by individual characters.

But we must not imagine that the whole huge Empire, the entire life of the people, at once became Christian when the Emperor set up the cross. The most mighty of forces cannot change in a day the customs and institutions of an Empire more than a thousand years old. The Emperor was still called *Pontifex Maximus;* even the succeeding Emperors, who forbade the rites of the ancient religion, nevertheless bore the same title. The statue of Victory still stood in the Roman Senate, and before every session libations and offerings were brought to it.[1] At the time when Constantine was having regular Christian preaching in his palace in order to convert the heathen of his court, the altars of the *Gens Flavia*, the imperial *Gens*, were smoking in

CHAP. III.] THE REVOLUTION STILL INCOMPLETE. 447

the cities, and the Emperor still bore the official title *Divus*, that is, he was still in his own person a heathen God. Especially in the western Empire the heathen were still greatly in the majority, and the ancient religion was still deeply rooted in the manners and customs, in the domestic and the public life. Heathenism was conquered, but it was far from being really subdued, still less extinct. In this new city on the Bosphorus, Constantine set up a colossal statue of himself. It was an ancient statue of Apollo. Its head was struck off, and a head of Constantine substituted. Also, inside the statue was placed a piece of what was supposed to be the holy cross, discovered by the Empress Helena. This is a kind of mirror of the age. A heathen body with a Christian head and Christian life at the heart; for Christianity was in truth the dominant power within, though externally Heathenism everywhere appeared, and would have to be gradually overcome from within. This unique character of the times is to be duly considered, if we are truly to estimate the actors on this stage. Only then can we judge Constantine fairly even in his faults, only then can we comprehend how Julian could form the purpose of restoring Heathenism, and also why his scheme would necessarily be wrecked.

Triumphs sudden and unexpectedly great bring with them the danger that the conqueror will under-estimate the strength of his opponent, and, by pushing his conquest too far, will evoke a re-action against him of the forces which still remain. Even Constantine did not escape this danger. After the victory over Licinius it seemed as if Heathenism had forever collapsed, and with ease could be completely put out of the way. Though the Emperor would not suppress Heathenism by force, yet he did not interpose when fanaticism and avarice destroyed the temples in some places. Though he would not compel the heathen to change their religion, yet he endeavored in every way to persuade them so to do. Large gifts of money were bestowed to enable the Church to distribute liberal charities; for, thought Constantine, the sermons would not reach all, some would be won by receiving support in a time of need, others by finding protection and assistance, others again by a friendly welcome and gifts bestowed as marks of honor. And the Emperor did not neglect advocating the claims of the Church in person. In regular sermons he tried to convince his court-circle of the truth of Christianity,[2] and was much delighted when one or another confessed to having been won over by him. The Church grew, and that more rapidly than ever before, but what kind of adherents were those who now thronged in, attracted by the sunshine of the imperial favor!

Worse than this, the Emperor now began to interfere in person in the internal affairs of the Church. Its position was one full of temptation for him. He recognized the greatness of the power which the Church and its hierarchy possessed. The unity of the Empire, which was the ruling idea of his life, would suggest to him the plan of making the compact unity of the Church contribute thereto. Reminiscences of Heathenism confirmed this purpose. Since the Emperor had been at the head of the heathen religion, how could he, now that the Empire had become Christian, fail to occupy a similar position without endangering his supremacy over the realm? How could he be simply a spectator, when, in the Arian controversy, the unity of the Church was threatened with dissolution? Thus Constantine began to interfere in the internal affairs of the Church. He called the council of Nicæa, he confirmed its decrees, and provided for their execution even with political machinery.[3] The Emperor determined what doctrines were to prevail in the Church, and banished Arius to-day and Athanasius to-morrow. And there were plenty of bishops who were content with this state of things, and recognized the Emperor as a kind of *Pontifex Maximus* over the Church, — only "a bishop over the external affairs of the Church,"[4] Constantine modestly called himself. For the Church was indeed surfeited with property and privileges. The Emperor, a poor financier, impoverished the Empire to enrich the Church. While the provinces were groaning under the pressure of taxation, money never was lacking to build a splendid church, or to buy costly robes or sacred vessels and richly adorned Bibles for a bishop. The bishops had the freedom of the imperial palace, they accompanied the conqueror into camp and battle; gold and honors were liberally bestowed upon them, and some of them at least were not ashamed to reward the "pious Emperor" (now his regular designation) with flattery. Byzantinism was already present in germ, and had begun to exert its power. Both the purity and the freedom of the Church were in danger of being lost. State and Church were beginning an amalgamation fraught with peril. The State was becoming a kind of Church, and the Church a kind of State. The Emperor preached and summoned councils, called himself, though half in jest, "a bishop," and the bishops had become State officials, who, like the high dignitaries of the Empire, travelled by the imperial courier-service, and frequented the ante-chambers of the palaces in Constantinople. The power of the State was used to the full in order to furnish a Propaganda for the Church, and in return the Church was drawn into the service of the State. Even at this time we find decrees of councils which threaten civil offences with ecclesiastical penalties, and, on the other hand, the bishops were invested with a considerable part of the administration of civil justice.[5]

Yet we should, I think, be in error, were we, on account of these mistakes, to regard the whole work of Constantine as a failure. Apart from all else, it is asking too much to expect, that State and Church would immediately assume their proper relations as soon as they first entered into an alliance. For indeed we are still endeavoring to solve this, the greatest problem of the world's history. But the recognition of what Constantine did ought not to hinder us from realizing the mistakes that were made, and the pernicious consequences for the Church which necessarily resulted. These errors paved the way for the re-action attempted by Julian, and let us say now, that what the Church suffered from the apostate Emperor was a well-deserved discipline.

The state of affairs became much worse under the sons of Constantine, who had inherited his bad qualities, ambition, harshness, and cruelty, rather than his good characteristics, and especially his statesmanship. All times in which a great revolution is accomplished bring many forms of corruption to the surface, and this period was no exception to the rule. It now became the fashion at the imperial court to be zealous for Christianity. He who wished to attain any success, had first and foremost to prove himself sound in this respect. Any appearance of lukewarmness towards Christianity, not to speak of inclination towards Heathenism, created a suspicion of political unsoundness. Many of the new converts, who but yesterday had been heathen, knew no better way of proving the sincerity of their conversion than by exhibiting fanatical hatred towards the religion whose adherents they would certainly still have remained, had not their imperial master become a Christian. Ambitious priests crowded around the Emperors, and sought to make themselves prominent, in order to gain wealth and station by the imperial favor. Zeal, which was rash though perhaps not ill-meaning, thought to do service to the Church by urging to deeds of violence against Heathenism, without realizing that the power of the world which bitterly opposes the Church cannot do it so much injury as those who endeavor to come to the rescue by worldly means. Men seemed to have wholly forgotten how long and earnestly the Christians had demanded religious freedom. Now that they had come into power, they refused their opponents the benefit of the freedom which they had won. Those who but now were persecuted became persecutors. "Emperors!" one of their spokesmen exhorts the sons of Constantine, "the temples must be overthrown and utterly destroyed in order that the pernicious error may no longer pollute the Roman world. The Supreme God has committed the government to you in order that you may cure this cancer. When the temples have been destroyed, and no trace remains of Heathenism, you will have conquered your enemies and extended your Empire."[6]

At first the three brothers, among whom Constantine had divided the Empire, were fully occupied with their family feuds. But, when Constantine II. had fallen, and the other two, Constans and Constantius, had become supreme rulers, the former over the West and the latter over the East, they really had recourse to violent measures against Heathenism. A law promulgated in A. D. 341 proclaimed: "The heathen superstition must cease, the madness of offering sacrifices must be extirpated; whoever contrary to this law dares to offer sacrifices shall suffer punishment without mercy."[7] Still more severe was the legislation of Constantius when he became sole ruler after the death of Constans: "The temples everywhere are to be closed, in order to deprive the heathen of the opportunity of sinning. He who offers sacrifices shall be struck down by the avenging sword, his property shall fall to the State treasury."[8] Though this law could not be strictly enforced, yet in many places the images of the gods were broken in pieces, and the temples closed, completely dismantled, or converted into Christian churches. Base passions mingled in this work. The property of the temples was partly stolen, partly came into the possession of the churches, and often might be seen in Christian houses of worship the glitter of gold and jewels which had formerly adorned heathen idols. Those who still adhered to Heathenism were compelled to conceal themselves. The agents of the police searched in every place, and those who took part in a secret sacrifice, or even wore a heathen amulet, were liable to suffer death.[9]

These measures had the result always reached when, in the conflict of spiritual forces, the party for the time being in power resorts to the employment of force. At first every thing gives way, and it looks as if the goal sought were to be reached easily and without labor. But if the opponent still possesses any power of resistance, this will gradually increase as a result of the attack; those who belong to that party come to know one another, and unite against the common foe. Then if circumstances favor them, especially if they find the right man for a leader, it may happen that the situation is suddenly reversed to the condemnation of those who attempt to wage a spiritual conflict with the weapons of the flesh.

Heathenism still possessed a latent power greater than those supposed who persuaded the Emperors that now it could be easily extirpated. The state of affairs in the West differed from that in the East. In the West it was principally the Roman aristocracy, who with few exceptions still adhered to their ancient religion, and with them the great mass of the people. In the East, on the contrary, Christianity had made much more progress among the masses, and a real aristocracy could scarcely be said to exist. In its stead there was an aristocracy of learning, whose hostility was far more dangerous to Christianity than the aversion of the Roman nobility. The youth still thronged to the ancient and illustrious schools of Miletus, Ephesus, Nicomedia, Antioch, and above all Athens, and the teachers in these schools were almost without exception heathen. There the ancient classics were studied, and the eloquence of a Libanius and of other highly cultured rhetoricians of the age was enjoyed. There the ancient heathen spirit was imbibed, and with it a contempt for barbarian Christianity. The doctrinal strife in the Christian Church was held up to ridicule, and, alas! with too much reason. For, according to the Emperor's favor and caprice, one doctrine stood for orthodoxy to-day and another to-morrow. To-day it was decreed that Christ was of the same essence with the Father, and all who refused to acknowledge this were deposed and exiled. To-morrow the court theology had swung round, it was decreed that Christ was a created being, and now it was the turn of the other party to go into banishment. The educated heathen thought themselves elevated far above all this in their classic culture. With what secret anger they beheld the way in which the temples were laid waste, the works of art broken to pieces, the memorials of an age of greatness destroyed, and all in favor of a barbarian religion destitute of culture. The old rude forms of Heathenism, indeed, they themselves did not desire, but the refined Heathenism of the Neoplatonic school seemed to them not merely the equal but the superior of Christianity. For they believed that in it they possessed whatever of truth Christianity contained, only in a much more refined form, wedded to culture and filled with the classic spirit. So they revelled in reminiscences of the bygone glory of Hellas and Rome, and fondly cherished the hope that better times would one day come, that the triumph of Christianity might be only of a transitory nature, and that the "Adonis-gardens" which Constantine had planted would soon wither.

These were the sources of the re-action against Christianity. Their spirit was embodied in Julian. In him it ascended for the last time the imperial throne, and made the final attempt to stop the triumphal progress of Christianity. But it succeeded only in giving to the

JULIAN'S EDUCATION.

world irresistible evidence that the sceptre of the spirit of Antiquity was forever broken.

Flavius Claudius Julianus was the son of Constantius, brother to Constantine, therefore a nephew of the great Emperor. His mother died when he was young, and he lost his father and all his near relatives, except his brother Gallus, in the bloody quarrels which devastated the imperial house after the death of Constantine. He himself was saved only by his youth; he was still an object of perpetual suspicion to the party in power, and this the more as his extraordinary and universal gifts began early to manifest themselves. The Emperor Constantius also began to regard him with distrust, and the result was that Julian in his fourteenth year was banished from Constantinople, conveyed to the castle of Macella in Cappadocia, and there closely guarded.[10] For a noble nature, and such was Julian's through and through, there is nothing more dangerous than thus to grow up under the burden of suspicion and in the midst of intriguing factions. Such a nature is driven, contrary to its essential character, into deceit. Julian learned from his early youth to conceal his real thoughts; he was compelled to cultivate systematically a hypocrisy which afterwards became the worst trait of his character. Worse still, it was thought in Constantinople that the best way to deprive Constantine's nephew of all political importance was to destine him for the Church. He was carefully cut off from all contact with Heathenism, his whole education was confided to ecclesiastics, and assumed a character severely religious. His time was divided between studies and services, even his recreation was an exercise of devotion. In his leisure hours Julian had to build a chapel to the martyr

Mamas[11] as a kind of amusement. That this training accomplished the opposite of what was attempted, need not surprise us, especially when we bear in mind what kind of a Christianity it was which was forcibly poured into the youth as with a funnel,—dogmatic controversy rather than heart-faith, dead ceremony rather than spiritual life. Julian never learned to know true Christianity: the imperial court was the worst imaginable place, and his training in captivity the worst imaginable means, for acquiring such knowledge. On the contrary he became even thus early estranged from Christianity. He would naturally hate a religion whose representatives had murdered his family, and whose priests were his jailers. Of course he did not dare to exhibit any signs of this disgust, but outwardly showed himself a zealous Christian, and even went so far as to enter the lowest grade of clerical orders. He became a reader in the Church,[12] and obtained the reputation of peculiar piety.

Even to the Emperor Constantius he now appeared not dangerous. He was set at liberty again, and spent some time in Constantinople, where the Sophist Hecebolius (a man at bottom wholly indifferent in religious matters, but who had become a zealous Christian for the sake of obtaining favor at court[13]) strove to fill Julian with contempt for the heathen gods, but evidently exercised no favorable influence over him. Then he was even permitted to go to Nicomedia in order to study philosophy and rhetoric there. But he had to give a promise to his teacher Hecebolius that he would not hear Libanius, the chief representative of the party which included the heathen philosophers and rhetoricians.[14] That which was forbidden became only the more attractive. Julian did keep his promise of not hearing Libanius, but he the more zealously studied his writings, and soon had established personal or epistolary relations with the chief men of those circles of heathen culture which have been described.[15] They conjured up all the splendor of the ancient world before his eyes, they opened the classics to him, and speedily won the youth for the ideas in which they lived. With what eagerness did he now study Plato and Aristotle; what inspiration he now drew from listening to the revelations of the Neoplatonic philosophy; with what a holy awe was he filled by the magic arts, the practice of which was a favorite pursuit in these circles! Here he believed himself to have found that for which his soul long had languished. How could men give up all this splendor for the sake of barbarian Christianity! It may be regarded as certain that Julian even then, in A. D. 351, returned to Heathenism, and, beside the rhetoricians of Nicomedia, it was principally the aged and illustrious Neoplatonist, Maximus of Ephesus who brought about his perversion.[16]

What influenced Julian was chiefly enthusiasm for Greek culture. Even in a religious aspect Polytheism seemed to him superior to Monotheism, because more philosophic. Neoplatonism filled the whole soul of the young enthusiast, and seemed to him to comprehend all the culture of the ancient world in a unified system. But of course his vanity had a great share in the matter, for he naturally received the most devoted homage among the Hellenists, and his rhetorical friends did not stint their flattery. Under the forcible measures then adopted by Constantius against the ancient faith, the heathen party had become more closely consolidated, and already cherished various schemes for the restoration of Heathenism, while Julian was already looked upon as the man who was one day to realize them.[17] He had, it is true, still studiously to conceal his predilection for Heathenism, and to appear outwardly as a zealous Christian and an admirer of Constantius; but his friends hoped for a time when he would be able to come forward openly in his true character, and that time was to come more speedily than even their boldest hopes could anticipate. Suddenly and unexpectedly to Julian, he was called away from his classic studies, and given a place in practical political life.

Things looked dark in the Empire. On the South-east the Persians were moving to the attack; on the North-west the Germans were pressing on, and had already overrun part of Gaul. Constantius stood almost alone, such gaps had family feuds made with poison and the sword in the once flourishing house of Constantine. Julian alone survived, after Gallus, his brother, had been murdered.

The Emperor determined to call Julian to his assistance. He was made *Cæsar*, and invested with the supreme command over the troops in Gaul. Julian was to repulse the Germans, while the Emperor undertook the defence of the eastern frontier against the Persians.[18] With startling rapidity did the young Cæsar now develop his wonderful gifts. He who had hitherto lived only for study, soon showed himself an able general and a sagacious ruler. Conscientiously dividing his time between the studies which he even now did not neglect, and his duties as a ruler, a model of simplicity in his way of living, pure and austere in his morality, sharing every danger and every fatigue with his soldiers,[19] he succeeded by a series of victorious battles in driving the Germans back over the Rhine, and in bringing peace to Gaul. Deified by his soldiers, he was also held in high honor by the inhabitants of the province. This aroused again the old suspicions in Constantinople, carefully as Julian avoided all that could provoke the Emperor, and studiously as he concealed his Heathenism above all. For while, in the select circle of his trusted friends, the ancient gods were still worshipped in the palace of Julian, he still appeared in public as a Christian.[20]

In order to prevent his becoming too powerful, the Emperor near the end of A. D. 360 recalled from Gaul the best legions, which were under Julian's command, nominally because he needed to use them against the Persians.[21] The legions refused to march, and proclaimed Julian *Augustus*. Even now Julian tried to placate Constantius; but, when the attempt proved fruitless, when Julian saw that it was a matter of life and death with him, he assumed the rank of Emperor, and advanced at the head of his army. He had already reached Dacia, when the news met him that Constantius had died Nov. 3, 361, on the march against the Persians. Without further resistance the whole Empire recognized Julian as Emperor, and he hastened to Constantinople. He made his entry there as a declared heathen. Although at the beginning of his campaign he had secretly sacrificed to Bellona, yet he had attended the church in Vienne.[22] But on the march he put an end to all ambiguity, and publicly offered sacrifices to the ancient gods. The Roman Empire once more had a heathen Emperor.

At first all was joy; for as universally as Constantius

was hated, Julian was welcomed as a deliverer. Even the Christians joined in this rejoicing. They too had found the arbitrary government of the last few years hard enough to bear. And if some who looked deeper began to feel anxiety, they consoled themselves by the reflection that even a heathen Emperor could not injure the Church so much as a Christian Emperor who used his power in promoting whatever seemed to him at the time to be orthodoxy in the dogmatic controversies of the age. And Julian proclaimed, not the suppression of Christianity, but only complete religious liberty.[23] He himself intended to be a heathen, but no Christian should be disturbed in his faith.

Julian was certainly thoroughly in earnest in this. To be a persecutor of the Church, was the last thing he would have thought of. Besides, he was much too fully persuaded of the untruth of Christianity and the truth of Heathenism to persecute. Julian was an enthusiast, like all the rhetoricians and philosophers who surrounded him. He regarded himself as called by a divine voice to the great work of restoring Heathenism, and this was from the beginning avowedly his object. And he was no less firmly convinced that this restoration would work itself out without any use of force; as soon as free scope was given to Heathenism it would, by its own powers, overcome Christianity. If the heathen would only cultivate their religion studiously, perform its rites zealously, and lead lives well-pleasing to the gods, then without doubt the Christians would become converted, and recognize the truth of Heathenism.

The Emperor himself was evidently in all respects a heathen from sincere conviction. In this regard at least he was honest and no hypocrite. The flagrant voluptuousness, which had corrupted the court, was banished, and a large number of useless officials dismissed.[24] The life of the court was to be simple, austere, and pure. Men had never before seen an Emperor who conducted himself with such simplicity, whose table was so economically supplied, and who knew no other employments than hard work, and devoted worship of the gods. A temple was built in the palace, and there Julian offered a daily sacrifice.[25] Often he might be seen serving at the sacrifice himself, carrying the wood and plunging the knife into the victim with his own hand.[26] He remembered every festival which should be celebrated, and knew how to observe the whole half-forgotten ritual most punctiliously.

He was equally zealous in performing the duties of his office as *Pontifex Maximus*. Everywhere he revived the ancient worship which had fallen into neglect. Here a closed temple was re-opened, there a ruined shrine restored, images of the gods were set up again, and festivals which had ceased to be celebrated, were restored. In this way, Julian was certain, Heathenism would be sure to renew its life. He expressly rejected all use of force. At the beginning of his reign he wrote to Artabius, one of the provincial governors, that he did not wish the Christians to be unjustly beaten and killed; and in a letter dated from Antioch, and therefore of the latter part of his reign, he forbids the compulsion of the Christians by force to attend the temples. "Blows and bodily injuries," he says, "are not the means by which to change a man's convictions." To him the Christian religion seemed an error which deserved pity, not hatred; a foolishness, a madness, which indeed must be cured against the will of the patient. "Though it is possible," he affirms, "to cure bodily sicknesses by violent operations, yet errors concerning the nature of God cannot be destroyed either by fire or steel. What does it profit if the hand does sacrifice, when the mind condemns the hand? It is only a new disguise outwardly applied, not a change of conviction."[27] Who would not agree with these sentiments? But it is of course another question whether or not Julian would be able to keep within the limits here so truly and wisely laid down.

Julian certainly did not wish to use force, yet he was much pleased when any one became convinced of the truth of Heathenism; and though his purpose was to leave to each the fullest liberty of choice, yet he must have been less convinced of the truth of his own position than he was, to have refrained from striving to win over others. His conduct at the funeral of Constantius was characteristic. He left to the Christians perfect liberty, he did not interfere, though in many churches the plaint over the death of the Christian Emperor became a complaint against his heathen successor; but he himself went through the burial ceremonies in honor of the deceased according to heathen ritual. When he had poured out the libation he invited the bystanders to follow his example. Those who did so were cordially greeted by him; those who refused were not compelled, they were free to do as they chose, yet the friendly smile with which he answered their refusal had something suspicious in it. Of course it was not long before one and another among those at court, who had hitherto been zealous Christians, and perhaps within a short time had ardently striven in behalf of the Nicene or the Arian views, made the discovery that after all Heathenism was really preferable to Christianity. They had hardly been men, had it failed to be so; and the enthusiastic Julian really believed that their conversion was his work, especially when the more cunning courtiers managed to delay a short time, and allow the Emperor to declaim at great length about the glory of the ancient religion, before the new light dawned upon them. What joy he experienced each time that one of the more illustrious individuals was won over to the ancient gods; and though he did not dismiss from his court any Christian solely for religious reasons, it was yet only natural that those who shared his views should stand in the most intimate relations with him. Soon conversions became plentiful; governors, officials, soldiers, made themselves proficient in the ancient cultus; and even a bishop, Pegasius of New Ilium, whom Julian had previously learned to know as a secret friend of the gods, when he had been the Emperor's guide to the classic sites of Troy, changed his religion, and from a Christian bishop became a heathen high-priest.[28] The long-closed doors of the temples were opened anew in many towns, and the altars of the gods now smoked again where their fires had long been extinguished. Julian really imagined that Heathenism was beginning to revive, and the temptation became very great to assist it by some little devices which were not quite honorable. But men, and especially enthusiasts, only too easily justify bad means by good ends. For instance, it was a favorite plan to put an image of a god by the side of the Emperor's statue. Those who paid the customary reverence to the Emperor might easily be regarded as having offered worship to the god; and, on the other hand, those who did not bow before the god invited the suspicion of disloyalty towards the Emperor.[29]

In the army this policy was carried still further. Military and religious ceremonies had always been mingled, and the strictness of military discipline naturally limited religious liberty. The monogram of Christ, which the standards had borne since Constantine, was banished, and its place was taken by the ancient Roman S. P. Q. R.[30] When the soldiers received their gratuities, a portable altar was placed at the side of the imperial throne, and near the altar a little box filled with incense. The soldiers were ordered to come forward one by one, and receive each his *congiarium*. Each one as he approached was expected to take a few grains of incense, and throw them into the fire on the altar. The Christians among the soldiers held back and delayed, but the officers emphatically assured them that it was an entirely innocent ceremony, since there was no image on the altar. Most of them allowed themselves to be persuaded, and did as they were bidden; a few preferred to go without the *congiarium*. Afterwards at the festal banquet the Christian soldiers crossed themselves as was their wont. Their heathen comrades laughed, and when asked the reason replied mockingly: "We laugh because you are still praying to Jesus Christ the moment after having denied him." The Christians sprang up in horror, now that they perceived the snare which had been set for them. Many of them rent their garments, and ran into the town, crying: "We are Christians! Every one may know it! If our hands have denied, our hearts have not!" A crowd collected before the imperial palace. Some went so far as to throw down at the Emperor's feet the money, which they were said to have gained by denial. The Emperor was placed in an unfortunate position. His purpose had not been exactly to seduce the soldiers into open denial of their faith; he regarded the ceremony perhaps as innocent, but it was ambiguous and instituted for the purpose of gradually accustoming the soldiers to ceremonies of that kind. If now the Emperor should punish these tumultuous soldiers, it might look like a persecution, and Julian did not wish that. If he left them unpunished, then military discipline would be imperilled. The Emperor arrested and condemned some soldiers, but expressly declared that this was not because they were Christians, but because they had revolted from their standards. Nevertheless all Constantinople was in an uproar. Immense crowds accompanied the soldiers to the place of execution; they were already honored as martyrs. Then Julian judged it best to pardon them.[31] But the consequences of the event were not averted by this. The mistrust of the Christians was now awakened against the Emperor, and would not be disarmed. Julian himself was hurried onward. That which he had hitherto not intended, was now carried out: all the higher officers who were Christians were removed or dismissed, and all Christians were rejected from the service of the court.[32] The gulf which separated the heathen Emperor from his Christian subjects had become visible.

A still worse influence was exercised by certain laws which Julian enacted[33] in order to correct the injustice of his predecessor, but which, as he well knew, were certain to affect the Christians most. Under the pretext of impartial justice, these laws concealed an injury to the Church, and Julian secretly rejoiced that it was so. Under Constantius the property of the communes had often been taken from them and arbitrarily applied to other purposes. Now all was to be restored, and that without any compensation to those now in possession. The property concerned had been partly used to meet the expenditure of the Emperor, but also, in part, to build churches. Temples had been changed into churches, and were now to be given back to the heathen cultus. Temples which had been destroyed were to be rebuilt, or their estimated value repaid out of the treasuries of the churches. Even private individuals who had bought in good faith the temple-lands were compelled to make restitution. Gold and gems which had formerly ornamented any image of the gods, but now adorned chalices, crosses, and evangelistaries in the churches, were to be broken out and restored to their former uses.[34] And this law was enforced with ruthless severity. For the governors knew that they would thereby gain favor with the Emperor, and the heathen mob already began to help here and there.

Julian not only rejoiced in this, and did nothing to soften the rigor of the law; but he even expressly approved of it, and mockingly said: "Indeed, the Galileans should rejoice: does not the command of the Gospel enjoin them to suffer evil?"[35] On the part of the Christians, fanaticism began to blaze up, and the first blood was shed. In Doristera, a town of Thrace, a Christian church had been changed back into a heathen temple; idols stood once more where the cross had been placed. On the eve of the day when the temple was to be dedicated with a great heathen festival, a Christian broke into the church and destroyed the idols. Then he gave himself up, and was executed. The Christians honored him as a new martyr.

The dream of a restoration of Heathenism nevertheless soon began to prove itself a dream. Though now surrounded by heathen only, Julian could not help feeling that he was really isolated in their midst. He himself was naturally a mystic, and lived in his ideals. His Heathenism was one purified by poetic feeling. But there was little or nothing of this to be found actually existing. His heathen friends were courtiers, who agreed with him without inward conviction; empty rhetoricians, who sought only the glory of saying fine things; men wholly indifferent and destitute of religion; or merry companions, whose first object was amusement, and who were glad to be released from the restraints of Christianity, but not under the penalty of submitting to still more rigorous restrictions from the Heathenism of their ruler. The Emperor was far from satisfied with his adherents. He often gave them severe lectures, accused them of being cold and indifferent, and blamed their license. They were no better satisfied with him. He was far too serious and severely moral for their tastes. They preferred the theatre to the temple, they liked amusement best, and found the daily attendance at worship and the monotonous ceremonies and sacrifices very dull. A measurably tolerant Christian Emperor would doubtless have suited them better than this enthusiastically pious heathen. Blinded as Julian was by his ideal views, he soon could not escape the knowledge that things were not going well. If Heathenism was to revive, it must receive new life within. The restoration must be also a reformation.

Strangely enough Julian felt compelled to borrow

from Christianity the ways and means for such a reformation. The heathen priests, like the Christian, were to instruct the people, and exhort them to holy living. The heathen, like the Christians, were to care for the poor. "If our religion," he writes to the high-priest of Galatia, "does not make the progress we could wish, the blame lies with those who profess it. The gods have done great things for us, above our hopes and petitions. But is it right that we should be satisfied with their favors, and neglect those things which the impiety of the Christians has cultivated, their hospitality to strangers, their care of the graves, their holiness of life? We should earnestly seek all these things." And then he proceeds to give the high-priest directions to instruct the people, to purge the priesthood from unworthy members, to prohibit the priests from going to the theatre and frequenting the taverns. Above all, he was to provide for the exercise of benevolence among the heathen as it was practised among the Christians. Alms-houses and hospitals were to be built, and the needy assisted. The Emperor himself appropriated abundant means, but the villages were also to be urged to auxiliary contributions. "We ought not," the Emperor says in conclusion, "to allow others to appropriate our virtues while the shame of indolence falls upon us. This may be called despising the worship of the gods." [36]

While new strength was thus to be infused into Heathenism, other measures were adopted to weaken Christianity. An imperial edict, June 17, A. D. 362,[37] forbade the Christians to act as teachers of the national literature, the ancient classics. It was, the Emperor explained,[38] a contradiction for Christians to expound

Homer, Thucydides, or Demosthenes, when they regarded them as godless men and aliens. He would not compel them to change their convictions, but also he could not permit the ancient writers to be expounded by those who took them to task for impiety. "If ye," he adds, "recognize any wisdom in the ancients, then prove it by imitating their piety towards the gods. But if, on the contrary, you believe that all their opinions are false, then go into the churches of the Galileans, and expound Matthew and Luke." It is true, this edict prohibited the Christians only from teaching the national literature, not from becoming the pupils of heathen teachers.[39] But this would necessarily be the immediate consequence. For when the Christians were prevented from teaching, the instruction came wholly into the hands of the heathen, and thereby gained a character so specifically heathen, and came into so avowed an antagonism to Christianity, that Christians could no longer be even hearers at such lectures. Thus the consequences of the edict reached much farther than its immediate scope. It cut the Christians off from all culture, and became to them an actual prohibition of culture. Thus also they were excluded from all the higher offices which required education; they were excommunicated from the society of educated men. This was just what Julian wished. To the complainants he answered: "Keep your ignorance; eloquence is ours. Your doctrine has only one word: Believe! Then be content with faith."[40] He expressly declared that the worshippers of the Carpenter, the followers of the fishermen,[41] had no claim to culture.

This, of course, was not a persecution, if the use of force alone makes a persecution, yet it was a persecution, and in a sense a worse one than any which went before. Julian tried to deprive the Christians of that which should be common to all men, — education; he disputed their right to the intellectual property of the nation. They were really no longer to be treated as men.[42] Julian had already gone as far as this. Nevertheless he had to confess to himself that the restoration of Heathenism was making no progress worth speaking of, but that on the contrary the aversion to it increased steadily. And, though he was too proud to pay much regard to this, yet his own feelings became daily more excited and imbittered. He found himself more and more isolated in the world to which he had tried to present the best thing he knew, — the classic heritage of Greece, — only to discover that the world had no taste for it. He spent his whole strength, he sacrificed himself, he lived only for the Empire over which Providence had made him lord, and yet found himself alone in his endeavor. Even his heathen friends, the philosophers and rhetoricians, kept at a distance. He had invited them. Very few came; most, and those the principal ones, excused themselves. Had they too no longer any heart in the matter, concerning which he and they had once been so enthusiastic at Nicomedia and Athens? Or did they already despair of the success of his work?

With such thoughts as these, Julian journeyed to Antioch, in Syria, in order to make preparations there for the great campaign he purposed to make against the Persians. There new disappointments awaited him. He found the shrines of his gods forsaken and desolate. The grove of Daphne in the neighborhood of the city, once a famous sanctuary of Apollo, and where oracles had been imparted at the sacred spring, was in a deplorable condition. The spring was filled up, the temple in ruins. In the grove itself was a Christian chapel in which rested the bones of the martyr Babylas. Julian commanded the immediate restoration of the temple, and the exhuming of the martyr's bones. The Christians obeyed, but as in solemn procession they carried the relics to another church, Julian could not help hearing them sing, in full chorus, the words of the Psalm (xcvii. 7): "Confounded be all they that serve graven images, that boast themselves of idols."[43] Starting up in a rage, Julian ordered some soldiers to attack the procession. They arrested some of the Christians, and he was about to order their execution, but came to himself, and discharged them. His noble nature showed itself once more; he did not wish to persecute.

The temple of Apollo was restored with the greatest splendor. Julian went there to offer a sacrifice to the god. He expected to find a multitude of worshippers, but no one even brought oil for a lamp or incense to burn in honor of the deity. Only an old man approached to sacrifice a goose.[44] It did not help matters when Julian gave the Antiochians a long lecture on the subject of this neglect of the god.[45] It only exposed him the more to their biting gibes. They called him "the Bear" because of his long beard; they scoffed at the frequency of his offerings, saying that it was no wonder that meat was getting dear, when the Emperor himself was the butcher.[46] Shortly afterwards, the newly restored temple burned down in the night.[47] Now the Emperor's wrath knew no bounds. He ascribed the guilt to the Christians; and although the temple, as is probable, caught fire through the fault of a heathen philosopher, who carried a dedicatory lamp about in it without due precautions,[48] many Christians were arrested and tortured. The Church had its martyrs once more; and Julian, discontented with himself and the whole world besides, advanced to new measures. The cathedral of Antioch was closed and its property confiscated.[49] Julian decreed that the Christians, whose God had forbidden them to kill, should not be intrusted with any office with which judicial functions were connected.[50] He explained that the Galileans were not to be persecuted, but pious men were to be preferred. This was enough to exclude the Christians from all offices.[51] Day and night the sacrifices smoked, and their flesh was distributed to the soldiers. Some of them murmured at it. Julian had them arrested and executed.[52] In front of the great fountain in Antioch, an altar was erected, and the spring was solemnly dedicated to all the gods. Then with this water they sprinkled the market, and the provisions which were brought thither, the meat and the vegetables; and Julian enjoyed the thought that now the Christians could not eat or drink any thing without polluting themselves with the water consecrated to the idols.[53] It seemed as if the times of Galerius had come back. Worse still was the Christians' lot in the provinces. In many places the heathen gathered, and plundered and killed the Christians. Julian everywhere took the side of the heathen. " What does it matter," said he, "is it then a crime if one Greek kills ten Galileans?"[54] Of course such words, from the Emperor, were the signal for fresh persecutions; and Julian permitted it to be so.

More and more heavy became the atmosphere of Antioch. What happened was exaggerated by report.

Every night, it was narrated, the Emperor had some Christians executed, and in the morning their bodies floated down the Orontes.[55] Julian himself became more and more restless. He hurried from temple to temple, brought sacrifice after sacrifice; he knelt for hours before his gods and covered their statues with kisses. Then at night he sat in the silence at his writing-table, and gave vent to his bitterness and disgust with every thing. Then he wrote his works full of brilliant wit, thought out and expressed with Greek refinement, but full of bitterest hatred especially against the Galileans and their Carpenter's Son. Writing did not make him calmer, but only more restless and bitter.

Finally, his immense preparations for the campaign against the Persians were finished. Julian started, after finally setting over the Antiochians a wretch as governor, with the remark, that the man did not deserve to be a governor, but they deserved to be governed by such a one.[56] The campaign was to be like that of a second Alexander. Julian purposed ridding the Empire forever of its most dangerous enemy. The heathen set all their hopes on this campaign. If the Emperor returned victorious, then the victory of Heathenism was assured. The Christians were silent. The thrill as of an expected judgment of God went through the world. When the rhetorician Libanius scornfully asked a Christian priest, "What is your Carpenter's Son doing now?" the other replied, "He is now making a coffin for your Emperor."[57] Julian, too, felt gloomy forebodings. His ever-increasing superstitiousness sought for signs, and saw signs, in every thing. Now various deformities in the sacrificial victims filled his soul with anxiety, or his horse shied, or he discovered some other evil omen.

This mood passed as soon as he stood at the head of his army. The commander awoke within him once more. He had sketched a bold plan, and at first all went according to his wishes.[58] The legions advanced victoriously Eastward as far as the Tigris. Ctesiphon was taken after a brilliant passage at arms. Prudent men among the Emperor's counsellors now advised him to be content with these fruits of victory, but Julian's restless spirit urged him forward. Just as he, living wholly in reminiscences of the past, had taken the ancient heroes for his examples, so he now determined to imitate Alexander. In order to exclude all thoughts of retreat, he burned his fleet upon the Tigris. Then the army was compelled to advance. They marched on and on into the great plains. The enemy was not to be seen; the Persian light horse retreated further and further. Thus the position of the Romans became each day more critical; they were continually receding from their bases of supply. The soldiers began to murmur. Vainly did Julian represent to them in eloquent words that to retreat was much more perilous than to advance, vainly he showed them that victory was near. If the enemy had been in sight before them, these veteran legions, which he had led to victory on the Rhine, had followed him. But here in the hot sandy plains they could not endure dragging themselves onward day by day without seeing a single foe. With a heavy heart Julian was forced to command a retreat. The Persians had waited for this moment. Their troops of light horse attacked the Romans on every side. Ever skirmishing by day and never resting at night, poorly supplied with provisions, — thus the legions had to make their way back.

Julian could not conceal from himself that his position was extremely critical. How discouraged he must have felt as after the ceaseless efforts of the day, he lay sleepless in his tent! What had become of all his dreams of the restoration of the ancient glory of Greece and Rome! One morning he sent for the priests, and said that in the night the Genius of Rome had appeared to him, just as once before in Gaul during the night before the day on which the soldiers had proclaimed him Augustus; only now the horn of plenty which the Genius bore was reversed, not held on high as before. He had sprung up to detain the vision, but the Genius had left the tent and quickly disappeared. The priests offered sacrifices, sought for signs, but finally had no other counsel to give except to avoid a battle if possible. But how was this possible, when they were surrounded by enemies? That very moment was heard again the Persian battle-cry. Julian put himself at the head of the legions, and once more Roman valor sustained its reputation, once more fortune smiled on him. With desperate courage the legions pressed forward and gained a complete victory; with shouts of joy they escorted the Emperor to his tent. But scarcely had he laid aside his armor to rest, when again came an attack of the Persians from another quarter. Without putting on his armor, Julian hastened to the scene of battle. Vainly his friends strove to restrain him: in advance of all the rest he charged the enemy. They had already begun to waver, when a spear struck the Emperor in the thigh. With a loud cry he sank to the ground. Carried to his tent, he lived a few hours longer, and died in the night of June 26, A. D. 363.[59]

At least this was his, a hero's death, one worthy of

an ancient Roman. It seemed as though the old world was in him to arise once more in the form of a hero, and then utterly perish. Julian's fate was deeply tragical. Richly gifted, daring and courageous, a born general, eloquent in speech, full of spirit, a noble nature, lord of himself, and ready to sacrifice all for his country, what might he not have been! What might he not have done for the Empire! But all these rich gifts were turned to destruction, for himself and for the Empire, because failing to recognize the ways by which God had been leading the nations, he attempted to turn back the current of history: because, possessed with the delusion of Heathenism, he tried to force it upon the Empire, after the world had already attained the higher light, Christianity. The cry with which Julian fell is variously given. Some say it was: "Nazarene, thou hast conquered!" others: "Sun" (Julian was particularly devoted to the worship of the sun-god), "thou hast betrayed me!"[60] Both sources ascribe to him the cry of a soul undeceived; and, whatever the words may have been, his thoughts must have been of this nature. Continuous disappointment, this was the punishment which Julian had to bear for his offence. For was it not his own fault, that he was deceived, and continued to deceive himself and others? Filled with youthful enthusiasm he hoped to see the glory of the ancient world revived, and yet all his labor and zeal did not avail to kindle one spark of true life in those burnt-out ashes. He was deluded in holding that the antique world, in whose behalf he was so enthusiastic, was still capable of life. He did not mean to persecute, he meant only to give freedom; and yet at last he was driven to act as a tyrant and a persecutor of the

Church. He was deluded in supposing that he could turn the world back again without the use of force. After Christianity had once gained the victory, every form of opposition to it must necessarily end in being Anti-Christian. Julian's intention at first was to be simply not a Christian, a heathen, but against his will he was more and more forced into Anti-Christian antagonism to the Church. His life became a contest between himself and the Nazarene. This he felt, this was the cause of his restlessness, of his bitterness and his deep anxiety. He called for a judgment of God, and it came in the plains beyond the Tigris.

Even if the fatal spear had not struck him there, yet his part had been played to the end. Returning with a defeated army, he would not only have had to renounce all thoughts of restoring Heathenism, but would have had difficulty in maintaining his position on the throne. Athanasius would have been right in any case. When during the reign of Julian, the friends of the illustrious teacher expressed their anxiety and fear, he responded only: "*Nubecula est, transibit!*" — "It is only a little cloud, it will pass!"[61] Heathenism was to give a proof that its life was exhausted. That proof was now given. The re-action under Julian was its last effort; after that failed, Heathenism collapsed all the more rapidly. In Julian, ancient Heathenism fell, crying out: "Nazarene, thou hast conquered!" The victory of Christianity over Heathenism was complete.

Was the victory pure and perfect? Yes, looking back over the whole conflict, we may say that this victory was the purest ever won. For it was won by witnessing and enduring, by loving and suffering, by pouring out innocent blood. But what is pure in this sinful world? Even the development of the Church was not immaculate, even there sin intrudes, though the Lord governs it, and in spite of human sin, is guiding it to the goal of perfection. It is sorrowful to see that already were sown the first seeds of errors, which in course of time would grow and bring forth other and different conflicts. During the conflict with Heathenism a legal element obtained a footing in the Church. This was later to pervert Christ's institution of grace more and more into a governmental institution. Already was laid the foundation of a hierarchy which in the course of the centuries was, it is true, to render the Church powerful and glorious, but also to put the Lord Jesus himself into the background. Already a worldly element had penetrated into the Church. In the time of peace just beginning, this element was to enter more and more and to render the Church itself worldly. Though Church and State through Constantine's momentous achievement had joined hands to work together, yet a terrible series of conflicts was to come between the two powers, struggles which held centuries in suspense. The conflict with external Heathenism was over, the struggle with the Heathenism in the Church was to take its place. For though outwardly conquered, Heathenism was not yet completely subdued within; but as in each of us "the old man" perpetually fights against "the new man," so in the history of the Church the ancient Heathenism is ever rising from the depths of the natural man to do battle against the new life of Christianity. This conflict is not ended. The history of the Church is only the story of this conflict. Therefore the peace which the Church won is as yet no perfect peace, but only marks a new phase of the struggle, which is not yet fought out. Indeed, to-day we are in the midst of it; for stronger almost than ever, the heathen spirit in modern guise is wrestling against Christian thought and life, and it almost seems as if the questions of the time should be gathered up into *the* question: "Shall we remain Christians, or become heathen again?"

May then these pictures from the past heroic age of the Church serve as instructive illustrations for to-day. May we above all learn from them, that in the conflict which we have to wage only one thing is victorious, — faith, living faith, confessing with joy, working by love, and enduring in hope. In this faith we, together with the confessors and martyrs, look forward to a victory other than that which they won, the victory which the Lord will bring in His great day. That victory will be wholly pure, wholly perfect. After that victory comes no more conflict, but eternal peace.

NOTES.

BOOK I.. CHAPTER I.

[*Notes added by the translators are enclosed in brackets.*]

1. Eusebius, H. Eccl., iv. 26. Melito, addressing the Emperor, says: "Our philosophy first flourished among the barbarians, but having flowered among the nations under your government during the glorious reign of Augustus your ancestor, it became, especially to your dominion, an auspicious blessing. For since that time the Roman power has grown to greatness and splendor. Whose desired successor you have become, and will be, together with your son, if you preserve that philosophy which was the foster sister of the Empire, and began its existence with Augustus" (τῆς βασιλείας τὴν σύντροφον καὶ συναρξαμένην Αὐγούστῳ φιλοσοφίαν). **2.** De Virtut. et Leg., § 7. **3.** [Epigr. i. 67, xiii. 3. Merivale, Hist. of the Romans under the Empire, vi. 232, *sq.*; Norton, Evidences of Gen. of the Gospels, i. 50, *n.*; Ed. Rev., cxxxix. 6, 1874. Pliny, Ep. ix. 11. For the value of the sesterce see Marquardt u. Mommsen, II'dbuch d. röm. Alterthümer, v. 70; De Champagny, Les Césars du 3º Siécle, i. 37, 469, *sq.*] **4.** [iii. Eleg. 13. 59-60.] **5.** [Germ. 37.] **6.** Cf., for the entire chapter, especially: Friedländer; Darstellungen aus d. Sittengeschichte Roms; Boissier, La religion romaine d'Auguste aux Antonins, Paris, 1874 [2d ed., 1879]; [Marquardt u. Mommsen, II'dbuch d. röm. Alterthümer, Bd. vi.; Fisher, Beginnings of Christianity; von Döllinger, Gentile and Jew in the Courts of the Temple of Christ; Merivale, History, c. liv.; De Champagny, Les Césars, T. iii., iv., Tableau du monde romaine]. **7.** [Friedländer, iii. 487.] **8.** Sat. 17. **9.** Adv. Colotem., c. 31. **10.** [Hist. vi. 54.] **11.** Suet. Aug., c. 35. **12.** [Boissier, i. 4, *sq.*; Marq. u. Momm., vi. 5, *sq.*] **13.** De Anim., c. 39; ad Nat., ii. 11. These names are to be found in the *Indigitamenta*, or registers. They are indeed but epithets of the Deity, and show very plainly the abstract character of religion among the Romans, who lacked fancy, and whose entire nature was thoroughly practical. **14.** Cato, de re rust. passim. **15.** Pro dom., 1. **16.** Cf. Boissier: la relig. rom., i. 12 (1st ed.). **17.** De bell. Gall., vi. 17. **18.** Hist. nat., vi. 22. **19.** Adv. gentes, vi. 7; "Civitas omnium numinum cultrix." **20.** Macrobius, Sat., iii. 9, 7. [Marq. u. Momm., H'dbuch Bd. vi., 21.] **21.** Dion, li. 16. **22.** Jos., de bell. Jud., v. 38. Philo, de Virtut. et Leg., 40. **23.** Corp. inscr. lat., iii. 75. **24.** Letronne, Inscr. de l'Egypte, i. 206. **25.** Orelli, 1993. **26.** Orelli, 2047, 5909. **27.** Ann. xv. 44. **28.** Ov. Fast., iii. 525; Am. iii. 13; Hor., Od. iii. 18. **29.** Amphitr. ii. 2, 211 [840]. **30.** Orelli, 4859 [ii. 351]. **31.** iii. 46. **32.** Non posse suaviter vivi sec. Epic., 121 [xxi.; Goodwin: Plutarch's Mor., ii. 191]. **33.** [Marq. u. Momm., vi. 438; White and Riddle, Dict. 2,098; Friedl., iii. 493.] **34.** Cf. Varro, de ling. lat., vii. 2; Capitol. Marc. Aurel., c. 4. **35.** [Telamo, Ribbeck, p. 44; Boissier, i. 49.] **36.** [Sallust, Cat. 51, 52. Merivale: Conversion of the Rom. Emp., 25, 187, *sq*.] **37.** Lucret., i. 62-101. **38.** [Nat. Hist., ii. 7 (5); xxviii. 1 (2).] **39.** Antiq. Rom., ii. 67. **40.** Geog., i. 19. **41.** [Aug., De Civ. Dei, vi. 10.] **42.** [*Ib*., vi. 5.] **43.** [Hypot., iii. 2, *sq*.] **44.** [Geog., xvi. 35 (761).] **45.** [Apol. 17.] **46.** Plin., Nat. Hist., xxviii. 2 (4). **47.** Suet., Aug., c. 70, 90, 91. **48.** [Sat., ii. 149.] **49.** Hist. iii. 20. **50.** Instit., ii. 2 [?]. **51.** Tac., Ann., vi. 12. **52.** Dion, lx. 23. **53.** Suet., Claudius, c. 22. **54.** Suet., Nero, c. 56. **55.** An inscription styles Vespasian: *conservator ceremoniarum publicarum,* and *restitutor œdium sacrarum.* Or., 2304. **56.** Letronne, Inscr. de l'Egypte, i. 241. **57.** Nat. Hist., ii. 7 (5). **58.** Pitra, Spicileg. Solesm., ii. p. xli. **59.** [*Apocolocyntosis*, lit., pumpkinification. Cf. Meriv., Hist. Rom. Emp., v. 601; West. Rev., July, 1867, p. 49, *sq*.] **60.** Ovid, Ep. ex Ponto, i. 37-40; Juvenal [iii. 60-90, vi. 390]; Tacit., Hist., i. 22; Minucius Felix Octav., 21. **61.** De leg., ii. 8. **62.** Hist. xxv. 1: Neu quis in publico sacrove loco, novo aut externo ritu sacrificaret. **63.** *Ib*., xxxix. 16. **64.** Corp. inscr. lat., i. 196. **65.** [Dion, i. 16, xliii. 2.] **66.** Orelli, 4737. **67.** Bull. de l'inst. arch., 1864, p. 154. **68.** Inscr. de l'Algerie, 3712. Cf. Or., 7395. **69.** [Friedl., ii. 204; Fisher, Beginnings of Christ., 65, n.] **70.** [Tusc. Disp., i. 11.] **71.** [Ep. lii.]. **72.** [Alc., ii. 14 (condensed and paraphrased); Homer, Il., v. 127; Cf. Plato, Rep., x. 618, Jowett, transl., ii. 461.] **73.** [Phædo, 85; Jowett, i. 434.] **74.** Propert., iv. 1. **75.** [1225-8; Plumptre, Trag. of Soph., 105, 435. Cf. in Cic. Scr., ed. Klotz., iv. 3, 380; Inc. Auctor. Consol., 36.] **76.** [Il., xxiv. 527-8.] **77.** [Bergk, Poet. Lyr., Græc., p. 1064 (Fragm. Adesp., 97); cf. Stobæi Florileg., ed. Meineke, iv. 102 (P. K.); Nägelsbach n. hom. Theol., 228; Friedl., iii. 651.] **78.** [De Ira, iii. 15. Cf. Lactant. Inst., iii. 18, 19.] **79.** [Odyss., xi.

488.] 80. [Od., lvi. (Analecta, ed. Brunck, i. 112); Campbell's Eng. Poets, xii. 47.] 81. Cf., e.g., Virgil, Æn., vi. 734. 82. Rep. vi. 31; Tusc., i. 31 [Cf. Cic. Scr., ed. Klotz, iv. 3, p. 381]. 83. [Ep. Mor., 120, 14 (breve hospitium); *ib.*, 102, 26 (Dies iste . . . æterni natalis).] 84. [De Is. et Osir., ed. Reiske, vii. 505; Goodwin, iv. 135-6.] 85. Inscr. lat., ii. 1877. Cf. Withrow, Catacombs of Rome, 435, *sq.* 86. Orelli, 6674. 87. Nat. Hist., vii. 55. 88. Lucret., iii. 37 [840-2]. 89. Non posse suav. vivi sec. Epic.; [Goodwin, ii. 104. Cf. Trench, Lectures on Plutarch, p. 117.] 90. Cf. Zeller, Philos. d. Griechen, iii. 1, 740.] 91. Agric., 46. [Cf. Seneca, Ep., 63, 16.] 92. [De Clem., i. 6; De Benef., i. 10; Ep. 97.] 93. [Contra Stoicos, ed. Reiske, x. 436; Goodwin, iv. 408. Cf. Animine an Corp. Aff., 1.] 94. [Cf. Boissier, i. 288, *n.*] 95. Strabo, in Jos. Antiq., xiv. 7, 2. 96. [Philo, in Flaccum, § 8.] 97. Cf. Fisher, Beg. of Christ., 67, *sq.*; Schürer Neu, test., Zeitgesch., § 31; Friedl., iii. 506, *sq.*; De Champagny, Rome et la Judée, c. iv.] 98. [Juv., iii. 13-16, vi. 426-31; Martial, Epigr., xii. 57.] 99. Jos., Antiq., xiii. 8. 4; xiv. 10. 11-12. 100. Jos., Antiq., xii. 3. 1; Philo, leg. ad Caium, § 23. [Corn is not mentioned in these passages.] 101. In almost every city there was a storehouse for the sacred things deposited by the Jewish people. Philo, de Monarchia, ii. 3. After some wavering the Roman government sanctioned the transportation of these offerings to Jerusalem. 102. Philo, de Mon., ii. 1; Josephus (de bell. Jud., vi. 9, 3) estimates the number of visitors at the Feast of the Passover, including those belonging to the city of Jerusalem, at 2,700,200. 103. [Tacit., Hist., v. 2-3.] 104. [*Ib.*, v. 4.] 105. xiv. 105-6. 106. Tacit., Hist., v. 4. 107. [Sat. i. 5. 100.] 108. [Hor., Sat., i. 9. 70; Juv., xiv. 104; Mart., Epigr., vii. 82. 6; xi. 95. 2, 4, 6; vii. 30. 4; Petr., S., 68. See also Farrar, Life of St. Paul, Am. ed., i. 667, and ref.] 109. [De Sup., ed. Haase, iii. 427; Ap. Aug. de Civ. Dei, vi. 11.] 110. Jos., Apion, ii. 40: "There is no city of the Greeks or of the barbarians, nor any nation whatsoever, whither our custom of resting on the Sabbath has not come, and by which our fasts, and lighting up lamps, and many of our prohibitions as to our food, are not observed."

CHAPTER II.

1. Ep., 53, 8-11, 90, 27, *et al.* 2. [Cf. Lightfoot, Philippians, 268 *sq.*; Hurst and Whiting, Seneca's Essays, 32, *sq.* and ref.; Fisher, 169; Boissier, ii. 52-104.] 3. De Ira, ii. 9. 4. [Nigrinus, 15.] 5. Præf.

6. [On this chap. cf. Tholuck's Essay on the Nature and Moral Influence of Heathenism, transl. by Professor Emerson, Bib. Repos., vol. ii.; Fisher, chap. vi.; *ib.*, note and references, p. 197; Pressensé, Christian Life and Practice in the Early Church, transl. by Annie Harwood-Holmden, Book iii.; Schaff, Hist. Ap. Ch., Bk. ii. c. 1; Hist. of Ch. Church, c. v., § 86, *sq.*, and references; Lecky, Hist. of Europ. Morals from Augustus to Charlemagne; Schmidt, Essai historique sur la société civile dans le monde romain et sur sa transformation par le Christianisme; and other works referred to in Chap. i. n. 6.] **7.** Athen. Deipnosoph., xiii. 34. **8.** [Rep., viii. 563; Jowett, ii. 401.] Cf. Cic., de Republ., i. 43. **9.** Poet., 15. **10.** Xenoph., Œcon., iii. 12. **11.** Contra Neæram sub fin. **12.** Plut., Pericl., 24. **13.** Athen., xiii. 583. **14.** *Id.*, xiii. 583, 585 [591, 590]. **15.** [Plut., Vit. Rom., 22; cf. Thes. cum Rom. sub. fin. (vii. ed. Sinteris); Val. Max., Hist., ii. 1, 4; Tert., Apol. 6.] **16.** Plin., N. H., ix. 117. **17.** De Benef., vii. 9. 4 [cf. *id.*, De Vita Beata, xvii. 2.] **18.** De Spectac., 25. **19.** Juvenal, vi. 350. **20.** Propert., ii. 6, 27–34; Senec., Controv., v. 33; Tacit., Germ., 19. **21.** De Benef., iii. 16, 2. **22.** vi. 223. **23.** Apol. 6. **24.** [De Benef., iii. 16.] **25.** Ovid, Am. i. 8, 43; iii. 4, 37; Senec., Consol. ad Helv., 16, 3. [De Benef., i. 9.] **26.** Juvenal, ix. 19-22; Min. Fel. Octavius, 24. **27.** Tert., ad Nat. i. 15, Apol. 15 [9]. **28.** Juv., vi. 379–397. **29.** [Ad Marciam, xix. 2. Cf. Friedl., i. 394–400.] **30.** In the temple of Venus in Corinth there were more than one thousand prostitutes (*Hierodouloi*). They had great privileges, and sometimes presented to the goddess the vows and prayers of the city. Cf. Strabo, viii. 378. So, also, in a temple at Eryx in Sicily, where even Roman consuls and prætors participated in the impurity, believing that thus they made themselves acceptable to the Deity. Cf. Diod., iv. 83. **31.** [Orelli, 4626, *sq.* Cf. Friedl., iii. 503-7.] **32.** Joseph., Antiq., xiv. 7, 1. **33.** Dio, xxxix. 55. **34.** Cic., pro Rabir., 8; Suet., Cæs., 54. **35.** Strabo, iv. 188. **36.** Rep., ii. 375 [? Leges, xi. 918–20; Jowett, iv. 429, *sq.*] **37.** Polit., v. 2, 1. **38.** [Cic., De Off., i. 42. Cf. Döll., ii. 269.] **39.** Cato, de re nat., v. 4; Columella, i. 7. **40.** Cic., De Off., ii. 25; Columella, iv. Præf., 4. **41.** [Cf. De Champagny, Les Césars, iv. 337, *sq.*; Friedl., i. 54–63.] **42.** De Benef., iv. 28. **43.** [Suet., Oct., 42; Dion, liv. 11.] **44.** Cf. Spart., Sept. Sev., 19–23; Vopisc., Aurelianus, 35, 47, 48. **45.** [Suet., Ner., 31.] **46.** Ad Helv., x. 3. **47.** Plin., H. Nat., xiv. 142 [129]. **48.** Ep., i. 9; cf. also Seneca, De Tranq. Animi, c. 12. **49.** Ep., i. 13 [Melmoth, p. 26.] **50.** Ep., 88. **51.** [Cf. Boissier, ii. 48.] **52.** [xi. 185, *sq.*] **53.** ["According to the latest calculations, the circus in late imperial times must have contained 480.000 seats," Guhl and Koner, *Life of the Greeks and Romans*, transl. by Hueffer, p. 424. n. See,

however, Marq. u. Momm., H'dbuch d. röm. Alterth., vi. 486, n. 4.]
54. [Cf. C. I. L., iv. 1189, 1190, 1181.] **55.** [Cf. Lecky, Hist. of Eur. Mor., i. 298; Mart., De Spect., vii.; Epigr., viii. 30; x. 25; Tertull., Ad. Nat., i. 10; Friedl., ii. 268, notes and references.] **56.** [Panegyr., 33.] **57.** [Ep., vii.] **58.** [Art. Am., i. 167-8.] **59.** iii. 20. **60.** De Re Rust., i. 17. **61.** [Ad Attic., i. 12, 4.] **62.** [Verr., v. 3; Val. Max., vi. 3, 35. The man had broken a law prohibiting slaves from carrying arms.] **63.** Instit., i. xvi. 4. Nullum caput habet; L. 53, Dig. iv. 5, de capit. minut. **64.** L. 10, § 5, Dig. xxxviii. 10, de grad. et affin. **65.** Suet., De Clar. Rhetor., 3; cf. Columella, Præf., 10. Aged women even, who could be made serviceable in no other way, were chained before the door. Plaut., Curcul., i. 1, 76. **66.** Inexpiabili literarum nota, Valer. Max., vi. 8, 7; Inscripti vultus, Martial, viii. 75; cf. Cic., De Off., ii. 7. **67.** Juvenal, vi. 173-177. "Set a cross for the slave." — "For what offence has he merited punishment? What witness is present? Who has accused him? Hear! No delay is too long when the question concerns the death of a man." — "O fool, as if the slave were a man! He has done nothing? Be it so. It is my will. I so command. My will is reason enough." **68.** De Re Rust., ii. Plutarch, Cat. Maj., 5. **69.** Suet., Claud., 25; cf. Dion., lx. 29. **70.** Cf. Tacit., Ann., xiv. 42, *sq.* **71.** Phrixus, ap. Stob. Florileg. [Tit., lxii.], 39. **72.** Philemon, *Ibid.*, 28; cf. the well-known saying in Terence: "Homo sum, humani nihil a me alienum puto." **73.** Ep., 95, 33, 52; cf. De Benef., iii. 28, 1. **74.** De Benef., iii. 20, 1. **75.** Ep., 47, 1. **76.** [Boissier, who presents in general the most favorable aspects of Roman slavery, remarks that "no ancient writer expresses, either as a distant hope, or as a fugitive desire, or even as an improbable hypothesis, the thought that slavery might one day be abolished. . . . This was one of those radical reforms which could scarcely be expected in the regular course of things. . . . A change so profound that no one desired it, nor foresaw it, could not be accomplished without one of those revolutions which renovate the world." La Rel. Rom., ii. 404-5.] **77.** [Cf. Prof. B. B. Edwards in Am. Bib. Rep.. v. 138, *sq.*; vi. 411, *sq.*; vii. 33, *sq.*; Wallon, L'Esclavage dans l'Antiquité, 2d ed., 1879; Boissier, La Rel. Rom., ii. 345, *sq.*] **78.** [Theod., de Græc. affect. Cur. Disp., iii.; Opp., iv. 774; Bib. Repos., ii. 464; Clem. Alex. Strom., ii. 20 (62).] **79.** Eunuch., iii. 5. **80.** Ep., 53, 8-11. **81.** De Vita Beata, viii. 2. **82.** Duruy, Hist. des Romains, v. 431.

CHAPTER III.

1. Ep. ad Diogn., c. 6. I have allowed the passages cited from this Epistle to stand, although I cannot deny that my previously entertained doubts whether the letter is really as old as usually supposed have been strengthened by the treatise of Overbeck: Studien zur Geschichte der alten Kirche, i. Heft., s. 1-93. **2.** Cf. Kraus, Roma Sotteranea, S. 247 [284, 2d Aufl.; Northcote and Brownlow, Rom. Sott., 247; Withrow, The Catacombs, 241-2.] **3.** [Dial. c. Tryph., i.-viii.] **4.** c. 32. **5.** Apol. 46; [Plato, Tim., p. 28; Jowett, ii. 524.] **6.** [Orig. c. Cels., iii. 55.] **7.** [*Ib.*, iii. 59, 62.] **8.** *Ib.*, iii. 65. **9.** Minuc. Felix Octav., 32: "What temple shall I build to Him, when this whole world fashioned by His work cannot receive Him?" Orig. c. Cels., iii. 34. "We have refrained from honoring the Divinity by such means," i.e., by temples and statues. [Cf. Ante-Nicene Christian Library, xiii. 504; xxiii. 115. The language of the translations in this "Library," and in the Oxford "Library of Fathers of the Holy Catholic Church," has been freely used in the text.] **10.** Clem. Alex. Strom., vii. 5, 29: "Not the place, but the assembly of the elect, I call the church." **11.** Ep. x. 96. **12.** Apol. i. 65, 67. **13.** Apol. c. 39. **14.** [Hist. Eccles., iii. 37.] **15.** Legatio, ii. **16.** Apol. i. 63. **17.** c. 5. **18.** Apol. 44. **19.** Ruin., Act. Mart., p. 270; [ii. 145, ed. Galura.] **20.** c. Cels., i. 46. **21.** Cf. Orig. c. Cels., i. 2; iii. 24; Just., Apol. i. 45; Iren., adv. Hær., ii. 32. 4. **22.** Cf. on the miraculous powers of the early Christians: Bückmann in the Zeitschr. f. Luth. Theol. u. Kirche, 1878, ii.; [Blunt, Right Use of the Early Fathers, 3d ed., 310, *sq.;* Mozley, Bampton Lectures, 1865, p. 250, *sq.;* McClintock and Strong, Cyclopædia, vi. 320, *sq.*] **23.** Cf. Tert., De Coron. Mil., c. 3; Ad Ux., ii. 5; Orig. c. Cels., vi. 27. **24.** Tert., De Coron., 11; Ad Martyr., 3; De Exhort. Cast., 12; De Orat., 14, 19; De Jejun., 10, 12, 13. **25.** De Or., 29. **26.** Cf. Tertullian's treatise on Fasting, particularly c. 14, 16; Iren., ii. 31; Just., i. 61; Cypr., Ep. 11; Euseb., Hist. Eccl., v. 24. **27.** De Coron. Mil., 11. **28.** Tertull., Apol. 9; Minuc. Felix Octav., 30; Clem. Alex., Pæd., iii. 8; Orig. c. Cels., viii. 30. They abstained also from meat offered to idols. Just. c. Tryph., 34, 35; Tert., De Spect., 13. **29.** Tert., Apol. 31, 35; Ad Nat., i. 17; Minuc. Fel. Octav.. 18. **30.** In general the Church had not prohibited military and political service. "It is lawful to take part in public affairs." Clem. Al., Pæd., iii. 11. 110. There was also, however, a rigid theory. The Const. Eccl. Egypt., ii. 47, exclude from the number of catechumens every one who bore the power of the sword, or, as an officer of the State, was clothed in purple, unless he resigned his office. They excommunicate a Christian who voluntarily becomes a soldier: ii. 41. Cf., further, upon military service, Tert., De Idol., 19; De Cor. Mil., 11; Orig. c. Cels., v. 33; vii. 36; viii. 73–75: upon governmental offices, Orig. c. Cels., *ib.;* Tert., Apol. 38; De Pallio, 5, De Idol., 17, 18; Cypr., Ep. viii. **31.** Const. Ap., viii. 32; Tertull., De Idol., 4. **32.** Ign. ad Trall., 5; Tertull., De Pudic., 4; Ad Ux., ii. 8; De Monog., 11. **33.** Strom., ii. 8. 71. [?] **34.** Ad Ux., ii. 9. **35.** [Instr., iii. 11. 67.] **36.** Strom., iv. 19; Pædag., 1. 4. **37.** [Ap. Const., viii. 3. 20.] **38.** [Tertull., De Cult. Fem., ii. 11.] **39.** Cf. Clem. Alex., Pæd., iii. 10. 49. **40.** De Cult. Fem., ii. 11. **41.** De Cult. Fem., 1. 8; ii. 6. et al.; cf. Cyprian's treatise De Habitu Virginum. **42.** De Cult. Fem., ii. 13. **43.** Clem. Alex., Pæd., ii. 10. 96. **44.** Const. Æg., ii. 62. [*Vid.* Anal. Ante-Nic., ii. p. 475.] **45.** Clem Alex., Pæd., ii. 1. 10. **46.** Bunsen, Analecta Ante-Nicæna, iii. 88, 89; [*Id.* Hippolytus and his Age, iii. 144, 68.] **47.** Lact. Inst. Div., v. 15. **48.** De Coron. Mil., 13. **49.** Const. Eccl. Egypt., ii. 40. **50.** c. 19. **51.** Apost. Const., iv. 6. **52.** Orat., c. 11. **53** Ign. ad Polyc., c. 4. **54.** Const. Ap., iv. 17. **55.** [Acta Sanctorum, Maii, i. 371.] **56.** Tert., Apol. 46. **57.** Legatio [11]. **58.** Const. Apost., iv. 2 [ii. 63]. **59.** Const. Apost., iv. 2. **60.** Cf. Tertullian's treatise De Spectaculis, and the similar one by Cyprian [iii. p. 11, ed. Hartel., Opp. Spuria]. **61.** [Asin., ii. 4. 88.] **62.** Trinum., ii. 2. 58. **63.** De Offic., iii. 29; 1. 16. **64.** Seneca, De Clem., ii. 6; De Ira, i. 14. 3. **65.** Tac., Ann., iv. 63. **66.** Tert., Apol. 39. **67.** Ep. 19. **68.** Lact. Inst., vi. 10. 11. **69.** Ad Ux., ii. 4. **70.** Const. Ap. Copt., i. 17. **71.** Apol. 42. **72.** Apol. i. 67. **73.** Apol. 39. **74.** [Adv. Hær., iv. 18. 2.] **75.** Tert., adv. Marc., iv. 4; De Præscr. Hær., 30. **76.** Const. Ap., iv. 6. **77.** Tert., De Exh. Cast., 11; De Cor. Mil., 3; De Monog., 10. **78.** [Vit. Cyp., 2. 15.] **79.** The entire passage, Apol. 39, is of the highest interest, because it shows plainly that the Christian churches bore, at least in this relation, the form of Associations. An inscription from Lanuvium, of the year 136 (Or., 6086) gives us exact information respecting the Association of *Cultores* of Diana and of Antinous. It is a burial-club. Each member paid an admission fee of 100s. (about $5), and afterwards a monthly assessment of 5 *asses* (about 5 cents). On the death of a member 300s. were paid for his burial. Of this sum 50s. were divided among those members who were present at the interment. A part of the income of the society was expended in common banquets and festivities. Tertullian evidently refers to this custom when he sets forth so explicitly that the gifts deposited in the *arca* were not used for any such purposes. Cf. respecting these

Associations: Mommsen, De collegiis et sodalitiis Romanorum; [De Champagny, Les Antonins, iii. 417, *sq.*] **80.** Cypr., Ep. 60; Herm., Pastor, iii., Sim., 5. 3; Tert., De Jejun., 13; Const. Ap., v. 20. **81.** In Levit. Hom., x. 2. ["Invenimus enim in quodam libello ab Apostolis dictum: beatus est, qui etiam jejunat pro eo ut alat pauperem."] **82.** [Ep. iv. vi.] **83.** [Ambros., De Offic. Ministr., ii. 28; Prudent. Peri Steph. Hymn., 2.] **84.** Const. Ap., ii. 25, 31, 32; iii. 19; Cypr., Ep. 38. **85.** Cypr., Ep. 41. **86.** Const. Ap., ii. 4; iv. 3. Cyprian, Ep. 61 [ii., ed. Hartel, and Oxford ed., lx., transl. in Ante-Nicene Lib.] provides that support should be given, if needful, from the church treasury, to a converted actor. **87.** [Ignat. ad Polyc., 4; Const. Ap., iii. 3; Cypr., Ep. xxxv. (vii).] **88.** [Ap. Const., iv. 1-3.] **89.** [Tert., Apol. 39; Chastel, Etudes Histor., p. 104.] **90.** [Const. Ap., iv. 9; cf. i. Clem. ad Cor., 55.] **91.** [Const. Ap., v. 1; Alexand., Lit. in Bunsen, Anal. Ante-Nic., iii. 24; Cypr., Ep. 36 (xii.), 4 (v.), 5 (xiv.)] **92.** [Chastel, *ib.*, pp. 109-10; i. Clem. Rom. ad Cor., 1-2; Euseb., Hist. Eccl., iv. 23; Lucian, De Mort. Peregr., 13; Bib. Sac., x. 455.] **93.** Euseb., Hist. Eccl., iv. 23; vii. 5. **94.** [Ep. 59 (62).] **95.** Euseb., Hist. Eccl., vi. 43. **96.** Chrysost., Hom. 66; In Matth., § 3. **97.** Ambros., Ep. 63 [1044. 89.] **98.** Ambros., De Off., ii. 28. **99.** [Apol. i. 14, 15. Cf. Athenag. Sup. pro Christ., 1, 11; Theoph. ad. Autol., 14.] **100.** [Ad Scap., 1.] **101.** Pont. Vit. Cypr., § 9. **102.** Euseb., Hist. Eccl., vii. 22. **103.** [Cf. Chastel., Etudes Historiques sur l'Influence de Charité durant les Premiers Siècles chrét., Paris, 1853.] **104.** Ad Autol., iii. 11. **105.** Ad Scap., 2; [Apol. 37.] **106.** [Ad Nat., i. 17; cf. Apol. 35.] **107.** Apol. 33. **108.** Ep. vi., xiii. **109.** Tert., Apol. 46. **110.** [Mart., Pol. xiv., in Patr. Apostol., Op. ed. Zahn, p. 154.] **111.** [Ruinart, Acta Martyr., i. 191, ed. Galura.] **112.** Euseb., De Martyr. Palæst., c. 8. **113.** Ruin., Acta Mart., p. 150. **114.** [Cf. Withrow, The Catacombs of Rome, p. 103.] **115.** [Cf. Withrow, *ib.* 294-9; Northcote and Brownlow, Rom. Sott., 73, 245, 250, 310.] **116.** Cf. Orig. c. Cels., viii. 38. **117.** [Mart. Polyc., c. 4.] **118.** [Ep. 82 (Ed. Oxf. 81).] **119.** [De Mortal., c. 17.] **120.** Cf. treatise De Fuga In Persecutione. **121.** [Ep. 4 (Oxf. ed. 5).] **122.** Diod., iii. 12, 13, gives a description of the misery of those who worked in the mines: "No mercy is there, no respite allowed either to the sick, or the maimed, or to women. Without distinction they are all compelled by blows to labor until, reduced to despair, they perish in their misery." **123.** Ruinart, Acta Mart., p. 395 [ii. 295, ed. Galura]. Cf. Tert., Apol. 50; Cypr., De Mortal., p. 233. [c. 15.] **124.** Ruinart, Acta Mart., p. 144 [i. 332, ed. Galura].

BOOK II., CHAPTER I.

1. Roma Sott., i. 318 [North. and Br. Rom. Sott., 122, *sq.*]; Insigni scoperte nel cimetero di Domitilla in Bull. di Archeologia cristiana, [Ser. i., 1865]. Cf. Theol. lit. Zeit., 1876, p. 291; [Harnack in Princeton Rev., July, 1878, p. 257, *sq.;* Kraus, Roma Sotteranea, p. 127, *sq.* (142, 2d Aufl.)]. **2.** Octav., c. 5. **3.** [*Ib.* 6.] **4.** [*Ib.* 8.] **5.** *Ib.* 12. **6.** *Ib.* 10. **7.** ["Molestum illum volunt, inquietum, impudenter etiam curiosum."] **8.** [*Ib.* 10.] **9.** Tac., Hist., v. 3; Tert., Apol. 16; [Ad Nat., 11, 14;] Minucius Felix Octav., c. 9. **10.** P. Raffaele Garucci: il Crocifisso graffito in casa dei Cesari, Roma, 1857; Becker: Das Spottcrucifix im römischen Kaiserpalast, Breslau, 1866; [Kraus: Das Spottcrucifix vom Palatin, Freiburg i. Breisgau, 1872; Parker, Hon. J.H.: Historical Photographs, No. 107, Oxford, 1870; Aubé: Persecutions de l'Eglise, La Polémique Païenne, Paris, 1878, p. 96, *sq.;* Caricatures, etc., by J. Parton, pp. 25–6; Univ. Quart., July, 1879, p. 338.] **11.** Octav., c. 9; cf. Eus., Hist. Eccl., iv. 15; [A. N. L., xxii. 463.] **12.** Orig. c. Cels., iii. 44. **13.** *Ib.* iii. 75. **14.** Acta Epipodii et Alexandri [Ruinart, i. 166, ed. Galura]. **15.** Octav., c. 8. **16.** *Ib.* 12. **17.** [Apol. 38.] **18.** Cf. Tert., Apol. 42. **19.** [Æn., i. 278.] **20.** [Tert., Apol. 4.] **21.** [According to the Acta, Ruinart, i. 350, ed. Galura, Achatius was a confessor. Other martyrologies, however, represent him as a martyr. Cf. Smith and Wace, Dict. of Christ. Biog., i. p. 11.] **22** [Apol. 5. . . . portio Neronis. . . .] **23.** Christ. Kortholt: de persecutionibus eccl. primævæ, Kiloni, 1689. For later works I would refer particularly to Aubé: Histoire des Persecutions de l'Eglise jusqu'à la fin des Antonins, 2d ed., Paris, 1875; Overbeck: Ueber die Gesetze der röm. Kaiser von Trajan bis Marc. Aurel. gegen die Christen, in den Studien zur Gesch. der alten Kirche (1875), S. 93, *sq.;* Wieseler: Die Christenverfolgung der Cäsaren bis zum dritten Jahrh., Gütersloh, 1878. [Thiel: altröm Rechtsanschauung bez. d. polit. Stellung d. chr. Relig., Tüb. Th. Q'schr. 1855. 2.; Le Blant: les Bases juridiques des poursuites dirigées contre les martyrs, compt. rend. de l'Acad. des Inscr. Par., 1868. For the Acts of the Martyrs, see Theodor. Ruinart: Acta prim. mart. sincera et selecta, 2d ed., Amstel., 1713. The references in these notes are to this edition, unless otherwise stated. Other sources of information are: Martyrol. Hieron., in Migne's Patrol. Lat., tom. xxx. 449; Martyrol. Roman., ed. Baron, 2d ed., 1589; Menolog. Græc., ed. Urbini, 1727; Euseb., Hist. Eccl.; the works of the Apologists; Lactant., De Mort. persecutorum; Biographies in the Acta Sanctorum Boll.; in Les petits Bollandistes Vies

des Saints, Bar-le-duc, 1872-74; and in The Lives of the Saints by Rev. S. Baring-Gould, 1872-77.] 24. [These general laws were, as stated by Kraus, Lehrbuch d. Kirchengesch., i. pp. 55-6, (1) the *lex Julia majestatis*. Its transgression — either facto, or verbis impiis, murmuratione contra felicitatem temporum, or cœtu nocturno and coitione clandestina, illicito collegio — was punished with death: humiliores bestiis objiciuntur vel vivi exuruntur; honestiores capite puniuntur. The same penalties were appointed for (2) *sacrilegium* — which could be committed by refusing the sacrifices due to the gods and to the Genius of the Emperor: sacrilegi et majestatis rei convenimur; summa hæc causa, immo tota est. Tert., Apol. 10. This charge took away a freeman's privileges, so that he could be put to torture like a slave, . . . majestatis causa, in qua sola omnibus æqua conditio est. Cod. Justin., L. iv., de quæst., ix. 41. Beside torture, burning and crucifixion could be employed. (3) *Magia, superstitio malefica*. A law of the XII. Tables affixed the penalty of death to the crime of incantation. An offender could be thrown to the wild beasts or crucified. Ipsi autem magi vivi exuruntur. Sentent. v. 23, 17. The Christians could bring on themselves the accusation through exorcisms. The law forbade keeping books of magic, and could be applied to those who had the sacred Scriptures. (4) *Superstitio externa*, or *peregrina; religio illicita*. Acts xvi. 21. The penalty was banishment for the higher classes, death for the lower. (5) From Trajan's time the law against brotherhoods (Hetæriæ) was applied to the Christians.] 25. De Rossi, in his investigations, is the first to have drawn attention to this circumstance. Cf. Kraus, Rom. Sott., S. 49, *sq*. [2d ed. S. 53, *sq*.; Northcote and Brownlow, R. Sott., 49, *sq*.] Following exactly the custom of the burial-clubs which Severus had sanctioned by a general edict (Dig. xlviii. 22. 1), the Christians, according to Tertullian (Apol. c. 39), contributed *menstrua die* in order to support and bury the poor. Of special interest is the inscription found at Cherchell [anc. Cæsarea] in Africa (Renier, Inscr. de l'Algerie, 4025) [Kraus, R. Sott., S. 58, 2d ed.], where a Christian who gives an area, or burial-place, calls himself "*cultor verbi*," a designation which is evidently formed from the custom of calling the members of such burial-clubs *Cultores Jovis, Cultores Apollinis* et *Dianæ*. Cf. also G. Heinrici: Die Christengemeinde Korinths u. die religiösen Genossenschaften der Griechen, Ztschr. f. wiss. Theol., 1876, S. 405 ff. 26. Wieseler (Die Christenverfolg., etc., S. 1, *sq*.) has called in question the opinion that the Christians were regarded by the heathen as Jews. He refers particularly to the fact that according to Tacitus they were already called Christians by the populace in the Neronian persecution. This is correct, but on the other hand it appears from Tacitus's report that they were persecuted not as Christians, but on account of the shameful deeds attributed to them, particularly the setting the great fire. The heathen, it may be assumed, did not everywhere attain at the same time to a knowledge of the difference between Christians and Jews, and, doubtless, this discovery was first made in Rome. This being so, the heathen could give the Christians a special name, and still at the same time regard them as a fraction of Judaism. There are no instances before the time of Trajan in which Christians are condemned on account of a *collegium illicitum*, or for holding a prohibited religion. So far, indeed, Wieseler is right: Christianity did not first become an unlawful religion by the decree of Trajan. It had always been this, though not at first so recognized. It is also true that trials of Christians did not first begin in consequence of Trajan's rescript. Pliny assumes that there had already been such, even in Rome itself; only he had never had an opportunity to be present at one. At the same time Pliny's letter shows plainly that these trials were still somewhat novel. 27. Suet., Claudius, 25. Cf. Tert., Apol. 3; [ad. Nat., i. 3; Justin, Apol. i. 4; Theoph. ad Autol., i. 12; Lactant., Inst. iv. 7; Lightfoot, Philippians, p. 16, n.] 28. Tacit., Ann. xv. 44; Suet., Nero, 16. Cf. on the burning of Rome, and the Persecution, particularly Schiller: Geschichte des römischen Kaiserreichs unter Nero (Berlin, 1872), S. 415, *sq.*; Aubé: Persecutions, etc., 74, *sq.*; Hausrath: Neutestament. Zeitgesch., iii. 93, *sq.* 29. i. c. 6. [Lightfoot's Transl.] 30. Sat. i. 155, *sq.*

CHAPTER II.

1. No writer before Orosius (vii. 7) makes this persecution extend beyond Rome. De Rossi's attempt (Bullet. di Archeol. Crist., Dec. 1865, p. 90, *sq.*) to prove its extension, from Pompeian inscriptions, was unsuccessful. Cf. Aubé, De la legalité du Christianisme dans l'Empire Romain pendant le premier siècle. Comptes Rendus, 1866, ii., p. 134, *sq.*; also printed in his "Persecutions de l'Eglise," p. 407, *sq.* 2. Suetonius, Domit. 12. 3. Xiphilinus, Epit. Dion. Cass., lxvii. 14. 4. [Domit. 15.] 5. Cf. Zahn, Hirt des Hermas, p. 44, *sq.*; [*contra*: Lightfoot, Philippians, p. 22, *sq.*; Clement of Rome (Appendix), p. 256, *sq.*; Harnack in Pat. Apost. opp., ed. iii., Fasc., 1. p. lxxxviii.; Withrow, Catacombs, p. 56, *sq.*] 6. Euseb., H. Eccl., iii. 20. 7. Ep. x. 96 (97); [Trajan's answer, Ep. x. 97 (98)]: cf. Aubé, lib. cit., p. 207,

sq.; Overbeck, lib. cit., p. 111, *sq.;* Wieseler, lib. cit., p. 14, *sq.* **8.** Apol. 2. **9.** [Tert., Apol. 50. See Oxf. Transl., p. 105, note, for collection of passages.] **10.** [Just. M., 2 Apol. 2.] **11.** [De Spect., 1.] **12.** Iren., Adv. Hær., iii. 3. § 3.; cf. Lipsius, Chronol. d. röm. Bischöfe, pp. 170, 263, 272. Telesphorus was martyred A. D. 135 or 137. Bp. Alexander's martyrdom is probably legendary (*Ibid.*, p. 167). **13.** Ruinart, Acta Sinc., p. 23, *sq.* These Acta are based on fact, though containing legendary embellishments. [The references are to the second ed., Amstel. 1713.] **14.** Tert., Ad Scap., 5. **15.** Hadrian's edict adressed to Minucius Fundanus I hold to be genuine, against Keim (Theol. Jahrb., 1856, p. 387, *sq.*), Overbeck (lib. cit., p. 134, *sq.*), and Aubé (lib. cit., p. 262, *sq.*). Its insertion in Justin M., 1 Apol. 68, is a strong proof of its genuineness, which cannot be set aside without the hypothesis of interpolation, of which there is no evidence. Of course, if the Emperor (as above authorities assume) really is made to say that Christians are not to be punished as such, but only for other offences against the laws, then the edict could not be genuine. But this interpretation is not necessary. Without violence the edict may be explained as on p. 263. **16.** Euseb., H. Eccl., iv. 23. **17.** *Ibid.*, iv. 26. I believe the *Edictum ad commune Asiæ* to be spurious, in spite of Wieseler's defence of it (lib. cit., p. 18, *sq.*). **18.** Apol. 37. Ad Scap., 5. **19.** [Pantænus, Euseb., H. Eccl., v. 10.: "Dumb folk," Min. Fel. Octav., 8; cf. 31.] **20.** [1 Apol. 1.] **21.** *Octavius* used to be regarded as of later date than Tertullian; but now the view constantly gains ground that Tert. used *Oct.*, and that the latter belongs to the time of Marc. Aurel., cir. A. D. 180. *Theophilus ad Antolycum* is of about the same date. **22.** [1 Apol. 55]. **23.** [1 Apol. 5, 46.; 2 Apol. 8, 10.] **24.** [c. 9.] **25.** [Adv. Græc., 2, 3, 25, 26.] **26.** [Apol. 17; cf. De Test. Anim.] **27.** Tusc., i. 39; Ad. Attic., x. 18, 1. **28.** [M. C. Frontonis Epp. ad Antonin. Imp. et invicem, I., Ep. 1: *Pullus noster Antoninus aliquo lenius tussit: quantum quisque* in nidulo nostro *jam sapit, tantum pro te precatur.*] Fronto ad Marc. Cæs., iv. 12. **29.** Aulus Gellius, xii. 1. **30.** Orelli, 2677; Mommsen, Insc. Neap., 1092. **31.** Henzen (Annali dell' instituto di corresp. archeol., 1844, pp. 1-111. [Wolf., F. A., von einer milder Stiftung Trajans, *Programm*, Berl., 1808.] Peter, Gesch. Roms, iii. p. 514, *sq.* **32.** c. 26. **33.** Jul. Capitolin., Antonin. 8.; Lamprid., Severus, 56. **34.** Ep. i. 8; ii. 5; v. 7; vii. 18. **35.** Orelli, 6669. **36.** Ep. vi. 3; vi. 32. **37.** Ep. i. 8; vii. 18. **38.** Orelli, 114; 6042. **39.** Ep. v. 19; ii. 6; iii. 19; viii. 16, 19. **40.** Dig. i. 1. 4. [*Utpote cum jure naturali omnes liberi nascerentur, nec esset nota manumissio, cum servitus esset incognita; sed postea quam jure gentium servitus invasit, seculum est beneficium* *manumissionis. Et cum uno naturali nomine homines appellaremur, jure gentium tria genera esse cœperunt: liberi, et his contrarium servi, et tertium genus liberti, id est, qui desierant esse servi.*] Cf. Becker-Marquardt, II'dbuch d. röm. Alterthümer, v. 197, *sq.*; Overbeck, lib. cit., p. 170, *sq.* **41.** [iv. 4.] **42.** Especially De Champagny: Hist. des Antonins [Paris, 1866]; Schmidt [Charles], Essai historique sur la société civile dans le monde romain et sur sa transformation par le Christianisme, Strasb., 1853; Thiersch: Politik und Philosophie unter Trajan und Hadrian und den beiden Antoninen. On the other hand Overbeck, l. c., is inclined to under-estimate the influence of Christianity. **43.** Orig. c. Cels., viii. 68. **44.** [1 Apol. 1-3. Oxf. Transl. in the main.] **45.** [vii. 73; ix. 42; viii. 59. These and the following are from Long's Transl.] **46.** [iv. 23, 34; ii. 13; iii. 5; v. 31.] **47.** [xi. 3.] **48.** [Epp. ad Marc. Antonin. Imp. de Nepote Amisso: Ep. 2.] **49.** [ii. 16; vi. 54; ii. 5.] **50.** [ἀσεβείας: the better reading is 'Ασίας, "the teacher of Asia;" cf. Zahn in Pat. Apost. Opp., ed. iii., Fasc. ii., p. 150.] **51.** Much has recently been written about the date of Polycarp's death. The majority now follow Waddington, who (Mémoire sur le chronologie de la vie du rhéteur Ælius Aristide [Memoires de l'Acad. des Insc., etc., Tom. xxvi., Part I., 1867. p. 203, *sq.*]) makes Feb. 23, 155, the date. Gebhardt [Zeitschr. für hist. Theol., 1875, p. 377] holds to 155 or 156. [Cf. Lipsius, Zeitschr. für wiss. Theol., 1874, p. 188; Hilgenfeld, *Ibid.*, p. 120, note, 325, *sq.*; Zahn, lib. cit., p. 148; Lightfoot, Contemp. Review, May, 1875, p. 838; Aug., 1876, p. 415.] Wieseler (lib. cit., p. 34, *sq.*) seems to me to have hit the mark. **52.** Cf. Wieseler, lib. cit., p. 104, *sq.* **53.** [2 Apol. 3. "Impaled," this is Uhlhorn's translation (an den Pfahl gehängt) with Maranus. The words are ξύλῳ ἐμπαγῆναι. Valesius, Heinichen (in Euseb., H. Eccl., iv. 16 § 3), also Gildersleeve (Apologies of Justin, N.Y., 1877, p. 213), Otto in loc. (3d ed.), translate "fastened in the stocks." Otto in ed. 2. (i., p. 175) translates it "crucified;" and if we bear in mind (1) that the connection seems to favor a capital punishment, — Justin would hardly refer to the hatred of Crescens as satisfied and the rage of the heathen as glutted by putting him in the stocks. — (2) the frequent use of ξύλον with the meaning *cross:* then "crucified" will perhaps appear a not unnatural interpretation.] **54.** Apol. 5. [*Fulminata* appears in an Inscr. of Tarquinii, Bullet. dell' Institut., 1830, p. 198; White and Riddle, Dict., s. v.] **55.** Adv. Græc., 4. **56.** Euseb., H. Eccl., iv. 26. Acta Symphor., Ruinart, p. 78, *sq.* The edict there cited, and which Neander (ch. Hist., 2d Am. ed., i. p. 108) holds to be genuine, is surely spurious. **57.** Euseb., H. Eccl., v. 1. The persecution began A.D. 177. **58.**

Orig. c. Cels., viii. 39, 40, 69. On the situation of the Church cf. Keim, Celsus' Wahres Wort [Zürich, 1873], p. 268, *sq*. Aubé (lib. cit., p. 342, *sq*.) vainly tries to shift the blame from Marcus Aurelius, and to represent the persecution as insignificant. **59.** Orig. c. Cels. [i. 28, 32, 38, 62; ii. 9; i. 67; ii. 29, 32; i. 68, 71; ii. 41, 42; ii. 15, 13, *sq*., 20, 24, 54, 55.] ii. 55. **60.** [*Ibid.*, ii. 63, 70.] **61.** *Ibid.*, iv. 3. [Keim, *Ibid.*, p. 46.] **62.** *Ibid.* [v. 5], iv. 23. [Keim, *Ibid.*, p. 51.] **63.** [*Ibid.*, iv. 23, 74, 78, 80, 81, 86, 88, 98.] iv. 99. [iv. 62; Keim, *Ibid.*, p. 63.] **64.** Strauss: Der alte und der neue Glaube, p. 228 [3d Eng. ed., Lond., 1874, vol. ii., p. 37.] **65.** Strauss, pp. 200, 202, *sq*. [Eng. ed., ii., pp. 11, 13–15.] **66.** [Orig. c. Cels., i. 27; Keim, *Ibid.*, p. 11.] **67.** *Ibid.*, viii. 63 [Keim, *Ibid.*, p. 135.] **68.** *Ibid.*, viii. 66, 67 [Keim, *Ibid.*, p. 136.]

CHAPTER III.

1. [Jul. Capitolin., Vita Marc. Aurel., 28.] **2.** [Dion. Cass., Hist. Rom., lxxvi. 15.] **3.** Athenagoras, Leg. pro Christ., 26. **4.** Philostrat., Vit. Sophist., ii. 7. **5.** Athenag., l. c. **6.** [This last inscription may be found in Gruter (Insc. Ant., Amstel., 1707, 4 vols. fol.) p. 748, 7.] **7.** [These words *in æternum renatus* occur in an inscription Corp. Insc. Lat. vol. vi. 1. (510), where may be found a collection of inscriptions referring to the Taurobolium and Kriobolium.] **8.** [Refutat., iv. 28, *sq*.] **9.** [Hierocles, Phot., Bibl. Cod., 214.] **10.** [Porphyry, Plotini Vita, 10.] **11.** [Apparently condensed from Plot., Ennead., iv., lib. i., 1.] **12.** [Præf. lib. de philosophia ex oraculis, cited Euseb., Præp. Ev., iv. 7.] **13.** Philostrat., Vit. Apollon., iv. 24. **14.** *Ibid.*, iv. 45. **15.** *Ibid.*, vi. 10. **16.** *Ibid.*, iv. 3. **17.** [*Ibid.*, viii. 10, 12.] **18.** [*Ibid.*, viii. 30. Uhlhorn says "in the island of Rhodes;" Philostratus mentions this version of the story, but connects the voice from heaven with Crete, not with Lindus in Rhodes.] **19.** De Rossi, Insc. Christ. urbis Romæ, p. 9. **20.** Ad Scapul., 4. **21.** Apol. 37. **22.** [Euseb., H. Eccl., v. 21.] **23.** Cf. passages in Tert., de Spect., 1, 3; de Idolol., 13, 14; de Cultu Fem., ii. 11. **24.** Tert., de Coron., 1. **25.** Tert., de Idolol., 14. "*Sed enim plerique jam induxerunt animo ignoscendum esse, si quando quæ ethnici, faciunt, ne nomen blasphemetur.*" Cf. de Cult. Fem., ii. 11. **26.** Tert., de Fuga in Pers., 12. **27.** [On this subject cf. Lightfoot's Essay (Philippians, p. 179, *sq*.), and Fisher (Beginnings of Christianity, p. 550, *sq*.)] **28.** [Yet how strong was this bond may be seen from Clem. Rom., Ep. i. ad Cor., particularly the portions recently discovered (cc. 58–63.)] **29.** [Dial. c. Tryph. 39.] **30.** Tert., Apol. 32, 39. **31.** Orig. c. Cels., viii. 68.

CHAPTER IV.

1. Dion. Cass., Hist. Rom., lxxii. 4. Hippolyt., Refutat., ix. 7. **2.** Euseb., H. Eccl., v. 21. Hieron., de vir. illustr., 40, 42. Of course the details of the story awaken incredulity. **3.** Tert., ad Scapul., 4. **4.** Spartian. Sever., 17. **5.** Tert., de Fuga in Pers., 12; Ruinart, p. 120. **6.** Euseb., H. Eccl., vi. 1, 2, 5. **7.** Ruinart, p. 86. **8.** *Ibid.*, p. 26. **9.** Lamprid., Alex. Sever., 28 (29); 50 (51); 48 (49). **10.** No more is implied in the words of Lampridius (21 (22)): *Judæis privilegia reservavit, Christianos esse passus est.* Cf. Görres, Zeitschr. für wiss. Theol., 1877, p. 48, *sq.* **11.** Jul. Capitolin., Maximin., 19. **12.** H. Eccl., vi. 28. **13.** Lipsius, Chronol. d. röm. Bischöfe, p. 194, *sq.* **14.** [Euseb., H. Eccl., vi. 17. Pallad., Episc. Helenopol. Hist. Lausiaca, c. 147. (Migne, Patrol. Lat., vol. lxxiii. p. 1091.)] **15.** Origen, in Matt., xxiv. 9; Euseb., H. Eccl., vi. 28; Firmilian, Ep. ad Cyprian, Ep. 75, 10. [We number Cyprian's Epp. according to the edition of Hartel (Wien, 1871), coinciding with the Oxf. Transl.] — On the whole subject cf. Görres, Zeitschr. für wiss. Theol., 1876, p. 526, *sq.*, and the review of it by Harnack, Theol. Lit. Zeitung, 131 März.] 1877, p. 167. **16.** Euseb., H. Eccl., vi. 34, 36.; Jerome (Chronic., *ann.*, 256.) calls him the first Christian Emperor. **17.** Cyprian, Ep. xi. **18.** De Lapsis, 8. **19.** For all these details, cf. Cyprian's Epp. and de Lapsis. **20.** Euseb., H. Eccl., vi. 39. **21.** Lipsius, lib. cit., p. 210, doubts the martyrdom of the last two, and regards them as only confessors. Cf. also Kraus, Roma Sotterranea, p. 142 [Northcote and Brownlow, Rom. Sott., p. 142.] **22.** Euseb., H. Eccl., vi. 41. Cf. Ruinart, Acta, p. 124. **23.** Martyrolog. Roman., May, 3d. **24.** Euseb., H. Eccl., vi. 39. **25.** [Greg. Turon., Hist. Franc., i. 28 (Migne, Patrol. Lat., lxxi. p. 175, *sq.*) Tillemont, Memoires, &c., iii., p. 299, *sq.*] **26.** Cypr., Epp. 19, 17, 13, 5. **27.** Cypr., Ep. 22. **28.** Cypr., Ep. 40. **29.** Ep. 11. [Oxf. Transl. in the main.] **30.** Cypr., Ep. 49; de Lapsis. **31.** Cypr., Epp. 58, 59; Lib. ad Demetrianum. **32.** Euseb., H. Eccl., vii. 11.; Acta Cypriani, Ruinart, p. 216. *Sanctissimi impp. Valerianus et Gallienus præceperant, ne in aliquibus locis conciliabula fiant, ne cœmeteria ingrediantur.* **33.** Cypr., Ep. 80. **34.** Otherwise Lipsius, lib. cit., p. 222; cf. Ambrose, de Offic., i. 41. **35.** Cf. Kraus, lib. cit., p. 91, *sq.* [Northcote and Brownlow, p. 88.] **36.** Euseb., H. Eccl., vii. 13, 23. **37.** The view is very generally taken that Gallienus proclaimed Christianity a *religio licita:* So Neander, Gieseler, Herzog (Kirchengesch. p. 55), Görres (Zeitschr. für wiss. Theol., 1877, i. p. 606), and even Mason (The Persecution of Diocletian (Cambridge, 1876), p. 29.) Eusebius knows nothing of any such edict, and narrates the martyrdom of Marinus as under Gallienus (Hist. Eccl., vii. 15). Marinus is usually placed under the usurper Macrianus, but without evidence. Keim (Aus dem Urchristenthum, p. 130, note 1.) recognizes no edict of toleration from Gallienus. **38.** Cf. Cypr., Epp. 18, 20. **39.** Cypr., Ep. 17. **40.** According to Cypr., Ep. 20, the confessors had distributed *milia libellorum pacis*. **41.** Cypr., Ep. 21.

BOOK III., CHAPTER I.

1. [The title of the treatise is *De testimonio animæ*, and the phrase "the soul by nature Christian" does not occur in it, but Apol. c. 17. Still the phrase fairly describes the subject of the treatise.] **2.** [Orig. c. Cels., i. 30.] **3.** Ad Scapul., 2. [Oxf. Transl.]; Apol. 24 [Oxf. Transl.] **4.** Cf. Burckhardt, Die Zeit Constantins d. Gr., [Basel, 1853; p. 333, *sq.*] Wietersheim, Völkerwanderung, iii. pp. 163, 483. **5.** Lactant., de Mort. Pers., 27. **6.** Vopisc., Probus, 14. **7.** Vopisc., Numerian., 14, 15. **8.** [Zosimus, ii. 10 (ed. Bekker, p. 75, l. 11.)] Aurel. Vict., Hist. Rom., Cæs., xxxix. 48. Lact., de Mort. Pers., 10: *ut erat pro timore scrutator rerum futurarum*. **9.** Lact., *Ibid.*, 10, 11. **10.** Panegyr. Incerti, v. 12: *Recipe Jupiter quæ commodasti*. [Panegyr. Vett., W. Jaeger, Norimb. 1778, i. p. 353.] **11.** Joh. Malalas., xii., p. 310. **12.** Lact., de Mort. Pers., 10. **13.** Cf. Ep. of Theonas (Routh, Reliq. Sacr., iii. p. 43, 9.) which I regard as belonging to this period. **14.** Lact., de Mort. Pers., 15. **15.** Lact., Inst. v. 2. *Mordacius scripsit — composuit enim libellos duos non contra Christianos, ne inimice insectari videretur, sed ad Christianos ut humane ac benigne consulere putaretur*. **16.** Lact., de Mort. Pers., 11. **17.** Ruinart, p. 302, *sq.* **18.** Opinions still differ about Constantine, yet a reconciliation seems approaching. Till recently, by setting aside the testimony of Lactantius (de Mort. Pers.), the persecution has been explained as arising solely from Diocletian's political views and his personal attitude towards Heathenism, but Mason (lib. cit.) goes to the other extreme. He makes Diocletian a kind of Constantine who was only forced against his will to play the part of Decius. Cf. the review by Harnack (Theol. Lit. Zeitung, 1877, p. 169.) The truth lies midway between. **19.** Hierocles is designated by Lactantius (Inst. v. 2, and de Mort. Pers., 16) as the real fountain-head of the persecution. **20.** Euseb., Vit. Const., 50, 51. Lact., de Mort. Pers., 11: *hanc moderationem tenere conatus est, ut eam rem sine sanguine, transigi juberet*. **21.** Euseb., H. Eccl., viii. 2; Mart., Palæst. proleg., 1. Lact., de Mort. Pers., 13. Cf. Mason, lib. cit., App., p. 343. **22.** "*Legitime coctus*" (Lact., de Mort. Pers., 13.) **23.** Ruinart, p. 382.

(Acta Saturnini, Dativi, &c.) 24. Euseb., H. Eccl., viii. 6. § 8. 25. Ibid., § 10. 26. Euseb., Mart. Palæst., 3. § 1. Mason (lib. cit., p. 212) believes that in the *Passio S. Sabini* the edict is to be found in a more authentic form. But the whole character of this *Passio* renders this doubtful. 27. The inscriptions still often quoted, in which Diocletian is described as the destroyer of the Christian name, I hold to be spurious. Cf. Mason, lib. cit., p. 217. 28. Euseb., H. Eccl., viii. 11. § 1. 29. Lact., de Mort. Pers., 21. 30. Cf. on *Mutilation*, Keim, Aus dem Urchristenthum, p. 198, *sq.* 31. Euseb., H. Eccl., viii., and Mart. Palæst. 32. Euseb., H. Eccl., viii. 12. Ambrose and Chrysostom treat them simply as martyrs; Jerome (ad Jonæ, i. 12.) expressly justifies them. Otherwise Augustine, De Civit. Dei, i. 26. 33. Euseb., H. Eccl., viii. 17. Lact., de Mort. Pers., 34. 34. Euseb., H. Eccl., ix. 1-8.

CHAPTER II.

1. [Euseb., Vit. Const., i. 40.] 2. Euseb., Vit. Const., i. 28-32. Differently Lact., de Mort. Pers., 44. 3. Constantine's course is viewed as wholly political by Burckhardt (lib. cit.). Keim (Der Uebertritt Constantins d. Gr. zum Christenthum, Zürich, 1862) brings out the religious motives. With Zahn (Constantin d. Gr. und die Kirche, Hanover, 1876) these become still more prominent. Cf. also Dieckhoff (Rostock Theol. Zeitschr., 1863, iv. 1.) 4. Lact., de Mort. Pers., 48. *Hactenus flet, ut sicut superius comprehensum est, Divinus juxta nos favor, quem in tantis sumus rebus experti, per omne tempus prospere successibus nostris cum beatitudine nostra publica perseveret.* 5. Euseb., H. Eccl., ix. 9. 6. I stand by this view of the cross-story. If Keim (lib. cit., p. 23, *sq.*) has shown many of the details to be incredible, even impossible, that does not rob the story of a historic basis. And when Zahn (lib. cit., p. 14.) gets rid of the story by saying that the Crucified One could have shown His cross to Constantine only as a means of salvation, but not as an instrument of magic, he makes a twofold mistake. For, first, when Constantine told the story, the cross was no longer to him a mere instrument of magic, and, second, Zahn ignores the fact, that God does condescend to those who are only on the way to faith. 7. Hitherto it has been assumed (even by Herzog, lib. cit., p. 59) that there were (besides the one issued by Galerius, A.D. 311) two edicts of toleration, one A.D. 312, and one 313. It is true Keim [Theol. Jahrb., 1852, p. 217] had shown that this was a mistake, but from the circumstance that the edict of 313 refers to limitations of toleration, he concluded that Constantine and Licinius must have issued together, in 312, an edict which tole-

rated Christianity only at a disadvantage. Zahn (lib. cit., p. 33) and Mason (lib. cit., p. 327, note) have shown that the references of the edict of 313 are not to any previous edict, but to the no longer extant *directions to the officials* which accompanied the edict of Galerius, A.D. 311. There was no edict of A.D. 312. [For the edict of Milan see Euseb., II. Eccl., x. 5.] **8.** [Migne, Patrol. Lat., viii. p. 180; Cod. Theodos., xvi. 2. 1-7; Euseb., H. Eccl., x. 7.] **9.** [Euseb., Vita Const., i. 42; ii. 21, 45; iv. 26, 28; H. Eccl., x. 6.] **10.** [Cod. Theodos., xvi. 2. 4.] **11.** [Sozom., H. Eccl., i. 8; cf. Aug. Serm., lxxxviii. (ed. Bened., T. v.) and the comments of Jac. Gothofredus in Cod. Theodos., ix. 12. 1; ix. 18. 1.] **12.** [Migne, p. 119, *sq.;* Cod. Theodos., ix. 40. 2.; Cod. Just., ix. 47.] **13.** [Migne, p. 293, *sq.;* Cod. Theodos., xv. 12. 1, 2; Socr., H. Eccl., i. 18; Sozom., i. 8; Euseb., Vita Const., iv. 25.] **14.** [Migne, p. 198; Cod. Theodos., ix. 3. 1.] **15.** [Celibate and childless: Migne, p. 189; Cod. Theodos., viii. 16. 1. Adultery: Migne, pp. 298, *sq.*, 307, *sq.*, 312, *sq.;* Cod. Theodos., ix. 7. 1, 2; ix. 9. 1. Rape: Migne, p. 194; Cod. Theodos., ix. 24. 1. Incest: Migne, p. 397; Cod. Theodos., iii. 17. 1, 2; Cod. Just., v. 5. 3. Divorce: Migne, p. 353, *sq.;* Cod. Theodos., iii. 16. 1.] **16.** [The exposure of children does not seem to have been expressly forbidden, but Constantine sought to suppress it by removing all the motives for it, and Christian writers unequivocally condemned the practice. Cf. Lactant., Inst., vi. 20. *Tam igitur nefarium est exponere quam necare;* Cod. Theodos., xi. 27. 1, 2; v. 8. 1, with the comments of Gothofredus; Cod. Just., vi. 8. 1.] **17.** [Migne, p. 121; Cod. Theodos., xi. 27. 1.] **18.** [Migne, p. 236, *sq.*, 397; Cod. Theodos., xi. 27. 2.] **19.** [Migne, p. 214, *sq.*, 223, *sq.;* Cod. Theodos., iv. 7. 1.] **20.** [Euseb., Vita Const., iv. 18, 23; Cod. Theodos., ii. 8. 1; *venerabili die solis,* Cod. Just., iii. 12, 3.] **21.** [Euseb., Vita Const., iv. 19, *sq.;* Migne, p. 73, *sq.;* Cod. Just., iii. 12. 1, 3; Schaff, Ch. Hist., ii. 106.] **22.** [Migne, p. 202; Cod. Theodos., xvi. 10. 1, 3; Euseb., Vita Const., iii. 55, 58; iv. 25.] **23.** [Cod. Theodos., ix. 16. 1, 2; Neander, Ch. Hist. (2d Am. ed.), ii. p. 20, n. 4.] **24.** [Euseb., Vita Const., iv. 62; cf. Heinichen in loc. (vol. iii. p. 566); the meaning of Constantine's words is doubtful.] **25.** [Euseb., Vita Const., iv. 62.] **26.** On the persecution by Licinius, cf. Görres: Kritische Untersuchung der Licinianischen Christenverfolgung, Jena, 1875. **27.** Euseb., Vita Const., i. 51-53. **28.** *Ibid.*, ii. 20. **29.** This is plain from the subsequent edict of Constantine in A.D. 324. [Cf. Euseb., Vita Const., ii. 30-41; Migne, Patrol. Lat., viii. p. 265, *sq.*] **30.** Cf. Görres, lib. cit., p. 104, *sq.* **31.** Euseb., Vit. Const., ii. 5. **32.** *Ibid.*, ii. 56. **33.** [*Ibid.*, iii. 49.] **34.** [*Ibid.*, iii. 3.] **35.** [Julian Imp., Cæsares (ed. Spanheim, 1696, p. 329, c.)]

CHAPTER III.

1. Ambrose, relat. Symmachi respondet (Ep. i. 18. § 31, *sq.*, p. 886); relatio Symmachi, urbis præfecti (§45, p. 872) state that the altar was removed by Constantius. **2.** [Euseb., vita Const., iv. 17, 29, 55.] **3.** [*Ibid.*, iii. 16-23; Sozom., H. Eccl., i. 17, 20, 21.] **4.** Euseb., vita Const., iv. 24. **5.** [Cf. Cod. Theodos., De Episcopali Judicio, 1.] **6.** Jul. Firmic., Matern. de Errore Profan. Relig. [17. cf. 21, 29.] **7.** Cod. Theodos., xvi. 10. 2. **8.** *Ibid.*, xvi. 10. 4. **9.** [Cf. *Ibid.*, xv. 10. 6; ix. 16. 1-6; Ammian. Marcell., xix. 12. 14: *Si qui remedia Quartanæ vel doloris alterius collo gestaret . . . pronunciatus reus capitis interibat.*] **10.** [Ammian. Marcell., xv. 2. 7; Sozom., H. Eccl., v. 2.] **11.** [Socr., H. Eccl., iii. 1; Theodoret, H. Eccl., iii. 2; Sozom., H. Eccl., v. 2; Greg. Naz., Or. iii. p. 58 D (ed. Morell., Colon., 1699.)] **12.** [Socr., H. Eccl., iii. 1; Sozom., H. Eccl., v. 2; Greg. Naz., Or. iii. p. 58 C.] **13.** [Socr., H. Eccl., iii. 1, 13.] **14.** Libanius (ed. Reiske, 3v. 8°, Altenburg, 1784-1797). Epit. i. p. 526, *sq.* On this part of Julian's life cf. Friedrich Rode, Gesch. der Reaction Kaiser Julians gegen die Christl. Kirche, Jena, 1877, p. 27, *sq.* **15.** [Socr., H. Eccl., iii. 1; Rode, p. 30.] **16.** [Cf. Socr., H. Eccl., iii. 1.] The exact date is given by Jul., Ep. 51, in which Julian writes (near the end of A.D. 362) that he had been a heathen eleven years. Cf. Libanius, Prosphon., i. p. 408; Rode, lib. cit., p. 31. **17.** On Julian's inner history, cf. H. Adrien Naville, Julian l'Apostat et sa philosophie du Polythéism, Paris, 1877, p. 5, *sq.* **18.** [Jul. ad Athen., p. 277 A; Ammian. Marcell., xv. 8. 4-17; Rode, lib. cit., p. 40.] **19.** Ammian. Marcell., xvi. 5. 4-6. **20.** [*Ibid.*, xxi. 2. 4. Rode, lib. cit., pp. 34, 41.] **21.** Zosimus, iii. 8. **22.** Ammian. Marcell., xxii. 5. 1; Vienne, *Ibid.*, xxi. 2. 5. **23.** [Ammian. Marcell., xxii. 5.] **24.** [*Ibid.*, xxii. 4; Socr., H. Eccl., iii. 1.] **25.** Socr., H. Eccl., iii. 11. **26.** [Libanius, Panegyr., i. p. 394, *sq.*] **27.** Jul., Epp. 7, 42, 43, 52. [Rode, lib. cit., p. 50, *sq.*] **28.** An Ep. of Julian in Hermes [Zeitschr. f. classiche Philologie, ed. Hübner, Berlin, 1874, iv. p. 98; cf. Rode, lib. cit., pp. 39, 69.] **29.** Greg. Naz., Or. iii., pp. 75, [83 B; Sozom., H. Eccl., v. 17; Theodoret, H. Eccl., iii. 16, *sq.*] **30.** [Greg. Naz., Or. iii. p. 75 D; Sozom., H. Eccl., v. 17.] **31.** The story is told, Greg. Naz., Or. iii. [p. 84, *sq.*]; Sozom., H. Eccl., v. 17. Rode is inclined to doubt its truth, but it rests on good evidence. **32.** [Socr., H. Eccl., iii. 13; Theodoret, H. Eccl., iii. 8.] **33.** [Cod. Theod., x. 3. 1; xii. 1. 50; xv. 1. 8, 10; Cod. Just., xi. 69. 1. Sozom., H. Eccl., v. 5; Theodoret, H. Eccl., iii. 6; Philostorg., vii. 4.] **34.** Sozom., H. Eccl., v. 5. [Cf. Libanius, Epit. i. p. 564, Greg. Naz., Or. iii. p. 86 D, *sq.*] **35.** [Socr., H. Eccl., iii. 14.]

36. Jul., Ep. 49 to Arsacius, High-priest of Galatia, and Ep. 63 to Theodore, High-priest of Asia. 37. Jul., Ep. 42. 38. [The law may be found, Cod. Theodos., xiii. 3. 5.] 39. Rufinus, H. Eccl., i. 32 [also Theodoret, H. Eccl., iii. 8] erroneously gives the law the latter meaning. [Against this, Julian's words Ep. 42: "We would not throw any obstacle in the way of the youth (among the Christians) who wish to go (to classic lectures)" are decisive. On this whole subject cf. Ammian. Marcell., xxii. 10. 7; xxv. 4. 20; Theodoret., H. Eccl., iii. 8; Socr., H. Eccl., iii. 12, 16.; Greg. Naz., Or. iii. pp. 51, *sq.*, 97.; also Rode, lib. cit., p. 66 and note.] 40. [Greg. Naz., Or. iii. p. 97 B.] 41. [Cf. Greg. Naz., Or. iv. p. 122 D.] 42. [Cf. *Ibid.*, iii. p. 51, *sq.*] 43. Rufinus, H. Eccl., i. 35 [Sozom., H. Eccl., v. 19, 20]. 44. [Jul., Misopog. (ed. Spanheim), p. 363.] 45. The Misopogon, the chief original document on Julian's stay in Antioch. 46. [Jul., Misopog., p. 338, *sq.*, 360, *sq.*, et passim. On Julian's sacrifices cf. Ammian. Marcell., xxii. 14; xxv. 4; Sozom., H. Eccl., v. 19; Socr., H. Eccl., iii. 17.] 47. Ammian. Marcellin., xxii. 13. 48. [*Ibid.*, xxii. 13. 1, 3. Misopog., pp. 346, 361.] 49. [Ammian. Marcellin., xxii. 13. 2; Sozom., H. Eccl., v. 8; Theodoret, H. Eccl., iii. 12.] 50. [Rufinus, H. Eccl., i. 32; Socr., H. Eccl., iii. 13.] 51. [Theodoret, H. Eccl., iii. 13.] 52. [*Ibid.*, iii., 15.] 53. [*Ibid.*] 54. [Greg. Naz., Or. iii. p. 92 A.] 55. [Greg. Naz., Or. iii. p. 91 B.] 56. [Ammian. Marcell., xxiii. 2. 3.] 57. [Theodoret, H. Eccl., iii. 23; slightly different, Sozom., H. Eccl., vi. 2.] 58. [On the campaign cf. Ammianus Marcell., xxiv., xxv.; Theodoret, H. Eccl., iii. 25; Sozom., H. Eccl., iii. 12, *sq.*; Zosimus, iii. 11-29, &c.] 59. Ammian, who was in the army, narrates Julian's death, xxv. 3. 1. The doubt whether the fatal spear came from among the Persians, or from some one in the Roman army, is of very early origin. The heathen [notably Libanius, Socr., H. Eccl. vi. 1, 2] accused the Christians of treacherously murdering the Emperor; but the way in which Ammian mentions this rumor gives no ground for the accusation. 60. [Philostorgius, H. Eccl., vii. 15; Theodoret, H. Eccl., iii. 25; Sozom. vi. 2.] The cry, "Nazarene (*or* Galilean), thou hast conquered," is not found earlier than Theodoret, and cannot therefore be regarded as possessing much evidence in its favor. Here, as often, legend has put into the mouth of the hero a word not really historical, but expressive of the real historical situation, and therefore, when once invented, always brought into the story. 61. [Rufinus, H. Eccl., i. 32; Socr., H. Eccl., iii. 14; Sozom., H. Eccl., v. 5; Theodoret, H. Eccl., iii. 5: yet no one of these contains exactly the form *nubecula est, transibit.*]

INDEX.

Abeona, 31.
Abgar Bar Manu, 265.
Abitina, 410.
Abonoteichos, 318.
Abraham, 82.
Achatius, martyr, 234.
Acte, 94, 246.
Adonis, myth of, 32, 33; gardens, 443, 454.
Ælian, 313.
Æschylus, 72, 120; monument to, 192.
Æsculapius, 59, 319.
Agatha, 308.
Africa, 19, 59, 83, 111, 113, 127, 273, 342, 356, 376, 410, 425, 431.
Agape. See *Love-Feast*.
Agrippa, King, 122.
Agrippa, the lake of, 103.
Agrippina, 94.
Alcibiades, 97, 99.
Alemanni, 362.
Alexander the Great, 65, 98, 473, 475.
Alexander Severus, 272 *sq.*, 313, 317, 334, 359 *sq.*
Alexander of Abonoteichos, 318-320, 325.
Alexander, Bishop of Jerusalem, 369.
Alexandria, 17, 20, 25, 60, 64, 113, 356, 368 *sq.*; Jews in, 83, 84; church of, 220.
Almsgiving. See *Church*.
Alps, the, 68, 424; Pass of St. Bernard, 30.
Amatius, 262.
Ambrosius, 360.
Ammonius, 326 *sq.*
Amulets, 17, 63, 317, 452.
Amphitheatres, the, 124 *sq.*
Anacreon, 74.
Anatolia, 368.
Andrew, the apostle, 220.
Anna Perenna, festival of, 43.
Annona, 55.
Anti-Christ (Nero), 248 *sq.*
Antinous, deification of, 62, 487.
Antioch, 17, 20, 83, 113, 262, 362, 369, 402, 442, 453, 461, 470, 472; benevolence of church of, 203; missionary centre, 219; cathedral of, 474; numerous membership of its church, 402.

Antiochus the Great, 83.
Antipas, martyr, 251.
Antium, 245.
Antisthenes, 144.
Antoninus, Arrius, 262; Pius, 262 *sq.*, 264; Marcus Aurelius. See *Marcus*.
Anubis, 314.
Aper, 308.
Aphrodite, 144; Anadyomene, 98; Cnidian, *ib.*
Apollo, 36, 39, 296, 319, 447, 470; the Milesian, 407.
Apollodorus, 98.
Apollonia, 369.
Apollonius, 356.
Apollonius of Tyana, 279, 331-333.
Apologies, 266 *sq.*, 391 *sq.*
Apologists, 266 *sq.*, 281, 331 *sq.*
Apostles' Creed, the, 348.
Apostles, church of the, 442.
Apostles, death of (Peter and Paul), 249.
Appian Way, the, 67, 83.
Apuleius, 314, 320 *sq.*
Aquila, 221.
Arcadia, 46.
Arius, Arianism, 449, 463.
Aristides, 265.
Aristotle, 97, 105, 132, 276, 326, 457.
Aristophanes, 47.
Aristophanes of Byzantium, 98.
Armenia Minor, 439.
Artablus, 461.
Artemidorus, 318.
Artemis, 45.
Arvales, the, 44, 60.
Aschera, 33.
Asia, 16, 33.
Asia Minor, 23, 32, 83, 84, 288, 342.
Asinius Pollio, 80.
Aspasia, 98, 99.
Astarte, 63.
Athanasius, 445, 477.
Athenagoras, 165, 166, 265 *sq.*, 296.
Athene, 37, 70.
Athens, 19, 21, 23, 25, 27, 29, 105, 264, 470.
Atheism, 51.
Atlas, Mount, 94.
Attellana, 120.
Atticus, 132.

501

502 INDEX.

Attys, 314.
Audientes, 389.
Augustus, 13, 15, 16, 24, 38, 52, 54, 57, 64, 109, 110, 121, 135, 136, 278.
Augustus (the title), 397, 406, 413.
Augustales, 59.
Aurelian, 110, 376, 395.
Aurelius. See *Marcus*.
Autolycus. See *Theophilus*.
Avidius Cassius, 293.

Baal, 33.
Babylas, 369, 471.
Babylon, 82, 219.
Babylonia, 83.
Bacchanalia, the, 64.
Bar Cochcba, 254.
Barnabas, 155; on giving, 197.
Bartholemew, the apostle, 220.
Basilides, 357.
Bellona, 459.
Benevolence, of the Christians, 191-204; not a virtue of antiquity, 191 *sq.*; instances of among the heathen, 273 *sq.*
Bernard, St., the Pass of, temple of Jupiter in, 30.
Bethlehem, 442.
Bible, a heathen, 330.
Bishops, 201, 349-351, 450.
Bithynia, 255.
Black Sea, the, 111.
Blandina, 255 *sq.*
Bosphorus, 436, 442, 447.
Britain, 18, 83, 145.
Burial-clubs, 195, 238.
Byzantinism, 449.

Cadiz, 15.
Cæcilius, 224; arguments against Christianity, 225-231.
Cæculus, 31.
Cæsar, Julius, 105, 109, 123; his superstition, 52; his deification by the people, 56; his scepticism, 75; the title, 397, 412 *sq.*; the Cæsar-gods, 59.
Caius, 126.
Caligula, 60, 71, 96, 100, 136.
Callistus, catacomb of, 222.
Campania, 30.
Camulodunum, 19.
Candelifera, 31.
Candle hymn, 183, 184.
Candidus. See *Vesprontus*.
Cannæ, 123.
Canon. See *Church*.
Capitol, the, 55, 123.
Capitoline Hill, 315.
Cappadocia, 360, 455.
Captivity, The, 82.
Caracalla, 276, 310, 320, 359.
Cardea, 31.
Carlsburg, 320.
Carpenter, Jesus the, 188, 469, 473.
Carthage, 264, 339, 351, 357, 370, 375, 378.
Cassius, C., Speech of, 136, 137.
Catacombs, the, 103, 222, 238, 368, 372, 374, 376.
Catechumenate. See *Church*.

Cato, 30, 75, 134, 135, 275, 285.
Celerinus, 378.
Celibacy, laws against, 102, 174; relation of Christianity to, 175.
Celsus, 158, 159, 229, 233, 269, 278 *sq.*, 293, 296-306, 334, 353.
Ceres, 32.
Ceylon, 36.
Chaldeans, 63, 65.
Charlemagne, 443.
Cherchell, 400.
Childlessness, 102.
Children, 102; effect of slavery upon, 138; rights of, 182 *sq.*, 272 *sq.*; baptism of, 183; training of, 273; charities for, 273 *sq.*
Chrestus, 242.
Christ, 66, 152, 155, 156 *sq.*, *passim*; a heathen counterpart to, 279, 331-334. See *Jesus*, *Carpenter*, *Nazarene*.
Christianity, aids to its extension, 21, 90; its influence on the study of nature, 68; effect of its offer of eternal life, 77, 160; first introduced true benevolence, 110; true humanity its product, 141; its restorative power, 143; relation in, between faith and life, *ib.*; expected universal dominion, 152; its resources in opposition to Heathenism, 152; impression made by it on the heathen, 153 *sq.*; how preached, 156, 157; for the poor and sinful, 157-159; recognized the rights of children, 182; transformed the relation between masters and servants, 184, 185; required benevolence, 191; its encounter with the Roman State, 217 *sq.* (see *Persecution*); its absolute claims, 218; how first diffused, 221; by whom received, 221-223; by whom despised, 223-226; early preached in Rome, 241; first collision with Heathenism, 249; completion of its separation from Judaism, 253; became an illegal religion, 255; influence, 264-282; method of the Apologists in its defence, 266 *sq.*; attack of Celsus on, 158, 159, 297 *sq.*; re-action in, 336-354. See *Christians*, *Church*.
Christians, the early, refuse to worship the Emperor, 60, 61, 233, 234; congregational life among, 164, 165; their conduct, 165-190; surrounded by heathen customs, 171-173; charges against, 226-234; why adjudged guilty of treason, 231-234; how protected, 238, 239. See *Benevolence*, *Church*, *Martyrdom*, *Worship*.
Church, the, its discipline, 173, 174, 339-342, 344, 377 *sq.*; regulated duties of master and slave, 186-7; *collegia illicita*, 237; martyrs of, 247, 249, 253, 260, 262, 288-291, 295 *sq.*, 339, 356-359, 366, 368-376, 405 *sq.*, 410, 415 *sq.*, 439, 472; purity and simplicity of, 249; as a community, 270; its influence, 270, 271 *sq.*, 402; of the people, 339 *sq.*; persecutions of, flight from, 211, 212; the ten, 236; under Nero, 245-250; Domitian,

INDEX. 503

252 *sq.*; Trajan, 255–262; Hadrian, 262 *sq.*; Antoninus Pius, 262 *sq.*; Marcus Aurelius, 287–297; Commodus, 356; Septimius Severus, 356 *sq.*; Maximinus the Thracian, 360; Decius, 373; Gallus, 373; Valerian, 373; Gallienus, 376; Diocletian, 407–411; Galerius, 412–417; Maximinus Daza, 419–423; Maxentius, *ibid.*; Licinius, 438–440; Julian, 468 *sq.*; a conventicle, 336 *sq.*; pietism, 337; in time of persecution, 339 *sq.*, 367 *sq.*; tradition, 347 *sq.*; canon, 348; naturalization of, on earth, 344; officers of, 349–351; polity, 349–352; ecclesiasticism in, 350–352; its confessors, 372, 377–381; almsgiving and benevolence of, 202, 203, 370, 469; worship, 372, 386–389; catechumenate, 387 *sq.*; and State, 443 *sq.*, 449 *sq.* Cf. also *Bishops, Creed, Deacons, Laity, Lapsed, Lord's Supper, Presbyter, Priest.*
Cicero, 34, 43, 63, 64, 69, 74, 132, 193, 272, 276, 285.
Circus, the, 124.
Circus Maximus, 119, 122, 123.
Claudiales, the, 59.
Claudius, 19, 54, 57, 61, 96, 109, 128, 134.
Clemens. See *Flavius*.
Clement of Alexandria, on marriage, 175.
Clement of Rome, 153 *sq.*, 247.
Cleophas, 262.
Colchester, 19.
Commodus, 273, 306, 309, 334, 338, 355.
Como, 274.
Competentes, 389.
Confessors. See *Church*.
Constans, 452.
Constantius, Chlorus, 412; brother of Constantine, 455; son of Constantine, 452–462, 466.
Constantine the Great, 413, 419–452, 455 *sq.*, 462, 478; II., 452.
Corinth, 17, 23, 59.
Constantinople, 436, 459, 465.
Conventicle. See *Church*.
Cornelius, 368.
Corn-laws, 109.
Council, the supreme, 85.
Crassus, 104.
Creed. See *Apostles', Church*.
Crescens, 269, 290.
Crete, 86, 333.
Cross, the, and Constantine, 425–431; punishment of the, abolished, 434.
Ctesiphon, 474.
Cunina, 31.
Curubis, 374.
Cybele, 63.
Cynics, the, 147.
Cyprian, 199, 201, 208, 211, 351, 353, 366 *sq.*, 369, 372, 374 *sq.*

Dacia, 395, 459.
Dalmatia, 398.
Damascus, 89.
Danube, the, 15, 18, 24, 66, 83, 85.
Daphne, 470.
Deaconesses, 177, 198, 201.

Deacons, 349.
Decius, 201, 237, 361, 365, 373, 411, 445.
Delphi, 41, 59.
Demeter, 323.
Demosthenes, 98, 469.
De Rossi, 222.
Diana, 48, 59, 313, 362, 487.
Diaspora, the, 82.
Diocletian, 146, 317, 330, 393–414, 444.
Diognetus, Epistle to, 166, 167, 268, 486.
Diomed, 70.
Dionysius of Alexandria, 374; of Halicarnassus, 49.
Discipline. See *Church*.
Dispersion, the, congregations of, 85.
Dioscurus, 360.
Divorce, introduction of, into Rome, 99.
Docetists, 346.
Domitian, 128, 132, 237, 252, 333.
Domitilla. See *Flavia*.
Domna. See *Julia*.
Dorystera, 466.
Druid worship exterminated, 19.
Druidess, 398.

East, the, 17, 19, 20, 25, 42. See *Orient*.
Easter, 389.
Ecclesiasticism. See *Church*.
Edessa, mission centre, 219.
Educa, 31.
Egypt, 32, 56, 83, 86, 127, 355, 376; materialistic tendency of its religion, 32; animal gods of, 66.
Eifel, the, 113.
Elagabalus, 310, 315, 334, 359 *sq.*
Elder. See *Presbyter*.
Eleusis, 98, 161, 323.
Elis, 59.
Emesa, 333.
Emperors, Age of the: its materialism, 32; the Julian, 140; the soldier, 145; worship of, 56 *sq.*, 233; principles which led them to persecute, 234–236.
Empusæ, 316.
England, 16.
Ennius, 285.
Ephesus, 17, 59, 83, 332, 362, 453, 457; seven sleepers of, 445.
Epictetus, on happiness, 70.
Epona, 32.
Ergastula, the, 135.
Esus, 39.
Euripides, 140.
Europe, 19.
Eusebius, 338, 360, 426 *sq.*, 429.

Fabian, 67.
Fabianus, 368.
Family, the, 97 *sq.*, 174 *sq.*
Fasts, 171.
Faleria, 43.
Farinus, 31.
Faustina, 274.
Felicitas, 41, 357 *sq.*
Fetish, a, Nero's worship of, 63.
Fidenza, 195.
Flavia, the *gens*, 89.
Flavia Domitilla, 252.

504 INDEX.

Flavianus, 376.
Flavius Clemens, 252 sq.
Flavius Philostratus. See *Philostratus*.
Florence, 106.
Flores, 132.
Forculus, 31.
Forum, the, 147.
France, 47, 113.
Franks, 361.
Freedmen: their pernicious influence on Roman society, 139 sq.
Friedländer, 123.
Fronto, 228, 269 sq., 272, 285 sq., 294.
Fucinus, lake of, 128.
Fulminata, 292.
Fulvia, the *gens*, 89.

Gabinius, 105.
Galatia, 468.
Galen, 76, 116.
Galerius, 395, 403, 405–419, 422 sq., 427, 472.
Galileans (Christians), 466, 469, 472 sq.
Gallienus, 313, 376.
Gallus, Emperor, 373.
Gallus, brother of Julian, 455, 458.
Games, public, 119–131, 434; importance of, in ancient life, 119 sq.; renounced by the early Christians, 229 sq.
Gaul, 18, 19, 25, 60, 66, 83, 105, 311, 412, 458 sq., 475. Gauls, the, 63.
Genius of Rome. See *Rome*.
Gentiles, the, 87.
Genuflectentes, 389.
Germanicus, 317.
Germany, 47, 145.
Germans, 26, 104, 361, 395, 443, 458 sq.
Geta, 320, 358.
Getulius, 262.
Gladiatorial sports, 190.
Glyphon, 319.
Gnosticism, 338, 344–349.
Golden Ass, 320 sq.
Gospel, the, 148.
Goths, 311, 362, 373, 395.
Gracchi, the, 71.
Greece, 18, 23, 25, 26, 32, 45, 59, 66, 71, 72, 83, 89, 90, 97, 130, 470; its influence on Rome, 19 sq.; in promoting unbelief, 34, 47.
Greeks, the, their worship, 33 sq., 98; fickleness, 47; conception of the other world, 73; early purity, 97; ignorance of true family life, 98; importance to them of the theatre, 120; lack of humility, 144.
Greek language, its prevalence, 20; religion, 45; idealized Nature, 33; humanized its deities, 34.

Hades, 74.
Hadrian, 62, 262 sq., 265, 273, 275, 280.
Ham, descendants of, 97.
Heathenism, multiplicity of its deities, 29; its homogeneity, 36; causes of its strength in the Roman Empire, 41 sq.; its centre of religious unity, 60; demanded new gods, 65; its bankruptcy, 73; its hopelessness, 75, 90; its great defect, 130, 143 sq.; re-action of, 143, 308–335.
Heaven, a heathen, 321.
Hecebolius, 457.
Hegesippus, 253.
Helena, 432, 447.
Hellenists, 457.
Herbart, 130.
Hercules, 36, 129; Pillars of, 15; worshipped, 36.
Here, 34.
Hermes Paytnuphis, 38.
Hesiod, 346.
Hierocles, 404, 407.
Hilaria, 314.
Hilarianus, 410.
Hippolytus, 323.
Homer, 70, 72, 73, 114, 346, 469.
Horace, 87, 101.

Iazyges, 292.
Ida, Mount, 86.
Ignatius, 262.
Ilium. See *New Ilium*.
Illyrians, 362.
Illuminism, 92.
Immortality, belief in, 67, 73 sq.; disbelief in, 75 sq.; influence of the Christian assurance of, 77, 155 sq.
India, 127, 220.
Infanticide, practice of, 101.
Influence of the Church. See *Church*.
Inscriptions, 16, 38, 41, 43, 44, 56, 67, 75, 98, 104, 124, 125, 272–275, 315, 320 sq., 486.
Irenæus, 352.
Isaiah, 80.
Isis, 63, 65, 314, 322 sq., 325.
Isidorus, C. Cæcilius Claudius, 135.
Israel, 80; its mission twofold, 81 sq. See *Judaism*.
Italy, 15, 19, 25, 83, 106, 137, 414, 424 sq., 431.

Japhetic nations, the, 97.
Jerusalem, 38, 60, 85, 104, 239, 252 sq., 262, 369, 442.
Jesus, 222, 252, 262, 297 sq. See *Christ, Carpenter, Nazarene*.
Jewish Christians, 254; theology of, 346.
Jews, 60, 63, 65, 83, 245, 252, 296; heathen expectation of their supremacy, 80; their dispersion, 81 sq.; their chief business, 84; privileges of, *ib.*, 85; religious unity, 85; hated, 86 sq.; influence of, 87 sq.; persecuted the Christians, 239.
Judaism, 80, 81–91, 253 sq., 298.
Judas, brother of James, grandsons of, 253.
Julia, 94.
Julia Domna, 278, 333; Mæsa, 333; Mammæa, 333, 359.
Julian, 442 sq., 447, 450, 455–477.
Juliana, 360.
Julian house, the, 142.
Junius Rusticus, 290 sq., 294.
Juno, 34, 36, 38, 43, 325.

INDEX.

Jupiter, 34, 35, 36, 39, 46, 65, 78, 144, 252, 292, 335, 399, 412; Ammon Anubis, 38.
Justin Martyr, 260, 265-268, 281, 290 sq., 353; his conversion to Christianity, 165 sq.; description of Christian worship, 162, 163; testimony to Christian conduct, 166, 167.
Juvenal, 53, 57, 84, 86, 101, 123, 247, 314.

Kephro, 374.
Kriobolium, 322.

Labarum, 425, 432.
Lactantius, on benevolence, 198.
Laity, 351.
Lamiæ, 316.
Lanista, the, 126.
Lanuvium, inscription from, 487.
Lapsed, treatment of the, 340, 343, 377 sq.
Larissa, 264, 321.
Lases, 45.
Latin language, its diffusion, 29.
Laurentius, 201, 374 sq.
Laws against the Christians, 255, 257, 294, 365, 373, 374, 393, 405, 408, 410 sq., 438 sq., 466, 468 sq.; general laws employed against them, 237, 490; favoring Christianity and against Heathenism, 418, 428, 431-436, 441, 452 sq.
Legacy-hunting, 103.
Lent, 389.
Leonides, 356.
Leontopolis, 83.
Libanius, 453, 458, 473; testimony to Christian women, 182.
Liber, Father, 41.
Liberty, religious, 392 sq.
Libya, 85.
Licinius, 423, 431, 438, 440, 447.
Limentinus, 31.
Livy, 53, 63, 64; on the state of morals in Rome, 95.
Locutinus, 31.
Logos-Doctrine of Justin Martyr, 268.
Lollia Paulina, 100.
Londinium, 19.
Lord's Day, 339. See *Sunday*.
Lord's Prayer, 389.
Lord's Supper, 163, 372, 374, 378, 386, 388.
Louis XIV., 142.
Love-feast (*Agape*), 228, 257, 358.
Lucian, 270, 318-320, 324-326, 333; his testimony as to the state of morals in Rome, 95.
Lucina, 31.
Lucina, St., 222.
Lucius, 323.
Lucius, Bishop of Rome, 368.
Lucretius, 49, 51, 76.
Lugdunum (Lyons), 294 sq.
Luke, 469.
Lutetia (Paris), 317.
Lydia, 83.
Lyons, 24. See *Lugdunum*.

Madaura, 320.
Marcella, 356, 455.
Marcellus, 405 sq.

Marcia, 355.
Marcion, 199.
Marcomanni, 280.
Marcus Aurelius Antoninus, 45, 121, 123, 146, 264 sq., 269 sq., 272, 276, 278 sq., 287, 293 sq., 306 sq., 309, 311, 319; on Christianity, 284. See *Meditations, Church*.
Marie Antoinette, necklace of, 100.
Marinus, 376.
Marriage, in Antiquity, 97 sq.; influence of Christianity upon, 174-178.
Mars, 36, 45.
Marseilles, 19.
Martial, 24.
Martyrdom, 205-213.
Martyrs, the, honored the Emperor and the laws, 206, 207; spirit toward their persecutors, 208, 209; the Scillitan, 208; not fanatics, 210; their steadfastness, 212, 213. See *Church*.
Mæcenas, Tower of, 244.
Mæsa. See *Julia*.
Magic, 316-321.
Mamas, 455.
Mammæa. See *Julia*.
Mary, wife of Cleophas, 262.
Maternus, Julius Firmicus, quoted, 451.
Matthew, the apostle, 469.
Maxentius, 413, 423-426, 429, 431.
Maximian, 413 sq.
Maximinus Daza, 317, 414, 419, 423, 431 sq.
Maximinus the Thracian, 360.
Maximus, 457.
Medea, 46.
Meditations of Marcus Aurelius, 270, 276, 282-285, 287.
Mediterranean, the, 14.
Melito, 13, 59, 294, 296.
Melytta, 32.
Menander, 44.
Mesopotamia, 280.
Messalina, 95, 96.
Metras, 369.
Middle Ages, the, 146, 147.
Milan, edict of, 399, 427-429, 431.
Miletus, 453.
Miltiades, 265, 296.
Milvian Bridge, the, 241, 426, 431.
Mimus, the, 120.
Minucius Felix, 265; the *Octavius* of, 224, 266.
Miracles, their continuance, 169.
Missions, means of diffusing Christianity, 220.
Mithras, 63, 314 sq., 324, 331, 335.
Moloch, 32.
Monotheism, 51 sq.; its superiority to the heathen cults, 88.
Montanus, martyr, 376.
Montanus, Montanism, 338, 342-344.
Morals, state of, in ancient heathenism, 92-149; of the early Christians, 165-190.
Moses, 86.
Musculus, Titus Lollius, 67.
Mutilation, 415.
Mysteries, the, 293, 322-326, 330.
Mythology, 328.

Nationality, its significance before and after Christ, 22.
Nazarene, 476 sq.
Neoplatonism, 326-330, 380, 400, 403 sq., 407, 416, 454, 457.
Neptune, 32.
Nero, 55, 57, 61, 62, 63, 71, 80, 93, 103, 115, 116, 123, 136, 275, 393; progress of Hellenism under, 19; Golden House of, 111; law of, against pulling down houses for speculation, 112; his interest in public games, 119; persecution under, 237, 247-252.
Nerva, 253, 273.
New Ilium, 463.
Nicæa, creed of, 449, 463.
Nicomedia, 20, 396, 407, 409, 412, 432, 442, 453, 457, 470.
Nihilism, 51.
Nile, the, 15, 20, 32, 66; cataracts of, 15.
Noah, 88.
Numerianus, 398.
Numidia, 357.
Numidicus, 370.
Nundina, 31.

Octavia, 246.
Octavian, 106.
Octavius, the, 223 sq., 266.
Œta, Mount, 129.
Officers of the Church. See *Church*.
Olives, Mount of, 442.
Oneirocritica, 318.
Orantes, 389.
Orbana, 31.
Orestes, 45.
Orient, the: insufficiency of its cults, 89. See *East*.
Origen, 297, 304, 352 sq., 356, 360, 366, 391 sq.; on alms-giving, 200; on early mission-work, 220.
Orontes, the, 20, 66, 314, 473.
Orphans, 202.
Osiris, myth of, 32.
Otho, 112.
Ovid, 43, 54, 101, 129.

Pætus, Thrasea, 49.
Paganism, its worship destitute of devotion, 161; a State-religion, 235. See *Heathenism*.
Palatine, the, 71.
Palestine, 20, 81, 83, 90, 122.
Palladium, the, 65, 315.
Pan, 43.
Pandateria, 252.
Pantænus, 265.
Panthera, 298.
Pantheus, 313, 316.
Paraclete, the, 342.
Paris, 19, 39. See *Lutetia*.
Parthians, 280, 293.
Patræ, 45.
Paul, the apostle, 68, 77, 93, 103, 148, 151, 185, 219, 222, 238, 242, 249.
Paulus, martyrdom of, 209.
Pedanius Secundus, 136, 137.
Pegasius, 463.

Penelope, 97.
People, Church of the. See *Church*.
Pergamus, Pergamum, 59, 251.
Pericles, 97.
Perpetua, 357-359.
Persecutions. See *Church*.
Persians, the, 361 sq., 376, 395, 458 sq., 470, 473-475.
Persius, 101.
Pertinax, 273.
Peter, the apostle, 219, 249.
Peter, martyr, 409.
Petronius, 30, 48, 49.
Pharisees, the, 88.
Phidias, 71.
Philip, the Arabian, 360, 365; the Asiarch, 289 sq.
Philippi, 89.
Philo, on the Roman Empire, 16.
Philosophy, its growth in power, 146; its small influence upon the people, 148.
Philostratus, 279, 331-334.
Phrygia, 83, 342, 413.
Phryne, 98, 99.
Phylæ, 38.
Pietism. See *Church*.
Pilate, 69.
Pindar, 72.
Pionius, 209.
Placentia, 273.
Plato, 58, 97, 192, 276, 324, 326, 331, 457; his contempt for the laborer, 105, 158; on slavery, 132; his desire for a revelation, 70.
Plautus, 43, 192.
Pleasure, the fundamental characteristic of ancient life, 67.
Pliny, 49, 53, 58, 75, 116; the Younger, 124, 223; on life in Rome, 117; on the Games, 129; letter to Trajan, 162, 255; his public charities, 274 sq.
Pollio, Asinius, 24.
Pontianus, 360.
Ponticus, 295.
Pontus, 439.
Plotinus, 326-328.
Plutarch, 44, 74, 76, 78.
Polity. See *Church*.
Polybius, on Roman piety, 30.
Polycarp, 208, 288-291.
Pompeii, 113, 122, 125.
Pompey, 30.
Poppæa Sabina, 61, 89, 115, 246.
Porphyry, 330.
Porta Capena, 83.
Porta triumphalis, 124.
Poseidon, festival of, 98.
Potamiæna, 356.
Pothinus, 295.
Potina, 31.
Pozzuoli (Puteoli), 333.
Præneste, 106.
Prætorian Guard, 310, 314, 334, 424.
Praxiteles, 71, 98.
Presbyter, 349-351.
Priest, 351.
Prisca, 403.
Probus, 263, 395.

INDEX. 507

Proculus, 334, 356.
Propertius, 26.
Proselytes of the gate, 88.
Proteus, 331.
Protocletus of Cæsarea, 360.
Ptolemy Epiphanes, 56; Auletes, 105.
Publius, 263 sq.
Publius Rutilianus, 319.
Pudens, 263; martyr, 359.
Puteoli, 219.
Pythagoras, 70, 331, 334.
Pythia, 41.

Quadi, 282, 292.
Quadratus, 265.
Quinctilian, 53, 193.
Quinta, 369.

Redemption, the need of, felt, 78; looked for from the East, 79.
Reformation, 443.
Reformers, 348.
Religion in antiquity, 29 sq. See *Greek religion, Roman do., Heathenism*.
Renan, 300.
Retiarii, the, 125.
Revelation, book of, 250.
Rhine, the, 18, 24, 127, 145, 459.
Rhodes, 19.
Rhone, the, 207, 296.
Roman Empire, its providential relation to Christianity, 13 sq.; united the cultivated nations, 14; its roads, 15, 219; intercourse in, 16; its universalism, 21 sq.; spread of unbelief in, 46 sq.; of the gospel in, 220.
Roman religion, deified the State, 34 sq.; juridical and external, 35; its Emperor-worship, 38; attempts to restore it, 54 sq.; consisted of ceremonies, 55.
Romans, the, their endowment, 15, 68; decline, 99 sq.; laws, 63, 132, 136, 141, 490.
Rome, 13–20, 22, 24–26, 34, 35, 39, 41, 42, 44, 45, 61, 64, 66, 67, 71, 84, 88, 90, 119, 122, 123, 130, 135, 139, 143, 245, 315, 376, 425 sq., 428, 431, 436, 453–455, 476; a Babel of religions, 62 sq.; number of Jews in, 83; morals of, 95, 99, 105 sq.; population of, 108; its buildings, 110 sq.; a mission centre, 220; Bishop of, 262, 355, 360, 368, 374; Genius of, 475.
Romula, 407.
Romulus, 49.
Rosmerta, 39.
Rousseau, 71.
Rufinus, 67.
Rumina, 31.
Rusticus. See *Junius*.
Rutilianus. See *Publius*.

Sabazius, 322.
Sabbath, the Jewish, Roman observance of, 63; ridicule of, 83.
Sabina, the martyr, 213. See *Poppæa*.
Salona, 399, 413.
Samnites, the, 125.
Samosata, 324.
Sardinia, 355, 368.

Sardis, 13.
Sarmatians, 409.
Saturn, 79, 359.
Saturninus, 369.
Saturus, 359.
Saviour, the, 148.
Scævola, Mucius, 129.
Scepticism in the Roman Empire, 51 sq., 71.
Scipios, the, 71.
Scriptures, reading of, in Christian homes, 183.
Scythia, 220.
Sebaste, 439.
Senate, the Roman, 94, 96, 356, 363, 365, 395.
Seneca, 50, 61, 70, 74, 94, 100, 101, 103, 109, 115, 117, 129, 141, 144, 148, 194, 331; on the aim of philosophy, 72; on suicide, 73; on human depravity, 77, 78; on the Jews, 87; ethical essays of, 93; on tranquillity, 93, 118; on heathen morality, 95.
Septimius Severus, 110, 276, 278, 310, 313, 333 sq., 356.
Serapis, 38, 64, 65, 314.
Serenus Annæus, 93, 94, 118.
Severus. See *Septimius, Alexander*.
Sicily, 83.
Sextus Empiricus, 51.
Simeon, 262.
Simonides, 72.
Sirona, 39.
Sixtus II., 201, 374.
Slavery, ancient, 131 sq., 435; effects of, 138 sq.; held to be necessary, 141; Christianity and, 184 sq.; its amelioration, 275 sq.
Smyrna, 17.
Socrates, 69, 98, 144, 324 sq.
Solon, 106.
Sophocles, 72, 120, 324.
Sositheus, 132.
Spain, 18, 19, 45, 50, 59, 83, 105, 124, 376.
Sparta, 45, 59.
Spectacles, public. See *Games*.
Speratus, 357.
State, the, dependence on religion, 146. See *Church*.
Stoicism, its mediating theology, 51; its exclusiveness, 148.
Stoics, the, 70, 140, 144, 283 sq., 326.
Strabo, 52; on the necessity of superstition, 50; on the Jewish dispersion, 83.
Strauss, 303 sq.
Suetius Certus, 125.
Suetonius, 79, 241, 242, 252.
Sulla, 106.
Sunday, 162, 435. See *Lord's Day*.
Switzerland, 25.
Syene, 38.
Symbolum, 389.
Synagogues, the, 85, 219.
Syria, 18, 32, 45, 66, 83, 113, 207, 265, 470.

Tacitus, 18, 26, 76, 79, 104, 137, 220, 223, 245 sq., 251 sq.; his faith in the gods, 49; on the Jews, 86; on sabbatical year, *ib*.

Tagis, 401 *sq*,
Talmud, 254.
Tangiers, 405.
Taprobrane, 36.
Tartarus, 74.
Tarvus, 39.
Tatian, 157, 268, 293.
Taurobolium, 322, 325.
Taurus in Cilicia, 83.
Telesphorus, 262.
Temple, the Jewish, 104, 252.
Terence, 144.
Terminalia, 408.
Terracina, 274.
Tertullian, 52, 100, 123, 157, 259-261, 264, 269 *sq*., 277, 292, 334, 338, 353, 391 *sq*.; on the *Agapæ*, 163; on the conduct of the Christians, 167, 168; eulogy of Christian marriage, 175 *sq*.; on luxury in dress, 178 *sq*.; on the public shows, 189, 190; on liberty in giving, 199; on the law-abiding spirit of Christians, 207.
Thascius Cyprianus. See *Cyprian*.
Thebaid, 369.
Themistocles, 97.
Theophilus, 207, 266.
Thessalonica, 89, 264.
Thirty Tyrants, the, 395.
Thomas, the apostle, 220.
Thrace, 466.
Thracians, the, 125.
Thucydides, 469.
Thule, 25.
Tiber, the, 83, 134, 314, 431.
Tiberius, 51, 83, 88.

Tigellinus, 103.
Tigris, 474, 477.
Titus, 80, 121, 123, 195.
Tortures, 317, 379, 410 *sq*., 415.
Toulouse, 369.
Tradition. See *Church*.
Trajan, 58, 121, 127, 236, 237, 255, 261 *sq*., 264, 272-274, 287, 292, 356, 365, 393; his rescript to Pliny, 240, 257 *sq*.

Ulpian, 276.
Utica, 375.
Ulysses, 73.

Valeria, 402; the *gens*, 89.
Varro, 50, 132.
Velcia, 273.
Versailles, court of, 143.
Vespasian, 55.
Vesta, 65, 78, 315.
Vestals, the, 54, 62, 125.
Vienne, 294 *sq*., 459.
Virgil, 54, 58, 114; the Fourth Eclogue, 80.
Victoria, 78, 368.
Victory, statue of, 446.
Vitellius, 112, 113.

Women, low estimate of, in antiquity, 97 *sq*., 177 *sq*.; simplicity of Christian, 178 *sq*.; benevolence enjoined on, 198; improved position of, 271 *sq*.
Worship, family, 183. See *Church*.

Zeus, 60, 72.

www.ingramcontent.com/pod-product-compliance
Lightning Source LLC
Chambersburg PA
CBHW051159300426
44116CB00006B/377